The BIG TRIP

YOUR ESSENTIAL GUIDE TO GAP YEARS, SABBATICALS AND OVERSEAS ADVENTURES

CONTENTS

HOW TO USE THIS BOOK

This book is designed to provide information you need to plan a trip of a lifetime, whether a gap year after finishing school or a lengthy (and well earned!) sabbatical from the rat race. The first part, Travel Smarts, looks at everything you need to know to get started, including what to expect when you arrive in your destination and all the paperwork you'll need to organise beforehand. The Tailoring Your Trip section is about organising your trip in a way that works for you and suits your interests – do you want to work to make some extra money or gain a new skill, volunteer in a community or take on the festival circuit? It's worth reading to see what's out there.

For more specific planning there are the destination chapters in the book's third part. These chapters look at the regions of the world and are a good place to start if you can't make up your mind where to go. Finally, there's the Directories section, a list of contact information for useful organisations that you can use as further resources while planning your trip, whether departing from Britain and Ireland, North America, Australia or New Zealand.

We've made this book as up-to-date as we can, but remember that prices do go up, currencies fall and a million other things can happen before this book even hits a bookshelf. But the secret to good travelling is to stay flexible and stay up-to-date.

THE BIG TRIP

Gap years and extended overseas adventures used to be the sole domain of recent school graduates. The history of such forays dates back to the 17th century, when upper-class British kids would complete their education by taking the 'Grand Tour' in Europe. The goal was a simple one: to experience the museums, paintings, culture and, more importantly, wines that they'd studied or read about in school. For a few months they'd tour the continent, though most only went as far as Italy (probably something to do with the wine). All of them returned with enough stories, souvenirs and memories to last a lifetime.

Fast-forward a couple of hundred years. Cheap flights and open minds have meant that even more people are taking a year off to embrace a world outside of their own. Of course, graduates still take the chance to celebrate the escape from school books and dull history lessons, but now everyone from couples with young kids to those in middle-age and even retirement are also making the exciting leap into the unfamiliar. No matter what demographic you may be part of, there are more options than ever to fill your time with rewarding experiences, whether backpacking or taking part in exchange programmes, working holidays or volunteering placements.

This seemingly endless list of options from around the globe can be as daunting as it is exciting, but making sense of it all is what this book is for – *The Big Trip* is designed to help you unite your dreams with distinct destinations and inspirational experiences, and to provide you with all the expert advice needed to get you on the road and back again. After that, all that's left to be done is to let the life-changing trip begin.

WHY GO?

There is only so much you can understand about the world from school, documentaries, the news and your circle of friends on social media. There's no substitute for getting out there to see, hear, taste, touch and smell the realities of what the world is. And, most importantly, there is nowhere better to learn about yourself than from outside your comfort zone.

Travel in foreign lands, away from the securities of home, friends and family, certainly has the power to take you there. Along the way you'll open yourself up to be enthralled, inspired, amused, amazed, bemused, enriched, empowered and – yes – even scared. It's a heady mix of emotions, but one that few people ever get tired of. When was the last time you heard of someone looking back at their life and wishing they'd travelled less?

The reason for this is that travel has the power to change your life for the better, often in ways you'd never imagined. For some travellers, such as Matt Phillips, it was coming to the stark realisation that fear was playing too large a role in his life. His lesson: dying wouldn't be his life's greatest tragedy, not truly living it would be. He has happily never looked back, and now travels the globe for a living while working for Lonely Planet. For others, it may be something as profoundly simple as finally grasping that wealth has nothing to do with a bank balance.

For many travellers it may be more practical, perhaps provoking an unexpected change of career: what starts out as a vacation ends up a vocation, a passion becomes a profession. Take the economics graduate who thought he was bound to work in an accounting firm but did a stint with a music distribution company during his gap year. He was so inspired he's been in the music business ever since. Similarly, Amanda Allen-Toland, who volunteered to work as a youth ambassador in Bangkok on an international development programme on AIDS, could not have predicted the positive impact her volunteering experience would have on her career. Upon returning home she moved on to work as a programme manager for the Asia Pacific Business Coalition on HIV/AIDS in Melbourne, Australia.

'It's paid dividends for me. It led me into an area I wanted to be in with a higher level of responsibility, excellent pay and job satisfaction. It's the icing on the cake. My experience working and living in Thailand was so fantastic that even if my next role had been making fruit shakes, I'd do it all over again.'

But it's not all about life-changing realisations or your career. Just like those

ESCAPING THE PARENT TRAP

So maybe your parents aren't so keen on you going away for months on end. They're probably making noises about going to university, settling down or getting a good job in a bank. They really need to move on. Here are our best arguments to stop them fretting and get them shelling out for airline tickets:

- **Protective research** If you can tell them about the place you're visiting, it can be reassuring. Everyone's going to freak out when they don't know where someone's going, but if you can explain your itinerary it will seem more real. Helpful facts ('They all speak English', 'There's more than 30,000 tourists every year and they all seem okay' or 'It's one of the safest cities in Central America') can also be useful. You can even get them to read a few chapters of this book so they can see you're taking this trip seriously.

- Get involved **Get your parents to help out with the planning and show them a detailed itinerary – they can even check progress on your blog. Show them you've got a budget and you have a time limit on the trip. You can always make changes to itineraries later, but let them know when you do veer off the itinerary to save the grey hairs and panicked phone calls.**

- **Phone home** Create a schedule for phoning home, texting or whatever (there are more tips in Part One, p71). Make sure it's reasonable (calling every hour is crazy, but only ringing once a month could lead to parental tears) and stick to it.

- On course **Prove you're committed to the trip by doing a course (see Part Four, Directories, for more clues on how to do this). Learning to speak a language, taking a first-aid course or even picking up some basic travel skills are all good ways to show that you're taking this seriously.**

- **Insurance is reassurance** Show them you're prepared for the bad stuff by getting good travel insurance that will cover any emergencies.

- Career building **This is your trump card. Explain that this trip could help your career and point to a few people whose careers have been demonstrably aided or improved by travel.**

It's important to take time to see the world in a different light; a morning boat trip on the Ganges

ESCAPING FROM WORK

Negotiating time out from work (or resigning) is the most important, and potentially hardest, obstacle to overcome for many travellers. If you're keen on staying within the same organisation it's key to plan your conversation with your employer carefully, especially if you work for a company that doesn't have a policy on extended leave or where no precedent has been set. Here are some tips:

Do your homework If you work for a large organisation, consult your company's staff handbook, staff intranet and human resources department to get yourself up to speed on its leave provisions. Investigate if anyone else has taken time out and, if so, discreetly sound them out. Find out the company's general attitude to people taking extended periods of leave: is it openly supportive or the reverse? Armed with this information, you can plan your negotiation strategy accordingly.

Know exactly what you're asking for **How much time away are you requesting? Will you settle for less? Do you want the same job once you return? Are you willing to quit? If so, are you going to be upfront about this, or will threatening to resign be the secret weapon that will give you leverage in your negotiations?**

Offer solutions Draw up ways in which you can be replaced temporarily so that continuity is ensured and minimum expense incurred by the company. In this way you will be making life as easy as possible for your boss by doing the thinking and planning for them.

Sell the benefits **Put forward your case for how your time abroad is going to benefit both your company and you: in many cases, such as volunteering, you may return with new skills that will benefit the workplace.**

Play by the rules **When negotiating it's wise to stick with well-worn tactics such as listening, expressing your wishes without being aggressive and showing that you can see things from your employer's point of view. Even if you've decided to quit if you don't get what you want, leaving on good terms will pay dividends in the future. On your return it's possible the company will reconsider its position, but not if you've burnt all your bridges and made enemies by telling them where to shove their job.**

Get any agreement in writing If you've been successful in getting an agreement in principle from your employers, get it in writing. Make sure this includes the dates of your leave of absence, what position (or level of position) and salary you'll return to and whether your pension or other company benefits are affected.

Negotiating voluntary redundancy **If during your homework you get wind of the fact that your company is looking to cut costs and staff, get in first and offer to take a voluntary redundancy package and you might just leave with a nice fat cheque to help fund your adventure.**

© Lonely Planet

Make your trip more comfortable and do the research to figure out exactly what you'll want to get out of it

Grand Tourists of hundreds of years ago, you'll also gather friends and experiences that will be valuable for the rest of your life. Whenever someone mentions Kenya you'll remember marvelling at the great wildebeest migration in the Masai Mara, or if you meet a New Zealander, Canadian or Scot you'll be able to regale them with stories of exploring their beloved mountains and meeting their fellow citizens. These intangibles will stay with you your whole life.

WHY NOT GO?

We're going to be honest: no trip is always easy. Travel brochures can turn out to be studio-shot trickery and there may be times when you're sick, broke or just lonely and homesick. But with a bit of preparation you can minimise the lows and maximise the highs.

Before you go there's always the money to think about. Travel can be expensive and even volunteering can come with a pretty big price tag. We've got a few tips on making your dollars, pounds, euros and baht go further (see p32), but you may have to prioritise and work out how long you can afford to be away. Would you rather spend your winter working at a ski resort in the Alps, leaving your summer free to journey around Europe by train and budget airline? Or would you rather volunteer in Nepal helping rebuild homes after an earthquake? Or do you just want to trek to Machu Picchu then take your sore feet home? After balancing up time and money, should your gap year really be a gap month? Either way, we've got you covered and can help you come up with a budget that will make it work.

Lots of travellers worry about personal safety, and from the way much of the world's dangers are sensationalised in the media, it would be easy to find a reason not to visit most places, be it Addis Ababa, New York, Rio de Janeiro or Paris. However, the situation on the ground – particularly in relation to travellers – often bears no resemblance to what is being depicted in the news. Your best guide to determine a level of safety that you are comfortable with is via government agencies, such as the UK's Foreign and Commonwealth Office or the US Department of State, which produce up-to-date travel advisories on every country on the globe (see p40).

And then there's the environmental concern. Although modern aeroplanes are producing less carbon emissions than previously, their pollution is still an issue, as is the potential for tourists to bring problems to sensitive regions. However, if travel is done responsibly it has the power to provide great benefits, both to the hosts and the visitors. This book will show you how to keep your carbon footprint tiny and how to respect the countries you're visiting to prevent damage to fragile environments and cultures (see p76). At the risk of getting overly sentimental, travel should bring the world closer together.

21 BIG TRIP TRAVEL EXPERIENCES

HAND-PICKED BY LONELY PLANET'S TRAVEL EXPERTS

Exploring the temples of Angkor (Cambodia, p226)
This complex of 1000 temples, shrines and tombs, some being dramatically devoured by trees, rises out of the jungles of northern Cambodia. At its heart is Angkor Wat, the largest religious structure ever built – it is arguably the most inspired monument ever conceived by the human mind.

Diving the Great Barrier Reef (Australia, p188) An underwater nirvana, this incredible reef stretches more than 2000km along Australia's northeastern coast. Dive (or snorkel) below the surface and share its tropical waters with 400 types of coral, 1500 species of fish and numerous sea turtles, whales, dolphins and porpoises.

© Anton_Ivanov / Shutterstock

Trekking to Machu Picchu (Peru, p277) Gawping down at Machu Picchu from the Sun Gate after a lung-busting four-day hike along the Inca Trail is a rite of passage for travellers.

© aphotostory / Shutterstock

Walking the Great Wall of China (China, p203) Not a single wall, but an awe-inspiring maze of walls and fortifications that stretch for an astonishing 8850km.

© Marques / Shutterstock

Finding peace and perfection at the Taj Mahal (India, p241) It might be the most recognisable building in the world, yet it still hides plenty of secrets.

© turtix / Shutterstock

Hiking in Grand Canyon National Park (USA, p263) This mile-deep canyon is nature's cathedral. To hike down to its floor is to walk through two-billion years of geologic time.

© IlexImage / Getty Images

Soaking up the ancient history of Rome at the Colosseum (Italy, p163) There's nothing like a feisty Roman monument to rev up your inner historian, and the Colosseum performs brilliantly. A testament to raw, merciless power, this massive 50,000 seat amphitheatre is the most thrilling of Rome's ancient sights.

Witnessing Iguazú Falls (Brazil–Argentina, p281)
Mind-bogglingly mighty, particularly the plummeting waters at Garganta del Diablo (Devil's Throat).

Observing the intricate details of Alhambra (Spain, p168)
This palace complex is perhaps the most refined example of Islamic art anywhere in the world.

© Matt Munro / Lonely Planet

© Pete Seaward / Lonely Planet

© Mark Read / Lonely Planet

Embracing nature in the Galapagos Islands (Ecuador, p282) Nowhere else on earth does the animal kingdom turn the tables on humanity quite like on the Galapagos Islands. Afloat in the Pacific Ocean, 1000km from mainland Ecuador, it's a place where visitors can often feel more like the exhibit than the observer.

© Alexander Safonovy / Getty Images

Get spiritual inside Aya Sofya (Turkey, p295) Church, mosque and museum in one, Aya Sofya is a structure unlike any other on the planet – defying easy categorisation just as it defied the rules of architecture when it was built almost 1500 years ago. It is a huge, almost cosmic space, with a sense of vastness unmatched in its ancient era.

Sailing around Dubrovnik (Croatia, P169) The city's storybook fortifications have become famous as the setting for King's Landing in *Game of Thrones*, but it's the crystal waters lapping at their foundations and the surrounding islands that can provide the greatest playground.

© haraldmuc / Shutterstock

Getting lost in the medina of Fez (Morocco, p313) Fez's old town (Fès El Bali) is a tangled, unmappable labyrinth that dates back more than a thousand years.

©Sergej Onyshko / Shutterstock

© Jonathan Gregson / Lonely Planet

Playing Indiana Jones at Petra (Jordan, p295) The reality of the rose-red, rock-hewn facade of the Treasury at Petra is as extraordinary as Hollywood fiction.

Climb above the jungles at Tikal (Guatemala, p281) Mexico might have the most well-known Mayan sites, but it's Guatemala's that give the biggest thrills. Once a city the size of Rome, Tikal is now haunted with jungle ambience – wind through vines, animals cries and the occasional cacophony of birds to find age-old pyramids.

© Dreamer4787 / Shutterstock

© Simon Dannhauer / Shutterstock

Going on safari in the Serengeti (Tanzania, P313) No other park in the world spawns such a magnificent wildlife spectacle. Every year more than a million wildebeest, accompanied by hundreds of thousands of zebras (and predators in tow), make the 3000km, eight-month return trip to the Masai Mara. A 'Great Migration' indeed.

Lounging in Santorini (Greece, p168) Why settle for golden sands when you can have red and black beaches, backed by 300m multi-coloured cliffs?

Breathing in life on Haida Gwaii (Canada, p265) It's a place where bears roam, bald eagles and old-growth rainforests soar, and sea lions and orcas frolic offshore.

© mitchFOTO / Shutterstock

© Michael Nolan / Getty Images

© Puripat Lertpunyaroj / Alamy Images

Crossing Shibuya Crossing (Japan, p203) With neon canyons, giant video screens and streets teeming with humanity, Shibuya Crossing is the Tokyo you've seen in the movies. This is one of the world's busiest pedestrian crossings, where five roads meet and up to 1000 people cross in every direction.

© Sean Pavone / Shutterstock

Tramping, kayaking and cruising in Fiordland National Park (New Zealand, p183) The scale of this wilderness on New Zealand's South Island is mind-blowing enough, but its primeval atmosphere seals the deal. It's a landscape of jagged peaks, pristine lakes, sheer fjords and ancient glacial valleys dripping green and twitching with such birds as kiwi and takahe.

Losing sleep at the Edinburgh Festival Fringe (Scotland, p172) The biggest festival of performing arts anywhere in the world, the Fringe takes place over three weeks every August. You can attempt to see it all, but with some 3400 shows in 300 different venues, it's simply not possible. But you'll enjoy trying.

TRAVEL SMARTS

PART ONE CONTENTS

GET PLANNING

If you're tired of flicking through travel magazines and websites, looking wistfully at your dream destinations thinking 'One day...', then it's time to get serious. Travel is always on everyone's list of things to do, but why not put it as your number-one priority? Planning might sound boring but once you start buying guidebooks, imagining your itinerary and working out where to go, you'll feel like you're actually doing it.

TIMING

As well as finding the best time to visit your destination (see the destination chapters in Part Three for details on when to visit specific regions), you need to find the right time for you. Is there a big project finishing up at work that may clear the way for some extended time off? Are your high-school or university studies coming to an end? Or are you about to retire? No matter what stage of life you're at, travel is a great way to find the time (and inspiration) to work out what you want to do next.

The classic 'gap year' (as it's known in the UK) occurs just before university study, and it can start as soon as you drop your pen after the last exam and finish just in time for enrolment. The risk of taking this traditional time away is that you may fall out of step with some of your friends – you might be starting university a year later or entering the job market after them. This might seem like a big difference, but if you stay in touch with your buddies at the other end, they might help you get a job or tell you which courses to avoid.

If you've already started down your career path you may worry that stepping out of it to travel will interrupt your climb up the corporate ladder. But the perspective gained and knowledge learned during your adventure may actually allow you to grab a higher rung upon return, or perhaps even discover a shiny new ladder that leads to greater heights. In short, you may miss some opportunities by being overseas, but you'll also see even more possibilities – you might even find out that you want to study overseas or volunteer (see p141).

Lastly, it's always a good idea to give yourself time to relax before heading away. And you'll need to ensure you have the money to get you through your trip. You can get a rough idea of costs by heading to the Money & Costs chapter (p32).

CHOOSING YOUR DESTINATIONS

India, Southeast Asia, Australia, New Zealand and South America are perennial favourites with travellers, but you have the freedom to choose. Are there places you've always wanted to see or know more about? You might be inspired by something you studied, such as the ruins of ancient Greece or crumbling Aztec ziggurats. You may want to trace your family's roots; with ancestral DNA tests becoming all the rage, more and more people are heading out to previously unforeseen places on their family tree. Others choose more concrete family connections, visiting relatives abroad to learn about their way of life or to save on accommodation costs.

Another rewarding way to target potential destinations is to follow your passions. If skiing is your thing, why not investigate the possibility of doing a season in the Alps, Rockies or New Zealand? Or take it one step further and train to be an instructor (p155), perhaps giving you the potential to make a living from doing something you love in future. If you've been engrossed in wildlife documentaries for years, think about volunteering with a conservation organisation that helps protect iconic African animals in their natural environment. Or simply plan on an extended overland safari through East Africa or Southern Africa (or both!).

With time for a long trip, most travellers look at doing several stops, with younger ones often including a destination where they can work (see p115) to get cashed up before heading out again. The round-the-world ticket (see p158) can be the perfect way to skip around the globe.

If you have decided to team up with your best friend or the love of your life to travel, you'll likely need to plan much of the itinerary together. A good alternative can be to look at doing some legs of your journey alone and others together. If your boyfriend would rather surf in Indonesia while you explore China, it's easy enough to meet up in Hong Kong before heading on to Europe. Check the Who With chapter (see p84) for a few more ideas on travelling with friends and partners.

RESEARCHING YOUR DESTINATIONS

Once you've chosen a few destinations to visit you can start finding out a little more about them, including the best time to visit and the local customs and culture. You'll get a closer look at what individual places have to offer and start working out which towns or cities you'll include on your itinerary – are you more New York than New England, more Milan than Ko Pha-Ngan?

There's a more serious side to research, including details such as immunisations, visas and other precautions, which will be different depending on where you go. Remember to be sure to check government travel advisories (see p40) before booking, and again before travelling (travel insurance should cover you if the situation has changed).

INTERNET

Chances are you'll have started your research by Googling a few destinations. The quality of the information you'll find will vary, though the internet can have some of the most up-to-date information from travellers. **Lonely Planet's Thorn Tree** (www.lonelyplanet.com/thorntree) is a good example, as travellers post questions about destinations they're interested in and they're often answered by travellers who've recently been to the same places.

Two other sites worth exploring are **Lonely Planet's Destinations** (www.lonelyplanet.com/destinations), which offers profiles of destinations from across the globe, and the **CIA Factbook** (https://www.cia.gov/library/publications/the-world-factbook/index.html), which takes a more technical look around the world, including comments on roads and telecommunications.

Tourism Websites

Another popular way to find information is from tourism websites. Their helpfulness can vary widely; you'll see when you read a few of them that they often specialise in 'brochurese', a gushing language where every island is a 'secluded paradise' and even a hole in the ground can be described as 'a boutique getaway subterranean retreat'. They're good for basics and usually have plenty of inspiring pictures, but they're really trying to sell their destination. That said, some are very useful, such as those from **California** (www.visitcalifornia.com), **Germany** (www.germany.travel), **New Zealand** (www.newzealand.com) and **Western Australia** (www.westernaustralia.com).

Travel Websites & Apps

There are countless websites and apps that provide information and ideas. Here are some of the more helpful ones:

- **Euan's Guide** (www.euansguide.com) A guide to accessible destinations for people with disabilities.
- **Instagram** (www.instagram.com) Pure visual inspiration.
- **Nomadic Matt** (www.nomadicmatt.com) Budget guides and advice about various destinations.
- **RoadTrippers** (https://roadtrippers.com) Provides ideas and sights to see while plotting a road route from A to B.
- **Snapchat** (www.snapchat.com) With its Snap Maps, you'll be able to see what (and where) people are checking out in various destinations.

Online Travel Agents & Bookers

Several websites offer booking services and also provide destination guides, which can be a good way to get an idea of what a destination is like and what the major attractions are. Even if you don't book with them, they can give you some good ideas on places to head for or (if you want to get off the beaten track) avoid.

Here are a few:

- **Expedia** (www.expedia.com)
- **SafariBookings** (www.safaribookings.com)
- **Travelocity** (www.travelocity.com)
- **Viator** (www.viator.com)
- **Trailfinders** (www.trailfinders.com)

GUIDEBOOKS

Okay, so being a company that sells guidebooks we're always going to tell you that they are essential tools for travelling – they offer information on places to stay and eat, detail what to see and give you language basics and cultural insights.

Most travellers prepare for their trip by buying a guidebook so they can read up before they leave. It gets you excited about your destination before you get there. But before doing so you should work out a rough itinerary, so consider just browsing a bookshop or library until you have a good idea where you're heading. Multi-country books that cover areas such as Europe or Southeast Asia can keep your options open, and you can always buy a new or used book on the road if you change your itinerary.

Selecting Your Guidebook

There's a confusing array of guidebooks on the shelves in most bookshops, but flip through them and see which one suits you. As well as various options from Lonely Planet, other popular brands include Bradt, DK, Fodor's, Frommer's, Let's Go, Michelin, Moon, Rick Steves, Rough Guides and Time Out. Before parting with your hard-earned cash, ask your friends and family which books they've used.

When you're in the bookshop, read through the guidebooks a little and compare edition dates (bearing in mind though that latest may not always be best – having the most recent book is no use if it's wrong), hard information and reviews. Which book has a style that suits you? For instance Lonely Planet's *Best of...* and *Discover* guides are full of colour pictures and highlights of top sights, while our traditional blue-spine guidebooks feature fewer images but hold copious information on destinations big and small. How easy are they to navigate and find what you're looking for? Does the publisher have a policy that rules out writers accepting freebies for positive coverage? Some books will go into greater depth on activities such as hiking, cycling or surfing, so if you're basing your whole trip on doing these activities, check the coverage in different books. You might also consider a specialised guidebook that concentrates on whichever aspect of the trip you're most interested in.

Also think about how long you plan to spend in each destination, as this will influence the level of detail you will want from your guide. For example, in Lonely Planet's *Europe* guidebook, Paris is covered in 19 or 20 pages, which is fine if you're taking a short trip. If, on the other hand, you're travelling around the country, the equivalent *France* book might be better as it gives Paris a whopping 100+ pages. If you need even more depth, you should try a city guide, which gives the 'City of Light' capital around 400 pages, or if you're on a brief visit, *Pocket Paris* has 200+ pages, and the *Best of Paris* and *Discover Paris* both have around 258 pages, including a lot of snappy colour photographs.

TRAVEL AGENCIES

With internet booking booming over the past few years, the writing seemed to be on the wall for local travel agencies. However, the good ones have continued to prove their worth and have survived by offering things you can't get on the web, such as advice on where to go. These agencies can also help with booking tricky connections and telling you which vaccinations and visas you'll need. Their brochures can be a good source of free information and even if you don't want to go on an organised tour, you can get a good feel for a country's major sights from the full-colour pictures in these glossy publications.

Travel consultants are often widely travelled and most will be happy to share their experiences with you. However, many consultants work on commission, so they may be keen to make the deal and won't want to waste too much time if it's not going to result in a booking.

PAPERWORK

If travelling is all about being free, then why does paperwork take up so much time? It's boring but important stuff and it may mean waiting in a few long lines or reading lengthy documents, but you really can't leave home without it. The more you research the easier it will be once you're on the road – everyone's heard stories about travellers who get sent home before they even board their flight because they didn't have the right visa or their passport had expired (or close to it). They're easy problems to avoid if you use the advance-planning tips in this chapter.

PASSPORTS

When overseas, your passport is your main form of ID, with visas and entry stamps showing that you have a legal right to be in a country.

You'll need to carry your passport with you in most destinations. You should avoid handing it over to anyone for long periods of time, though when checking in at hotels or hostels it's common to give it to the desk clerk to sign you in. When you apply for a visa, you'll entrust your passport to embassy staff, which can sometimes mean being without your passport for a period of a few weeks.

KEEPING A COPY

When you haven't got your passport in your possession it can be reassuring to know that you have a record of all the important details on it – making it easier to replace if you lose it. You should always copy down your passport number – some travellers keep it in their journal – but putting all the relevant details (or an image of the photo page taken on your phone) in an email to yourself is an even better way of ensuring you have all the info recorded. Additionally, having a printed scan or photocopy of the photo page of your passport can be handy when you don't have photo ID.

EXPIRY DATES & BLANK PAGES

If you've already got a passport, check its expiry date. Many countries require that your passport is valid for at least six months after your planned return date, even if you're only intending to stay for a few days. Depending on where you're travelling, you'll also need enough blank pages for stamps and visas. Some immigration officials demand that their entry and exit stamps (or visa stickers) go on clean pages only (though usually if you ask nicely they'll put the stamps on a partially used page).

GETTING A PASSPORT

Getting a passport is a simple enough process no matter where you live. Your national government website will have details of where you can apply (see Directories in Part Four), but many post offices should be able to give you forms and process your application. What you'll require in order to apply depends on your home country (so check websites for latest changes), but generally you'll need proof of citizenship (such as a birth certificate), photo ID (driving licence) and at least two identical photos of yourself (in a portrait style).

You'll also need to pay a fee and provide any evidence of a name change. Some countries have strict rules regarding the photos (no smiling, no hats etc) and their websites will be the best guide for this. In Australia, for example, photos must be signed by a guarantor. Some US outlets (they're listed on the US State Department site) include photography facilities, which will cost you a little more but can be a good way to ensure you get a useable photo.

Some countries require you to sit an interview, a simple process of checking your application and making sure you have the correct documentation. Other countries let you apply online and you can post in relevant documents.

Costs

Depending on where you're from, you might have the option of getting more pages in your passport, which can push the price up. If you really get the travel bug, it can be worth getting a passport with more pages, but generally a cheaper one will do the trick.

At the time of research, the cost of a passport (if applying in your home country) was:

- **Australia** A$282 (10-year validity); A$142 (5-year validity, for under-16s and over-75s)
- **Canada** C$160 (10-year); C$120 (5-year)
- **New Zealand** NZ$180 (10-year)
- **UK** £72.50 (10-year, online application); £85 (10-year, paper application)
- **USA** US$145 (10-year, first-time); US$110 (10-year, renewal)

Standard Issuing Period

Again, different countries promise different results. Sometimes there can be complications such as not having the right type of photos or not providing the correct information, which will complicate the application process, so check the details on the relevant country's website.

- **Australia** 3 weeks (must be done in person at participating Australia Post outlet)
- **Canada** 10 working days (if applying in person at passport office); 20 days, plus mailing time (if applying by post from Canada or USA)
- **New Zealand** 10 working days (online application is possible)

- **UK** 3 weeks (online application is possible)
- **USA** 4 to 6 weeks

Fast-Tracking

If you need your passport in a hurry, most countries will fast-track applications for an additional fee to the passport cost (see examples of total costs below). In some cases, such as in the USA, you may need to prove the necessity of the emergency passport.

- **Australia** Priority (two business days, plus mailing time): A$468
- **Canada** Urgent (end of next business day): C$270; Express (2-9 business days): C$210
- **New Zealand** Urgent (up to 3 business days): NZ$360; After hours call-out (same day): NZ$730
- **UK** Paper or Online Premium (4 hours): £177; Fast Track (1 week): £142
- **USA** Expedited (2 to 3 weeks) or expedited at agency (9 days): US$205; various private expediting agency fees (24-hour to 5-7 business days) US$199-429, excl passport/govt fees

ELECTRONIC PASSPORTS

Most countries have already introduced the electronic passport, which has a small built-in computer chip that stores the passport holder's information, including a photograph. These passports are also called biometric passports, because they use facial-recognition technology so your facial features can be quickly scanned to see if they match the passport you're carrying. Most also now hold fingerprint information. Electronic passports are slightly more vulnerable to damage and most come with warnings not to bend, wet or fold your passport.

LOST OR STOLEN PASSPORTS

Although we advise you to keep your passport with you at all times, losing it is a fixable problem. You should report it straight away to your nearest embassy or high commission (which should be listed in your guidebook). If your country doesn't have diplomatic representation in the country you're in, you should try a neighbouring country to your own. You may also need to notify local authorities, but check with embassy staff as there may be a quick way to resolve the situation. If your passport has been stolen, go straight to the police and ask for a police report which you can take to the embassy or consulate.

You'll generally have to show the embassy another form of photo ID, so they can issue an emergency passport. This is the time to bring out the photocopy of your passport (or to print out/show the image of it that you emailed to yourself earlier). Replacements usually cost a little more but will get to you quickly, and you may even be issued with an emergency passport on the same day.

If you had visas in your lost passport, you'll need to replace them by going to the nearest consulate of the issuing countries.

DUAL/MULTIPLE CITIZENSHIP

Every country has different rules about dual/multiple citizenship (and some may not allow it at all), so check the passport websites. And if you do travel with more than one passport, don't advertise it to immigration officials as it tends to raise more questions than answers.

If permitted, you can be a dual/multiple citizen if your parents (and sometimes grandparents) were born in another country. With passports from two or more countries, you may be able to switch between them for more affordable visas. But if travelling between neighbouring countries you should stick to the same passport – if you entered and left Thailand on a British passport, don't try to enter Malaysia on your Australian passport as the officials won't find the exit stamp and will wonder how you got into the region.

VISAS

As you may know, a visa is a stamp or document in your passport that says you may enter a country and stay there for a specific amount of time. Usually they're issued by the embassy, consulate or high commission of the country you're intending to visit. They're attached to or printed in your passport and require a photograph or two which will be kept on file and may be added to your passport.

Depending on your country's diplomatic relations with the destination you're planning to visit, you may not even need to get a visa to enter a country (see below). You'll need to check though, because without a visa (or with the wrong kind) you might be sent home before boarding your plane.

Applying in advance is usually the best idea, though most visas are active from the date of issue, so if you get a six-month visa to China and you visit seven months later, it will have expired. If you've got a flexible or lengthy itinerary it might be better to apply on the road. If you do apply in advance, however, you may be given a greater choice of visas. For example, some countries may offer a six-month visa if you apply through the embassy, but if you turn up at the border you'll only have the option of a 30-day version.

DO YOU NEED A VISA?

When you review your itinerary, remember that every country could potentially require a visa. Be aware that international relations often shift while you're away, so you may find that a country that was fine when you left could require a visa when you arrive at the border. The best place to find out the latest rules is the embassy site of your destination, and a good portal to many of these sites is **Project Visa** (http://projectvisa.com), which links directly to the visa pages in the maze that constitutes most embassy sites. You should check for every country you plan to visit – and check again just before you leave.

Commonly, countries that have trade agreements (such as the European Union) or are neighbours (such as Canada and the USA) don't need visas between them. The Schengen Agreement between European countries, for example, allows many European nationals to travel freely between their countries, but it also means that non-Europeans need only apply for a single Schengen visa to visit several European destinations. The US has a Visa Waiver Program (VWP) for many countries it's friendly with, though citizens of these countries must still apply online (US$14) for an Electronic System for Travel Authorization (ESTA) at least 72 hours before departure. Canada now has something similar – the Electronic Travel Authorization (eTA) – which costs C$7.

APPLYING FOR VISAS

Applying for visas isn't necessarily a nightmare, though if you have to go to an embassy or organise an invite into a country (as is still the case with Russia), it can require some preparation. Allow some time before you travel to organise your visas, just in case you get knocked back or need to supply more information. Don't forget to add visa costs into your budget (see Money & Costs, p32), as they can range from £10/US$15/A$20 to £50/US$275/A$250, and remember that, like passports, they can cost more for rush jobs.

An embassy website should tell you if you need to organise a visa in advance or if it's possible to get it on arrival – some countries offer both options, and how you apply might affect the cost of the visa. It's often cheaper to apply before you travel, and online applications can be even better options; for example, if an Australian applies online for an e-visa to Brazil the cost is A$57, but to apply at an embassy or by post costs a whopping A$216.

TIPS

1. If you do need to get a visa, find out at what times the embassy or consulate is open and what documentation you'll need. Get there ahead of this time and be prepared to queue. This preparation will prevent you from wasting days hanging around an embassy that's only open for an hour a week.

2. If you want to be really prepared, bring along a set of passport-sized pictures. These are good for visa applications, police reports if you get anything stolen, and other unforeseen paperwork. You don't have to get new pictures every year, but think of how cheap they are back home and how much of a pain it will be to find a place to get them done at 3am in Nepal.

Whether you visit the embassy or apply for a visa when you arrive at your destination, you'll need to make sure you have passport-style photos and money to buy your visa. Many embassies allow you to download application forms which you can bring with you to an interview or post them in with your passport. The forms generally ask for personal information (date of birth, mother's maiden name, marital status, occupation, etc) as well as information about your trip (length of stay, arrival/departure dates and, possibly, an address where you'll be staying), so if you have to apply at an embassy make sure you have this information with you. You'll also be asked which type of visa (see p28) you'll need.

If you do have to go to the embassy in person, arrive early and allow lots of time for long queues. No matter how petty or bureaucratic they might seem, you should be polite and friendly to the embassy staff, partly because they can be helpful if they like you, but also because reviewing hundreds of applications is a hard job.

Going to an embassy is still the preferred way to get a visa for many travellers, but if you do a postal application be prepared for it to take longer and don't expect to get too much help from embassy staff. ('You'll find all this information is on the website, goodbye...').

Better travel agents and specialised visa-agents can organise visas for you for a fee, so it's generally more affordable to organise it yourself. Using agents is only useful when there are complicated applications, such as those requiring invitations or negotiating complex bureaucracy.

Of course, obtaining a visa when you land in a country is the easiest method with a transaction at the immigration desk, but never assume you can do this, especially if you're getting a working holiday visa (see p116).

Bear in mind too that visa requirements can change based on the transport you used to enter a country. For instance, if you fly into Ethiopia you can get visas on arrival at Addis Ababa Bole International Airport, but if you go overland you have to arrange them in advance at an embassy.

When you do get your visa (sometimes posted back to you, sometimes by a return visit to the embassy), check that the dates and details are correct. Mistakes do happen and you should make sure it's all okay before you leave.

TYPES OF VISAS

There are five basic visa types: transit, tourist, business, student and working holiday. You're most likely to use tourist, student or working holiday visas, though transit visas are worth thinking about for stopovers. The tourist visa usually lasts for 30 to 90 days and is designed for visitors who are taking in the sights and won't be working. If you're studying (usually at university level – short courses don't require a student visa), the student visa is for you. Your school at home or in your destination should help you apply for this.

The working holiday visa is just the ticket if you want to mix vocation and vacation. The idea behind this visa is that you're just working short-term and some visas won't allow you to work in your career field, so it can be important what you write as your occupation when you apply for this visa. In practice it's very difficult to police this ('Your field is landscape gardening – have you mowed any lawns while you've been in the country?'), but there are random crackdowns. For more on working holiday visas see p116.

The transit visa is for brief stays in a country when you're heading on somewhere else in the next day or two (some countries only allow one-day transit visas). If you're heading overland through a country or stopping over, then a transit visa will get you in and out in a hurry.

Don't get a transit visa if there's a chance you might stay longer, because immigration people are tougher on transit visas than tourist visas.

Finally, business visas are for when you're working in a country and will require sponsorship by a company. They require major hoop-jumping on your part and from the company who will sponsor you, plus you'll be bonded to that company and unable to work anywhere else in the country. Because of these complications, most people only use these visas to relocate or do business in another country.

Single or Multiple Entry?

A single-entry visa allows you to enter (and leave) a country once, while a multiple-entry visa lets you come and go several times. With the practicality and flexibility of the latter, there comes a greater cost – so choose wisely. Multiple-entry options can come in handy if you're going to use one country as a base to visit neighbouring nations.

TICKETS

AIR

Travel doesn't feel real until you buy your ticket, right? But shopping around, picking favourable dates and buying at least three months in advance are all wise things to do. For types of tickets to suit your trip, head for the Transport Options chapter (p89).

Seasonal Limits

Think carefully about your departure date, because the price of your ticket will depend on this. Try to avoid departing during school and major national holidays, as all airline fares are at their peak during these times.

When to Purchase

Ideally, you should start looking for bargain fares eight to 12 months in advance of your departure date. However, statistically speaking, the lowest price will fall between 47 and 60 days before your flight (see The 9 Best Flight-Booking Hacks, opposite). You may get cheap tickets at the very last minute but this is rare, even if seats are still available. Unfortunately, many of the best deals will require you to pay in full soon after booking. And special or bargain fares often don't allow changes or carry heavy change penalties (which are rarely covered by your travel insurance).

Maximum Time Limits

If you are travelling for more than a year, it's likely you won't be able to use the return portion of your ticket. This is because it is virtually impossible to find a ticket that allows you to be away for more than 12 months. It may still be cheaper for you to buy a return (rather than a single fare) and simply not use the return flight. And arriving in most countries on a one-way ticket is also very problematic (or unacceptable) at immigration.

Cancellation Penalties

These vary considerably but cancelling your ticket once it's booked may mean you lose the entire value of your ticket. (Most travel insurance policies protect against unavoidable cancellation fees, such as health emergencies or government travel advisories being placed on your upcoming destination).

Refund Policy

There is always a chance that you may want to extend your travels. If you do this and don't use a certain portion or sector of your airline ticket, it is unlikely you'll get a refund. Most airline tickets are sold on a 'non-refundable if part used' basis. And don't rely on what you're told about refund value by overseas travel agents or airline office staff – staff in Nairobi, for example, don't know all the rules of a discounted ticket sold by an agent in another country. If you are entitled to a refund, it can usually be arranged only through the travel agency you purchased your ticket from (and it may take months). This isn't terribly useful if you're travelling in the middle of Africa.

THE 9 BEST FLIGHT-BOOKING HACKS

Former NGO director Clint Johnson shares the tips and tricks he's learned while travel hacking his way around more than 120 countries at Triphackr (http://triphackr.com).

1. **Book at the right time** According to studies, the magic number ranges from 47 to 60 days before your departure date.
2. **Fly into alternative airports** Flying into London's Gatwick, Luton or Stansted airports may save you a bundle compared to Heathrow.
3. **Book a layover that's actually your end destination** Skiplagged (https://skiplagged.com) will help you find hidden city fares with this trick. Just don't check any bags!
4. **Take advantage of flight deals and error fares** Sites such as The Flight Deal (www.theflightdeal.com) and TravelPirates (www.travelpirates.com) share deals across social media. Error fares occur often and most airlines will honour these. Book quick!
5. **Sign up for newsletters** Newsletters from major airlines are a great way to stay on top of the cheapest fares, and find out how to earn extra miles and frequent flyer points.
6. **Join frequent flyer programmes and earn miles** There are three main global airline alliances where miles can be transferred between airlines.
7. **Set up fare alerts 90 days before a flight** If the price drops substantially, you can book it early. Use sites such as Kayak (www.kayak.com), Skyscanner (www.skyscanner.net) and Google Flights (www.google.com/flights).
8. **Book by the fare instead of the destination** Kayak offers the 'explore' tool and Skyscanner allows you to search 'everywhere' by month, which shows you the lowest fares around the world for a particular region.
9. **Fly on Tuesdays, Wednesdays and Saturdays** An easy way to save money.

Change Penalties

There are three main types of changes: name changes, date changes and route changes. It's very rare that a name change will be permitted. As regards dates, there are usually restrictions on changing your departure date from your home country. However, when travelling on a long multi-staged trip, the dates of onward flights can often be changed (subject to seat availability). Although in many cases date changes are free, quite hefty fees can be levied depending on the rules of the ticket (and the policies of the travel agency and the airline(s) concerned). In some cases, tickets will allow no date changes at all. Route changes may be possible but usually attract a fee, and where they are permitted there is likely to be a stipulation as to how many route changes you're allowed (often only one).

Comparing Prices

Shopping around for the best flight prices will significantly reduce your spend. Hopping between several **budget airlines (see p92)** can be cheaper than a **round-the-world ticket (see p89)**, and going **overland (see p95)** can cut the price tag if you've got the extra time.

Airlines, online travel agents and flight search engines increasingly offer newsletters and/or alerts that you can subscribe to, and you can even be informed when specific destinations are on sale. Signing up for a few of these as much as a year before you travel can give you a clearer idea of how fares vary.

Buying from Airlines

For short-haul flights, buying from airlines is almost always the best plan. For long-haul flights it's almost always the worst plan. Check the Air section in the Getting There portion for the region you'll be visiting (see destination chapters in Part Three, p156) for details about which airlines fly there.

Buying from Specialist Travel Agents

A good specialist travel agent will be familiar with all routes that airlines fly and will have up-to-the-minute information on discounted fares around the world.

For specialist travel agencies operating in the UK and Ireland, see p339. For those in North America, see p346. Australasian options are covered on p343.

Buying from Online Bookers

The web has a plethora of great sites and flight aggregators to help you find flight bargains. Some of our favourite reliable options are:

- **Adioso** (https://adioso.com)
- **Cheap Tickets** (www.cheaptickets.com)
- **Ebookers** (www.ebookers.com)
- **Expedia** (www.expedia.com)
- **FareCompare** (www.farecompare.com)
- **Google Flights** (www.google.com/flights)
- **Hotwire** (www.hotwire.com)
- **Kayak** (www.kayak.com)
- **Last Minute Travel** (www.lastminutetravel.com)
- **Matrix Airfare Search** (http://matrix.itasoftware.com)
- **Momondo** (www.momondo.co.uk)
- **Opodo** (www.opodo.com)
- **Sky Auction** (www.skyauction.com)
- **Skyscanner** (www.skyscanner.net)
- **Travelocity** (www.travelocity.com)
- **Viator** (www.viator.com)
- **Zuji** (www.zuji.com) Hong Kong- and Singapore-based site.

OVERLAND

Buying tickets in advance for overland travel can be a good money saver. Many train passes are available only to foreigners, so if you wait to arrive in the country it may be difficult to buy a pass like the Eurail ticket (see Transport Options p89).

INSURANCE

Accidents happen, sickness can hit even the healthiest people, luggage gets stolen and there are a thousand other things that could really ruin your trip. Travel insurance at least prepares you for some of them. Many nations have reciprocal health agreements, so British travellers, for instance, can use Australian health services, but this is limited to only medically necessary (and urgent) care and doesn't cover expensive ambulance services. Insurance has its benefits, and can sort you a ticket home. You may need to bring a health card from home to use another country's medical services.

WHAT INSURANCE DO YOU NEED?

Read the fine print and look for user reviews before choosing your insurance policy – the price may look tempting, but it's not a saving if the company doesn't pay claims. Some other important factors to look for are:

• **Activity coverage** Study the list of activities you're covered for. Often a policy will cover one or two bungee jumps, but charge twice as much if you want to go gliding, for instance. If you want to try snowboarding or scuba diving, ask about them as they're often not included. Also, look at the list of sports you're allowed to play.

• **Acts of war and terrorism** No policy covers for nuclear, chemical or biological warfare, but some do insure you against acts of terrorism.

• **Cancellation** Good policies will cover you for flight and train cancellations, which can be handy when you've pre-booked accommodation.

• **Extensions** If you decide to extend your stay, ensure your policy can be easily extended too, and that you only pay for the difference in cost between the two periods rather than having to take out a fresh policy for your additional time.

• **Geography** Make sure you and your insurance company are on the same map. What do they understand by 'Europe', for instance? Are Turkey and Russia included? Premiums go way up when you volunteer in Canada and the US.

• **Government warnings/advisories** If you go to a country that your government has advised against visiting (see p40), it will usually invalidate your insurance. Make sure you know your insurance company's exact policy on this. Some insurance policies will still pay out if your claim is within seven days of your destination being named, and others won't. This means you need to regularly check your government's relevant website when you're away.

• **Illegal activities** Most policies won't help you out if you get up to anything illegal.

• **Luggage & valuables** If you're taking a laptop, phone or other valuables, check they're covered, as some policies require you to declare them upfront and give serial numbers. Cheap ones may require you pay more for valuables.

• **Pre-existing conditions** If you've got high blood pressure, diabetes, asthma or any other illnesses, make sure they're covered. Usually you're okay if your condition is diagnosed and stable, but all policies vary.

• **Receipts & serial numbers** Keep receipts and serial numbers at home for anything you might lose on your travels.

• **Sufficient cover** Buy a policy that covers repatriation – you really don't want one that only covers evacuation to the nearest medical facility rather than back to your home country. And check how much your medical excess will be (ie how much you'll have to pay before your insurance company picks up the tab).

• **Who pays?** Check whether you have to pay for healthcare and claim the money back, or whether the company will pay the providers direct. If the former, you'll need to keep all documentation. If you have a medical problem, some policies will ask you to call a centre back home where an immediate assessment of your condition will be made. Before you go try out your travel insurance company's 24-hour emergency hotline to make sure that it's working and easy to work your way through. You'll find reliable insurance options on p338 for British travellers, p342 for North American travellers and p345 for those from Australasia.

MONEY & COSTS

No-one likes penny-pinching, but if you have a finite budget there is only one certainty: the less you spend per day, the more days you can spend on the road. Some travellers go overboard with fixed budgets and draconian 'no splurge' rules, but we think a budget should be a flexible guide. Would you really want to miss out on seeing whales thumping the ocean next to your boat just to save a few dollars? Or say 'no thanks' to a safari through Kenya, or hang out in a hostel rather than the hippest London club just because your budget didn't include it?

Good budgets allow for new possibilities and give you the chance to enjoy the odd bit of serendipity. Plus you could discover a few savings along the way or take a job to pay it off later (see p115). While you don't want to be throwing money away, being miserly and haggling over every last dong (yes, that's what Vietnamese money is called) in a Hanoi market won't make you many friends among locals

BUDGETING

The best way to start budgeting is to try and gauge what your expenses will be while you're away and then see how long the money you have will last. Up-to-date guidebooks to your destinations will give you a pretty good idea of prices, but checking the internet, especially local blogs, can also help as prices can rise quickly.

While you're reading a guidebook, look for activities you might want to do or a course that could make your trip more worthwhile (see p148). A tour could be the best way to get out of a major city if you don't have your own transport. Think about comfort levels. Do you want to blow some extra money on a plush Fijian resort after a couple of weeks of tough island-hopping in the Pacific? It's difficult to plan for everything, so build a bit of 'fat' into the budget so you can stay in a nice hotel when you need to, or allow cash to get a taxi when you're in a hurry.

Sometimes you'll have no choice but to spend more to get things done quickly – the Russian visa, for example, can almost double in price depending on how quickly you need it. Allow a little bit of money for emergencies such as missing a plane or needing to take a taxi, and if you don't have any emergencies you can blow it all on your way home (or put it away for your next foreign foray!).

No matter how thoroughly you plan it, no budget will capture everything or every eventuality, so overestimating is always a good idea – if the guidebook says a meal in Indonesia will cost 15,000Rp (£0.78/US$1.04/A$1.41), you might want to round it up in your currency (£1/US$1.25/A$1.50). This means you'll factor in a bit of a fudge factor for price changes and currency fluctuations, which can happen when your own currency falls on financial markets.

EXPENSES

Working out your expenses will give you a good idea of how much you'll spend. Start with the big-ticket items which are often closest to what you'll actually spend when you're away (as they won't change much and you can get a clear quote when you book).

PAYPAL

If you're addicted to online shopping, you'll know about PayPal (www.paypal.com). This web-based financial tool lets people transfer money into and out of your bank or credit card accounts without giving them the account details, plus you can buy and sell almost anything online. It's a good alternative to wired money if you have easy access to the internet.

BEFORE YOU GO

Plane Tickets

Your plane ticket will be the biggest pre-trip expense, and prices vary widely depending on where (and when) you are travelling. Start your comparison shopping online as much as a year before your planned date and you'll soon have a good idea on what you'll need to spend to get your trip truly underway. For approximate prices on round-the-world (RTW) tickets, check the Transport chapter **(see p89)**. Don't forget the budget carriers **(see p92)** which offer deals year-round, as well as some charter airlines that don't turn up on some search engines.

It's now rare for airport taxes not to be included in advertised prices of flights, but in some countries you might have to pay this at the airport in the local currency. This is often mentioned in the guidebook, or if it's unclear you could call the airline to verify how and where the taxes are paid.

Visas

Don't forget visas when working out your expenses. Sometimes they're free, but if you need a few they add up to a hefty total. Travelling in East Africa for example, visas for Tanzania (US$50), Kenya (US$50), Uganda (US$50) and Rwanda (US$30) add up quickly. By doing some research however, this price can be reduced slightly by buying an East Africa Tourist Visa (US$100), which covers the latter three countries. If you're travelling across many borders, try to work out how long you'll stay in each country so you can get the best-value visa, and choose routes that enable you to avoid the more costly multiple-entry visas (see p116).

Travel Insurance

Skimp on your travel insurance and it will come back to bite your bruised arse. A cheap policy can be a waste of money if it won't pay out, and it may not cover you for everything you'll want to do or all the places you want to go (see p109).

Immunisations

Go to your local travel clinic or surgery at least eight weeks before you depart to discuss which vaccinations are necessary, and also if antimalarials are needed. Some jabs may be free but most will cost you – for your first trip to Southeast Asia, Africa or Central America the total could be several hundred dollars or pounds sterling. Check out the Health & Safety chapter for more information on immunisations (see p39).

Equipment

Given the amount of costly specialist travel gear available, you could spend thousands kitting yourself out if you so choose. However, you probably won't need half of what you think you do. A few key pieces of equipment will make your trip easier, such as a money belt, padlock and small head torch, but think about your destination and whether you'll really need the gear. It's usually best to pack light, and if you realise you do need that one piece of kit you didn't bring, it's often easy enough to find it while on the road. Borrowing equipment or buying second-hand might be a good way to crunch costs.

Buying a tent and sleeping bag will add hundreds to your total (and weight to your bag), so think carefully if you'll get enough use out of them to justify the spend. Equipment can often be rented cheaply while travelling, and it saves you having to carry it for the duration.

Luggage

You'll need to invest in a good bag that will suit every moment of your trip (see Choosing Your Bag, p55), so add a decent amount to your pre-trip budget for this. An uncomfortable bag can bring daily misery.

ON THE ROAD

The destination chapters (see Part Three, p156) include costs, which will help you get an idea of basic on-the-road expenses, and once you've decided on a destination you can get a better idea with the help of a guidebook. Prices do go up, particularly in tourist hotspots, so some travellers get their estimates of on-the-road expenses and add 20%. Others monitor their budget as they go and adjust it as they discover unexpected costs.

THE TIPPING POINT

If you're not prepared, tipping anxiety pounces on you just as you're wiping the corners of your mouth. However, doing a little research before arriving in the destination (most guidebooks provide advice on this topic, as do apps such as GlobeTipping - Tipping Calculator & Advisor) will alleviate any stress or possible offence. Importantly, it will also allow you to more accurately budget your costs before departing.

Tipping varies from country to country and the best approach is to stick with local customs. If you're not sure what to do, look at what other people are doing around you. For instance in some cultures leaving without tipping may result in a waiter chasing you down the street, while in other places, such as Japan, leaving a tip is seen as rude.

Accommodation

In terms of your on-the-road costs, where you rest your head each night will be your biggest expense. Work out how many nights you'll be staying in each type of accommodation and multiply this by the room rate. Even if keeping your spend down is paramount, don't forget to allow yourself a few nights in a motel or hotel for those days when you just want to get away from the hostel. You can make some savings by camping if you've got a tent, or by couchsurfing (**see p105**). And if that motel room is looking too pricey you can always share to drive costs down.

Travelling out of season is another way to cut costs and you can check the destination chapters for advice on off-season prices for specific places (see Part Three). Booking ahead can sometimes be a good way to grab a bargain, but if you've got a flexible itinerary you can make savings by finding cheaper places as you travel.

Food & Drink

You'll likely be on the move more than you would be at home, so you'll need to account for eating a little more too in your budget. Plan on at least three square meals a day in your calculations, plus a few coffees and snacks along the way. If need be, you can scrimp on some meals by cooking for yourself when staying in a hostel or hotel with kitchen facilities, and by stocking up at supermarkets for packed lunches.

A good approach for budget travellers is to allow for a restaurant meal about once a day so you don't miss out on sampling great Italian pasta, true Mexican burritos and a million other signature dishes. After all, experiencing local cuisine is a major part of travel. Whatever you do to save money, don't forget to factor in the odd tip (see The Tipping Point box, opposite).

If money isn't so tight or you're travelling to experience great cuisine, do some research before you arrive in various destinations and make reservations at some of the signature restaurants so you don't miss out by arriving and finding them all fully booked or closed for holidays. The prices of meals in such establishments are covered in guidebooks, which will help you calculate your spending.

Sightseeing

Be sure to factor in admission fees for galleries and museums as these can add up. If need be, look out for discounted or free times and days, and note that a student card (see p38) usually gets you a discount.

Entertainment

OK, so you may need to think about a few club cover charges or perhaps the odd ticket to a performance such as a *M□ori hangi* (traditional feast and dancing) or a Japanese *noh* (opera), but there's a lot of free entertainment to see on the street. Ask at a local tourist office for free events or check out posters and flyers around universities, libraries and other public venues.

Shopping

You'll definitely want to allocate a small portion of your budget for souvenirs – from colourful *kramas* in Cambodia to a traditional Ghanaian drum – but if you're going away for a while you'll probably also need to replace your clothes and other travel goods along the way. There will be bargains in some countries, such as buying clothing in Asia.

Communication

With free Wi-Fi spreading widely, you shouldn't have to worry about the costs associated with keeping in touch with people at home, be it email, Facetime/Skype, WhatsApp etc. Between hotspots you can write messages on your phone/laptop and then send them when you find your next signal. Check the Staying in Touch chapter (p71) for all the options.

Laundry

Launderettes usually cost more in time than money, so budget for a trip per week. Handwashing in the sink will save you some money, though it's not allowed in some hostels (and drying your clothes in colder climates is an issue). In many places across Asia, Africa and South America it's cheap and easy to have your lodging do your laundry.

Transport

On a day-to-day basis, particularly in cities, you'll do plenty of walking – how better to see the sights? But you'll still need to budget for some public transport and taxis.

When you're planning your itinerary, you can work out the costs of larger trips (from one city to another) by bus or train using guidebooks. If flights are involved, do a little research online as early as possible to determine costs. Work out the costs of the big tickets and it might be more affordable to get a rail pass (see p95) or to use the hop-on/hop-off bus (see p97).

Activities

This is another important splurge to plan for, as you need to enjoy your trip as well as balance the budget. Some of these one-off costs can be eye-wateringly expensive, such as a permit to track mountain gorillas in Rwanda (US$1500) or Uganda (US$600), but they are often once-in-a-lifetime opportunities. You'd regret skipping them, and these experiences are actually good value given you'll be talking about them for the rest of your days.

MONEY PRACTICALITIES

TAKING YOUR MONEY WITH YOU

Travelling for months on end requires a significant amount of savings, and carrying it all with you as cash would be as unnerving as it is unwise. The general rule is to mix different methods: credit and debit cards; pre-paid travel cards; and cash (local currency and US dollars). Once you're on the road the best idea is to use a money belt and look at some good personal security measures (see p49).

Credit & Debit Cards

With contactless payments on the rise, you can skip handling much cash and just tap your debit or credit card for your purchases on the road. If you're given the option of paying in your home currency or the local currency during the transaction, always choose the latter or you may be stung with unfavourable exchange rates (the same can be said when withdrawing cash). In some cases, using a credit card also offers insurance on purchases, which comes in handy for large spends.

Getting money on the road can be a simple matter of using your debit card to withdraw cash from your bank account back home (cash advances on credit cards are to be avoided at all costs due to interest charges). There are numerous smartphone apps for locating ATMs and your bank card will usually have words such as Cirrus or Maestro on it to indicate which network you can use.

Search these popular networks to see if they cover your destinations:

- **Mastercard/Cirrus** (www.mastercard.com)
- **Mastercard/Maestro** (www.maestrocard.com)
- **Visa/Plus** (www.visa.com/atmlocator)

Be warned however that debit and credit cards may not be the cheapest option, with your bank charging loading and transaction fees (on both purchases and withdrawals).

Enquire at your bank and credit card company about this before you depart – it may be worth opening another account elsewhere that doesn't sting you with fees. For those in the UK, **Money Saving Expert** (www.

moneysavingexpert.com/travel/overseas-card-charges) documents the best accounts for international spending. In Australia, check **Savings Guide** (www.savingsguide.com.au). While on the road you may find that some merchants charge a fee for the onerous task of pushing your credit card through their machine, which makes credit cards less attractive for these functions.

Lastly, before you pack your cards check that they are not going to expire while you're away, and contact your bank and credit card company to let them know you're off overseas.

Prepaid Travel Cards

Prepaid travel cards are much like the travellers cheques of old, but without the same hassles. You load them prior to travel and then use them as you would a debit card when abroad, either paying for goods or withdrawing cash. If the card is lost or stolen, as long as you contact the provider, you won't lose any money. An advantage over debit cards is that you can lock in a rate of exchange if you so choose. There are numerous providers, so shop around as fees and rates of exchange vary. **MoneySavingExpert** in the UK provides up-to-date rankings of the various providers (www.moneysavingexpert.com/credit-cards/prepaid-travel-cards). In Australia, **Finder** provides similar reviews (www.finder.com.au/travel-money).

Cash

Cold hard local cash is certainly handy at times, but carrying too much of it can be risky if you lose your wallet or get robbed. A good option is to put a day's worth of spending money in a spare wallet so that you don't have to dip into your money belt while out and about (thus advertising your main stash of money) – and if the worst happens, handing over this wallet with this limited amount of cash during a mugging isn't the end of the world.

Before departing on your trip it's wise to get a small amount of your destination's local currency, usually just enough to get a taxi into town and pay for a few nights' accommodation in case something goes wrong (it's always better to acquire this before reaching the airport, as exchange bureaus there offer poor rates). If your bags get lost or the ATMs are out of action, those yuan you got before arriving in China will be more valuable than any transaction fees. Savvy travellers will also carry some US dollars for larger emergencies – it's generally accepted everywhere.

Changing foreign cash back or into other currencies as you travel can be difficult (see p38) and small amounts are almost unchangeable with commissions and other fees factored in – better to donate to a charity at the airport than hang onto them.

Wired Money

Also called 'money transfers', this is your real get-out-of-jail emergency option. You're better off using some of the other options before calling your loved ones or friends to wire you some money. Why are we so down on this method? Firstly, there's a whopping fee to wire the money, then there's trying to find the wired-money company's office and you'll have to pull out a government-issued piece of ID to get the money.

But when you're really in desperate need, wired money is quick (it can take ten minutes to get to you) and you'll receive it in local currency so you can start spending as soon as you leave the wired-money office.

Wired-money companies include:

- **MoneyGram** (www.moneygram.com)
- **Western Union** (www.westernunion.com)

CURRENCY CONVERSION

Currency exchange rates change daily and one day a moneychanger will offer a great rate, the next your country's currency nose-dives and you'll be wondering if the friendly folks at the moneychanger's aren't ripping you off. Most travellers don't worry too much about daily exchange rates, but currency converters come into their own when you're crossing borders and you need to know how many Chinese yuan you'll get for your Thai baht. You can stay up-to-date online, and it's a good idea to install apps from these sites:

- **Oanda (www.oanda.com) Has good online and app converters and a printable cheat sheet that gives you rates.**
- **XE (www.xe.com) Also has online and app converters and offers an email alert of currency changes.**

CHANGING MONEY

Whenever you change money, whether it's with a bank or a bloke on a street corner shouting 'Best price for US dollars!', moneychangers will take a cut. Make sure you know upfront how this will work. Most places take a percentage, though some may add a small fee and others just offer bad rates which cover their cut, so make sure you're clear on the rates before you make the deal.

Rules for changing money include:

- **Bigger is better** Change large amounts all at once rather than in several small transactions. This may mean having large amounts of cash on you, but dividing your money is the best idea (see p49).
- **Denominational switcheroos** Beware of getting too much local currency, as in some destinations it's almost worthless. In Cambodia, for example, most traders accept US dollars and will give you change in Cambodian riel which ironically aren't as well accepted in Cambodia. In Cuba, it's the opposite and you can save money using Cuban dollars, which are better than using the US cash. Check your guidebook for the best currency and ask for it in all exchanges.
- **Keep your receipts** Some destinations need you to hang onto these, but they also come in handy when you're trying to work out which place to go back to for a good rate.
- **Street dealers can be hustlers** If it seems too good to be true when a guy comes up to you on the street and offers you the best rate you've heard, it probably is. And be careful as black-market trading is illegal in many countries.

DISCOUNT CARDS

Discount cards will make it cheaper on the road and are available to students and young people. They offer good deals on everything from hostels to museums, so good that there's a roaring trade in fake cards in backpacker hangouts such as Bangkok and Cairo. It means you'll probably be asked for your student card from home when you're looking for a discount.

International Student Identity Card (ISIC)

The **ISIC** (www.isic.org) offers almost 150,000 discounts in over 130 countries, including everything from cinema tickets to flights and carbon offsetting. Check their website for your destinations and see how much value you can get out of the card.

The **ISIC** card lasts for 12 months, is available to full-time students (there's no upper age limit) and costs vary depending on the country of issue (£15/US$20/A$30). Applications are available online or at any of the branches listed on the site (usually travel agents such as STA

Travel). You'll need to provide evidence that you're a full-time student.

International Youth Travel Card (IYTC)
If you're not a full-time student the **IYTC** is available from the **ISIC** (www.isic.org) if you're under the age of 31 when you apply. It's valid for 12 months and has many of the same benefits as the ISIC (£12/US$20/A$30).

European Youth Card
If you're under 26 (30 in some countries) and heading to Europe, the **European Youth Card** (www.eyca.org) offers discounts on insurance, concerts, museums, transport and more in 49 different countries. Wherever you see the pink EC logo, it indicates that the place offers advantages and discounts to cardholders. It costs between €5 and €19 depending on where you buy it, lasts for a year and is available online.

Hostelling International (HI) Membership
If you're going to stay in a hostel, this card is crucial as it will give you a discount rate at **Hostelling International** (HI; www.hihostels.com) hostels as well as a few other discounts elsewhere. HI is so massive that even some independent hostels will sometimes give discounts to HI members. At last count HI had over 4000 hostels worldwide, which can be searched through its website. You can get a membership card at any HI hostel or through your local branch online. A one-year card costs £5/US$6.50/A$9).

BARGAINING & HAGGLING

In most parts of the world the price on the tag is what you pay, but there are a few places out there in which bargaining is part of the transaction. Your guidebook should give you a good idea of whether it's okay in a given destination – it's definitely not cool for galleries, museums and most hotels. Markets are usually the venue for haggling, though it's sometimes okay in retail stores.

At some point haggling stops being fun for everyone and becomes hard work for the seller who could be serving someone else while the annoying foreigner is trying to shave a few cents off the price. You'll rarely get prices the locals get, so stay polite and keep smiling so that the seller enjoys haggling with you. Chances are they've seen all your tricks before ('I'm really walking away now. No, I really am.') and will have a price in mind when haggling starts. Most importantly, keep some perspective. You're probably paying a lot less than you would at home and a little difference to you could mean a lot to the trader.

HEALTH & SAFETY

There are scammers and shifty characters in every country on the planet, but there are many more good-hearted people who look out for visitors' wellbeing. While they may steer you away from a dodgy currency trader or two, they won't help your immune system get tuned into the bacterial environment you're in. But there's no need to be alarmed. With a few simple precautions you can avoid most hassles and enjoy your trip without any incidents.

BEFORE YOU GO

IS YOUR DESTINATION SAFE?

No matter where you go there are always some risks. Governments monitor these risks and offer regular updates on places that they perceive have risks or potential incidents. While your own government will publish information specific to your nationality, we advise you to check a few of these updates to get an overall picture of the situation. You should also register for alerts about the country you're travelling to, if you can. This means that the info on any potential problems will be delivered into your inbox while you're on the road and you can work out if it's time to hightail it out of the country.

The best travel advisory services include:

- **British Foreign & Commonwealth Office** (FCO; www.gov.uk/foreign-travel-advice) Straight-up advice by country.
- **Government of Canada** (https://travel.gc.ca/) Advisories by country, among loads of other useful travel information.
- **New Zealand Foreign Affairs and Trade** (www.safetravel.govt.nz) New Zealand site that's also good for Pacific islands.
- **Australian Department of Foreign Affairs and Trade** (www.smarttraveller.gov.au) Subscribe and register your trip to receive alerts.
- **US Department of State – Bureau of Consular Affairs** (www.travel.state.gov) Read individual country advice and the Worldwide Caution Alert. Register with the Smart Traveler Enrollment Program (https://step.state.gov) for updates.

PRE-TRAVEL CHECKUPS

It's a good idea to check in with your doctor eight weeks or so before you hit the road to get a checkup and find out if there are any health issues that might affect your trip. Ask your doctor about any medications you might need to take with you, and look at getting a bigger prescription to cover the trip. If you're doing any diving while you're away, you may need to get a certificate of fitness for some dive centres. Ask about any ongoing problems you might have, such as hay fever or asthma, and how they might be affected in some of the countries you'll be visiting.

A stop at your dentist is a definite must too, as your teeth will be hit with new pressures from life on the road, so best to make sure they're in good condition when you go. Tooth trouble can be painfully inconvenient (and expensive) when travelling.

If you wear glasses or contacts, you should check in with your optometrist before you go. Bring a good supply of cleaning solutions and a few disposable contacts, which will stay sterile until you crack them open. Even if you prefer contacts, take a spare pair of specs because you may need them. If you live in a country or travel through one where prescription contacts are affordable, consider stocking up.

IMMUNISATIONS

The expression 'prevention is better than cure' could have been coined for immunisations. The basic principle behind immunisations or vaccinations is that your body will be given a tiny amount of a virus so that it can build up immunity for when you're exposed to the full-blown nasty virus.

You'll need to visit your local doctor or a travel clinic at least eight weeks before you travel to ensure there's enough time to take full courses of immunisations. Doctors can generally advise on what jabs you'll need, but they'll probably just be looking at a site like **Centers for Disease Control and Prevention** (www.cdc.gov/travel) and clicking on your destination. You should check the

Directories (Part Four) for other websites about immunisations to make sure you're well informed. It's also worth reviewing immunisations you may have had as a child, such as tetanus, diphtheria, tuberculosis and polio, to see if they need to be topped up.

If you can't complete a course of vaccinations, your protection against a disease won't be full, so make sure you organise a good schedule with your doctor well before you go. Of course, no matter how sweetly your doctor distracts you, needles will hurt and you may need to organise the rest of your day around experiencing minor side effects, such as slight fever and a numb arm. If you need to take antimalarial drugs, you may have to start your course of drugs before you go, depending on which ones you opt for (see p42).

All your immunisations will be recorded on an official certificate and it's a good idea to take this with you on your travels, as some countries require you to show you've been immunised against yellow fever and other diseases. Some travellers even attach it inside their passports with elastic bands.

MEDICAL KIT

Medical kits are as essential as insurance – as soon as you don't have one, you'll realise how crucial they are. Travel clinics sell a range of medical kits with names such as 'overland', 'expedition', 'independent' or 'rock'n'roll', which are designed for all kinds of travellers. They usually cost between £30/US$50/A$60 and £50/US$80/A$110.

It can be slightly cheaper to make your own medical kit and tailor it to your destination. It's better to make the kit comprehensive and keep extras of some items for emergencies (you don't want to be hunting for a pharmacist at 4am to buy water-purifying tablets).

Following is a list of the medical-kit basics:

- Prescription medicines, including antibiotics and antimalarials.
- Antidiarrheals – loperamide is probably the most effective, or the preventive Pepto-Bismol.
- Antifungal cream.
- Antihistamine tablets for hay fever and other allergies or itching.
- Calamine cream or aloe vera for sunburn and other skin rashes.
- Cough and cold remedies, and sore-throat lozenges.
- Eye drops.
- Indigestion remedies such as antacid tablets or liquids.
- Insect repellent (DEET or plant-based) and permethrin (for treating mosquito nets and clothes).
- Laxatives (particularly if you're headed to an area where there's little fibre in the diet).
- Oral-rehydration sachets and a measuring spoon for making up your own solution.
- Over-the-counter cystitis treatment.
- Painkillers such as paracetamol and aspirin for pain and fever, and anti-inflammatory drugs such as ibuprofen.
- Sting-relief spray or hydrocortisone cream for insect bites.
- Sun lotion and lip salve with sun block.
- Water-purifying tablets or water filter/purifier.

First-Aid Equipment

Stow this in your checked-in luggage because anything sharp will get confiscated if it's brought on as hand luggage:

- Antiseptic powder or solution (eg povidone-iodine) and/or antiseptic wipes.
- Bandages and safety pins.
- Digital (not mercury) thermometer.
- Gauze swabs and adhesive tape.

- Non-adhesive dressings.
- Scissors.
- Sticking plasters (adhesive bandages).
- Syringes and needles – ask your doctor for a note explaining why you have them to avoid any difficulties.
- Tweezers to remove splinters or ticks.
- Wound closure strips.

If you're going to really remote areas, you'll also need the following:

- Antibiotic eye and ear drops.
- Antibiotic pills or powder.
- Blister kit.
- Dental first-aid kit (either a commercial kit, or make up your own – ask your dentist for advice).
- Elasticated support bandage.
- Emergency splints (eg SAM splints).
- Triangular bandage for making an arm sling.
- Sterile kit with an intravenous-fluid giving set, blood-substitute solution and other intravenous fluids.

Health Documents

Here's a checklist of health-related information you might need to bring with you – some of it may not be relevant to your destination:

- Blood group.
- Contact details of your doctor back home.
- Copy of the prescription for any medication you take regularly.
- Details of any serious allergies (drug or otherwise).
- Health card or contact details for your national health service.
- Letter from your doctor explaining why you're carrying syringes in a medical kit.
- Prescription for glasses or contact lenses.
- Proof of yellow-fever immunisation.
- Summary of any important medical conditions you have.
- Travel-insurance emergency numbers and the serial number of your policy (see Insurance, p31).
- Vaccination certificate.

STAYING HEALTHY ON THE ROAD

When you're away you're likely to be run-down and off your guard for viruses and villains alike. But there's no need to get paranoid if you take a few simple precautions and use some common sense.

MALARIA

This disease provokes much debate among travellers. Aside from the backpacker myths (and you'll hear plenty of them, including the one about rubbing gin on yourself!), the facts are that malaria has been found in more than 100 countries globally and can be potentially fatal. The disease is commonly spread by mosquitoes, though not every mosquito bite results in malaria.

You're generally less at risk of getting malaria in Asia than in the more infamous malarial zones of sub-Saharan Africa and South America, though there are some high-risk areas in Asia. In many parts of Southeast Asia – especially areas of eastern Thailand and western Cambodia – there is a rise in resistance of the malarial parasite to commonly used antimalarial drugs. So the best prevention is to use several different preventive methods.

Antimalarial Pills

The bad news is that those crafty mosquitoes have developed resistance to several antimalarial pills, so a doctor will need to prescribe different pills from region to region. You need to start taking the pills before you leave, so that they'll reach maximum protective levels in your body before you arrive at your destination. And when you're away you must be really conscientious as it can be easy to forget to take your pills. Note that popping your pills will still be required after you get back or any parasites you picked up will go on a spree in your body. This can mean up to four weeks after you've left a malaria-prone area.

You can find a full list of antimalarial drugs and their possible side effects on the websites of **Centers for Disease Control and Prevention** website (www.cdc.gov/malaria) and **NHS fitfortravel** (www.fitfortravel.nhs.uk/advice/malaria).

You'll need to check on the latest news and most effective pills because mosquitoes keep developing new immunities, but at the time of research some antimalarial drugs included:

- **Atovaquone-proguanil (Malarone)** Good for both prevention and treatment of malaria; not for very young children, and very expensive so not ideal for longer trips.
- **Chloroquine** Long-standing drug generally not recommended in Asia and elsewhere due to resistance; useful if you can't take other drugs; can be difficult with other medications.
- **Doxycycline** No drug resistance reported yet, but it's probably only a matter of time; side effects include diarrhoea, sensitivity to sunlight and vaginal thrush; not for pregnant women or children under eight.
- **Mefloquine (Lariam)** Developed when chloroquine resistance was becoming widespread, though resistance has developed in Thailand and Cambodia; ask your doctor about side effects; note that it's not recommended during pregnancy.
- **Primaquine** The most effective medicine for preventing P.vivax. But it can't be used unless you've been tested for a glucose-6-phosphatase dehydrogenase (G6PD) deficiency.

FIRST AID COURSES

Depending on where you're going and how far off the beaten track you'll be, a pre-departure first-aid course can be a good idea.

As well as listings in the Directories chapter (Part Four), try these international options:

- **Red Cross (www.redcross.int) Find your local Red Cross branch for first-aid courses that can include childcare and workplace specialisations.**
- **St John Ambulance (www.sja.org.uk, www.stjohn.org.au, www.sja.ca) With offices in the UK, Australia and Canada, this organisation conducts reliable first-aid courses.**

Cover Up

The best way to stop a mosquito biting you is to not give it any flesh to bite. Even if you're taking antimalarials, you should take these simple precautions to avoid bites as you can't get immunisations for some diseases such as degue fever. Wearing long sleeves, long trousers and socks will leave only a small area exposed – in some countries this can just mean changing into your 'longs' at dusk and dawn, but in areas where you're preventing dengue-fever mosquitoes (such as Central America, Southeast Asia and even northern parts of Australia) you'll need 24-hour protection. Treating your clothes with permethrin will help repel the little monsters.

Using a mosquito net at night is another essential, and often you'll be supplied with them in good hostels, but check for holes and protect your own net on your travels by rolling it in another bag. When buying your own net look for one that is treated in permethrin. If you're eating out, look for places that have mosquito coils (see p44) or bug zappers – the constant crackling might not make for great dining ambience, but it's better than slapping your dinner companion to get yet another mosquito.

Finally, biting insects are attracted by many variables: body heat, body odour, chemicals in your sweat, perfumes, scented soap and types of clothing, so consider avoiding perfumes and scented soaps as well as steering clear of activity that makes you hot and sweaty when you know mosquitoes will be around.

Repellents

Despite the many 'jungle strength' and 'mozzie blitzkrieg' brands on the market, the most effective mosquito repellents contain DEET (diethyltoluamide) – check the label for these magic letters and you'll be alright. DEET is very effective against mosquitoes and other bugs and one application lasts up to four hours, although if you're sweating in the heat it won't last as long. The higher the concentration of DEET, the longer it will last. The optimal concentration is around 50%, although there are some longer-acting formulations with lower strengths of DEET. You should try a test dose before you travel in case of allergies or skin irritation.

Lemon eucalyptus–based natural products have also been an effective alternative to DEET (although DEET is probably still your best bet in high-risk areas). Other natural repellents include citronella, but these tend to be less effective and last less time (up to an hour), which makes them less practical.

There's a whole industry in repellents, including DEET-soaked wrist bands, electric vapour mats (that gradually burn chemicals), even electrified 'tennis racket' swats and, the traveller's favourite, mosquito coils. Although illegal in some countries and a bit of a fire hazard, burning a mosquito coil while you sleep is often a good way to get rid of the buzzing blights, plus they're cheap, relatively portable and usually available in camping shops.

You can often buy packs of coils in mosquito-prone countries, but make sure that they don't contain formaldehyde as their active ingredient, and try not to put them right next to you when you're sleeping. Plug-ins, which go into a power socket and disperse slowly, are another option if you know there won't be blackouts at your destination or generator switch-offs.

MALARIA & LONG HAUL TRAVEL

If you're planning on travelling in a malaria-prone area for six months or more, antimalarial pills can get expensive. You have two main options: continue taking them or stop. If you decide on the latter (discuss this with your doctor before you go), you need to be extremely vigilant about avoiding mosquito bites, plus you need to be very clear about where your nearest doctor is and have a good idea of symptoms of malaria. Unlike with other diseases, you don't build up immunity to malaria with time, so you're still at risk of getting it, even if you've been in a risk area for ages.

EATING & DRINKING

Bali belly, Montezuma's revenge, the Rangoon runs and tourist trots – it's almost a rite of passage to get diarrhoea from eating something bad while you're on the road, but at the time it can really blow your plans. Most problems are the result of food, with poor hygiene usually to blame. Diarrhoea and dysentery (bloody diarrhoea) are transmitted in this way, but there are also some diseases such as hepatitis A (common in travellers) and typhoid (uncommon).

Less-developed countries are particularly prone to it, but diarrhoea could equally strike in a cafe at home. When you travel, you'll being eating out more and relying on other people to prepare your food safely. There are a few simple precautions to minimise your risk of getting something nasty. Here are some food-and-drink hygiene tips:

• Avoid food that has been peeled, sliced or nicely arranged as this means it has been handled a lot.
• Avoid ice cubes in drinks; they may have been made from contaminated water.
• Drink bottled water or canned drinks when you're not sure of water quality and don't have an option to purify it. This can mean brushing your teeth with bottled or purified water as well.
• Eat only food that's freshly prepared and piping hot – avoid the hotel buffet like the plague.
• Raw fruit and vegetables are hard to clean. Only eat them if you know they've been washed in clean water or if you can safely peel them yourself. Bananas and papaya are good fruits to eat in the tropics.
• Remember that food can get contaminated from dirty dishes, cutlery, utensils and cups, and blenders or pulpers used for fruit juices are often suspect. Bring your own cup or spoon or clean those in the restaurant with a wet wipe.
• Tinned goods and powdered milk are usually safe (check 'best before' dates).
• Most breads and cakes are usually safe, though avoid cream-filled goodies because bugs such as salmonella love cream.

If you do get diarrhoea, don't panic. Traveller's diarrhoea usually strikes about the third day after you arrive and lasts about three to five days. As well as being caused by poor hygiene, other causes can include jet lag, strange food (including too much coffee) and your new lifestyle. It can make a comeback in the second week, though you will build up immunity so it should be less severe.

The most important aspect of treatment is to prevent dehydration by replacing lost fluid and to rest. You can drink most liquids, except alcohol, very sugary drinks, and dairy products. Oral-rehydration sachets can be useful but aren't essential if you're usually healthy. Starchy foods such as potatoes, plain rice or bread are believed to help fluid replacement, and you'll need to stick to a bland diet even after you start to feel better. Antidiarrheal tablets are of limited use, as they 'block you up', preventing your system from clearing out toxins and making certain types of diarrhoea worse. They're only really useful as a temporary stopping measure, for example if you have to go on a long bus journey.

Sometimes diarrhoea can be more serious, with blood, high fever and cramps (bacterial dysentery), or it can be persistent and bloody (amoebic dysentery) or persistent, explosive and gassy (giardia). All these diseases need treatment with specific antibiotics. If you're going to a remote area far from medical help, you may want to consider taking antibiotics with you for self-treatment of diarrhoea. However, it's generally better to seek medical advice to diagnose which type of diarrhoea you have and determine which antibiotics you should be taking.

Safe Drinking Water

Even the clearest, cleanest water can harbour nasty illnesses, so water purity will be an issue in many countries. Water can carry diarrhoea, dysentery, hepatitis A and typhoid, particularly in countries where infrastructure is limited and shared water may not be actively monitored.

Drinking bottled water is the obvious answer. It's best to stick to major brands of bottled water (though 'pirate' brands do appear), and make sure the seal on the lid is not broken (as bottles can be refilled with water from any old river). If you're in any doubt, choose carbonated water (for example plain soda water), as this is harder to counterfeit.

Bottled water can be costly, not just to your pocket but also to the environment, with millions of discarded and unrecycled plastic bottles having a severe environmental impact in many countries. Plus if you're trekking or travelling off the beaten track, bottled water is just not practical and may not be available in remote areas.

In these situations, you'll have to carry some means of making safe drinking water with you. Chlorine and iodine are the most popular chemicals, and at optimal concentrations both kill bacteria, viruses and most parasites (one exception is cryptosporidium). They're both available as tablets or liquids ('tincture' of iodine), and iodine is also available as crystals, usually at pharmacies, travel clinics and outdoor stores. They will come with instructions about dosage and use, which you should follow closely if you want to use them at their most effective.

Make sure you have more than one means of purifying water in case one method fails (for example, take some iodine as well as a pump-action purifier).

If the water is cloudy, no chemical in the world can help you because organic matter neutralises the chemicals. This will happen when you're going off the beaten track and taking water from a surface source (ie river, puddle or lake), instead of from a tap. This is when you'll need a filter/purifier. There are tons of different types on the market, and they can be expensive and break down easily, but specialist outdoor shops can usually recommend the best options.

ACCLIMATISATION

It can take a while to adjust to a new destination, but changes in temperature and altitude require some special consideration. Your body has an amazing capacity to adjust, but you'll need to help it along in extreme circumstances.

Beating the Heat

Avoiding serious problems such as heat exhaustion and heatstroke is all about drinking enough water to replace the amount you're sweating out. Cool water is best. Alcohol, tea and coffee, no matter how refreshing they seem, actually make you lose fluids. Don't wait until you feel thirsty before drinking; thirst is a very bad indicator of your fluid needs, and if you're thirsty, you're already dehydrated. Keep your own clean water, ideally in your own bottle to avoid plastic waste, and take regular drinks. If you sweat a lot, you may need to supplement your water intake with rehydration salts.

Physical activity will obviously make you hot, so your body will have to work even harder to stay cool during exercise. If you're active in a tropical climate, take it easy during the first week, building up slowly as you acclimatise. Avoid overexerting yourself (and this includes overeating) during the hottest part of the day; it's the perfect time for a siesta.

As far as clothing is concerned, you need to choose clothes that will protect your skin from the sun (and insects) but won't make you too hot. Sunburn makes your body less able to cope with the heat. Loose, light-coloured clothing made of natural fibres such as cotton will help you cope with the heat – ironically, dark colours, though 'cooler', will absorb the heat more.

Tanning might be an option at home, but with different conditions (holes in the ozone layer over the southern hemisphere or higher altitude, for example) it's probably not worth it. Too much sun will age your skin and increase your risk of skin cancer. The best tip is to stay covered up with clothes and hats. These provide by far the best protection from harmful rays (much better than any sun lotion). A wide-brimmed hat keeps damaging rays off all those easily forgotten bits: nose, ears, back of the neck, bald patch etc. Protect your eyes with sunglasses that block out UV rays. If you're using sun lotion, make sure it's strong and waterproof and reapply it as often as you need to. The sun is usually at its most intense between 11am and 3pm, so do as locals do and have a rest in the shade.

Remember, you can:

- Still get burnt on a cold day if the sun is shining.
- Fry on a cloudy day (because clouds let through some UV radiation) and in the shade (from reflected light, often off water).
- Get sunburnt through water (snorkelling can leave you smouldering).
- Cover up with a shirt and don't forget to use plenty of water-resistant sun lotion.

Cold Climate

Extreme cold, especially if you're trekking or just travelling through highland areas, can have as much of a serious impact as the sun. In the desert it can get freezing when the sun goes down, as there's nothing to retain the heat. Wearing the right gear is the best idea and if you're going in and out (which you will be if you're sightseeing in a museum, then heading somewhere else for lunch, for example),

5 URBAN MYTHS – FOOD

You'll hear many a not-so-wise old traveller give you tips on the road, but don't believe most of what you hear. Checking health conditions in a country you're visiting in a guidebook will help you out, but other travellers probably won't have any special medical knowledge. So ignore the following:

1. One bite and you're sick!

Your stomach's natural defences (mainly acid) can cope with small amounts of contaminated foods, so if you're not sure about something, just don't pig out on it.

2. If it smells good, it's all good.

Bugs and bacteria are just as attracted to those good smells as you are and smell really isn't an indicator of bacteria content.

3. Germs can't survive the burn of spicy food.

The only reason to add spice is for flavour, and it can disguise bacteria but won't kill them.

4. Milk is always good for you – my mother told me.

Unpasteurised milk can transmit a lot of diseases, including TB and salmonella, though boiling it will kill off many bugs.

5. What could go wrong with ice cream – it's frozen, right?

Freezing can kill off bacteria, but if power cuts are a factor, the food may have been refrozen several times, making it vulnerable to bugs.

wearing several layers that you can remove as temperature changes is a good idea. Food equals heat, so make sure you eat regularly and get sufficient calories in cold climates.

Another chilling problem is dehydration (cold makes you urinate more) so, much like in a hot climate, you should drink water often. The cold can also give you constipation and sunburn (especially at high altitude). Worse problems are general body cooling (hypothermia), or localised cooling (usually affecting hands and feet), called 'frostbite'.

Altitude

Above 2000m the lack of oxygen tends to make you a little loopy, particularly if you fly straight to a high place such as Lhasa (Tibet), La Paz (Bolivia) or Cuzco (Peru). Symptoms of mild altitude sickness kick in when you first arrive and include headache, nausea, loss of appetite, difficulty sleeping and lack of energy. Mild symptoms of altitude sickness just require rest, but more serious cases can be fatal so should be treated quickly.

If you're trekking you'll need to look seriously into acute mountain sickness (AMS) and consult with your travel-health clinic or expedition organiser. An authoritative website with a good section about AMS is www.fitfortravel.nhs.uk. Before you leave, check that your insurance covers altitude sickness. Discuss the effects of high altitude with your doctor if you have any ongoing illnesses such as asthma or diabetes, or if you're taking the contraceptive pill.

If you are trekking or climbing, the best way to prevent AMS is to ascend slowly. Sleep at a lower altitude than the greatest height you reached during the day, and allow extra time in your schedule for rest days. Drugs such as acetazolamide (trade name Diamox) are sometimes used to prevent AMS. However, taking drugs is no substitute for proper acclimatisation. If symptoms persist or worsen you must descend. You must never continue to climb if you have symptoms of AMS.

WOMEN'S HEALTH

Periods

Your cycle may be affected by time changes and the novelty of travelling, but, like jet lag, it should fall into sync with your new destination. You may find your periods stop altogether when you're away, affected by change of routine and various stresses (but do a pregnancy test if you think you may be pregnant). Or they might become heavier. If you suffer from PMT, be prepared for it to be worse, especially when you're trapped on a local bus where you have to nurse your neighbour's chickens. Take plentiful supplies of remedies you find helpful, as they may not be available in your destination.

If you think you may need contraception, consider starting the pill before you leave – it can reduce PMT and makes periods lighter and regular. Packing a silicon menstrual cup will alleviate the need to buy sanitary products while on the road.

Vaginal Infections

Hot weather and limited washing facilities make thrush (yeast infection) more likely when you're travelling. If you know you're prone to the infection, it's worth taking a supply of medication with you.

The Pill

If you think you'll need this while you're away, see your doctor, a family-planning clinic or your local women's health organisation before you leave. Timing your pill-taking can be tricky if you're crossing time zones, and diarrhoea, vomiting and antibiotics used to treat common infections can all reduce its effectiveness. The pill has also been linked to blood-clot formation, usually in the calf muscles or lungs (especially when you're not moving around a lot), so advice on deep-vein thrombosis (DVT) is particularly relevant to women. If you're going to be in a high-altitude destination (above 3700m), ask your doctor about alternative contraceptives.

There are more than 20 different types of pills, so take a plentiful supply of your medication with you to avoid switching to another brand. In some countries, oral contraceptives may not be readily available.

STAYING SAFE ON THE ROAD

While much is made of the external dangers we face when travelling, whether it's crime, terrorism or getting ripped off, one of the biggest threats can actually be ourselves. Travelling is an exciting and enlightening experience, and it inspires people to push their boundaries. But sometimes this can go too far, resulting in serious injury or death. If there is one rule to follow, it is this: if you wouldn't normally attempt it at home, don't try it in an unfamiliar land. Never dabbled with drugs? Then experimenting with them abroad is an even worse idea (besides the health ramifications, the laws are often much more strict in foreign countries). If you'd never dream of riding a motorcycle at 100mph down a motorway without a helmet in your homeland, don't give it a go in Brazil.

There are also some problems that you'll encounter on the road which you can only be protected against with preparation. Most people you meet will be friendly and helpful, but it can pay to be on your guard sometimes and set yourself some basic safety rules.

PERSONAL SECURITY

Not everyone is going to try to rip you off but in crowded, heavily touristed areas such as markets, busy squares, on public transport or even at tourist information centres, pickpockets have been known to operate. You'll probably be most at risk when you first set out because you may not be looking for potential dangers.

Make sure you know where your valuables are at all times – dividing them between a few different places is always a good idea. If your hostel or hotel looks trustworthy, you can leave some valuables in their safe or in your own locker. Bringing a money belt lets you stow your most precious belongings, usually your passport, the bulk of your cash and credit cards. The money belt should be worn under your clothing (baggier gear will hide it better, and don't leave straps showing as they can be easily cut) and it should never be taken out in public. Save your fumbling for a credit card for the privacy of your hostel room, and take your passport out in advance if you know you'll need it during the day.

So what about spending cash? A good idea is to carry a so-called 'dummy wallet' with a day's worth of spendings, and perhaps some expired bank cards to go with one of your active ones. Having either pickpocketed or taken during a mugging isn't the end of the world. Always keep a little spare cash and a credit card stashed somewhere just in case too – this could be your bag back at the hostel if it looks secure.

If you're travelling with a group, you can often make a base camp, where one of you will mind all the bags while the others go to buy tickets or get food. This can be a good technique, but secure your bags to avoid their easy theft – one traveller reported having their bags scooped up at an Indian railway station by enterprising thieves with their own luggage trolley.

Vulnerable Spots

Obviously, busy tourist spots will attract pickpockets and some may even work in groups, so avoid being distracted while another member of the gang dips into your pockets. Transport is equally vulnerable, so make sure your bag is looped around your leg on short hops and padlocked down for longer trips, especially on overnight train journeys. The other big danger is when you're drinking. Chances are you'll lose sight of your daypack and some opportunistic local will make the snatch, so keep it under your table (especially in streetside cafes, where a passing motorcycle snatch is possible) and loop your arm or leg through a strap. Just as you would at home, you should avoid lonely and remote areas at night. Public places can be good as there's little chance of violent crime, but don't forget about the pickpockets who love the busy spots. Visit public ATMs whenever possible and be discrete when you type in your PIN.

Make sure you're riding in registered taxis (check a guidebook to your destination for the local situation), and if your driver seems to be heading somewhere remote, make a polite enquiry and think about getting out. Taxi drivers can be saints in some places (especially when you're out late and need to get home fast) and satans in others ('Sir, what about a shortcut via my cousin's bar? You love it!'), so think about getting the mobile number of a good taxi driver when you encounter one.

In the Hostel

There are thousands of different hostels and, frankly, some of them are as secure as a baby's candy. Look for lockable doors and lockers where you can use your own padlock. Big hostels will use lockers that have computerised locks, which are also fine. Some places have left-luggage areas, which are good for leaving your bag in after you check out, but make sure they're lockable and not generally accessible. Some hostels even have safes, which are good for valuables so long as they're actually safes and not just a plastic bag under the counter. It won't hurt to ask to see the safe if it sounds dubious.

Everyday life at the hostel can present chances for thieves. Be sure your room is secure and try to keep the door locked at night (even when it gets hot), as even a charging mobile phone could be too tempting to a passer-by. When you sleep, it can be a good idea to keep your money belt in your pillowcase, as even the most out-of-it sleepers will wake up when someone's tugging at their pillow. Make sure your valuables are secure when you go for a shower – take them with you if the room is unsafe. Don't forget that your fellow travellers are just as likely to swipe your valuables as locals.

You should avoid giving your room number to strangers, particularly if you're a solo woman, and if you do want to arrange meet-ups with locals, look for public places. If a stranger asks where you're staying, you can be general (in a city with several hostels 'a hostel' is a fine answer, but if there's only one hostel be vaguer), or you can lie outright and tell them later when they've earned your trust.

In the Hotel or Guesthouse

With your own room in a hotel or guesthouse you are of course offered more privacy than at a hostel, and you need not worry about sleeping with your money belt in your pillowcase. That said, when leaving your room you should use the safe for valuables, if there is one. If there isn't, check with the front desk to see if they have one that you can use.

The same rules apply as per hostels in relation to keeping your door locked, left luggage and avoiding letting strangers know exactly where you're staying.

In Case of Mugging

Muggings are rare, as most theft of valuables is based on sneaky grabs rather than threatening someone with a weapon. In the unlikely event of a mugging, stay cool and give the muggers what they want quickly. Give them the money you have at hand (or a dummy wallet you use just for daily spending) and most muggers will take it and run, but some will ask for your money belt, camera and phone. Give it up, and your insurance should cover the loss. If you've got an escape route planned, make a run for it as most muggers won't follow, especially if you shout for help.

Once you're away from your assailant, make for the police station and report the robbery. You'll need some paperwork for the insurance claim and, if you followed the earlier advice about stashing some extra money and credit cards, you'll be okay until you can get replacement cards and passport. Remember to report stolen credit cards as soon as you can, so your mugger won't have too much of a spree.

Scams

Every traveller on the road will warn you about some great scam they claim happened to a guy they ran into in Bangkok or Amsterdam, or was it San Francisco? Some are just good urban myths, but there are plenty of real ones too. Most scams are about money, so if you're careful with yours then you won't be anyone's 'walking ATM'. In a few cases they may be about your personal safety (such as kidnapping scams), though these will often be covered in travel advisories (see Is Your Destination Safe? on p40). Some scams will be about helping a stranger while their accomplice is cutting the bottom out of your daypack. The trick is to remain sceptical enough to stay safe without closing yourself off to good experiences (see My First Roman Holiday boxed text, p53).

You can't make generalisations about scammers: sometimes it's a charming man offering to sell you gems at a bargain price, or it could be a shy kid wanting you to kick a football around with them. Most scams revolve around asking you to do something that goes against your common sense, but because that guy is so charming or the kid is so cute you'll find yourself thinking about it. Stick to your safety rules and you'll be fine.

Scams change as quickly as scammers do, but guidebooks will give you the latest and Lonely Planet's Thorn Tree (www.lonelyplanet.com/thorntree) is always quick to pick up on scams. Here are a few recurrent ones:

- **Changing money on the black market** It's always difficult to know what you're getting on the black market. Sometimes the rate will be really bad, sometimes notes will be counterfeit. Our favourite is the fake policeman who just happens to arrive when you hand over your money and 'confiscates' it.
- **Credit/debit card numbers** Due to the advent of contactless payments, or the ease of using someone's card number online, card fraud is all too easy these days. Carefully watch your card in restaurants to see that a second bill isn't rung up, or that the card isn't being surreptitiously cloned with an unnecessary swipe – and always, always, always cover the keypad if entering your pin on handheld devices or at an ATM. Check online to see if your balance has any unknown jumps. Be careful when using your credit card online in internet cafes. If it's a good place it's fine, but some

5 FREE APPS FOR STAYING SAFE

A mobile phone can be your most valuable safety tool on the road, which is a good reason to sort a local SIM or a decent data plan from home.

1. BSafe

This app allows you to create a 'social safety network' of contacts who will be notified in case of an emergency or in situations where you feel unsafe, and hit the panic button.

2. Companion

For extra safety when walking around at night or in sketchy neighbourhoods, this app texts a link to a live map of your walk to your pre-selected 'companions'. If there's a problem the app will ask you if you're OK or if you want to call the police. If you don't respond within 15 seconds, the app will notify your companions.

3. Citymapper

Simply punch in your desired destination in one of 39 urban areas in some 21 countries, and this app will show you how to get there via all methods of local transport.

4. Maps.me

This app allows you to download maps to use offline anywhere in the world.

5. Bugle

This app is designed primarily for people who don't want to take their phone with them when they're out. Users set the time limit and their emergency contacts in their phone are alerted by email and text if they don't check in within the limit.

places have password-detection software or hardware which will swipe your numbers for use later.

- **Fake police** In Africa, India, Central and South America, official outfits might sometimes fool you into thinking someone is a policeman. They'll demand to see your passport and order you to pay a fee for some fabricated reason. Hang on to your passport and money, and always ask to see ID. If they're the real deal, you can always ask to sort this out at the real police station. There have even been examples of this in Australia.
- **Gem or carpet deals** These are classic scams where someone will offer you a deal of a lifetime. Either they'll offer to send your recent purchase home or a bargain on gemstones that you could resell for a fortune. Of course, the expensive gems or carpets are worthless or they'll never send your purchase home for you. Another variation is designer clothing that's either fake or stolen.
- **Offers of food & drink from friendly strangers** Whether you're on a bus, in a bar or restaurant, or in someone's home, be careful about sharing a drink or a snack with someone you don't know. Travellers can be drugged and their possessions stolen. This seems to be particularly prevalent in the Philippines.
- **Practising English** You've just met someone cute at a tourist attraction and they're keen to practise their English with you. They'll suggest a local cafe and before you know it, you'll get served with a massive bill. Yep, the attractive English-speaker and the cafe staff have it all sorted out, so you have to part with a lot of cash for your one drink. Another variation involves an art gallery and a charming young artist.
- **'There's shit on your shoe'** In this gem someone taps you on the shoulder to tell you that a bird has just let drop on your shoe.

As you look down, the 'helpful' stranger's accomplice swipes your wallet and runs.

KEEPING IT LEGAL

Just as you should respect the people you're visiting, when you're in a foreign country you're actually bound by its laws. Your embassy and other authorities can't help you when you break local laws and you could find yourself doing jail time (or worse, in countries with capital punishment). High-profile cases have shown that bringing prisoners home can be very difficult – Australians will know of the Bali Nine's sentences for drug smuggling, while many Brits will be familiar with Laura Plummer's three-year jail term for bringing 300 prescription painkillers into Egypt while on holiday. Saying you had 'no idea' something was illegal isn't a defense.

The best protection is to do some research about the country you're visiting (a guidebook will usually make it clear). Even if locals are experimenting with drugs, it doesn't necessarily mean they're legal, and foreigners are usually more visible so getting caught is more likely.

Sex & Drugs

Tourist haunts seem to attract people selling drugs and you can get sick of people trailing after you offering 'Ecstasy, coke, marijuana, whatever you want'. But in some countries where drugs seem easy to come by, they may actually be illegal. Using drugs overseas can often mean getting mixes that vary in quality from lethally pure to throat-lozenge placebos ('Man, I was so high last night and it weirdly cleared up my cough.'). The real danger is that you never know what you're getting. You'll also be in an unfamiliar environment, so panic attacks and anxiety are more likely side effects. With HIV infection rates higher in many destinations than

MY FIRST ROMAN HOLIDAY

As if I wasn't worried enough by my first trip overseas, I had to read the section of my Rome guidebook called 'Dangers & Annoyances', which told me that the moment I got off the train I'd discover 'thieves are very active in the area around Stazione Termini'. In the days leading up to my first international flight, people elaborated on the devious means by which I'd be robbed blind, including Romani women who threw babies at you and the second you caught them would cut every bag off you while dipping into your pocket for your wallet, passport and every last stick of gum.

I arrived anticipating robbery. Catching the train in from the airport, I eyed the couple opposite me, convinced they were hardened thieves working the train for chumps who hadn't read the Dangers & Annoyances section. When they pulled out a package I braced myself in case they tried to throw it at me. It was cheese. They ate for a while and saw me staring so they offered me some.
It could be poison or, at the very least, a tranquiliser. But I risked it. And the soft milky taste was worth it. 'Mozzarella di bufala', the man explained. He told me it was from his home town, where he and his wife had just been, so they had plenty. He wasn't a thief, just a man proud of his hometown produce.

The expression 'taken with a grain of salt' is a Roman one. It was used to describe a king who wanted to become immune to poison, so he took small amounts of toxins with just a grain of salt to make it more palatable. Paranoia should be served with a sack of salt, while kind offerings from strangers generally taste good enough already.

George Dunford

at home, intravenous drug use is even more risky overseas. And if you're using Larium as an antimalarial, you'll need to be careful of side effects as Larium itself can be mind-altering.

Another concern with drugs is trafficking. No matter how much you're offered to 'just carry one package', it's never worth it and customs people mean it when they ask 'Did you pack that bag yourself?', so you'll bear any penalties for carrying drugs.

Don't carry a package for anyone unless you know exactly what's in it (including stuffed toys and wrapped gifts) and keep an eye on your bag at airports. Finally, before you get involved with the drugs industry (even as a customer), consider the impact on local communities, as local people can get caught up in a lucrative but illegal and dangerous black market.

Sex with a new partner could result in acquiring a sexually transmitted disease (STD, also called STI for 'sexually transmitted infection'). Get any symptoms such as an abnormal vaginal discharge or genital sores checked out as soon as possible. Some STIs don't show any symptoms, even though they can cause infertility and other problems, so unprotected sex while you're away should be followed by a checkup when you return home. Insist on the use of a condom to be safe. Bear in mind that rubber breaks down in heat, so store condoms deep in your pack and check for holes before using them. Safe sex is even more important when you're overseas because of the higher infection rates of HIV (in 2016 there were 20 million people living with HIV in East and Southern Africa, with almost 800,000 new cases that year alone). Not only are infection rates higher, often due to lack of safe-sex education, but medical resources will be limited.

GLOBAL ISSUES

After a browse of the headlines you could be left wondering if it's even safe to go outside your front door. But the news does give you the world's worst. You should plan your itinerary around the best and safest. You may not be able to do anything about some issues such as natural disasters, but being aware of the risks is the best preparation you can have. After reviewing a few travel advisories, you might reconsider your itinerary, but you should definitely keep an eye on current events for potential dangers.

Natural Disasters

Hurricane Irma's devastation of the Caribbean in 2017, the Nepal earthquake of 2015 and the Indian Ocean tsunami of 2004 were all tragic events that made many people rethink their travel plans. But these events were freaks of nature that had little warning – is there any way you can prepare for a natural disaster? Even 'safe' destinations, such as New Zealand with its several active volcanoes, are vulnerable to geothermal activity and earthquakes, but people still flock there in the thousands.

Most travel advisories warn of impending natural disasters. Watching the news will also keep you aware of the latest developments. In the event of a natural disaster, your embassy will track down travellers, and local authorities will be aided by international Non-Governmental Organisations (NGOs). To get more information (and possibly make yourself a little paranoid) about what to do in a blackout and similar situations, check out the disaster pages at **Centers for Disease Control and Protection** (www.cdc.gov/disasters).

Terrorism & Political Unrest

Just as disasters are ruled by natural forces, terrorism and political unrest are huge events rooted in history and social systems beyond a traveller's control. Reading up on the history of your destination can be useful, as you'll develop an understanding of the political situation and the likelihood of a revolution or clash of religious groups. A guidebook can also tell you more about regions where political unrest could be a particular problem – Kenya, for example, has dangerous pockets on the remote border with Somalia where there has been conflict for years, but the vast majority of the country sees little trouble. Travel advisories (see Is Your Destination Safe? on p40) are good indicators of what may happen in a country. You should, of course, avoid any political activity when you're overseas, including political marches or rallies as they can become violent.

Terrorism has become even more unpredictable with a global campaign waged by organisations such as the so-called Islamic State and the militant group Al-Qaeda. Obviously, increased security in airports has reduced the dangers, but if you see any suspicious activity you should report it to airport authorities or police. Some travel advisories warn about threats of terrorism, so if you can get a regular alert for your destination it will inform your choices.

GET PACKING

Everyone will have advice on what you should pack for your trip. Some people swear by sarongs (handy for wearing, lazing on or keeping the sun off) while others want to bring their hairdryer. It really just depends on your own comfort level, but it's universally agreed that travelling light is the best policy.

CHOOSING YOUR BAG

BACKPACKS

This is definitely the most practical way to carry stuff, even if you're not constantly on the move. It's worth paying a little more when it comes to a backpack, because it will be your constant companion and home for most of your trip. There are all sorts of snazzy designs, but your main concern should be comfort.

This is not a last-minute purchase. Buy your backpack six weeks in advance, pack it and take an experimental walk of your neighbourhood for an hour (get used to the stares of people, because backpackers are pretty conspicuous). It's better to work out before you go if it doesn't fit or if there's a manufacturing fault. Keep the receipt in case it doesn't work out.

Travel Packs

The preferred option of most backpackers is a bag with a zip that runs around the sides and top. This type of bag lets you open it completely, which can be handy when your last pair of clean underpants is buried at the bottom, or you want to make sure everything is in there. Plus it's easy to pack and unpack (and you'll do this often).

Good travel packs come with features that push the price up but are worth it. A zippered flap that will cover your harness is handy for flights. A detachable shoulder strap and side handles are also really useful when you need to pass your bag up to a porter or carry it other than on your back. You'd be surprised how biased some hotels can be against backpacks, and 'transforming' it into a large soft suitcase by zipping up the harness and using the carry handles often fools a snooty concierge.

Your zips need to be able to lock together and some bags come with a combination lock, though a decent padlock from a hardware store will do. Make sure your backpack has good back support, because you'll be wearing it for at least an hour most days when on the move. Most backpacks have good internal frames that are better than rigid external ones. Another handy feature is a bottom compartment, so you can roll up a sleeping bag or separate dirty laundry from clean.

And then there's the detachable day pack – another piece of baggage that will be your best friend by the end of your journey. These little beauties zip onto the front of your bag when you need to lug all your gear, or they can be worn on your front (it feels like being in a suit of armour) when you need to quickly pull out your passport in a train station. But wait, there's more! The day pack unzips, so you can carry it around separately and leave your big bag safely back in a locker at the hostel. They're usually big enough to carry around supplies for a day or even two, if you can pack lightly for a weekender.

Top Loaders
The top loader backpack is old school. It's basically a long tube with access through the top. These are best for trekking expeditions because they balance well – this is aided by compression straps down the sides to keep the weight as close to your back as possible. They are also considered more watertight and – importantly – you never have to worry about a broken zipper rendering them useless in the wilderness. They do have a reputation for being a real pain to get things out of, but there is an easy solution for this: coloured stuff sacks. Much like what you'd stuff your sleeping bag into, these sacks allow you to compartmentalise your top loader. One bag/colour for dirty laundry, one for clean socks and pants, another for shirts etc. This means you can empty your bag quickly, then find what you need in the relevant stuff sack. And it all quickly goes back in the way it came out.

TIPS

Carry a fold-down bag. You'll often find yourself suddenly overloaded with unexpected purchases, gifts or acquisitions. This way you won't end up wrecking your regular bag by trying to stuff a large carpet into it or have to buy a second bag. Mine folds down to about the size of a wallet.

Fitting & Fine-Tuning Your Backpack
Having decided which type to go for, now consider:

• **Fit** All backs are different, so get a pack that suits yours. Try all potential bags on with weight inside (most shops have small weights for this purpose). A good pack will have an adjustable internal frame that can be fitted to the length of your back and you should adjust this to get the perfect fit. Most big brands have male- and female-specific models (basically 'long' and 'short' ones), though tall women are often best off with the 'male model'. The key thing to remember is that the waist straps should fit nicely on your hips and take the brunt of the weight. The shoulder straps should be limited to simply keeping the bag snug to your back.

- **Size** The short answer is: 65L is big enough. Camping may require a bigger bag, but if you get much more than this, you'll probably overpack.
- **Strength** Cheaper models probably won't be as strong as a more expensive one. It's not always obvious from examining a backpack how durable it will be. Some materials seem light but are actually much more durable than heavyweight canvas.
- **Waterproofing** Getting a bag that's water-resistant will cover you when you're caught in the odd shower, but if you're doing water sports, waterproofing is necessary.

Backpacks are priced from around £75/US$100/A$175 to £250/US$350/A$400. We recommend the midrange packs (£150/US$200/A$250) for affordability, comfort and durability. You'll need to factor your pack price into your budget.

WHEELIE BAGS

You'll see people dragging this 'pet luggage' after them on wheels by the retractable handle. If you're staying in modern cities with good roads and pavements, these bags can save your back. Some are hybrid backpacks with soft sides, a detachable day pack and hideaway straps that mean you can wear the bag on your back when needed or zip harnesses away when that concierge is giving you the evil eye.

Investing in a bag with good wheels will make it easier to manoeuvre on cobblestones and other rough terrain. On stairs (and some destinations just don't do lifts) they can cause a real jarring on your spine as you lug them up one crunching step at a time.

Bear in mind that some cities – such as Venice – have made moves to ban them due to the incessant clattering of the wheels on the cobbled streets.

DAY PACKS

If you get a travel pack, it'll come with a good day pack, but if not, it's worth investing in one. A smaller bag is handy for your guidebook, camera, map, water bottle, medical kit and sun lotion, and you can stretch it when you want to stay out for a night somewhere.

If you're doing loads of walking, a strong, well-padded day pack is a worthwhile investment. If you're not a great trekker, a lightweight foldaway day pack is the way to go. Day packs are ideal as carry-on baggage on flights. A day pack will set you back from around £15/US$25/A$40 to £60/US$100/A$120 and is another cost to add to your expenses list.

COURIER BAGS

These one-strap, over-the-shoulder bags are great for hopping around town, but if you're wearing them by your side for long periods of time they can yank your spine out of shape. They're best for you if you twist them around onto your back, but then they're out of sight, which can make them less secure. Our final words of warning: one strap is easier for passing thieves to slash.

PACKING

Before you go you'll need to have a dress rehearsal, where you pack everything you think you'll need and see how well it fits in your pack. Chances are it won't, and you'll have to go back and reprioritise. Backpacker gurus reckon you should pack it all, then halve what you've got in there. Walk a lap of your neighbourhood with your fully packed bag just to see how it feels. Now you'll definitely feel like leaving behind that hairdryer.

Unless you're going somewhere really remote, it's worth remembering that you'll be able to buy supplies along the way, so if you rule something out you can often buy it later.

ONE BAG WONDER

Think you're doing pretty well on the packing front? Check out Doug Dyment (www.onebag.com) who swears by the 'single piece of luggage' rule. He's hard-core in the belief that you can go absolutely anywhere with just a lone piece of carry-on baggage. His lists will make you rethink everything you've brought. If you'd like to be a little less extreme but still super-efficient, check out Lonely Planet's illustrated book, *How to Pack*.

PACKING LISTS

Before you jump in and get packing, think a little about your destination(s), your potential activities and the climate. Overpacking will be annoying when you're on the road, so consider every item on our lists to see what will be really useful and what you might have to post home or, worse, abandon while you're away. We've organised the lists giving what's most important first and the more optional items further down, though depending on your destination some of these might be just as vital, such as antimalarial nets in Southeast Asia.

Security

- **Money belt** A money belt is useful – it's the safest way to carry debit or credit cards, cash, passport, tickets and other important items. Buy one that can be worn unobtrusively beneath whatever you're wearing, so bum bags (fanny packs to those from North America) are out. The most common types of money belt are worn either around the waist or the neck. They're not easy to get to, but thieves will find them similarly difficult to access. The fabric is important because plastic gets clammy, while leather becomes stinky. Cotton is ideal as it's washable and comfortable. Put any tickets, passport and paperwork in a plastic bag so they don't get damaged by sweat or water. Check out the belt's clasp or attachment.
- **Padlock & chain** Apart from securing the backpack, padlocks can fasten hostel and train-carriage doors. Chains are used to attach backpacks to bus roof racks or train luggage racks, though they can be heavy.
- **Waterproof pouches** Take one of these for your documents and money, especially if you're into water sports. There are also versions for your mobile phone, some of which even allow you to use your phone and take pictures without removing it from the pouch.
- **Personal security** Personal alarms, internal door guards and minisafes (attachable to radiators) are all things worth considering depending on where you're going. A metal Pacsafe outer web for your backpack will make it unslashable, but it may also flag up that you're carrying valuables.

Documents

Make sure all your important documents and photocopies (passport data and visa pages, credit card numbers, travel insurance policy, driving licence, tickets, vaccination certificates etc) are backed up before you go. Leave a set of paper copies with someone at home and take another with you (keeping it separate from the originals). Also scan them (or just snap images of them with your phone) and email the files to a loved one and yourself for an additional backup that can be accessed from the road if all hard copies are lost.

If you're planning to look for work at some point, make sure you have access to a current CV as it's tedious to update one from a busy Colombian internet cafe.

Sleeping

- **Alarm clock** Yes you're taking your mobile phone, but an alarm is a good idea for early morning trains, planes and buses, because there will definitely be times your phone is out of charge. A good loud watch will also do, plus it's more portable.
- **Sleeping bag liner or travel sheet** Even if you don't bring a sleeping bag, a liner or travel sheet can be helpful as a sheet in dubious hotels and hostels, or on overnight train journeys. The liner will also keep your sleeping bag clean.
- **Sleeping bag** A lightweight sleeping bag is a must if you want to be totally independent and travel around a lot.
- **Head torch** A head torch will keep your hands free and let you find stuff late at night in a dorm, when you're coming in late or leaving early, or if the electricity packs it in. It can also be handy for exploring caves and ruins. LED versions are the best as they don't blow bulbs easily and batteries last so much longer. Plus, battery life on your phone will become a precious commodity, so you don't want to have to count on it (and dropping it into a darkened toilet would be a nightmare).
- **Mosquito net and 3mm static cord** In malaria-prone regions a net is crucial. Even cheap hotels provide mosquito nets, but with your own net you can always be sure it's been treated with a mosquito killer (permethrin) and has no holes. Pack a 7m-long section of 3mm static cord – it will allow you to tie up your mosquito net if there's nothing obvious to hook it on, and will also be useful as a clothes line and to tie your bag down on the top of an African bus.
- **Pillow** If you have neck or back problems, a pillow can be a good addition. Types include inflatable head and neck pillows, inflatable neck cushions and compact pillows. Inflatable ones puncture easily, and even compact ones take up room. If you're travelling light, we recommend that you skip the pillow and nab a pillowcase from home instead, which you can stuff with clothes.
- **Tent** A small and very lightweight tent will save on accommodation costs, and can allow you to access some wilderness areas where there is no formal accommodation, but the inconvenience of packing it with you everywhere can't be underestimated. Renting for treks can be an option.

Eating & Drinking

- **Water bottle** Water bottles range in size from 500ml to 2L, though we recommend at least 1L for travelling. The collapsible-bladder water bottles take up very little room in your backpack when not in use, but they can be a pain to clean. You can save money by refilling a standard plastic bottle, but something sturdier will last longer and be more suitable for regularly purifying water.
- **Cup & cutlery** Your own cup and spoon will come in handy and help to avoid catching and spreading germs. Camping stores stock good knife, spoon and fork sets that lock together so they won't rattle around or get separated in the bottom of your pack.
- **Water purification** See p46 for your options.

Health & Hygiene

- **Toiletries** Most items are widely available – and often cheaper – but take any speciality products or favourite brands with you. Shower gels are better than soap and often do hair as well as body. Pour the large bottles into smaller ones for travelling and look out for concentrated soaps for washing clothes. Biodegradable soaps will reduce your environmental impact.
- **Towel** Cotton towels take up too much space in your backpack and never fully dry. Instead, choose a travel towel, made from either chamois (works wet and folds down tiny) or microfibre (works dry and packs down small). Microfibre towels are big enough to wrap around you, while chamois ones are generally much smaller.
- **Tampons or pads** Depending where you are, these can be hard to find. Consider purchasing a silicon menstrual cup before departing.
- **Contraception** Condoms are sold in most countries, but the quality can be variable (always check the use-by date) and it's best to come prepared with your own supply. If you use the pill, bring enough to cover your whole trip, as it is difficult to obtain in many countries.
- **Medical kit** See p41 for details.
- **Bath plug** Bath plugs are rare commodities in some cheaper accommodation. Double-sided rubber or plastic plugs will fit most plugholes.
- **Toilet paper** Unless you plan on packing a year's worth of your favourite roll, then you can acquire this on the road. A small packet of tissues can be useful at times when you expected toilet paper but they're all out. Toilet paper can block sewage systems in developing countries or places where there a septic tanks, so carry a plastic bag that will allow you to dispose of your paper later (in a bin or by burning it).
- **Washing line** If you packed a section of 3mm static cord with your mosquito net, you have this covered. If not a piece of string, or even dental floss, will do the job for this. But there are now inexpensive lines on the market that don't require pegs and include suckers and/or hooks to secure them on even the greasiest wall.
- **Antiseptic wipes** These are handy where clean water is in short supply (eating on the street or on a trek) and there are concerns about hygiene.

TIPS

There's no need to take lots of clothes to places such as Thailand, Vietnam or Bali. It's cheaper and more fun to buy them there.

Travel Essentials

- **Travel journal & pens** True, we live in an increasingly digital world, but there is still a thrill in receiving a postcard. And revisiting destinations through a journal you kept while travelling across the world a decade or two later is priceless (and battery life on your phone or laptop is precious).
- **Guidebooks, maps & phrasebooks** Essential for reading up on your destination and knowing what to expect. If weight or bulk is an issue, consider tearing out unnecessary pages or those from destinations you've already visited. If you do it carefully you can always leave these sections behind for fellow travellers to use.
- **Pocketknife** With a small fruit knife you can make a picnic from a baguette and a block of cheese. You can't go wrong with a Swiss Army Knife (or good-quality equivalent) with loads of useful tools. A Leatherman tool is also worth its weight in gold as they also include pliers and strong cutters. Unless you're camping or

hunting, you don't need a huge knife. Don't leave this in your carry-on bag, or it will be confiscated.

• **Sewing kit** Needle, thread, a few buttons and safety pins will mend clothing, mosquito net or tent.

• **Eye wear** Take your glasses (in a hard case) and contact lenses. Sunglasses are indispensable for both comfort and protection. If you wear prescription glasses or contact lenses, take the prescription with you, along with extras such as a case and contact-lens solution. Consider swimming goggles for pools.

• **Batteries** Depending on where you're travelling, bring spares for all your equipment. Always put new batteries in everything before you depart.

• **Gaffer/duct tape** Need a belt for your jeans? Got a hole in your tent? Backpack need repairing? The miracle-working tape saves you in the most unexpected situations.

• **Tea lights** Handy during power cuts, these are safer than regular candles. You can often buy them at your destination.

• **Lighter/matches** Given you won't be allowed on a plane at most airports with these on your person or in your bag, you'll need to acquire them while travelling (easier in cities).

• **Earplugs** Essential if you spend a lot of time in cities or take a bus with a driver who thinks he's Brazil's answer to David Guetta.

Clothing

If you're going to a few places you'll need to pack versatile gear, such as clothes that will get you into a club or perhaps even a Michelin-starred restaurant, but can also be worn day to day or when camping. It gets even trickier if you're flitting from climate to climate or between hemispheres.

• **Keeping cool** If you're travelling in hot climates you'll need a lightweight, loose-fitting wardrobe. Cotton will absorb sweat and keep you cool. Synthetics won't get so creased and they dry out quickly, but can get clammy. Take long-sleeved tops for protection from the sun and biting insects and for appropriate wear at religious sites. Take a hat and make sure it protects the back of your neck from sunburn.

• **Keeping warm** Several layers, topped by a good-quality jacket, will give you the versatility you need. Pack some thermal underwear which allows your body to breathe while offering good insulation. A fleece or pile jacket is lighter and less bulky than a thick jumper or sweater. You'll also need a lightweight, breathable, waterproof jacket. If you're travelling in cold extremes, consider the more expensive Gore-Tex mountain jackets. Take some synthetic or merino wool long johns and then wear your usual travel trousers. Don't forget your gloves and hat.

• **Waterproof poncho** Regardless of the weather, take one of these. You can use it to cover yourself and your pack, as a ground sheet or a sun awning.

Footwear

• **Boots/shoes** Unless you're doing lots of trekking, you probably don't need a full-on boot. Mid-boots are versatile because they give good ankle support and can pack away easily. Some travellers just wear trainers, though they won't be ideal for longer walks. Whatever you choose, non-waterproof shoes will let your feet breathe better than waterproof ones, which are really only useful if you're going somewhere cold.

Just like with a backpack, walk around the shop to see how new shoes feel, particularly before you buy them – and buy them a good few weeks before your trip as most shoes need breaking in. If buying boots for hiking, don't make the painful mistake of sizing them the way you'd do a shoe – you need extra room in front of your toes to accommodate movement while trekking downhill (if your toes even tickle the front of the boot when you kick a wall or the floor with the front of the boot in the shop, they are too small).

• **Water-sport sandals** Brands such as Teva and Crocs are good for day-to-day wear in warm climates, even if you're doing a lot of walking. You'll also need to wear them in grubby showers or when rock-hopping near the sea. More expensive pairs will last forever.

TIPS

Roll your clothes instead of folding them when you're packing. Less creases and more space!

Electronics

• **Adaptors** Many countries have different electrical plugs, so bringing an adaptor is vital. Check www.worldstandards.eu/electricity for a list of plugs and voltage by country.

• **Digital camera** Cameras in mobile phones have improved by leaps and bounds, so using yours may be a great shout. The main issues are running out of battery and storage, and not having the same zoom capacity of a quality stand-alone digital camera. If buying a camera, it's not always the number of megapixels that matters, rather it's the quality of the sensor and lens. Pack spare memory cards and batteries for when you can't find somewhere to upload your photos or recharge. Old-timers will tell you to get an SLR camera, but unless you're serious about photography it might be a little over the top. *Lonely Planet's Guide to Travel Photography* series has excellent tips on buying cameras.

• **Mobile phone** Wi-Fi is almost everywhere, so even if your phone isn't compatible with the mobile network where you're travelling it is still a great communication tool for email, social media, web and messaging via apps like WhatsApp. It's also great for your music playlists and as a GPS. See p72 for details about taking your mobile phone.

• **Laptops** A laptop can be used for content and music storage, video and image editing, and for writing/blogging, but it can be a very vulnerable possession. Get a chain and lock if you do decide to bring one and look at the lightest models if you're travelling a lot.

Extras

• **Books** Take a book for long journeys and swap it with other travellers on the road.

• **Games** Playing cards, chess and backgammon are universal, so you can always start a conversation with locals and travellers over a game.

• **Gifts** Take a few presents that people won't be able to get in your destination if you're staying with a family or using local guides.

• **Binoculars** A must if you plan on taking a safari or doing wildlife-spotting.

TAKE OFF

By the time you get through the emotional roller coaster of airport farewells, checking in and security checks, you'll be relieved to be just sitting on a plane. There's nothing too scary about surviving the airport and the flight, but if you know what you're in for you'll

be able to arrive fresh and ready to take on your destination.

BEFORE DEPARTURE DAY

On departure day you'll be preparing for some teary farewells, whether with your parents, your kids or your partner if you're travelling solo, so make sure everything's organised before then. Most of this preparation is fairly straightforward, but you can definitely save yourself some time and hassle by knowing what to expect and by doing a few basic chores.

SORTING YOUR CARRY-ON

Every airline has a slightly different policy about what you can and can't take on the plane, but details are freely available on their website. Usually you're allowed at least one bag which holds between 13lbs/6kg and 15lbs/7kg. You are often allowed a handbag or laptop bag in addition. On domestic flights you may be able to carry more, but on long-haul international flights they limit carry-on luggage harshly to avoid overstuffed lockers and cramming too much under passengers' seats.

You can fit a surprisingly large amount into your carry-on when you need to, but it's a good idea to get it organised before you go so you can sort out what goes in your main luggage (which you'll check in) and what you'll need with you while you're in flight. If you haven't got a bag already, look for one with an external pocket to keep your passport and tickets handy, as well as an internal pocket to keep other items such as your money or electronics more secure.

Recent security crackdowns have changed the rules on taking liquids onto planes. Airports have varying policies, but generally only very small amounts (less than 4oz/100mL) of liquids (including medicines, shampoo and suntan lotion) are allowed. Once through security you can still buy water or fill up your water bottle, but failing that just ask a flight attendant for water on longer flights.

Obviously, items such as razors, pocketknives and other sharp items can't be taken on board, so stow them in your check-in luggage, along with larger liquids you might need. Of course, narcotics, firearms, fireworks and pornography can't be imported anywhere without special permits, but look out for quirks related to medications. Greece, for example, considers codeine (common in a lot of painkillers) a narcotic, so check local laws and review your medication before you go.

Money

Getting a few bills in the local currency prepares you for any eventuality. Even if you're planning on carrying your money in another way, local money comes in handy for when the ATM breaks down or your hotel owner doesn't accept your credit or debit card. You can plan ahead by taking enough to get a taxi into town (in case public transport isn't running) and for your first night or two in a hotel if you haven't already paid online. That way you can go out and find a working ATM or a place to change currency in the morning.

DUTY-FREE

Okay, so this is the fun stuff. If you're planning to buy a digital camera, new mobile phone or other electrical appliance before you go, it might be a good idea to get it duty-free. This means you can avoid taxes in your own country (which can be substantial). Usually you'll have to have it sealed and keep your receipt so you can show it to customs officials (see p66), but the savings can be worth the hassle.

You can also buy alcohol duty-free. Most countries have restrictions on how much you can bring into the country. The US, for example, allows 1L, while boozy Australia lets you take in 2.25L. Check laws for your relevant destination or you may get slugged with duty fees on arrival.

SPECIAL REQUESTS

Airlines can take care of any passenger requests with a little advance notice. In-flight menus often offer kosher, vegan, low-fat and vegetarian options, which must be specified when booking your ticket. If you have oversized luggage, look at how you'll be expected to pack it and think about checking in early to allow time for this.

Travellers with disabilities should ring ahead and make sure there are adequate facilities, such as ramps for wheelchairs or facilities for guide dogs, available both in the airport and on the plane.

ONLINE CHECK-IN

It wasn't that long ago that passengers had to call an airline days in advance to confirm they were still planning to travel, then get their seats and boarding pass at the check-in desk. Now, most travellers are used to checking in online, picking their seat and downloading their boarding pass (generally 24 hours before the flight). However, depending on the airlines and airport involved, this isn't always possible – in the week before your flight, find out what options you have by visiting your airline's website.

Choosing Seats

Depending on when you check in and how busy the flight is, you may be offered a choice of seats. Window seats are great for views if flying during the day (trans-Atlantic flights often cruise over Greenland, which is astounding to see), and you never have to move to let someone past. But longer legs are best stretched in aisle seats, plus you can use the bathroom or take a walk without having to wake (or climb over) anyone. You can also try for an exit-row seat, which are located near the wing and the bulkhead doors so have a little more room. However, most airlines now charge extra for these.

AIRPORT

There's nothing quite as embarrassing as having your name hailed through the airport as you rush to the gate then stumble onto the plane with everyone staring daggers at you for holding up the flight. Another couple of minutes and the plane could have left without you. Avoid this drama by giving yourself plenty of time to get to the airport. Most international flights advise arriving at least two hours before departure (sometimes three if there's extra security). Some airports have train connections or bus shuttles, so build in some time in case you miss one. If you're going by road allow for traffic jams and other snafus.

CASH IN ON TIME TO SPARE

Airlines often estimate how many no-shows there will be on popular routes and overbook accordingly to ensure there are no empty seats on their flights. Of course, this doesn't always work out and there are times when there are more bums than seats (awkward). If this is the case, you may be asked at bag drop or check-in if you'd like to take a later flight – incentives can range from free meals and access to a members' lounge to a night in a luxury hotel, free flight vouchers and even cash. If nobody plays ball, the airline will simply have to choose someone to bump (or haul off, as United Airlines so infamously did to 69-year-old Vietnamese-American Dr David Dao in 2017).

BAG DROP / CHECK-IN

If you've checked in online and have your boarding pass, you just need to complete your bag drop before heading through security. There's a little more time pressure if you still need to check-in as this process tends to take longer. Either way, once you're in the airport look for one of the departures screens, which should list your flight, its departure time and its counter number/location. If it's delayed, complete the process anyway and relax on the other side of security sans checked luggage.

Before you check your bag, make sure it's got a label on it listing your name, address, airline and flight number. You can grab these labels at the check-in desk or bag drop area, and fill it in as you shuffle along the line. You may also want to check that everything you'll need for the flight is in your carry-on bag and that your passport and ticket info are handy. Tie up any loose straps or dangling ties on your backpack to avoid it getting caught and damaged on the airport's automated luggage belts (you may still be asked to take it to the oversized luggage belt). Padlocking your backpack's zipper is an option, but one that isn't recommended in the USA due to the Transportation Security Administration (TSA) screening of every checked item. There is now the option in the States to buy locks that are officially recognised as having a 'TSA-recognized locking mechanism' – this allows the TSA to open the lock without having to cut it off.

At the desk you'll be asked for your passport and ticket information. Then comes the moment of truth as you dump your bags on the scales – have you overpacked? Many travellers find that their checked-in luggage is over the weight restrictions, which means you'll have to do a quick reshuffle by possibly putting heavy items such as books in your carry-on luggage.

CARRY-ON ESSENTIALS

What you'll need on a flight depends on you. Prefer watching a movie to reading a book? Scratch the novel from your list. You might also need to add essential medications and make sure they fit the liquids policy (you can't take any liquids container larger than 4oz/100mL on the plane). Review this list to see what you'll need to add to your own list:

- **Passport, tickets (paper or digital), insurance papers, ID & money** Keep your passport and boarding pass handy so they can be easily checked then put away.

- **Valuables/fragile stuff** Anything of value that is at risk of theft or damage, such as jewellery, camera, laptop and binoculars.

- **Basic toiletries** Brushing your teeth or putting on some deodorant can freshen you up in the middle of a long flight.

- **Clothes** Bring clothes to suit your destination but also throw in something warm as flights can get chilly, even with the complimentary blankets supplied.

- **Earplugs** Useful for that loud snorer you might get stuck next to.

- **Entertainment** Games, novels, guidebooks, a travel journal or anything else for when the in-flight movie doesn't rate.

- **Pen** Useful for filling in immigration and customs forms.

If you're changing flights or transferring, your bag should be booked all the way through if flying both legs on the same airline (now is the time to confirm this). Sometimes, even if your bag is tagged for your final destination you may still need to pick it up at the end of the first flight to clear customs before dropping it back on a belt for the next flight – this happens if your first flight lands in the USA. Once your bag has been given the okay, you'll be given a luggage receipt and a boarding pass (if you don't already have one).

CUSTOMS & IMMIGRATION

Despite what you may have heard about body-cavity searches, inspections for departing passengers are pretty straightforward. Your bag will be X-rayed and you will have to walk through a metal detector or scanner. To speed things up there are some universal rules: remove all metal objects from your pockets, take off your jacket, remove large pieces of electronics from your bag and always be polite and courteous. It can be a good idea to put your keys, phone and other metal items in your jacket and just take it off and send it through the X-ray machine rather than dropping everything in the plastic tubs provided.

Things you cannot take on board include weapons, spray cans, explosives, flammable substances (including lighters) and liquids. You may be asked to step to one side and answer a few simple questions or to have your bag or electronic items swabbed.

Immigration formalities are much briefer, with the inspector often simply looking at your passport and waving you through. You may have to fill out a departure card, which has a few simple questions (reasons for leaving the country, flight number etc) and will be submitted upon departure.

MAKING SECURITY A BREEZE

No matter where you're flying in the world, there is always one thing standing between bag drop and your flight – security. If you don't leave enough time for this, or have included any items you shouldn't have in your hand luggage, there is a chance you may miss your flight. Some countries are stricter than others, with airports in North America, the UK, Northern Europe, the Middle East and Australia being ranked as the most stringent. To ensure a smoother passage through the security process, make yourself aware of the local regulations before packing your bags – these are usually covered on your airline's website, or on that of the relevant government (ie https://www.gov.uk/hand-luggage-restrictions for the UK, or www.tsa.gov for the US). And when in the security line at the airport pay attention to the posters or videos noting what else is required of you, such as removing shoes and belts etc.

Buying Duty-Free

Once you're through customs you can grab a meal and relax or do some last-minute duty-free shopping. The only items that tend to be good value are electronics, booze and cigarettes (as they are heavily taxed in most countries). You can also do duty-free shopping on board the plane, though the prices on most airlines are as high as the altitude. Make sure you don't exceed the duty-free allowances of the country to which you're heading (see p63).

IN-FLIGHT

The flight itself can be fun: your choice of movies, free food and drink, and maybe even a bit of a nap. Then there are the nightmare flights where you get trapped between a snoring granny and a crying baby. This is the reason earplugs were invented.

STAYING FLUID

Booze may flow freely on most international flights, but drinking too much is never a great idea. Apart from not wanting to arrive in another country half-cut, the plane's cabin is very dry and drinking alcohol will dehydrate you faster (worsening your impending jet lag). Water may be boring, but it's the best option.

STRETCHING YOUR LEGS

Sitting still on flights for longer than four hours has been shown to increase your chance of having a deep vein thrombosis (DVT), particularly if you are over the age of 40. Essentially this is a blood clot, typically in your lower legs, which has the potential to break up and cause more dangerous (sometimes deadly) blockages in your lungs or elsewhere. While the risk is low, it's still wise to reduce your chances by getting up regularly for a walk in the aisle. In-flight magazines and entertainment channels also often show a few exercises that you can do in your seat to help.

SLEEP

Getting a little sleep is also a good idea, and if you're lucky there might be a spare seat or two next to you so that you can stretch out for some zeds. Of course, you may also have someone next to you slouching over the armrest as they snore. However, if you stay relaxed (and use earplugs, if needed) you should get some shuteye. In economy you'll get a pillow and blanket and your seat will recline, but it's nothing like the flat-bed sleeping pods in first class (and no, they won't let you sneak through that little curtain to use an unoccupied one). Flights will try to create the time zone of your destination, so lights will be dimmed to simulate night and if you're arriving in the morning breakfast will be served right before landing. Try following this new routine to help with jet lag, but if you're too wired to sleep, watch a few in-flight movies, listen to some music and get up regularly.

Some travellers take sleeping pills, but they may leave you feeling groggy and make negotiating your way to a connecting flight difficult – they will also ensure that you're immobile longer during the flight, which increases your risk of a DVT.

IN-FLIGHT MEALS

Chicken or beef? Despite top chefs consulting on slick menus for airlines, you'll still be offered these basic choices on flights unless you've pre-organised a veggie or special-needs option. Many travellers opt for vegetarian or vegan meals because they believe these are better than meat-based meals, plus they come out first so you don't have to wait for the trolley to roll past. You can go for Hindu, low-fat or other options depending on your airline – budget airlines usually have fewer options, if they offer meals at all. An airline's origin and destination have some bearing on the type of food served, so if you're flying out of Japan you might get sushi or if you're on an Indian airline you could get a steaming curry and a yogurt lassi to wash it down.

TURBULENCE

Some turbulence during flights is fairly normal, and in some cases you may be asked to return to your seat and buckle up. Wearing your seatbelt when sitting is always a good idea, as some turbulence can be unexpected and severe. If you're the worrying type, know that planes are designed to withstand more stress than you'd think imaginable, including intense winds and lightning strikes.

TRANSIT BREAKS & STOPOVERS

If you're swapping from one flight to another, most airports have restaurants or cafés to pass the time. Other facilities can include prayer rooms, day rooms (for a snooze) and shower facilities. Singapore's (often ranked the world's top airport) offers a cinema, rooftop pool and free city tours (complete with a river trip) if your layover is longer than 5.5 hours.

Some brave travellers even zip into town if they've got a layover of more than four hours. This is risky, because you could miss your flight if you get caught in traffic or lost, and having to clear customs and security again, and possibly organise a transit visa, can take a long time.

When planning your flights, look into the option of an extended stopover, which would allow you a day or two to explore a different city or country. Some airlines and countries even encourage it – for instance, Icelandair has done wonders for its country's tourism by offering free layovers in Reykjavik en route between Europe and North America. And more recently, China has started to offer 144- and 72-hour transit visas for those flying through the country.

FEAR OF FLYING

Alternatively called 'aerophobia', 'aviatophobia' and 'aviophobia', fear of flying affects one in four people to varying degrees. If you've never flown before you'll experience some fairly normal anxiety, but if you find yourself having pronounced panic attacks or vomiting, it could be a serious fear of flying. If you already know you have a real fear, seeking out a little counselling or doing a course is a good idea.

Here are a few courses, ranging from psychological help to giving you a better idea of how planes work:

- **Fear Free Flying** (www.fearfreeflying.co.uk)
- **Fear of Flying Clinic** (www.fofc.com)
- **Fearless Flyers** (www.fearlessflyers.com.au)
- **Soar** (www.fearofflying.com) Offers courses to download.

If you suffer from mild aviophobia, prepare yourself mentally for the flight before boarding by doing some breathing exercises or meditation to focus yourself on the positive aspects of the flight. Getting a good seat could help, and not getting a window seat might make you feel like it's just a boring bus ride. Drowning your fears with alcohol will only add drunkenness to your anxiety. If you feel that you need something to calm your nerves, speak to your doctor beforehand about getting a mild tranquilliser prescribed.

TOUCHDOWN

'Please make sure your seat back and folding trays are in their full upright position as we are coming in to land' – could there be a sweeter sentence? It means you're about to touch down in your destination. Soon you'll start to hear people speaking differently and taste the air of somewhere new.

AIRPORT

CLEARING IMMIGRATION

For immigration, you need to fill out a

disembarkation card and (sometimes) a customs form. Usually, flight attendants will pass these around during your flight. Otherwise, look for them once you touch down – either on a table in the immigration hall, or being handed out by immigration officials.

Have a pen handy, because they're as rare as friendly officials in airports. Most countries ask for the address of a place you'll be staying at (a hostel or hotel address is fine – even one you've just copied down from a guidebook if necessary). Many landing cards ask for an occupation, which can be tricky. Keep it as innocuous as possible, especially if your job falls into a 'sensitive' category such as journalist or reporter. If you're on a working holiday visa, the profession you list might be one you'll be excluded from working in, so it's best to keep it vague.

You'll hand the disembarkation card over to an immigration officer with your passport. Generally they read it and may ask a few clarifying questions, though sometimes they're just bored and want to know about your holiday plans ('The wife and I always wanted to see the Lake District, actually.')

Possible sources of trouble include not having the necessary visa (although without one, most international airlines will refuse to let you on the plane in the first place), a passport that is due to expire within the next six months of your planned departure date, or a passport that is in poor condition.

The customs form is self-explanatory and, unless you are bringing in a video camera, bicycle, laptop computer or other specialised or electronic equipment, you'll probably have nothing to declare. If you have big-ticket items, avoid overestimating the value of your goods on the form, as it is likely to create hassles when going through customs inspection. Some countries also require you to declare how much currency you are carrying and may have limits on the amount of currency you can take with you when you go.

A few countries may have a health officer who can ask you to show an international health certificate with proof of yellow-fever (and possibly also cholera) vaccinations, so have this ready together with your passport.

BAGGAGE COLLECTION

Through immigration? Follow the signs (or exodus of passengers) to the baggage claim. Off-loading is usually not a speedy process, so be prepared to wait at a carousel for a while. In some airports you will be besieged by porters eager to assist you – refuse politely and organise your own trolley if you need one. Baggage loss is rare so relax, and only when everyone else has their bags should you go over to the baggage-claim desk and report it missing. If your bag does go missing, the airline should courier it to you when it's found, and compensate you if it's lost or doesn't make it back to you within a specified timeframe, so that you can go out and buy necessities or even a new wardrobe.

Sometimes as you leave the baggage-collection area, you'll be asked to show your baggage-claim tickets (often stuck to your boarding pass or passport), so don't lose these.

CLEARING CUSTOMS

At customs you can often choose between going through the green line (nothing to declare) or the red line (goods to declare). The green channel means you stroll straight through with only the chance of a random baggage search to slow you down. If that happens an officer will usually ask you to open your bags, do a quick check and wave you on. Sniffer dogs may also be used, so never try to bring drugs or other illegal substances into a country.

If you have something to declare, do so. This could simply be an oversight, such as nuts or a piece of fruit when landing in Australia (they are very hot on not bringing in any foodstuffs, so you may have to bin it before you go). You may be asked to pay an excess duty on whatever you're bringing in if necessary. They may also rifle through your bags just to see if everything's in order.

YOUR HOTEL IS CLOSED

A local (usually a taxi driver) tells you the hotel you have booked (or the attraction or store you want to see) is closed, but they can take you somewhere better. So you agree, and the driver makes a juicy commission for taking you to his mate's guesthouse or store. You then may be duped (read pressured) into buying dodgy gems or other products.

GETTING INTO TOWN

Unless you are being met by someone, you'll probably take public transport or a taxi into town. Some airports have special shuttles that go to certain hostels and hotels, which can be a good option if they're going your way. Your guidebook will outline all the options, including costs of each.

It will be at least two days before the public transport system makes sense, so make sure you know which stop you need to go to from the airport and where you'll need to get off.

If you've opted for a taxi, airport options range from cigarette-smoking nonchalance to in-your-face mania. Push your way through them to a rank if there is one (as these are often more dependable taxis), and confirm with a driver how much it will cost and that they have a meter to tally the price (rather than the more casual 'special tour price' made up on the spot). In many countries taxis are an easy, if expensive, ride into town, but do some research to see if your destination has specific scams or issues.

FIRST NIGHT'S SLEEP

If there is ever a time to book accommodation ahead, it is for your first night after arriving. Landing in a new city or continent for the first time, particularly after a long-haul flight, can be very disorienting. Knowing you have somewhere waiting for your weary head brings piece of mind, and also gives you an address for the immigration forms (see p68). Plus searching for accommodation with your luggage in tow when tired (and your internal compass doing circles) is nobody's idea of fun.

If it's late afternoon you'll usually be fine to check in, but if it's much earlier than 2pm few hotels will let you do so. That said, many will still allow you to drop your bag securely so that you can start exploring unencumbered. Others may not be staffed before 5pm, which means you have a couple of options: find a pleasant park or café to flop in until check in is an option, or search out somewhere to store your luggage. Often a train station will have lockers, and some museums will have cloakrooms where you can check in smaller items.

When you can check in, be sure and ask to see the room first. Even if you have a reservation you can still ask for another room. If a place really isn't what it's cracked up to be (websites exaggerate the truth, guidebooks date etc), always allow yourself the option to leave. If it's passable for the night, you can always search out a new place with fresh eyes in the morning.

COPING WITH JET LAG

There's a whole exciting destination waiting for you, but dumping your bags and immediately hitting the town might not be the best idea if you feel shattered. This is a big trip after all, so there's no need to rush. Give yourself a little time to adjust, maybe by putting your feet up in your room or going to a place nearby in case you start to flag halfway through.

Jet lag hits when you travel by air across more than three time zones (each time zone usually represents a one-hour time difference). Your body functions (such as temperature, pulse rate and digestion) are regulated by internal 24-hour cycles, so the flight will have put them all out of whack. Studies have shown that that your body will take about a day per time zone travelled through to fully adjust to your destination's clock. But the major effects, which can include fatigue, disorientation, insomnia, anxiety, impaired concentration and loss of appetite, will usually be gone within a few days of arrival. Until it does, you may find yourself wide awake in the middle of the night and tired during the day.

HOW TO MINIMISE JET LAG

- **Resting before you set off on your travels.**
- **Avoiding overeating, especially fatty foods.**
- **Setting your watch to your destination time zone when you board your plane.**
- **Limiting alcohol consumption on the plane and during your first few days in the country. Instead, drink plenty of noncarbonated drinks such as fruit juice or water. Also avoid coffee on the flight.**
- **Doing some exercise on the flight and at some point within 24 hours of arriving.**
- **Trying to go to bed in the evening at the appropriate time at your destination.**

STAY IN TOUCH

Are you checking in on social media or email before you've even left the airport?

OK, we admit it: one of the many joys of travel is sharing your adventures with the folks back home, and from the point of view of your loved ones it's fairly imperative.

But beware that daily tweets and updates from friends and family, not to mention using your phone as a GPS locator, are not as simple as they are at home – and the cost can come as quite a shock. And there is something to be said for switching off and fully immersing yourself in your destination – you don't want that long-sought-after moment of inner peace in a Tibetan monastery to be shattered by an incoming text. Think about switching off notifications and setting times when you engage with your phone.

Think about how you will keep in contact in advance, and let your family and friends know your plan; that way they won't be alarmed when they're not getting phone calls because they'll know that they should be checking on Facebook. Before you choose a mode of communication, though, consider your destination. There won't be much uploading of video in a remote village in Malawi, but in teched-up Singapore everyone will be texting on the train. Some web tools let you plot your itinerary for all to see (beware of privacy concerns – see the Cyberstalking & Online Scams boxed text on p74), but you can also just give your family an old-fashioned list of where you'll be when and use a phonecard or Facetime to call when you get there safely. A

good place to start investigating international SIM cards, mobile phones and phonecards is Ekit (www.ekit.com).

INTERNATIONAL PHONE CALLS

Remember, giving your family or friends a call from abroad is never a bad idea – they'll love you for it and it will help keep your parents from worrying. Making an international call is pretty similar no matter where you are. There's a code to dial out of the country you're in, plus a country code for the place you're dialling and the home number without the zero in front of the area code. For a full list of country codes head for **International Country Calling Codes** (www.countrycallingcodes.com), which also has useful instructions in its Quick Reference Phone Book section, including reverse-calling instructions for when you really have run out of cash.

Calling reverse charges (or 'calling collect' as it's called in North America) is quite expensive, and the operator will ask the person you're calling if they'll accept (and pay for) your call, but it's good for emergencies. To avoid calling in the middle of the night, use the world clock feature on your phone or check **Time and Date** (www.timeanddate.com), which has a handy time chart and a meeting planner, so you can work out times in several time zones at once.

Unless it's an emergency, avoid using a hotel phone as you will get stung for a much higher rate for calls. Following are some better options for making calls.

MOBILE PHONE

Whether or not your phone works overseas depends on its compatability with the local mobile phone system ('cell' phone in North America). Europe and Australasia mostly use the GSM 900/1800 network, which means that phones will work between these two regions (so long as your mobile company offers global roaming). North America mostly uses the CDMA and GSM 850/1900 networks, which means Americans usually can't use their phones in Europe and Australasia and vice versa (unless you have a 'world capable' tri-band phone). Japan and South Korea use CDMA and GSM 2100. For a more detailed explanation, see the 'Will my existing phone work in the country that I am travelling to?' section of www.ekit.com/ekit/MobileInfo/Guide. You can check your phone's specs in its instruction manual or call your mobile provider, and compare it to the network coverage in the countries you plan to visit, on a website like **GSMArena** (www.gsmarena.com/network-bands.php3) or, for Americans, **AT&T Travel Guide** (www.att.com/travelguide).

Global Roaming

If you bring your own phone, you'll need to set up global roaming (also called international roaming) before you go. No doubt you will hear horror stories about the stratospheric costs of global roaming charges – people have come home from trips to find themselves faced with bills for thousands of dollars. But with all the competition in communications these days, roaming prices are coming down, and the EU has passed laws that have eliminated roaming charges in Europe altogether.

You'll need to check with your phone company to see if it offers global roaming in the destinations you'll be travelling to. You should review your call plan before you go so that it suits your new global lifestyle and then keep those calls short – you'll definitely find it cheaper to text rather than call.

Don't forget to pack your charger and an

adaptor for the countries you'll be visiting (see p62). And make sure you switch off data roaming to avoid racking up a hefty bill as your phone strains to collect your emails and online messages on foreign networks.

Local SIMS

If you have a phone that's not SIM-locked (ie you can take your SIM card out and swap it easily with another one), you can buy a local SIM card (with or without data) when you arrive at your destination. This ensures you have the right network coverage plus you use a pay-as-you-go option to keep a lid on the bill. Often the SIM comes loaded with enough free credit to text your friends and family to let them know your new number.

For a long trip, you might want to pre-purchase an international SIM. Some providers are **Ekit** (www.ekit.com), **Keepgo** (www.keepgo.com) and **TravelSim** (www.travelsim.com).

Some phones are not compatible with different types of SIM cards, or their warranty may be voided if they are unlocked. In that case it may just be easier to buy a cheap handset when you get there.

INTERNET VOIP CALLS & MESSAGING APPS

If you can get access to the internet (see Free Wi-Fi, p74), you can make contact for free or very cheaply using VOIP (Voice Over Internet Protocol) or instant messaging services. Some of the most popular are WhatsApp, Facebook Messenger, WeChat, QQ Mobile, Viber, Skype, Snapchat, Tango, Google Allo, Google Duo, Google Hangouts and Line. Different apps provide different combos of voice calls, video calls, SMS and MMS. Most of these apps require the person on the receiving end to also have the app. But if some of your family can't cope with the technology, some VOIP services will allow you to call landlines around the world for free or at very low cost, such as **Skype** (www.skype.com), **Viber Out** (https://account.viber.com), **magicApp** (www.magicjack.com) and **Talk360** (www.talk360.com).

PHONECARDS

While phonecards are becoming less common, they are good to have as a backup, especially where mobile phones are not useable. You can often use payphones, other landlines or your mobile to ring the access number. They're available in newsagents, tobacconists, post offices and minimarkets, with the rates for popular countries on display. Generally, rates are much better than dropping coins in a public phone, though not as good as Skype.

When you buy an international phonecard you get a credit card–like piece of plastic with an access number and a hidden code on it. You dial the access number, punch in the code (to reveal it you might have to scratch away a protective seal), then dial your number. Usually there are helpful prompts telling you what you'll need to do next. When you're almost out of credit you'll be alerted by an alarm and you might be given the option to recharge the card.

Another kind of phonecard is the local one you can insert in payphones, in much the same way you'd use coins. Make sure you don't accidentally buy a local phonecard when you're after the international variety, or you'll get very bad rates for your international phone calls.

Finally, you can organise a phonecard from your phone company back home which will let you dial in to their network and the call will be added to your bill back home.

See Directories (Part Four) for details of local phone operators which offer this service.

CYBERSTALKING & ONLINE SCAMS

Don't get paranoid, but the information you put online about yourself can be used by some shifty characters. Usually it'll just be spam about penis enlargements (regardless of your gender), which can be avoided by having a disposable email address to use on your trip. In very few cases it could mean full-on cyberstalking, where someone will use information you post online to track you down. Avoid this by only ever giving vague ideas of where you are to strangers (a city might be okay but an address isn't), and only organise meet-ups in public places.

When in internet cafes, use a private window on your browser (or delete your history) and make sure you keep your passwords safe from prying eyes. Ask the cafe owner for help if you have difficulty with foreign-language browsers.

WI-FI

FREE WI-FI

Believe it or not, you can survive without being online 24-7. In fact, being offline can be one of the best things about travel. But when you absolutely must send that Facebook update, tweet or epic email, or when you want to chat on Skype, free or cheap Wi-Fi is readily available in much of the world. High-tech cities like Kuala Lumpur are swimming in free Wi-Fi spots, more airports are offering it as standard, and plenty of cafes and fast-food chains across Europe offer internet along with your coffee.

Travellers are often frustrated when their gadgets flag up a Wi-Fi spot but fail to connect. Often this is because the signal is too poor for your smartphone to obtain an IP address, and all the swearing in the world won't fix that. Where you do manage to connect, make sure you navigate only to secure sites if you're pushing any personal data around. An unsecured Wi-Fi point means other people could potentially see your internet traffic, so exercise some caution.

If you decide to take your tablet or laptop with you, this will give you the ultimate flexibility, but it does invite the risk of it getting lost, stolen or broken. Be sure to disable data roaming and use Wi-Fi. Keep it close to you when you are on the move and avoid pulling it out in public.

Download the free app **Wi-Fi Finder**, which has a database of Wi-Fi hotspots around the world and can be accessed offline.

PORTABLE WI-FI

If your phone is locked, a local SIM for it isn't an option and you don't want to rely on free-wifi hotspots, you can look into buying a portable Wi-Fi hotspot. Much like your internet router at home, this is a portable version with a SIM inside. Unlocked versions are widely available from tech shops or online, and allow you to put in local SIMs while travelling. Or you can buy one at home with global roaming enabled with a price plan on data, such as those offered by **Keepgo** (www.keepgo.com).

INERNET CAFES

Although dwindling in number due to the increasing amount of free Wi-Fi around the world, there are still many internet cafes around, particularly in backpacker areas. Some libraries and post offices act as internet cafes, with surprisingly zippy broadband connections. They charge for blocks of time (often from 15 minutes up) and some require registration. Avoid chain stores that lock you into membership cards as it can be difficult to find the next place if you're travelling around.

TRIP-SHARING APPS

If you want your pictures and videos to do most of the talking, try one of these trip-sharing apps:

- **Flipagram** Allows you to sequence your images and have them 'flip' along to any song, then post the result as a Facebook slideshow.
- **Instagram** The granddaddy of photo and video sharing. Famous for its editing options and filters to make even the dullest photos pop.
- **Livetrekker** Allows you to create a digital journal of your journey on an interactive map. You can add pictures, audio, video and text, creating a shareable multimedia diary.
- **Photobucket** Store, edit and share your images from anywhere while on the road.
- **Tripcast** Perfect for travellers who want to share every moment of their journey with loved ones at home. They will see every photo posted in real time, together with a location tag.
- **Touchnote** This fun (and money saving) app allows you to send photos from your travels as physical postcards. Once you've selected your photo and message, Touchnote will print and post the cards for you.

BLOGGING FOR BUCKS

You can make a little extra spending money if your blog is getting reasonable traffic. Services such as **Google Adsense** (www.google.com/adsense) plug ads into your blog based on your entries, so if you're blogging about Turkey it will include promotions for hotels in Istanbul. They work based on click-throughs so get your friends to click on the ads when they visit.

Another option is to get affiliate programmes with websites such as **Amazon** (www.amazon.com), so if you mention a book you can send people to a place where they can buy it and you get a share.

MY FIRST PASSAGE TO INDIA

I was expecting to come out of the airport doors in Mumbai and disappear in a locust crowd of beggars and taxi drivers. Everyone I knew had told me that my first few minutes would be terrifying. They made it sound as if I'd have to fight to keep hold of my luggage, possibly losing an eye in the processs. Instead, arriving in Mumbai after midnight, I found the airport all but deserted. I prepaid for a taxi at a booth and easily found my driver, and we set out for the city. Again, I was surprised – where were all the people? Mumbai at night was a city of men and dogs. Men lying in the street, pissing, riding motorbikes, smoking cigarettes – but nothing like the jumbled hordes I'd been led to expect.

All night outside my window there was the soft music of bicycle bells. In the morning, I was woken by female voices and rushed to the window to see three women in bright saris – fuchsia, turquoise, daffodil – crossing the road.

I'd arrived in the city with a gruesome cold (ironically, the only illness I would suffer in a year of Indian travel) so I spent my first day dazed in bed, watching Bollywood clips on MTV Asia and reading Pico Iyer. When I finally ventured out on the streets, the first person to approach me was a street vendor who tried to sell me a giant dropsical balloon, almost bigger than I was. This made me laugh. 'A smaller balloon?' he countered swiftly. Ah, the real India at last.

Rose Mulready

POST

SENDING MAIL

Old-school 'snail mail' will still be handy when you travel. If your package is valuable try **DHL** (www.dhl.com), **FedEx** (www.fedex.com) or **UPS** (www.ups.com). You can also look out for shipping agents who'll ship crates of one cubic metre upwards door-to-door – which can be affordable if you share space with friends.

Airmail is best for letters and postcards as it's quick, but if you're sending parcels home, surface mail is cheaper, though slower (it will take months to get home).

RECEIVING MAIL

The main way to get post on the road is using poste restante. This simply involves having your post mailed to a city post office for you to pick up. It should be addressed as follows:

Your Name
POST RESTANTE
Post Office name
Full address of the Post Office
Post code of the Post Office
Country

Most post offices hold poste restante mail for no longer than a month or so before binning it. The service works across North America, Australia, New Zealand, much of Europe and a couple of countries in Asia (Cambodia, India). Poste restante is also available at American Express offices if you have an Amex membership. Lastly, you can ask for mail to be sent to your accommodation – check ahead to see if this is an option.

BEING A GOOD TRAVELLER

It's easy to make sure your good time isn't making someone else's life tougher if you're aware of the culture you're visiting. Don't limit yourself to the suggestions here, as ethical considerations should inform all your travel. Volunteering (see p141) is another way you can make a difference to the places you visit.

RESPECTING LOCAL CULTURES

Confusing, frustrating, surprising and sometimes hilarious, cultural differences occur everywhere. Visiting another country means leaving your judgements at the airport and appreciating the difference. It's easy to feel threatened or scared in a new environment, but research before you go can prepare you for everyday encounters – see the destination chapters (Part Three) for a few ideas about the cultures you'll be visiting.

AVOIDING OFFENCE

All travellers feel stupid at some point in their trip. Everyday things you do may crack locals up or cause offence. and your best defence is an apology (needless to say, 'sorry' is a must-learn in every language) and a sense of humour.

Dress

Wearing the right clothes and headwear is more than fashion, it's also a matter of showing respect for local cultures. Flashing your flesh is a no-no in many countries around

THE BEST SITES & APPS FOR CREATING YOUR BLOG

If you want to share more than just the odd status update or photo with friends and family, you might want to start your own travel blog. These days there are lots of sites and apps that allow you to publish a blog for free and don't require more than basic computer skills to get it looking like it was put together by a professional.

Blogger (www.blogger.com)
Part of the Google portfolio, this is a reliable and trustworthy option. It ofers step-by-step instructions and lots of customisation options.

BlogPress (www.theblogpress.com)
Supports almost all popular blogging platforms including Blogger, Tumblr, WordPress and more. Features include an image and video uploader and social media site integration.

Medium (www.medium.com)
Another good option, Medium works well for story telling.

Penzu (www.penzu.com)
This site offers many types of blogging journals and plenty of inspiring examples. There are various levels of privacy/sharing available.

Tumblr (www.tumblr.com)
This is perhaps the best site to choose if you plan on featuring visuals. Images, videos and music are easy to incorporate.

Trips (www.lonelyplanet.com/trips)
This app provides a beautiful but intuitive way to share travel experiences, whether photos, videos or stories.

WordPress (www.wordpress.com)
This very popular platform is incredibly flexible regardless of whether you want to use it for writing, photography or both. It's possible to upgrade if you want your own domain name.

If you're not at all tech-savvy, you can purchase a travel blog package for a small fee per month. Blogging companies offer differing features and functions, but most include interactive maps, space for online entries, digital photo albums and personal message boards. Be sure to find out whether you can download the content of your blog once you're back home. Some companies offering it include:

- **Esplorio** (https://esplor.io)
- **MyTripJournal** (www.mytripjournal.com)
- **Off Exploring** (www.offexploring.com)
- **Travellerspoint** (www.travellerspoint.com)
- **Travel Blog** (www.travelblog.org).

The big downside with a blog is the time taken to update it. If you're in a backwater internet cafe with a shaky connection it can take ages to upload images and video, so find a reliable connection then do a few blog posts at once.

© Justin Foulkes / Lonely Planet

The three chedis at Wat Phra Si Sanphet, Thailand

the world, whether you're male or female. Did you know that men wearing shorts will even raise eyebrows in many African countries, or that shoes need to come off in every Japanese home? In Latin America, even the poorest people pride themselves on looking neat and clean, making your catwalk-fashionable slashed-up jeans best left at home.

Hospitality

Make sure you know what is considered polite and what is rude. In Japan, blowing your nose in public falls into the latter category, as does sitting or standing in a way that shows the bottom of your feet in Thailand. Eating and drinking is particularly ripe with potential offences. In some Asian countries sticking your chopsticks in your rice is considered rude, and in Australian pubs putting your glass upside down on the bar was once a challenge for the whole bar to fight. Guidebooks help on this front, but if in doubt, look around to see what locals are doing.

Religion

Being respectful in a place of worship such as a church, mosque or temple is fairly obvious no matter how many photo opportunities there might be.

A good start is dressing respectfully – long trousers for men and long skirts or trousers for women. You may need to remove your hat at some temples, while mosques require you to cover your head. At both temples and mosques, remove your shoes.

At Hindu temples, remove leather objects such as belts before entering. Don't point at Buddha images, especially with your feet. If you sit in front of a Buddha image, sit with your feet pointing away.

Showing Emotion

Losing your temper is never cool – getting angry in Southeast Asia or Japan just makes you look particularly silly and rarely achieves anything. In some parts of the world it is just not on for couples to show any emotion or physical contact towards each other in public, such as in Dubai where one couple was jailed for a year after being caught kissing on a beach. So read up on your destination and know what is considered rude and what is crossing the legal line.

Women

In many countries women travellers are still limited to some of the sights that they can visit. For example, women are usually not allowed in the main prayer hall of a mosque, or in various monasteries.

Taking Photos

A good image doesn't need to humiliate someone. Treating locals with respect when taking pictures means asking permission before you start popping a flash at them. Some people may ask you to send them a copy or you can show them the screen to see if they like the image. Some locals even charge money to have their photo taken, which you should probably also honour as they're your 'models'. You should also take care around religious sites, government buildings and even some bridges unless you know it's okay to photograph.

GREEN TOURISM

There's no doubt travel puts a strain on the environment, but there's a lot you can do to look after the planet. Start with offsetting the carbon of your flight and any other transport (see p93). Lonely Planet uses a sustainable icon in many guidebooks to highlight businesses that are minimising their environmental impact.

Handy resources for green travellers include:

- **AtmosFair** (www.atmosfair.de/en) A German non-profit organisation that offsets carbon from flights with investments in renewable energies.
- **Climate Care** (www.climatecare.org) A 'carbon trader' with a good carbon emissions calculator; also plants trees to counter the effects.
- **Responsible Travel** (www.responsibletravel.com) Site selling holidays from companies that fulfil strict responsible-travel criteria.

EASY BEING GREEN

Here are a few of the everyday things you can do to look after your destination's environment:

- Refill your water bottle from water dispensers or by purifying water.
- BYO shopping bags so you can refuse plastic bags from shopkeepers.
- Dispose of litter responsibly.
- Trekkers should take all disposable waste away with them. Batteries are particularly bad.
- Animal-based souvenirs, such as tortoiseshell trinkets, coral jewellery and seashells, should be left well alone.
- Take public transport, cycle or walk to reduce pollution.
- Choose accommodation that operates in an environmentally sustainable manner.

OVERTOURISM

Lonely Planet believes that tourism has the power to do good in the world. Done responsibly, it can provide rewarding and enriching experiences for travellers and those living in the communities being visited. And income generated from tourism can fund everything from wildlife conservation and sustainable development to poverty reduction and education. Yet, done poorly, its negative impacts can be just as widespread.

The overcrowding of certain destinations can alienate local residents, overload infrastructure, threaten cultural heritage and damage the environment. We take overtourism seriously and are constantly working to reduce its impact. Our goal isn't to tell travellers where they can and can't go, but rather to highlight important issues and to provide them with the facts to make their own decisions. That is why we ask our writers to do the following each time they are on the road: seek out destinations and businesses that operate in responsible and sustainable ways; provide concrete advice to visitors on how to minimise their negative impact in sensitive areas; and flag where there are problems.

Our global campaigns, such as 'Best in Travel', are also designed to open readers' eyes to lesser-known destinations and provide compelling reasons why to travel to them. This won't stop everyone from visiting Venice, nor will it cause everyone to flock to São Tomé and Príncipe, but it will spread the benefits of responsible travel and hopefully reduce the stress on places where tourism is currently unsustainable.

On a more finite scale, we also ask our writers to shed light on little-visited sights that are interesting alternatives to nearby ones that are experiencing overtourism.

REVERSE CULTURE SHOCK

First up, you have to prepare yourself for the idea that the home you left behind has gone. Your friends will be doing new things, your town will have moved on and even your family might have changed. Depending on how long you've been away, it might just be minor changes such as your mum cleaning up your room or a friend dyeing their hair a different colour, but the longer you've been away the greater the change.

You've changed as well, undoubtedly for the better. Everything you've seen and done has given you a better insight into the world. And having met real people on the road, and seen kindness and humanity close up, you'll find it hard not to be open to other cultures as you move forward through life. You'll even look at your home differently, even if you don't notice it at first.

INCOMING

If you know when you're coming home, make preparations. Organising a lift from the airport is a good idea because you may feel physically and emotionally exhausted – it's also just a wonderful feeling to be greeted by loved ones after a lengthy time apart. You'll be tempted to want to see everyone but don't organise too much for the week you arrive in case you need some time to catch up on sleep and to regain your strength. Perhaps send emails out and organise a reunion drink with your friends. Some travellers have a party with a display or projector flashing through their photos in the background – just don't turn it into a slide-show night, because no-one will be as interested as you are in your photos (yes, really).

WHAT'S NEXT?

Life at home is perfect for a while, but slowly you'll start getting bored, looking around for the next trip, the next wild adventure. So after a few weeks or months of catching up with friends and family and rediscovering your home town, you'll start asking the question 'So...what's next?'

ITCHY FEET

Just as with a good hangover remedy, some veteran travellers will tell you that the perfect cure for post-trip blues is more travel. But chances are you won't have enough money to hit the road again, so take things easy for a while. Enjoy looking back at your trip by perusing your images, watching your videos and reading your blog or hand-written journal (or even emails you sent while away). Perhaps also spend some time looking into where you might like to go next – the planning of future forays is often enough to capture the excitement again.

THE 'REAL' WORLD

So now you're home, it's time to get back into the 'real world', right? Not necessarily. Tony and Maureen Wheeler enjoyed their first trip together so much they started making guidebooks on their kitchen table once they finished. After years of work they transformed that kitchen table into the international guidebook company that produced this book and hundreds of others each year. There's something to be said for making your vacation into a vocation.

Getting your CV up to date and in order is probably the first thing to do. Don't forget to put anything you did while you were away on it, particularly if you worked or volunteered. Travel doesn't just belong under 'interests', because the ability to get yourself around the world and back again is an achievement in itself. And having your travels on the CV will also explain the gap in time since your last job or semester in school.

When it comes to applying for jobs or university courses, think about what you enjoyed while you travelled. You might have studied physics, but if you really enjoyed talking to people when you were away, maybe you should look at more social jobs. A really obvious 'travel' job is to work in the tourism industry by trying out as a travel agent, tour operator or even as a travel writer or photographer. These are all really popular gigs so there'll be lots of competition, but stick at it and let people know you're passionate about travel.

GIVING SOMETHING BACK

Once you've been around the world you'll appreciate your place in it. If you have enough money to go halfway round the world, you're probably much better off than many of the people you've visited. Some travellers stay involved by donating to charities that will help places they've visited. Others go a step further, volunteering internationally or locally to make a contribution.

DEAR ME

Don't forget to send yourself a postcard from the road. It sounds weird, but a little reminder of what you were doing or thinking during the last moments of your trip will be a good shot in the arm when you're back in the real world.

Returning home can be a shock but you can set yourself up to manage what comes next

TAILORING YOUR TRIP

PART TWO CONTENTS

WHO WITH?

So you picture yourself, luggage in hand, gazing into the distance of the open road. What do you see? Are you the enigmatic loner, roaming the earth? Or do you have your own entourage, rocking your own international travel party? There are advantages and disadvantages to travelling with or without companions, and even the most social people like to be alone sometimes.

SOLO

Ask any seasoned traveller and they'll tell you that the best way to travel is on your own. You never have to ask anyone what they want to do, your plan is always the most popular one and you never have to take anyone else's feelings into account. You won't have to compromise if your travel companions want to hit the art galleries while you'd rather be lying on the beach. It's all up to you.

Importantly, solo travel also offers you the definitive opportunity for self-reflection and development. There is no better way to get to know yourself better – you'll reveal strengths you never dreamed existed, and identify weaknesses that may have unknowingly been holding you back for years.

At home in our comfort zone we surround ourselves with people – friends, families, colleagues – who are all given different roles in how they influence the way we live our lives. When travelling alone, it's just you and you alone. With these influencers gone, you'll need to make your own decisions. It won't be long before your problem-solving capabilities increase, as will your self-confidence and your ability to act independently.

When you're on your own you tend to make more of an effort to meet new people. You start itching for conversation so you become more approachable. But there will be times when travelling solo will feel lonely, and you have to expect that. When that happens, make a call, send an email, write in your journal. You'll find you're actually having a better time than you thought when you start talking about it. Plus you can always join other travellers for group fun such as skydiving or a guided hike, then go your own way afterwards.

Getting sick when you're travelling alone is perhaps the most serious downside. You have to look after yourself and make sound judgements about the gravity of your condition. Are you too ill to travel? Should you see a doctor? These are questions that are much easier to answer with the help of someone else.

SOLO WOMEN

If you're a woman travelling solo, it's worth doing some cultural research before you head off. Whatever your destination, it's important to establish the status of women in local society, their cultural expectations and how they behave. In some cultures, drinking in bars (particularly on your own), smoking, wearing make-up and showing too much flesh (often quite modest by Western standards) may give the wrong signals to the local population. Try to dress in a way that blends in and shows respect to the people of your host country.

It's never wise to admit where you are staying or that you are travelling alone, so pretending that you are on your way to meet someone can be helpful in this regard. You'll still find that people are more likely to offer you hospitality because you are perceived as much less threatening than a man. However, keep your wits about you and be wary of accepting a drink or a snack from someone you don't know. Travellers being drugged, then robbed or worse, isn't unheard of.

Consider travelling with personal safety devices such as a whistle, doorstop alarm and capsicum spray – check if the latter is legal in the country where you're travelling (it may also not be allowed in your cabin baggage). Also be aware of your rights as a victim, as well as what threats the legal system may pose. For instance, in some countries such as the UAE, rape is considered akin to having sex out of wedlock, which is illegal and could see you thrown in jail for reporting the offence.

In various places around the world there are separate train carriages, waiting rooms, dormitories and queues for women as an added degree of security.

Realistically, depending on where you travel, you probably will get extra attention as a solo traveller. If you start to feel uncomfortable in a situation, get out, and never put up with any invasive behaviour. Check the Health & Safety chapter (p39) for more tips on safe travel.

FRIENDS

Sharing a travel adventure with a good friend can double the fun and halve some of the expenses. You can get twin rooms and share taxi and hire car bills. And there's the bonus of having someone to reflect on all those awesome travel moments with ('Are we really seeing this?'). When you get home you'll also have someone to help you with the post-travel blues by saying 'Remember when...'.

Of course there are pros and cons to travelling with company. So before you book that twin room in St Petersburg, ask yourself if there's anything that has always annoyed you

MY FIRST FRIENDS EPISODE

I was idly chatting with my old buddy Linda about how cool it would be to go to New York together and before I knew it, we were stowing our carry-on luggage in the overhead and splitting iPod headphones pumping what we decided would be the signature tune of our trip: Poison's 'Nothing But a Good Time'. Travelling with Linda was a blast. She was always there to laugh with, share a meal or room with, and lean on when I'd overdone it on the local brew.

But it wasn't always a smooth ride. We were spending more time together than you would normally, often 24/7, so patience inevitably wore thin sometimes.

Much to Linda's chagrin and frustration, I snored – she filmed the digital alarm clock showing some ungodly hour then panned to me snoring away like a trucker. And much to my disappointment, she got sick while we were away so I was left to explore the city solo while she shivered and hallucinated for three days, which was pretty rotten for both of us, and stopped me going to areas where I would've felt safer if I wasn't on my own.

But we still had great fun and crucially had been friends for so long that I had the freedom to say I wanted to check out the art galleries and the minutiae of department-store cosmetics – something that would've bored her senseless – while she headed off to East Village in search of rare Duran Duran on vinyl.

I felt like travelling with Linda was the best of both worlds – time together yutzing it up, and time apart communing with the city on our own terms.

Jane Ormond

GOING MY WAY

So you've decided your pilgrimage to the Toaster Museum can wait no longer. Only problem is you don't know anyone who is quite as excited about bread burning as you are – how can toast not float their boat?

There's always someone out there who wants to join you on even the kookiest missions. So how do you find a like-minded travel pal (preferably without a string of convictions)?

The Travel Companions branch of the Thorn Tree forum (www.lonelyplanet.com/thorntree) is a good place to start. You can look for posts or put one up yourself. There are also any number of apps that work well for finding people to travel with or to just take in specific sites, but here are some for you to start with:

- **Facebook** Joining one of the many travel groups on Facebook will enable you to search for people with similar interests. You can post where you are and what you want to do and see who is interested.
- **FlipTheTrip** Running in almost 5000 cities, FlipTheTrip allows you to contact travellers (or locals) in the same destination as you. You can also connect to chat with potential travel partners before you hit the road.
- **Meetup** This app aims to bring adventurers together to 'share, explore and learn'. It allows you to join events taking place in the area you are travelling in. The idea is that you'll meet like-minded travellers there.

Some websites can descend into sleazy hook-ups so make sure you're clear about your expectations upfront and check out your potential friends for the road by meeting up for a drink first. Another great way to bump into travellers before you go is at travel talks in bookshops or at local travel expos, so keep an eye and ear out for these.

about your travel partner. Are they cranky in the morning? Tight with the cash? Overly fond of the soundtrack to *Hairspray the Musical*? These traits can be charming in small doses and completely annoying in large, 24/7 doses. Even BFFs will need a break from each other so allow for a bit of 'own time'.

Travelling with a group of friends can be a lot of fun. It's often not as intense as the one-on-one scenario, but it does make it more difficult to make decisions that are going to suit everybody. Avoid this problem by breaking away from the group for a little while. If you set up a policy of letting people in the group do their own thing, then it will be easier further down the track. If things don't work out with the group, you might decide to take your Eurail ticket in another direction while the rest of your gang heads to Paris. Just hook up again later.

Sharing a trip with a friend or a group can save you money, but it's best if you're all quite evenly matched financially – you don't want to be the one quaffing Pinot Grigio while everybody else looks on in envy as they try to string out their cup of instant coffee. If you do have a little more travel cash, be prepared to pay for the odd drink or meal, but don't be left stuck with the bill all the time.

RELATIONSHIPS

If you're married or in a relationship, hitting the road together can be great – both romantically and financially. While two people can't travel as cheaply as one, depending on the destination they can travel as cheaply as one-and-a-half. For those in newer relationships it will also be a good test on how you get along under stressful situations and you might see new sides of your partner.

Even if you tied the knot a decade or more ago, you'll spend much more time in each other's company than you normally do and you won't have the usual support network of friends to moan to. Giving each other some space is always a good idea and if your partner wants to watch a movie while you're on safari, that's cool. Everyone sees a destination differently.

Being in a couple will mean you are less likely to make new friends – there's not the same drive to go out and meet new people, and other people might not find you so approachable. But if you strive to be open and friendly rather than insular you'll meet lots of fellow travellers, regardless of your relationship status.

Another issue to consider is money. On the road, more couples argue about every baht, rouble and złoty than anything else, so it's advisable to discuss your budget carefully. If you decide to have a joint cash pot, it's a good idea to allocate a certain amount each week for both of you to spend on whatever you want.

RELATIONSHIPS ON THE ROAD

While you may have left your home town happily single, you'll probably collide with that crazy little thing called love on the road. Who doesn't want to forget all the regular, boring bits of your home life and instead be in an exciting new city with a fascinating (and irresistible) new love? And while geography might get the better of these relationships when the return ticket calls, it's still one of the best parts of the travel experience and makes for the juiciest travel journals. If your budding relationship is with a local, be sure to read up on the culture to fully understand what you may be getting involved in. Safe sex is always advised (see p53), but it's particularly important when you're overseas.

WITH KIDS IN TOW

A big trip with the entire family might not be glamorous, relaxing or easy, but its rewards can last a lifetime. If you want to spend quality time with your children, help them learn, grow and gain a better understanding of the world and humanity, then travelling abroad is a great way to do it.

As a travelling family you'll talk and share experiences, which these days we often struggle to find time for in our busy lives. Babies, toddlers and teenagers may surprise you with their adaptability and affability when the hold of regular routines loosens. Watching your children engage with different surroundings can change your perspective and invigorate you with a renewed sense of wonder. As they blossom before your eyes in response to new encounters and experiences, it's hard not to share their excitement. Their questions will reveal the depths of their intelligence and the scope of their understanding, which in turn will enrich your appreciation of your children. Their horizons quite literally expand as they realise the world is bigger than their hometown or city, and with it comes an appreciation of cultural diversity, the seeds of tolerance and empathy, which will stay with them for the rest of their lives.

Travel with children also provides insights into local cultures that you often just don't get travelling childless. In most cultures children are welcomed, if not revered, and become the centre of attention. As a parent, you'll be caught up in the interest generated by your child and will have closer encounters with the locals as a result.

As advice on adventuring out into the world with your kids could fill an entire book, we created one – check out *Lonely Planet's Travel With Children*. But much of the advice here in *The Big Trip* still applies.

A FAMILY AFFAIR: MEET THE NORMANS

Stuart, Sue and their 10-year-old daughter Annabel packed up home in the UK and hit the road for a big trip in February 2016, and have so far (they are still on the move) travelled through Asia, Australia, Mexico, USA and Canada. You can follow them at www.normansrunningwild.com.

What inspired the trip? We've always loved travel but one day we asked ourselves a question – could we sell everything we owned and go off on a huge travel adventure? We then set about answering it. Over the next year we reduced a home full of belongings down to just three backpacks' worth.

What do you think the biggest lessons has been for Annabel? No matter how long you're in one destination, the time will come to move on, so Annabel has learned to be very adaptable to new situations and environments. She also understands that people around the world live very differently, and that there is no normal way of living.

What has been the most challenging aspect for you as parents? Annabel's future and wellbeing is often on our minds – we want to make sure she's still happy with travelling and our lifestyle. She's nearly a teenager now, so her life is changing in many ways that we need to be aware of.

What has been the most joyous aspect? Of all the amazing places we've visited and experiences we've had, the most joyous thing about our travel is the people we've met along the way. Kindness is everywhere.

How has it changed your life? It's changed our idea of what home means to us. And we've learned to trust in life and not try to plan everything. Travel opens the eyes to not only the world but what is possible for us as a family and the dreams we still want to live.

MEETING OTHER TRAVELLERS

You'll meet the most interesting people on the road. They'll fill you in on good places to stay and cool things to check out, plus they make great friends and travel companions. Never underestimate the travellers' grapevine; it's a powerful and up-to-date source of information.

Sometimes, though, you'll find yourself on the flip side where you meet travellers who do nothing but whine. Or you meet someone who appears to be laid-back and amusing, only to find out later that they're about as fun as a declined credit card and they've attached themselves to you like superglue. Luckily, developing an escape plan is easy enough.

Just change your plans a little – leave a place before they do, or stay on a bit longer when they depart. Unless you've really hit it off with a new travel bud, don't go signing up for any share-a-tent tours or treks into the middle of nowhere.

ON A TOUR

If kicking off your big trip on your own really doesn't appeal, an organised tour might be a good way of meeting like-minded people and take the intimidation out of first-time travel. You'll still feel like a traveller but your tickets, accommodation, food and activities will be sorted and you'll travel on a prearranged route in a group with a leader or guide. Tours can be a good alternative to going it alone in logistically difficult places such as Africa or China – you'll see the place without the day-to-day hassles, and any culture shock will be cushioned. Check the individual destination chapters (see Part Three) for some sample tour companies, or the Transport Options chapter, which lists international tour operators (opposite). When the tour comes to an end you'll be more familiar with the region and more at ease travelling onwards.

TRANSPORT OPTIONS

As the old saying goes, a journey of 1000 miles starts with a single security check. No matter where you're going, you're bound to spend time waiting for a train or queueing up for tickets or sitting next to someone who just won't shut up. Getting from A to B can be downright boring sometimes, but it's worth it. And sometimes you can spice things up. Mixing transport options can be an exciting bonus to your trip. Try cycling your way from Amsterdam (Netherlands) to Bruges (Belgium) with regular stops for local brews, or sit back and watch the vista wash by on a high-speed *shinkansen* (bullet train) from Tokyo to Kyoto. Look out for ways to keep your options open, as once you get on the road you'll hear about new places you'll want to go to and fall in with friends who might be going in different directions.

AIR

As close as we can currently get to teleportation, flying from one country to another is the zippiest way around the globe. Long waits in airports only build the excitement of getting on the plane and being transported from one culture to another. Thanks to budget flights and round-the-world (RTW) tickets, everyone's now a part of the jet set. There are a million destinations on the menu when you are flying.

E-tickets (electronic tickets) have made air travel much easier with online check-ins and no paper to lose. The internet has created literally hundreds of places to buy your ticket, so this chapter aims to help you work out which air ticket will suit you. A RTW ticket can represent the best deal, particularly if you're coming from Australasia where return flights to European and Northern American destinations are on a par with a well-priced RTW. The blossoming of hundreds of budget carriers has made it cheaper if you don't mind skipping a meal or taking a tighter seat. Don't forget to get your frequent-flyer points (see p93).

No matter which airline ticket you choose, prices will increase in high season. This is different for each destination, but is generally clustered around ideal weather (often summer, but for ski destinations it's winter) and school or public holidays. The lead-up to Christmas is hectic even in countries where Christmas isn't celebrated, as millions of people head home to be with families. Checking out low-season options can be good for the wallet, but if you are flying in high season you'll definitely have plenty of travel companions and the destination should be at its best.

ROUND-THE-WORLD (RTW)

Globetrotting really kicked off when airlines began to offer these babies. If you like things mapped out in advance and don't want to worry about how you'll get home if you run out of money, they can be very convenient. RTW tickets are primarily offered by large alliances of airlines, namely Oneworld, Star Alliance and SkyTeam. No airline can go everywhere, but because they pool together their routes, you can book through one airline and access the routes of all the others in the alliance. All three alliances offer price increases based on the miles you cover (usually 26,000, 29,000, 34,000 or 39,000), though Oneworld also offers one based on how many continents you visit (and how many individual flight segments there are). The number of stops is limited (usually between five and 15) and the basic deal doesn't allow backtracking over oceans. The tickets are usually valid for a year, and you need to start and finish in the same country (though not necessarily in the same city). You can make unlimited changes to the dates of your flights without penalty, but changing a destination attracts a fee, usually £95/US$125/ A$170. Some agencies offer the option to travel 'surface', meaning you'll fly into one destination in a country (say, Los Angeles) and fly out of another destination in the same country (such as New York). This gives you a good chance to see a country by travelling overland (see p95), but the mileage covered on the ground still counts towards your total. A travel agent can bundle a train or bus ticket with your ticket, but it's no problem to sort out an overland trip for yourself once you get to a country.

Here are the three major alliances:

- **Oneworld** (www.oneworld.com) This offers two versions: Global Explorer, a conventional mileage-based fare, and Oneworld Explorer, which is based on the number of continents covered (three to six – the three-continent fare is only available if you are departing from Asia, Europe or North America). Overland sectors are not counted in Oneworld Explorer flight segments. Oneworld has great global coverage and is particularly strong for South American destinations.
- **Sky Team** (www.skyteam.com) The weakest by some margin, this alliance is comprised of smaller airlines that are focused on the northern hemisphere, but it does have good coverage of Asia, particularly China.
- **Star Alliance** (www.staralliance.com) The biggest alliance and greatest number of airlines makes this a good choice for most destinations except domestic flights within Australia.

There are a handful of smaller partnerships between airlines. One good option is **The Great Escapade** (www.thegreatescapade.com), which has three airlines: Air New Zealand, Singapore Airlines and Virgin Atlantic. It allows 29,000 miles and unlimited stops, and is strong in Southeast Asian and Pacific destinations, but must commence in the UK.

You can check the rules and regulations of RTW tickets on these sites, which all have maps of their routes, so you can use them as planning tools and work out which alliance can get you where you need to go (see the map on p160–61 for some illustrated routes). All of the above include the big centres such as London, Bangkok, Singapore, Hong Kong and New York, but scan their destinations lists if you're looking for a more obscure spot (which can include Australian and Canadian destinations).

If you go through a travel agent you'll pay less than buying directly from the airline, and they'll take the headache of comparing routes and rules away from you. Specialist round-the-world travel agents can also piece together a route for you using the cheapest one-way tickets from any airline, which gets around the limiting rules of RTW tickets, and can even be cheaper if you are travelling out of Europe on a complicated route. Advantages of RTW tickets are the ease of changing flight dates, and the fact that alliances share frequent flyer points, so you can get them credited to your airline card of choice if you fly with a partner airline. RTW tickets can be particularly good value if you want to go somewhere that's normally expensive to fly to, eg Easter Island or Svalbard, as they only cost you mileage.

Prices for RTW tickets vary greatly depending on point of origin, class, number of stops and mileage, and sometimes seasonality. As a rough guide, you can expect prices to start around £2000 for a basic flight leaving London and taking in six stops. Australia suffers from limited competition on RTW tickets, so you're likely to pay more like A$3400 for six stops. US RTW tickets can be as cheap as US$1600 for a simple itinerary of three stops. No matter which RTW ticket you choose, make sure the price you're quoted includes airport taxes in the final cost – they often total more than US$400 (good agencies and airlines should be able to show you this upfront). For advice on how to choose your RTW destinations check the Round-the-World chapter (p158).

CIRCLE FARES

Most travel agents will look at you like you're a planespotting freak if you ask for one of these, but circle fares are a lot like RTW tickets. Circle fares let you explore a region with several stops, flying between continents in a circular direction, before returning to your point of departure. They're useful for long-haul trips in countries such as Australia and the US, or in regions such as the Pacific and Europe. These tickets are offered by the same alliances that offer RTW tickets. The popular Circle Pacific fare (taking in much of Asia, the Americas and the Pacific) is a good example of the kind of ticket you can get. It allows you to start in a major city such as Sydney and loop around to Perth, Hong Kong, then New York and Santiago (Chile) before returning to the point of departure in Sydney. This kind of ticket can be a great way to explore a few continents but does have to follow the circle-route path.

OPEN JAW

With this ticket you fly into one destination and out of another. Like the surface-sector option of the RTW ticket, you can enjoy a solid road trip between your two destinations, such as from Cape Town to Cairo. In Asia you could fly into Bangkok and out of Singapore, allowing you to loop through Cambodia, Vietnam and travel down the southern gulf of Thailand and into Malaysia before flying out of Singapore. Open-jaw tickets are rarely more expensive than standard return fares. They are also an excellent way of seeing a lot of Europe (fly into London and out of St Petersburg to see most of the continent) or North America (in through Canada, out through Mexico), particularly when using budget airlines to zip around other parts of a continent.

RETURN TICKET

Most travellers opt for a return ticket, the solid workhorse of the ticketing stable. The basic proposition is that you fly from your home destination to another place and then fly back from your place of entry. Within this structure there's lots of room to explore. Many travellers get a ticket with their return date a year after leaving, so they can either come home after a year or pay a small fee to stretch the return date out longer. Some cheaper tickets don't allow for any flexibility, so check conditions before shelling out your hard-earned cash.

ONE WAY

Designed for the directionless, one-way tickets are ideal if you don't know where you'll be going next. The downside is that for long-haul flights they can cost significantly more than half the price of a return ticket (sometimes even more than a return flight) so some travellers invest in a return ticket just in case. Some destinations have grumpy customs officials who won't let you in unless you have an ongoing ticket, but if you can show you have sufficient funds to support yourself for the length of your stay and still buy a ticket out, it's usually okay.

BUDGET AIRLINES

Cheap and cheerful or budget blues – it depends on your comfort levels. Budget airlines or no-frills carriers have made it more affordable for everyone to travel by offering flights that only give the bare minimum. You might not have a comfy seat that reclines and you'll have to skip a meal and the in-flight movie, but the savings can be worth it. Some airlines offer meals or video players for an extra fee, so beat the hidden costs by packing your own snacks and bringing your own entertainment (an iPad with headphones and a few movies loaded). Some budget operators save on costs by using secondary airports such as Stansted or Luton instead of Heathrow for London, or Westchester instead of La Guardia or JFK for New York. While you may save on the flight cost, you may have to travel longer to get there, so check your destination to avoid expensive taxi fares.

For lists of low-cost providers, check the Getting There section in the destination chapters of this book (see Part Three).

AIR PASSES

Another secret of the travel industry, air passes can be helpful if you're exploring a large country (such as Australia, Brazil or India) or a region (eg Europe or North America) in depth and need some flexibility with timings. Travel agents are usually in the know though you can check airline alliances and with individual airlines. The catch with air passes is that they're often not available from within a country, which means you have to buy them before you go. And with the increase in budget airlines, they don't offer the value they used to.

An air pass works much like a Eurail ticket (see p96), with various packages available based on how many flights you'd like over a certain period of time. The more flights and the longer you want to explore, the higher the price. Depending on where you go there will be a system of zones based on the length of each flight. For instance, Zone 1 in North America for the Oneworld alliance is any flight up to 310 miles (499km), while Zone 6 is anything over 2000 miles (3220km). For its Europe pass the maximum distance for a Zone 1 flight is reduced to 199 miles (318km), while Zone 6 is unchanged. Its Australia and New Zealand pass is broken into four zones, starting with Zone A (up to 480 miles / 773km) and finishing with Zone D (1011-1650 miles / 1626-2655km).

A basic North American itinerary could run Los Angeles–Boston–Washington, DC–Orlando–New York–San Francisco and cost around £450/US$600/A$800, while a European route could run London–Vienna–Budapest–Rome–Madrid–Paris–London and cost around £315/US$415/A$560. However, using Google Flights to create the same itineraries with one-way fares on various airlines (using set dates well in advance), the US flights could be bought for as little as £368/US$485/A$650 combined, with the European legs totalling around £200/US$260A$350.

The advantage of passes is generally the flexibility in timing, as you'll only need to set the first destination date, leaving the others open. But you'll need to know exactly where you want to go as you must lock in the route when you book your ticket. Be careful, however, as some airlines set their air pass price based on you being able to set the date of each journey 90 days in advance, and the cost can triple if you want to be have the flexibility of booking each leg on the day of travel (or double to book a week in advance).

TIP

Wanna buy a cheap ticket? While there are some great deals out there, there are also some big cons, but none more so than second-hand tickets. These are usually advertised on hostel noticeboards or in newspapers, when somebody has purchased a return ticket or one with multiple stopovers, and wants to sell a couple of unused portions of the ticket. Prices will be rock bottom, but these tickets are worthless unless the name on the ticket exactly matches the name on your passport.

FREQUENT-FLYER PROGRAMMES

Most airlines offer frequent-flyer programmes (also called 'air miles' in the UK and Canada), where you accumulate points for every flight which are redeemable for flights, and often goods and services too. You can also get points from hotel chains, rental-car companies and other travel-related traders. If you take a major long-haul flight (between Europe and Australia, for example) you'll probably accumulate enough points for a short domestic flight, which will come in handy on your trip, especially if you can use points on affiliate airlines.

Some frequent-flyer programmes require you to pay a small fee to join, though many are free. You'll definitely want to join the frequent-flyer programme of the company flying you over a great distance, but signing up for a few can also be rewarding. Some banks and credit cards offer frequent-flyer points on credit card purchases and other transactions, so check these partner programmes when you sign up.

Every programme has different rules about how soon your points will expire and how you can use them, so read the fine print for the best deal. Most programmes allow you to keep points for five years and you'll only be credited with them after you've made a flight. Quote your frequent-flyer number when you're booking and you should be able to see a note about your frequent-flyer points on your boarding pass. When you redeem your points your 'reward flight' will be limited to certain times (Christmas will be difficult) and may book out before a paid flight. Some airlines also allow access to their airport lounges to frequent flyers – these are great places to put your feet up and drink endless cups of coffee.

You'll receive a frequent-flyer card, but generally the number is more important than the card (you'll need it to book online and with travel agents), so make a note of it.

CARBON TRADING

With an average return flight from London to New York producing 1.52 tonnes of CO2, there's no doubt your flight will have a heavy impact on the environment. But there's a lot you can do about it. Many airlines offer carbon-trading options on most flights, where you can offset the damage your flight will do by spending a few extra dollars. But are they doing enough? Look closely at the measures behind an airline's carbon-trading policy and you might want to do more. If you want to calculate how much carbon your next flight will emit, check out the air travel CO2 calculator at **Climate Care** (www.climatecare.org), which will tell you how much CO2 your flight will produce and give you options for offsetting them. Options for offsetting include:

- **Carbon Neutral** (www.carbonneutral.com.au)

- **Climate Friendly** (https://climatefriendly.com)
- **Greenfleet** (www.greenfleet.com.au)
- **My Climate** (www.myclimate.org)
- **Offsetters** (www.offsetters.ca)

SEA

If you want a slow-paced trip, prepare for a slice of life on the high seas. Ship life will give you plenty of time to think between your destinations and can be a little cheaper. If you want speed, though, flying is your best option, because a journey of hours by air will take days by sea. For info on getting a job on a yacht see the boxed text on p135, and see p133 for information on working on cruise ships.

FERRIES

If you're looking at doing some island-hopping, ferries will become your favourite travel companion. On longer routes ferries double as seaborne bars or casinos, often because they can dodge local laws – the Calais–Dover ferry between the UK and France is notorious for boozy Brits buying up big. It can be a great party if your stomach can handle shots and the shifting seas.

Several ferry lines offer passes which give you unlimited travel over a limited period of time. If you can organise your travel well, they're a great way to explore the islands, but if you skimp and get a week to explore Scotland's Outer Hebrides, they might blur together like a big night on the whisky.

Some places are better served than others by their ferry services (Europe, for example); find out more about common ferry routes in the destination chapters (see Part Three). For a comprehensive list of ferry companies, head to **Interferry** (www.interferry.com), which lists members of this official ferry organisation.

FREIGHTERS

Freighters sound tough, but they're actually fairly cruisey. If you want to take it slow and hop off at a few ports along the way, a freighter might be just the ticket. Unlike a cruise, they're limited in passenger numbers so there are rarely more than a dozen aboard. Most freighters offer a cruise package, so you'll stop at several ports and see the seaside of a country (some port towns can be very grungy).

There's no need to work on deck as you can pay for a room that's fitted out a lot like a midrange hotel room, complete with TV and a kitchenette in the better rooms. Fares are calculated by the day and are around €85 to €110 per day. You'll need to be organised and cashed up if you want to take a freighter, because you'll have to make a deposit of a quarter of the total when booking, with the remainder due at least a month before you sail. Of course, it's not the quickest trip, with a transatlantic crossing taking at least 10 days, and with some return cruises stopping at several ports taking up to 70 days. Retirees are fond of taking freighter cruises, but if you're not into socialising with them you can always hide in your cabin and prepare for the next port.

The following can book freighter trips:

- **Maris Freighter Cruises** (www.freightercruises.com) Offers trans-Pacific, trans-Atlantic, South Seas and Europe-Asia-Australia routes.
- **Freighter Expeditions** (www.freighterexpeditions.com.au) Sails between all seven continents, as well as to the Pacific Islands.

CRUISE SHIPS

A luxury cruise is probably not what you're after if you're on a budget. While pricey, they have started to shed their reputation for attracting only older travellers, with new ships offering everything from climbing walls and surfing simulators to craft breweries and pool parties. Cruises now suit different lifestyles and all age groups. Destinations such as Antarctica and the Arctic are best experienced on a cruise, with its long slow approach.

To book a cruise, try these big providers:

- **Carnival** (www.carnival.com)
- **Celebrity Cruises** (www.celebritycruises.co.uk)
- **MSC Cruises** (www.msccruises.com)
- **Norwegian Cruise Line** (www.ncl.com)
- **P&O Cruises** (www.pocruises.com)
- **Princess Cruises** (www.princess.com)
- **Royal Caribbean** (www.royalcaribbean.com)
- **The Cruise & Vacation Authority** (www.tcava.com)

OVERLAND

Whether it's the essential road trip in a fast convertible to Las Vegas or the slow mosey of a camel ride to Samarkand, travelling overland is the best way to really see a country. Getting the bus or hopping on a train are great ways to get someone else to do the driving, so you can just lie back and watch the scenery pass by. Jetting around a country will, of course, be quicker and sometimes cheaper, but if you want to watch Italy gradually morphing into Switzerland or see New York's frantic metropolis slowly fade into countryside, taking a train is most definitely the way to go. Such trips may cost a little more than a budget flight, but you'll be free to take your time, especially if you hire a car.

You can find out more about specific overland trips by heading to the destination chapters (see Part Three).

RAIL

The idea of catching a train might sound like a throwback to travel a 100 years ago. On a state-of-the-art train network such as Japan's famous *shinkansen* (bullet train) or France's Train à Grande Vitesse (TGV) trains, however, train travel can be zippy and affordable. Someone else will be doing the driving, plus with many train stations centrally located you'll be dropped right into the centre of town. Train travel is always safer than juggling a road atlas as you drive on foreign streets, so you'll arrive stress-free. And if you're concerned about the environment, trains represent the most energy-efficient way of travelling.

In India you'll be riding iconic trains and routes packed with locals and in South America you might be sharing space with the livestock as well, so comfort can sometimes be difficult. Choosing a better class (see below) can sometimes get you out of 'cattle class'. If you're moving around a lot in one country or region, you should look at passes such as the Eurail or Interrail ticket, which has been helping transport travellers for decades.

Some train journeys are destinations in themselves. The Trans-Mongolian railway traces the slow changes of cultures and oscillating vistas from Beijing to Moscow. The northern route, the Trans-Siberian, is even more dramatic as it climbs through freezing temperatures and summery steppes. Other great journeys include Australia's Ghan, a desert trip that weaves its way to Uluru (Ayers Rock) in the country's red centre, or the run from China to Tibet that rises gradually to help travellers avoid altitude sickness.

Use some common sense when travelling on trains. All travellers should consider ways to secure their baggage, particularly if they're sleeping during any part of the journey.

Classes

All train services offer a variety of classes, from first-class sleepers with luxurious private compartments to single seats in crowded economy class. You might want to consider how far you'll be going when you're making your choice, as you might be okay in economy for an hour or two. In some destinations (India, for example) air conditioning could be essential and you may want to pay a little more for a cooler trip. Higher classes often book out early, so you'll need to reserve your seat in advance, though even lower classes can be packed. If you're sitting in the wrong class, a grumpy conductor will eventually catch up with you, so take the hassle out of the trip by sitting in your allocated seat.

Tourist-class tickets often cost more but are usually the most comfortable for travellers. In China a tourist-class ticket can include an air-conditioned waiting room, so while you'll pay a little more for these tickets, they can often be worth it, especially if a train's delayed and you've a long wait.

Timetables

Getting a timetable in advance will help with your planning, but all timetables will date so picking one up when you arrive can be very helpful. One of the better timetables is the huge **European Rail Timetable** (www.europeanrailtimetable.eu) which publishes a printed (£17.99) and digital (£11.99) edition each month. **Amtrak** (www.amtrak.com), which covers the USA, publishes its timetables on its website. Another good resource is **The Man in Seat 61** (www.seat61.com), which does a sweep of the globe's train services with suggested routes and links to local sights. It's particularly strong in Europe as it is the passionate project of a former British Rail employee.

Eurail & Other Passes

If you want a flexible way to see a country or a region, you should definitely pre-purchase a rail pass. Passes are usually valid for a limited time (seven, 14, 21 and 28 days are common) and allow either hop-on/hop-off options for unlimited travel (which means you'll be frantically trying to see as much as you can) or a certain number of trips. Prices increase based on the amount of flexibility you're after.

Passes are generally only available to foreigners and you will need to buy them before you travel (often they're not available in the country itself).

Popular passes include:

- **Amtrak** (www.amtrak.com) Offers passes for 15 days (8 segments) at US$459, 30 days (12 segments) at US$689, and 45 days (18 segments) at US$899. You'll need to collect your pass from a US station when you arrive.
- **BritRail** (www.britrail.net) Various passes covering England, Wales, Scotland and Ireland available to non-Brits, starting at £116 for all four countries for three days. Longer passes for four days (£144), eight days (£208), 15 days (£309), 22 days (£386) and one month (£455) are also available. Check individual trips as the pass may not be the best value, although it does include some ferries.
- **Eurail** (www.eurail.com) The granddaddy of all passes is available only to non-Europeans and must also be purchased in advance. There are two general options available: a limited number of days of travel in a given period, such as 5 days within one month (€468) and 15 days in two months (€919); or periods of continuous travel, ranging from 15 days (€597) up to one month (€942), two months (€1327) and three months (€1635). The passes allow travel to most European countries (except Britain) and include some ferries.

- **Indrail pass** (www.indiarail.co.uk/indianrail.htm) Given how popular they were prior to their discontinuation in late 2017, there's always a chance they may be reintroduced.
- **Interrail** (www.interrail.eu) The equivalent of Eurail for European citizens. Passes include 7/15 days of travel within one month (€325/480) or 15/22 days of continuous travel (€428/500). Discounts are available for those under 28 years of age.

BUS

Buses get a bad rap, particularly in the US. Sure, they can be slow (the cross-country route in the US takes at least 70 hours) and can get delayed in traffic, but they're budget-friendly and better for the environment than driving a car. At least with a bus you'll be sharing the carbon burn with your fellow passengers. Good bus journeys can even come with a movie screening, while bad ones come with an old woman who keeps falling asleep on your shoulder and an entertainment system that blares Cantopop. But you'll get into conversations with local people and fellow travellers and, much like on trains, you'll get to see the country glide by. Because buses are so common, timetables are harder to pin down than for trains. Check out local bus providers for the latest details.

Tour Buses

If you need a little more support, taking a tour bus can be a good option. You'll get to see the big sights with knowledgeable guides, and fellow travellers can make for good company. And if you're worried about costs, these trips will present you with a clear price that usually includes accommodation and meals. The downside can be that you'll be locked into an itinerary which might not suit you. Your fellow tourists often make or break the trip so look for a tour company that suits you.

Here are a few good tour options:

- **Contiki** (www.contiki.com) Offers European, North and Latin American, Asian and Australian tours for 18 to 35-year-olds ranging from three to 55 days.
- **Topdeck Travel Ltd** (www.topdeck.travel) Offers trips to Europe, Africa, North America, Australia and New Zealand from two to 58 days.
- **Trafalgar Tours** (www.trafalgar.com) A global provider with tours of North and South America, Europe, Asia, Australia and New Zealand.

Hop-On/Hop-Off Buses

Not to be confused with the similarly named big city sightseeing tours, these buses connect destinations within countries or regions. More flexible than a tour bus, these buses are geared towards backpackers, so you'll be delivered to a network of hostels and definitely make plenty of new friends with whom to explore your next destination. You can often stay at any stop for as long as you like (as long as your pass is still valid) and there are often optional side routes. Passes generally run for a limited time (a month can be a good length of time, but longer options are available) and some include add-on tours that can be good ways of getting to visit distant places when you don't have your own wheels. If you want to mix in some solo travel, you can always break away by hiring a car or cycling.

Here are a few popular options:

- **Bamba Experience** (www.bambaexperience.com) This service links many major cities within the USA.
- **Baz Bus** (www.bazbus.com) A longstanding operator that serves the South African coast between Cape Town and Durban and inland to the Drakensburg and Johannesburg.

- **Busabout** (www.busabout.com) Operates in Europe and the western USA, and offers maximum flexibility.
- **InterCity** (www.intercity.co.nz) New Zealand's biggest bus network offers several hop-on/hop-off passes.
- **Loka Travel** (https://loka.travel) A mix of bus tour and hop-on/hop-off service, it covers the east coast of Australia.
- **Moose Bus Adventures** (http://moosebus.travel) Operating in western Canada, it has routes linking Vancouver with Vancouver Island, Whistler and both Banff and Jasper in the Rockies.
- **Salty Bear Adventure Tours** (www.saltybear.ca) Backpacker-oriented van tours through the Canadian Maritimes with jump-on/jump-off flexibility.

OVERLAND TRUCKS

The monster trucks of the bus world, these behemoth vehicles boast oversized tyres, large ground clearance, portable kitchens and tents aplenty. Unsurprisingly, you won't find them linking Paris to Prague – instead their tours cover routes through more remote and challenging terrain, such as that found in Africa, the Middle East, Asia, Australia and South and Central America.

If you are fearful about travelling overland across a continent, joining an overland-truck tour is an attractive option for those who want their adventure packaged for risk-free consumption. Although these tours definitely don't come cheap, it's hard to put a price on the peace of mind that comes with safe and secure travel.

Most accommodation takes place in the form of camping, and many meals are prepared en route, so be warned that there isn't as much interaction with locals as there would be if you were travelling independently, staying in urban area lodgings and eating at restaurants.

In Africa you could easily join one running from Cape Town to Victoria Falls via Namibia and Botswana, before linking with another to take you to East Africa and beyond (Cairo calling?). Or journey from Tehran, Iran to Tashkent, Uzbekistan via Turkmenistan. Wild enough for you?

A few operators include:

- **African Trails** (www.africantrails.co.uk)
- **Dragoman** (www.dragoman.com)
- **Exodus Travels** (www.exodus.co.uk)
- **Intrepid** (www.intrepidtravel.com)
- **Oasis Overland** (www.oasisoverland.co.uk)
- **Truck Africa** (www.truckafrica.com)

CAR & MOTORBIKE

They pollute and get caught in traffic, but your own wheels can be very convenient. Taking a motorbike across the sludgy back roads of Cambodia or hiring a car for a romantic weekend away in Paris (with plenty of room for bulging shopping bags) will make your trip a lot more fun. It's budgetary insanity to take your own vehicle, so you'll usually have two options: buying a vehicle when you arrive or hiring one when you need it.

Whatever you do, make sure you sort out a licence that's going to work in your destination country and be sure to brush up on local laws. Common road signs and which side of the road to drive on are just some of the things you'll need to know before you hit the asphalt. Make sure your license is valid in the country you'll be driving through.

Just as with air travel, you can look at carbon-trading options to reduce the impact of your car or motorbike on the environment. The companies quoted under air travel can also offset your vehicle's emissions.

Licenses

If you've got a valid license at home, then you're halfway to driving in another country. Get an International Driving Permit (IDP) to act as a translation of your license – if you are stopped and asked for your license, you'll need to show traffic cops a copy of both. The IDP will only cover the type of licence you have, so if you don't have a motorcycle license, you won't be qualified to drive one just because you're in another country. In practice, many travellers ride mopeds and light motorcycles, particularly in Southeast Asia.

IDPs are available from your local automobile association or car club; check your section of the Directories (Part Four) for details.

Hire Cars

Hiring a car is a flexible way of enjoying all the freedoms an auto provides without the hassles of worrying about its maintenance. When you have a car, you'll be able to stop when you want, plan your own route and travel at your own speed. Hire costs will be based on a daily rate, typically including the Collision Damage Waver (basic insurance that is a legal requirement in many countries).

The excess (deductible) that you'll need to pay to cover accident damage before this insurance kicks in can run into the thousands, so having extra insurance to reduce this cost to zero is worthwhile. Rental companies charge a fortune for it, often up to 50% of the daily car rental rate (it's a real money spinner for them), but you can get an annual package from a separate insurer for a fraction of what you would pay the hire company for a week of it (single-trip excess insurance is also an option).

The only advantage of the option offered by the rental company is that you won't have to pay the excess up front after an accident – if you have separate excess insurance, you'll need to pay it before reclaiming it with your insurer.

Care hire excess insurance companies to look into include:

- **Insurance 4 Car Hire** (www.insurance4carhire.com)
- **Questor Insurance** (www.questor-insurance.co.uk)
- **Reduce My Excess** (www.reducemyexcess.co.uk)
- **Rental Cover** (www.rentalcover.com)

Most rentals are all-inclusive, but beware of mileage charges where you'll be charged if you exceed a certain amount of miles or kilometres. You can often pay more to drop your car off at a different destination to your point of origin, but work out if this is going to be cheaper. You'll also be stung with an additional fee if the car isn't returned with a full tank of petrol and if there are any unpaid parking fines or damages (they'll do a check when you leave and when you bring it back).

Some global hire companies include:

- **Avis** (www.avis.com)
- **Budget** (www.budget.com)
- **Europcar** (www.europcar.com)
- **Hertz** (www.hertz.com)
- **Thrifty** (www.thrifty.com)

Travel search engines such as **Kayak** (www.kayak.com) and **Skyscanner** (www.skyscanner.net) tend to offer much better deals than the global giants as they also scan local operators.

Buying

If you're in it for the long haul, then buying a car or motorbike of your own can be a good idea. Generally, a stay of a several months where you'll be regularly travelling is the best way to get value out of your car, but it can also be good to have the freedom to get away when you want. However, with rising fuel costs, parking fees, congestion levies and tolls to factor in, it will definitely be more expensive than using public transport for everyday travel.

Still keen to buy a vehicle? Buying a smaller vehicle will increase your fuel efficiency and minimise your pollution impact, so make sure you get the right car for your needs. You can often find cars advertised in hostels, in local classifieds and in used-car lots. There are several online forums that sell cars in specific countries, such as the local **Craigslist** (www.craigslist.org/about/sites) and **Gumtree** (www.gumtree.com). If you're in one of the big backpacker hang-outs (London and Sydney, for example), you can often buy a car from a traveller who's just made a trip in the car and is about to leave the country.

Once you've found a car, give it a good look over and take it for a test drive. If all seems well, then get a proper inspection done by an experienced mechanic if you're not mechanically minded. Some countries have automobile associations which will inspect cars for a fee.

Ridesharing

If you have an empty car going on a long journey, getting someone along for the ride makes sense for the environment as well as helping with the fuel money. If you're the passenger getting a lift, it will mean a bargain trip and maybe making some good friends on the way. Sort out the deal before you go. Some questions to consider include:

- Are you paying for all the fuel or going halves?
- How much luggage can you bring?
- Will you need to stay overnight on the way and will you need a tent or extra cash for a room?
- Can you have a say on the music selection? After all, a road trip is all about the music.

Unfortunately, there's no easy test for 'best friends forever' versus axe murderers, so be sure and check out a ride before you're trapped in a car with someone for several hours on a cross-country trip. A 'getting to know you' coffee or drink can be a good idea even if it's just to discuss what music you'll be listening to on the 12-hour drive up Australia's east coast. If you don't like the person who's offering you the ride, don't go. Solo women should be particularly careful and you may only feel comfortable travelling with couples or other women.

Ridesharing is most common in massive regions that have big traveller populations, such as North America, Australasia and Europe. Finding a ride is often fairly easy if you're on a busy travel route or in a backpacker hangout (such as Prague, London, Sydney or Amsterdam). You can start by casting an eye over a hostel noticeboard, and if no-one seems to be going your way, put up an ad yourself. There are plenty of services online that offer ridesharing, including:

- **Coseats** (www.coseats.com) Good for lifts in Australia
- **eRideshare** (www.erideshare.com) North American rideshare outfit with free registration.
- **Share Your Ride** (www.shareyourride.net) The US, Canada and Australia are served by this registration-driven portal.
- **Shebah** (http://shebah.com.au) Australia's first all-female ride-share company, which works like Uber (fee paying).
- **Thorn Tree** (www.lonelyplanet.com/thorntree) Lonely Planet's own bulletin board with postings under specific countries – especially good for out-of-the-way spots.

Most of these services have long disclaimers about how they take no responsibility for the rides they offer, which is all the more reason to make sure you feel comfortable about who you're going to get a ride with.

Driveaway Cars

This budget alternative to hiring a car is common in the US and works best when you want to drive on a long-haul trip that's a popular route, such as New York to Los Angeles. Basically, you'll drive someone else's car (often for a dealer, manufacturer or rental car agency, so the car could be brand-new) across the country. You'll need to be over 23 in some cases, have a government-generated Motor Vehicle Record from your home country and provide a deposit (at least US$350) to reassure everyone you're not going to steal the car. The time and date of the delivery will be specified and you'll have a maximum mileage, so there won't be much room for detours or going at your own speed. The company usually pays for insurance and you'll pay for all the petrol.

Finding a driveaway company can be as easy as skimming through the internet for 'Automotive Transport' and 'Driveaway Companies', or try **Auto Driveaway** (www.autodriveaway.com/driver).

Hitching

Hitchhiking is never entirely safe (ever seen *Wolf Creek* or *The Hitcher*?) and isn't really advisable, especially with better alternatives such as ridesharing. Warnings about checking out who you're riding with are crucial with hitching, and often you'll have to make a split-second decision based on what someone's car looks like. Not only is hitching risky, it can also be tedious waiting in the rain for the next ride.

BICYCLE

Cyclists the world over will tell you (sometimes as if they're members of a cult): four wheels bad, two wheels good. If you've ever eased around the windmills and green countryside of the Netherlands or chimed your bell as

TRANSPORT YOURSELF

- **Tut-tut for tuk-tuks (Thailand)** Tuk-tuks are ubiquitous, especially so in Bangkok where locals use them for short hops. Prices quoted to tourists are rather a rip-off, but they're worth taking once for the experience. Stick to the Skytrain, river ferries or taxis.
- **Going loco in a Coco (Cuba)** Cuba's small yellow egg-shaped 'Coco taxis' are costly, well-known tourist traps. Instead try 'colectivos', which are taxis running on fixed, long-distance routes, leaving when full. They are generally pre-1959 American cars.
- **Vaporettos in Venice (Italy)** The Venetian water-bus service, vaporettos are quick, frequent and network across the whole of the city. They cost a mere fraction of gondolas.
- **Hop onto a ferry (Greece)** Don't be put off by the sometimes confusing number of ferry routes and operators – sunning yourself on the deck during a four-hour crossing is a surprisingly relaxing way to travel. For journeys at night, it's worth paying for a cabin.
- **Long-tailing around Ko Phi Phi (Thailand)** A wonderful way to island hop in Thailand is by long-tail boat. Travelling in one is the essence of laid-back boho luxury.
- **Go by Greyhound (USA)** The sensible way to travel around the States is by plane, but the best way to see it is by bus. You'll get to see the sort of places found in road-trip movies, and meet a variety of usually friendly (and usually American) fellow travellers.
- **Take the tram (Stockholm)** If you have a burning desire to travel by tram, there are many places you can visit to do so (Budapest, Hong Kong, Istanbul, Lisbon, San Francisco, Vienna). However, the most underrated has to be the historic No 7 tram in Stockholm.

Jess White

you power past another cyclist on the Tour de France route, you'll know what they're talking about. Not only is it clean and green, it's fairly easy to maintain a basic bike and buying a bike is much easier than the paperwork and hassle of a car.

You can rent bikes almost everywhere, bike-share schemes are proliferating in major cities and some hostels may even have free bikes. The quality of rental bikes from hostels may not be great, but they'll be okay for short cycles around town. If you're after a better-quality bike, head for a local bike shop which will have shining mountain bikes and hybrids maintained by bike techs. They can also be good sources of advice on good trails and trips. In remoter parts of the world spare parts will be limited so stocking up on spare inner tubes and basic tools will be useful.

If you're thinking about some serious journeys, you'll want to bring your own bike. Most airlines will charge you extra to bring your bike and you'll want to pack it carefully in a bike box.

Once you've got a bike you'll need to obey local traffic laws, including those about wearing a helmet and drink riding. On short trips you can often take a bike on a train or bus, sometimes with a ticket for your bike but often for free. On long-haul trips you'll need to pack your bike away in a luggage carriage.

BICYCLING BEYOND FEAR

I had to stop pedalling. Not because of the blistering temperatures. Not to differentiate between the sting of tears and the smart of sweat on my sun-raw skin. Not even to recover enough for a full gulp of air. I stopped because beauty overcame me. As I crested a steep hill on that day's bicycle ride, I was stilled by a seeming mirage of multiple depths or a woodblock print made real – layer upon lighter pastel layer of hills stretching into the heat-faded distance.

I stopped too because of a powerful release of emotion. After nearly nine months of resolve-battering riding, my defences had finally disintegrated. And I shed proud and terrified tears of realisation that my 11,000km (6899 mile) bicycle journey from Morocco to Gibraltar, the long way around the Mediterranean Sea, was nearly over. Despite numerous warnings, my teammates and I would accomplish our goal.

The cautions still resonated. Before setting out, we had been repeatedly reminded how we would never survive. Worse, in each country we visited during the trip, we were asked our next destination only to be advised to avoid it because people across the border would commit terrible crimes against us. Which was, sure enough, never the case.

In principle, we knew that fear of the unknown distorts perceptions. But it wasn't until that sultry hilltop that I realised how, in practice, we had really and truly conquered fears – our own and others'.

Ethan Gelber

ACCOMMODATION

Whether it's just a place to stow your backpack or a cosy home base for a month or more, working out where you'll sleep is big part of planning. If you don't like where you're staying – too noisy, too far from the major sights in town or too cockroach-infested – don't forget you can always move on. Even if you're doing it all on the cheap, budget for a few splurges in a pricier place for when you want to relax a little or ditch the hostel crowd.

As a guide, you can check the costs table in the relevant destination chapter in Part Three to do rough calculations. If you want to book some or all of the accommodation online beforehand, there are plenty of websites that can help you do just that, often at a discount. Also try Lonely Planet's Hotels & Hostels (www.lonelyplanet.com/hotels).

HOSTELS

Staying in a hostel is a rite of passage for most travellers and, with facilities geared towards low or no budgets, plenty of fellow travellers and proximity to major sights, it's no wonder. Don't expect too many frills or room service because you get what you pay for at a youth hostel.

The deal is fairly straightforward: you get a bunk and a locker in a shared dormitory for a cheap rate. Some hostels charge less if there are more beds in a dorm, if you don't mind sleeping in a larger dorm with others. They also offer single and double rooms at rates that are usually slightly cheaper than at a budget hotel. There are common bathrooms (usually separate for men and women), kitchens and lounge areas that everyone can use. Some better hostels might add extras such as a café for when you can't face another home-made pasta, internet access and sometimes luxury facilities such as swimming pools, saunas, free surfboards or bicycles. Guidebooks will give you an idea of the good places and fellow travellers will quickly tell you if the next place you're booked into is shitty, but standards are generally high, particularly in busy cities.

Because hostels are backpacker epicentres, you'll meet lots of other people who are interested in the same things as you are. You'll soon have friends to visit sights with, and if you're staying in hostels in the same area for a while you'll bump into the same people again ('Hey, aren't you the guy who stole my towel in Khao San Rd?'). Some hostels have party reputations organising barbecues, talent contests or DJs in their on-site bars, or brilliant links to the local tourism industry so they can organise discount tours or activities. There will be times when you get exhausted, and the sound of 10 of your roommates rolling in drunk at 3am will not be conducive to a good night's sleep. For these times we recommend splashing out to stay in a B&B or hotel.

Look out also for hidden extras when you're staying at a hostel, with some owners thinking it's cool to charge extra for linen, car parking, showers and oxygen. It's not, and there's often a place nearby where 'extras' will be part of the price.

As well as the dependable **Hostelling International network** (HI; www.hihostels.com, see p39) there are often independent hostels which can be better or worse. The HI network has standards that their hostels comply to, while independents don't. Don't be shy of independents, but if places aren't included in your guidebook, it's usually for a reason. See the following online booking sites, which both have handy reviews from other travellers:

- **HostelBookers** (www.hostelbookers.com)
- **Hostelworld** (www.hostelworld.com)

HOTELS

If your funds allow, hotels offer a much wider range of accommodation options. You'll also get a room of your own and a variety of other perks depending on how much you want to pay. A good midrange hotel room will have a small TV, tea- and coffee-making facilities and an in-room minibar fridge. Beware of the latter, however, which usually has a budget-crushing mark-up on everything (yes, everything).

Some hotels will have restaurants and may include breakfast in your room rate, though you can always grab a cheaper bite at a local café to negotiate a few dollars off your room rate. A top-end hotel will have an excellent restaurant and/or bar, a gym and perhaps a pool too.

Budget travellers usually recoil from hotels, but sometimes the only place to stay in town might be a hotel, and when the hostel stops being fun a hotel can make a good escape route. If there are two of you, twin or double rooms can be quite affordable in a basic hotel.

GUESTHOUSES & B&BS

Short for 'bed and breakfast' (because that's exactly what they offer), B&Bs are common in Australasia, North America and the UK, while guesthouses (also called pensions in Spain and Italy) are common in Europe. With a few regional variations (Scots will almost force a hot breakfast of blood sausage on you despite protestations) they offer the same service. As private businesses, they can have the homely feel of staying at your favourite aunty's or they can be kitschy nightmares of porcelain kittens and teddy bears, depending on the owners. Pricewise they offer a good compromise between hostels and hotels, and often have the advantage of friendly owners keen to offer sightseeing tips.

You'll get a room of your own which will have limited furnishings, and breakfast is in a common dining room so you'll get a chance to meet a few of the other guests. B&Bs are often used by older travellers so they'll usually be fairly quiet, and loud music or drunken 3am returns could raise the eyebrows of the owners as they bring you your toast the next morning.

HOUSE-SHARING

Airbnb (www.airbnb.com) is at the forefront of this concept, where home owners can rent out their entire home or flat, or simply a room within it. The latter can be great value, though you'll have the owner to keep you company – reading reviews from previous visitors will give you an idea on their hospitality. Having the exclusive use of a property can be a similar cost to a room in a local hotel, but you'll likely have more space to play with, along with a kitchen for self-catering. Hosts also offer some great local advice on the destination.

CAMPING

Budget options don't come much better than this. In many parts of the world you'll just need to find enough ground to lay out your tent and you've got your night's accommodation. The only catch is that in many places pitching your tent will be illegal and fines will make it a less-than-budget experience.

Even if you have to fork out for a camping ground, this is still the cheapest option, and there'll be the bonus of facilities such as toilets, barbecue areas and possibly even laundries.

National parks, hostels and caravan parks will all let you put a tent up for very little cost.

LIVING IN

There's no better way to get to know a culture than to live and work among its people. You can expect to learn more of a language and make lifelong friends. Some hospitality jobs (see p121) will include board as part of the wage – which will usually be at the pub or guesthouse you're employed in. While the savings are great, you may find that living and working in the same place can be too much, especially if your employers are insane.

A lot about 'living in' depends on who you'll be living with, from delightful hippies who'll bake fresh bread for you to people who don't realise they're not your parents and give you curfews. Be sure to check them out with a phone call before agreeing to stay, particularly if they're in remote areas.

HOMESTAYS

These are great opportunities to live with hosts who may require you to work or study. It can be as simple as staying with friends, or it can be part of a formal programme that includes language classes.

Here are a few organisations that offer homestays:

- **Homestay Web** (www.homestayweb.com) A large site that requires registration and lists homestays around the world.
- **Homestay** (www.homestay.com) Options in 160 countries.
- **Responsible Travel** (www.responsibletravel.com/holidays/homestays) Coordinates homestays with locals in many locations around the world.

FARMSTAYS

These are ideal if you want to get out of the city and soak up the rustic lifestyle. Prices start at budget rates and you can reduce them with work around the farm. Hosts will advertise a private room and who they would prefer (some specify women, couples or students), and you can apply for a place in most parts of the world. Farmstays can include courses and training in everyday chores, so you may come home with a trade.

A few organisations that offer farmstays include:

- **Farmstays International** (www.farmstays.org) A service that includes Canada, USA, Australia, New Zealand and Argentina.
- **Help Exchange** (www.helpx.net) Lists host families, farms, hotels and B&Bs in Europe, Australasia and North America that provide free accommodation and food in exchange for unpaid labour.
- **Willing Workers on Organic Farms** (WWOOF; www.wwoof.net) Work in exchange for your food and board at this global network of organic farms. Membership varies depending on where you are visiting, up to £20/US$40/A$70.

COUCHSURFING

Thanks to sites such as Couchsurfing (www.couchsurfing.org) you can have access to a worldwide network of couches offered by fellow travellers who are happy to put you up for the night. Once you're registered you can search for couches. Be sure to carefully check the peer reviews from people who've visited before. You may find they are actually a great local guide. The idea is that it's expected you'll repay the favour to others down the line, which is where some of these sites fall down – there tend to be many more takers than givers.

ACCESSIBLE TRAVEL

BY MARTIN HENG

If you're reading this book, you clearly have the desire to travel. If you're worried that a big trip is out of the question, you needn't be. There are countless people with a disability who venture around the globe, and many of them are on the road now. There are even a few, including some with severe disabilities, who are making a living as travel bloggers. Those leading the way include quadruple amputee **Chris Koch** (www.ifican.ca), deaf-blind **Tony Giles** (www.tonythetraveller.com) and **Cory Lee Woodard** (www.curbfreewithcorylee.com), who has spinal muscular atrophy. These remarkable people may be exceptional, but they prove how indomitable the human spirit can be and how even the most severe disabilities can be overcome if you put your mind to it.

To make your big trip happen there are only two prerequisites: faith and conviction. This is not to say your journey will be easy. Everyone who has travelled with a disability knows that it's a lot harder, and takes infinitely more planning, than for someone who is able bodied. It's also more difficult to be spontaneous, although if you are to succeed you will need to be flexible and prepared for anything – whereas most people need a plan B, you may need a plan C or even D.

WHO WITH?

Your first decision will be whether to travel alone or with a companion. As in your daily life, only you know what you are capable of doing independently and what you need help with. There are many people with a disability who do travel solo, but the more severe your disability, the less likely it is. For example, there are many paraplegics who are happy to travel alone, but there are far fewer quadriplegics (tetraplegics) who do so. With diseases such as cerebral palsy or multiple sclerosis, it depends on how severely you are affected and how stable your condition is; again, there are many people with congenital conditions such as those who travel alone, and many who wouldn't be able to cope. When making this decision, it's important above all to remember that your home environment has probably been adapted quite specifically to suit your needs and that the further you travel from your home base – your comfort zone – the more difficult it will be to maintain your independence. Spending the day out alone in your home city is probably a doddle; a week in another city in your home country isn't too hard; a fortnight in a neighbouring country, when you throw in a language barrier, will take some preparation; and immersing yourself in a completely different culture and environment on a different continent will take some serious planning.

RESOURCES

The good news is that accessible, inclusive or barrier-free travel (useful terms to know for internet searches) has become a 'thing' in recent years. In 2016 the United Nations World Tourism Organization dedicated World Tourism Day to 'Tourism for All: Promoting Universal Accessibility', and as a result there are plenty of planning tools and resources at your disposal.

You're also not alone; there are numerous forums where you can ask questions or learn from other disabled travellers: the Travellers with Disabilities branch of Lonely Planet's Thorn Tree, Lonely Planet's Travel for All Google+ group, and several Facebook groups, the most active of which is the Accessible Travel Club. Also, your condition is probably not unique and, just as there is probably an organisation in your home country that represents your particular disability, there are likely to be similar organisations in countries you are visiting. Even if there are not, there is an umbrella, pan-disability organisation in almost every country. It will be well worth your while to contact relevant organisations before you leave for resources or advice you can tap into when planning and assistance you can access while visiting.

Lonely Planet produces the world's largest list of online resources for travelling with a disability – it's updated annually and free to download. Each year's edition of *Accessible Travel Online Resources* is useful for planning and when on the road as it contains hundreds of useful links.

It also allows you to immerse yourself in the adventures of dozens of seasoned disabled travellers, which provides inspiration and ideas on where to go and how to do it. Browse the specialist sporting and adventure travel organisations if adrenaline is your thing – you may be surprised to learn that everything from skydiving and scuba diving to skiing to surfing are all possible for people with a wide variety of disabilities. The country-by-country resources section contain links to a broad range of webpages, covering everything from public transport to NGOs, tourism management organisations and search engines for accessible facilities. You'll also find links to special assistance pages for all major airlines and airports. And if you feel the need to book parts of your trip through specialist accessible travel agents or tour operators, we also have most of the world covered.

Finally, you may find it handy to take with you Lonely Planet's *Accessible Travel Phrasebook*, which contains around 100 disability-related words and phrases in 35 different languages. Go to https://shop.lonelyplanet.com/categories/accessible-travel to download this title, and a selection of other free accessible city guides.

WHERE TO GO?

Your second decision is where to go. When asked, most experienced disabled travellers will advise not to base your decisions according to how accessible places are supposed to be. Rather, do as any able-bodied person would and ask yourself where you want to go. Although it has been said, memorably, that no amount of positive attitude will get you up a flight of stairs in a wheelchair, there is no doubt that you cannot survive a long trip – or perhaps even a shorter one – without a good dose of positivity and a willingness to engage with people you encounter. So decide where you most want to go, and make it happen!

It's obviously easier travelling in developed countries that have well-established anti-discrimination legislation and strong building codes, which are both in place and enforced. This includes most of western and northern Europe, North America, Australia and New Zealand, as well as affluent countries in Asia such as Singapore and Japan. These countries have the advantage of modern infrastructure – well-maintained pavements (sidewalks), kerb cuts, tactile paving, visual and audio alerts/alarms, good wayfinding signage and elevators – and public venues and facilities, including transport, that are more accessible as a result of both legislation and a strong history of advocacy.

There will also be a lot more resources at your disposal. For example, many cities have a public transport website and/or smart phone app with accessible filters that you can apply to plan your route. Some cities and even countries (eg Singapore) also maintain a database of accessible buildings, facilities and activities.

In this respect, best practice is found in those countries and regions whose tourism management organisations have invested resources in accessible travel. Flanders (Belgium), Germany and the UK are the undisputed leaders in providing excellent information and planning tools for travellers with disabilities or access needs. Spain, particularly Madrid and Barcelona (a veritable mecca for wheelchair users due to its accessibility), is close behind although some material is in Spanish only. And Portugal is the latest country to make significant efforts to tap into the large and growing accessible travel market.

Less-developed countries offer more challenges, as they do for any traveller, but by the same token the rewards and the sense of achievement are commensurately greater. Travelling in such countries is when you'll need to be at your most adaptable: accessible public transport is rare, ramps into buildings are uncommon, elevators may be unheard of, and even pavements are often absent or impassable. But this is not a reason to avoid these places. For starters, there is overwhelming anecdotal evidence (and the personal experience of this writer) that the kindness of strangers and people power can usually compensate for a lack of infrastructure – and this is true of developed countries too.

For instance, some of Bangkok's Skytrain stations are not equipped with elevators, but staff in these locations are very quick to approach a wheelchair user and will gather enough strong arms to ensure the person's safety as they accompany them up and down regular escalators.

In India, where the average daily wage is under ₹300 (US$4), it's very economical to hire someone to push your wheelchair around a tourist site or even to hire some muscle to lift your wheelchair up a flight of stairs. As mentioned above, a positive attitude won't remove an obstacle, but engaging positively with people you encounter almost certainly will. And travelling in less-developed countries is also where courage may come in useful: as pavements in Delhi are unusable in a wheelchair, it's actually better to take to the road – drivers there are already well used to avoiding a multitude of other forms of transport on the road, not to mention animals!

EQUIPMENT

When travelling with a disability, the likelihood is that you will be using equipment, whether to help your mobility or hearing. If this is the case, it's vitally important that you ensure you are as well prepared as possible for any eventuality. Most importantly, have your device serviced just before you leave. If your device requires charging, make sure that you have the necessary voltage converters, or that they are available en route. It's also worth finding out whether your equipment can be replaced or repaired in the destinations you're visiting and to take the contact details of equipment suppliers in countries you're travelling through. If there are spare parts that are hard to source but can be packed, try to make room for them in your luggage. As with infrastructure, you'll find that while in developed countries replacements and repairs may be more straightforward, in less-developed countries there is an abundance of ingenuity and resourcefulness.

MEDICATIONS

You may also be travelling with medications, in which case you should carry more than you think you'll need and not pack them all in the same bag – always have an emergency supply somewhere. Equally importantly, be aware that 'controlled substances' differ from country to country – particularly in the case of opioids and benzodiazepines (eg diazepam) – and you may need your medications to be authorised by a consulate or embassy before you enter a country. (The UAE is a good example.) In any case, carry a letter from your doctor certifying your condition and listing all the medications you need. It wouldn't hurt to carry prescriptions from your doctor with you – although they may not be valid in the countries you're travelling to, they may facilitate a local doctor prescribing the relevant medication should you run out. You should also make a note of the generic rather than the brand names of all your medications as brand names differ from country to country.

TRAVEL INSURANCE

If you're travelling with a disability, doing so without valid insurance is not a wise decision. Finding an insurer that will ensure you for pre-existing medical conditions at an affordable price might prove difficult, but we've highlighted a few good options that you can find in the Directories section for different regions. For British and Irish travellers, see p338, for North American travellers, p341 and Australasian travellers, p345. You may choose to take out insurance that excludes your medical condition, or else insure your equipment alone. If your equipment is insured in your home country, the insurer may extend that coverage overseas at a more reasonable rate than a specialist travel insurer.

TRAVEL THEMES

THE ADVENTURE TRAIL

Like the sound of having only a rubber tube between you and the wildest rivers Belize can serve up as you drift through a dark cave? Or perhaps hiking through the rugged volcanic wonderland of the Tongariro Crossing (New Zealand) just waiting for an eruption? You don't go halfway round the world to sit inside, so when you're planning your trip mix in a little adrenaline, sprinkle liberally with the great outdoors and wash the whole thing down with a shot of danger to make an adventurous meal out of your trip. If you're stuck for ideas, check out *Lonely Planet's Atlas of Adventure*.

Exploring national parks can give you a peek at the wildlife. Try cycling through Kenya's Hell's Gate National Park, with zebras, giraffes, impalas and buffalo all along for the ride. Sometimes the scenery itself can be more than spectacular, such as in the Canadian Rockies when hiking the Valley of the Ten Peaks trail in Banff National Park. Another favourite is the barren beauty of the Namib-Naukluft National Park in Namibia, where mountainous red dunes tower over baking salt pans dotted with ghostly forests of seemingly petrified trees. Or you can get another perspective while floating above it all by paragliding over epic landscapes and waterfalls in Iceland. You don't need to be a complete fitness freak to take on cheerful strolls such as the Cinque Terre (Italy) or easy day walks along the Pembrokshire Coast Path in Wales (UK).

TOP 20 ADVENTURES

Don't leave the USA without...
Hiking Zion National Park's Angels Landing Trail – just 8km long, but utterly unforgettable. The last 100m traverses a ledgy via ferrata route to a pedestal smack in the middle of the canyon, 460m above the canyon floor and the Virgin River below. Not for the faint of heart or the acrophobic.

Don't leave Australia without...
Riding Mt Buller's 40km Australian Alpine Epic Trail in the Victorian highlands – the only track in the country granted official 'epic' status by the International Mountain Biking Association (IMBA).

Don't leave Vietnam without...
Kayaking through sea caves and arches in Halong Bay. Many Halong tour boats carry kayaks, or they can be hired from operators and hotels on Cat Ba Island.

Don't leave Guatemala without...
Hiking 60km into Petén jungle to the spectacular ruins of El Mirador, a fascinating, largely unexcavated Mayan city. The vast Maya Biosphere Reserve is one of the most ecologically diverse regions in the world, home to giant anteaters, scarlet macaws, jaguars and pumas, plus hundreds of unique plants and trees.

Don't leave Indonesia without...
Climbing ancient Borobudur. The world's largest Buddhist monument features massive temple spires that sprout from the Kedu Plain valley floor, all set against a backdrop of countless volcanic peaks, including the volatile Mt Merapi.

Don't leave Brazil without...
Taking a tandem hang-gliding flight from Pedra Bonita over Rio de Janeiro, landing on a beach below. Check that the operator is certified by the Brazilian Hang-Gliding Association.

Don't leave Myanmar without...
Learning how to paddle a skiff with one leg across Inle Lake. Fishermen here are famous for paddling their watercraft with one leg while they toss their large nets into the water with both hands. It's even more difficult than it looks.

Don't leave Cambodia without...
Cycling around Angkor Wat, a 12th-century World Heritage-listed monument and the world's largest religious site, close to Siem Reap. Ride from crumbling tower to ancient pagoda to serene pond, basking in boundless positive vibes.

Don't leave Iceland without...
Venturing into a volcano. Iceland is home to the world's only volcano that can be explored from the inside: Thrihnukagigur, east of Bláfjöll Mountain, which hasn't erupted for 4000 years. Using an open elevator, subterranean explorers experience a journey into the Earth as they're lowered 120m into the magma chamber.

Don't leave Georgia without...
Paragliding over the Caucasus Mountains. With a range of launch sites countrywide, from 500m to

2500m high, paragliding the Caucasus is a serene experience that will linger long after feet touch terra firma.

Don't leave Madagascar without...
Going caving in Ankarana National Park, where you can explore some of its 140km of subterranean rivers and caves – just watch out for the cave-dwelling crocodiles.

Don't leave Japan without...
Skiing Mt Fuji. In Shinto it's the embodiment of nature itself, for Buddhists it's a gateway to another world. There is something special about skiing or boarding down the beautiful, conical Mt Fuji – the most iconic peak in Japan.

Don't leave Bolivia without...
Cycling the world's biggest salt flats, Salar de Uyuni, a disorientating, surreal and unforgettable experience. In the vast white expanse, you'll encounter Dalíesque standing rocks, brightly coloured hot springs and miraculous colonies of chinchillas and flamingoes.

Don't leave Laos without...
Scrambling up the 100 Waterfalls Trek. Accessed via Nong Khiaw village, ankle-tickling water is a constant chaperone for this 10km ascent that involves ropes and rickety bamboo ladders beside cascading waterfalls.

Don't leave Turkey without...
Paragliding from one of the highest commercial sites in the world, perched atop the 1960m *Mt Babada*□. It's a 30-40 minute thrill ride back down, landing on the postcard-perfect Ölüdeniz Beach. Almost as adrenaline-pumping is the 4WD journey up to the summit and the brief instruction session – 'Run. Fast. Don't stop.'

Don't leave Nicaragua without...
Exploring the excellent diving and snorkelling around the Corn Islands on the Caribbean coast, with wrecks and reefs accessible from the beach.

Don't leave Botswana without...
Hiking into the sacred Tsodilo Hills to examine some of the 4000 prehistoric San rock paintings – it's an outdoor art gallery like no other.

Don't leave Samoa without...
Going underground in one of Samoa's incredible caves, such as Pa'ape'a Cave on Upolu (with its population of Polynesian swiftlets) or Dwarf's Cave on Savai'i, a surreal subterranean lava tube leading into the underworld.

Don't leave Oman without...
Exploring Jabal Shams and Wadi Ghul, 'Arabia's Grand Canyon', and daring to do the nerve-wracking Balcony Walk around the rim.

Don't leave Tahiti and French Polynesia without...
Trying outrigger paddling, which is a way of life in French Polynesia. You can still opt for the traditional dug-out experience, or go for the comfort of a modern sea kayak, so you can stow camping gear and set off to discover your own empty patch of paradise.

THE FESTIVAL CIRCUIT

The riotous clatter of drums at a street party, the serene meditations in a temple in honour of the gods or the 'kerang' of a rock gig taking it to volume 11 – festivals come in many forms. Some travellers plan their whole trip around the festival circuit, attending gigs such as the UK's Glastonbury and the USA's Burning Man in the Northern Hemisphere before heading south to party down in Rio's epic Carnaval or catching the Big Day Out gigs in Australia or New Zealand. You can do your research and plan a whole route around festivals. Alternatively, you can just show up and see what parties you can join, but be warned that festival-going is a mission not to be accepted lightly. Hotels book out months in advance, tickets go on sale up to six months before and hard-core attendees start working on outfits as soon as last year's festival ends.

But it's not all wild dancing and sampling local brews. Religious festivals are about proving you're devout through elaborate rituals – such as Ramadan, the Muslim festival practiced in many countries that requires fasting during daylight hours. After 70 days of fasting, food is savoured at the Eid al-Adha, Ramadan's official end. The end of Buddhist fasting, Vassa, sees Asian monks leave monasteries with alms bowls and the release of banana-leaf boats at river festivals. Days of fasting could explain some local crankiness, so realising that festivals can impact peoples' daily lives helps in showing respect.

Religious festivals aren't all about abstinence though. At Turkey's Mevlâna Festival and

Glastonbury Festival, UK, takes centre stage when it comes to live rock and pop, creative craft villages and nightlife

SIX FESTIVALS TO BLOW YOUR MIND

HOLI (INDIA & NEPAL)

The Festival of Colour, as it has come to be known, is primarily a Hindu festival and it's celebrated with wild parties and crazy colour fights across large parts of India and Nepal. It's a celebration of the victory of one's inner good over evil.

AGITAGUEDA ART FESTIVAL (AGUEDA, PORTUGAL)

One of the most recognisable symbols of this vibrant Portuguese festival is the installation of hundreds of colourful umbrellas suspended above one of the city's streets. Other parts of the urban landscape, like park benches, stairs, and power poles, are also painted in colourful examples of street art, creating an enchanted atmosphere. The festival aims to promote new musical and artistic projects, with numerous local and international acts taking to the main stage, which is free. The festivities extend over three weeks so there's plenty to pack in.

PINGXI LANTERN FESTIVAL (PINGXI, TAIWAN)

It's a stunningly luminous sight. Close to 200,000 lanterns are released into the night sky at the start of the new Lunar Year. According to ancient legend, the lanterns were originally lit to let Pingxi villagers, who had fled their homes under the threat of outlaw raids, know that it was safe to return. Over the hundreds and hundreds of years, the lanterns have come to represent a release of bad habits and an aspiration to achieve positive ideals. You'll have a night you'll never forget.

MAINE LOBSTER FESTIVAL (ROCKLAND, NEW ENGLAND, USA)

What started as a community initiative to boost interest in local seafood has become a world-regarded festival celebrating the superior quality of the region's marine produce. If you feel the need to burn off some of this extravagant eating, the festival organisers have cooked up some fun activities. Join the Lobster Crate Race, where competitors hop from crate to crate across the open water.

CARNEVALE (VENICE, ITALY)

Aside from dapper gondoliers cruising the city's canals, there are few images as iconic to Italy's water-circled city as the masked partygoers at the world-famous Venice Carnevale. The festival was originally a licence to indulge in heedless pleasure, with masks worn to protect participant's identities. Today, decadence is still on the table, with more than three million visitors joining in the fun.

BORYEONG MUD FESTIVAL (BORYEONG, KOREA)

Time to get down and dirty. Many Koreans believe that the mud in Boryeong contains healing properties so, as any self-respecting health fanatic knows, this means it's time to get all your friends together and get completely covered in the stuff from head to toe. It's a family-friendly affair with activities that range from mud races and slides, to the more sedate mud facials and body painting.

Day of the Dead, the colourful and iconic Mexican festival, being celebrated in Oaxaca, Mexico

Fruits and bells hanging from of a devotee in Thaipusam festival at Batu Caves temple, Kuala Lumpur, Malaysia

Egypt's Moulid of Sayyed Ahmed al-Badawi, Sufi Muslims attempt to attain oneness with God by chanting and dancing into a trance. In Haiti the voodoo Fete Gede involves a visit to the cemetery to dance with the dead, and Mexico's *Día de los Muertos* (Day of the Dead) sees candlelight meals for the recently departed placed on flower-covered altars. Macabre marzipan shaped into skeletons, skulls and other emo themes are relished by kids.

Of course, there are big bashes such as Edinburgh's Hogmanay New Year's party, Sydney's simply fabulous Gay and Lesbian Mardi Gras and London's Notting Hill Carnival. Special mention must go to Rio's Carnaval, which kicks off with streetside *bandas* (bands), each party having its own fancy dress code. The event climaxes with a massive street parade and much drinking and debauchery. California's Burning Man is a community art project on a grand scale with a five-mile camp that gathers to sculpt, dance, topless-cycle and eventually incinerate an enormous human effigy.

Not weird enough? Head for Turkey's Camel Wrestling festival where the ships of the desert spar to shove each other out of the ring. Looking for something tougher than an eyebrow ring? The Hindu Thaipusam festival in Malaysia and India sees body piercing taken to the next level with some participants dragging offerings of milk jugs by hooks buried into their skin. Pyromaniacs converge on the Shetland Islands for Up Helly Aa, where wannabe Vikings toss burning torches on a longship they've spent a year building, then spend the night drinking and dancing as it burns.

For more specifics on festivals, see the individual destination chapters in Part Three.

JOBS

Work may be the 'curse of the drinking classes', as Oscar Wilde quipped, but sooner or later you may need to top up your wallet whether you're drinking or not. Getting a job while you're overseas can also be a great way to build your CV – working internationally always impresses potential employers, plus it can be a good way to sample a couple of jobs to see if it's a career you want to pursue when you get back home. And if a job overseas doesn't work out you can always move on with no hard feelings. Plus there's seasonal and casual work that's ideal for commitment-phobes, and because the expectation from employers is that you'll only work for a while before moving on to explore more of the world.

This chapter looks at a few of the common traveller jobs, from teaching English and freelance writing to fruit picking and working as au pair, and provides tips on what you'll need to do most of these jobs and what you should bring with you to help the job hunt. Of course, if your career from home is transferable and more lucrative, then you can seek out similar roles while on the road. If you can be a digital nomad – working on freelance contracts from home while abroad on your laptop – you can avoid searching for local employment altogether. Working out the visa situation is tricky for all options, even for digital nomads (visa and tax laws on this front are still a very grey area) – rules change too quickly and you should look online for the latest information, but information here was correct at the time of research.

Getting the right mix between travel and work is the key. You don't want to go half way around the world to be stuck in an office in New York or be trapped waiting tables 24/7 in a Pacific island paradise. Some travellers keep a tight budget when they're working to save up for a big trip, while others hop away for weekends to break up their working weekdays – this is particularly easy from London with more than 30 countries accessible by budget flight.

No matter what job you end up doing on holiday, it will feel more exciting just because you'll be doing it in another country. Even washing dishes in Lisbon will get you inside a Portuguese kitchen and a whole culinary culture – you can learn how to make *alcatra* (beef roasted in red wine and garlic) and enjoy a few after-work drinks with genuine locals. Long nights working as a bouncer on the door of a Moscow club might seem dull, but you'll be talking to people every day (great for learning local slang) and you'll get to hear local bands and DJs that you never would have access to back home. When you do finally return, your stories about jobs – the good, the bad and the ugly – will be much better than some of the postcard moments other travellers had.

READY TO WORK?

Before you hit the road you should do some research about your destination and look at how likely it is that you'll be able to find work, not to mention check out local pay rates. There's not much use in showing up at a place where the exchange rate is terrible and you're competing in a market with high unemployment. Many countries have a minimum wage, and if you surf a few local job sites you can often find how much specific jobs will pay. This will be invaluable when a potential employer says 'But this is what I pay everyone.'

Language is another good piece of knowledge to take with you. If English is your only language, you may need to focus on English-speaking countries. English is an international language but without the local lingo you might be limited in the kinds of jobs you can do. If you have a smattering of the spoken local language, you can likely get by in basic jobs and maybe even work in hospitality. If you're looking at office jobs, you'll need to have some developed language skills, particularly with written language. Interviews will be near impossible if you can't speak the same language as your potential boss, so consider language lessons if you're heading to a non-English-speaking nation.

VISAS, TAX & RED TAPE

No matter where you want to work, you'll need to sort out a visa. Working without one is illegal and you can be deported for 'working black', as it's often called. If you're 30 years old or younger (and in some cases under 35), there are almost 60 countries that offer some form of working holiday visas for various citizenships, which allow you to work or study for up to 24 months (most are limited to a year). Some go by different names, such as IEC (International Experience Canada) work permits in Canada. Citizens of Australia, Canada and New Zealand have the most options to play with.

In the past the US has been very difficult to secure work in, but if you're a post-secondary student (or recent graduate) with Australian or New Zealand citizenship, you are able to apply to the US for a J-1 12 Month Work and Travel Visa. If you're from the UK, the J-1 visa is your best hope of getting into the 'land of the free'. This visa requires sponsorship from a company, so big companies, nanny or au pair agencies and cultural exchange groups can organise sponsorship. At the time of research the US government was considering making cuts to the J-1 exchange visitor programme in five categories, which include Summer Work Travel, Camp Counselor, Intern, Trainee and Au Pair.

For citizens of the US, options are more limited. There are trial reciprocal arrangements with Australia, but other than that Americans will be relying on sponsorship, so arrangements such as internships or cultural exchanges can be a good option. See the Directories chapter in Part Four for relevant visa sites.

Taxes are another issue for working internationally. Whatever country you're working in, you'll contribute to its taxation system. This tax will often be taken directly from your salary unless you're working in an illegal 'cash in hand' job. Just like working without a visa, getting caught not paying tax can come with tough penalties for travellers, though many industries such as hospitality still rely on this method. Of course, if you've paid too much tax (which is common if you're working for less than the full financial year), you might be able to get some of your **tax back**. Check the sites below for details on this, or cut through the red tape by using a service such as **Tax Back** (www.taxback.com).

Here are some sites that will give you more specific information about tax in the countries you might visit:

- **HM Revenue & Customs** (www.gov.uk/government/organisations/hm-revenue-customs) Information for all UK tax issues.
- **National Insurance** (www.gov.uk/national-insurance) Get a national insurance number here to work in the UK.
- **Australian Taxation Office** (www.ato.gov.au) Click on 'Individuals' then 'Coming to Australia' for FAQs; get your Tax File Number (TFN) here.

• **New Zealand Inland Revenue Department** (www.ird.govt.nz) New Zealand's tax laws made simple.
• **Inland Revenue Service** (www.irs.gov) US tax authority which issues essential social security cards and explains federal tax.
• **Canada Revenue Agency** (www.cra-arc.gc.ca) Apply for your Social Insurance Number (SIN) and find out more about Canada's tax system.
• **European Job Mobility Portal** (http://ec.europa.eu/eures) Has information about most countries in the EU.

LOOKING FOR WORK

With a curriculum vitae (CV; aka 'résumé') to write, application letters to send and then interviews (sometimes several rounds), applying for jobs is never easy, but it's worth it when you get that first pay cheque, especially after you've had a couple of months of the bank balance dribbling away during travel.

The first step is to get your CV in order. Think carefully about what to include and how to represent yourself in the best light. You should try to summarise your work experience and include job titles, dates and tasks you did in each position, plus any training you have or awards you may have won, or memberships of clubs or societies. Some people include hobbies though these are fairly optional. If you're not sure whether the information belongs in your CV, ask yourself how it will help you get the job.

The web is filled with tips and advice on writing a good CV, and many employment agencies and job sites offer good formats for CVs, which can be handy to get the hang of local terms and ideas. A good basic site is **CV Tips** (www.cvtips.com).

Bring a soft copy on a USB key or email it to yourself – you can then customise it to a specific job on your laptop or in an internet café, then print it out if you need hard copies. Depending on where you are, many employers will want you to apply by email or via their website, but hard copy is always handy for face-to-face interviews and written applications.

If you're staying at a hostel, its noticeboard can be a good place to start looking for jobs. Otherwise, there is no shortage of online options to start your search:

• **Australian JobSearch** (www.jobsearch.gov.au) A government-run job site.
• **Backdoor Jobs** (www.backdoorjobs.com) This site has adventure and alternative options in the US and beyond.
• **Careerbuilder** (www.careerbuilder.com) A US-based site for work in the 50 states.
• **Dice** (www.dice.com) A US-based site that focuses on global roles in the tech industry.
• **Escape Artist** (www.escapeartist.com) Huge US site that includes global jobs and a free online newsletter.
• **Eurojobs** (www.eurojobs.com) A huge free-to-access jobs board linking to hundreds of organisations looking to employ both non-Europeans (with the correct work permits) and Europeans.
• **Fish4Jobs** (www.fish4.co.uk) A UK recruitment site listing global jobs.
• **Gaijin Pot** (www.gaijinpot.com) Jobs and study opportunities in Japan.
• **Gorkana** (www.gorkana.com) For PR and journalism jobs in the UK and elsewhere.
• **Idealist** (www.idealist.org) This site focuses on roles with organisations that work to make the world a better place.
• **iAgora** (www.iagora.com/work) Specialises in entry-level jobs and internships in Europe – mostly for free, with some subscription-based.
• **Indeed** (www.indeed.com) Aggregates job listings from across the web.

- **JobBank USA** (www.jobbankusa.com) A US job site with searches by job, state and city.
- **Jobs Abroad** (http://jobs.goabroad.com) Part of Go Abroad, a good US travel site, listing international job programmes. Other subsites include Intern Abroad, Study Abroad, Teach Abroad and Volunteer Abroad.
- **Jobs.ie** (www.jobs.ie) An Irish site that's good for Ireland but has global reach.
- **LinkedIn** (www.linkedin.com) A global work network. You'll need to set up a profile, but it alerts you to jobs that suit your experience.
- **Monster** (www.monster.com) A truly global company which has offices in the UK, USA, Canada, Australia and most European and Asian countries. Register and create a digital CV and contact job experts.
- **Pay Away** (www.payaway.co.uk) An excellent UK website with jobs advice, an email newsletter and jobs bulletin board.
- **Reed.co.uk** (www.reed.co.uk) British job site with listings in the UK and abroad.
- **Seek** (www.seek.com) Global job site with focus on Australia, New Zealand and the UK.
- **SimplyHired** (www.simplyhired.com) It offers an email alerts service and lets you save your job searches.
- **The-Dots** (https://the-dots.com) A network for those who work in the creative industries.
- **Undutchables** (www.undutchables.nl) Netherlands-based site with jobs and advice especially for multilingual people.

Most jobs will require you to write application/cover letters and sit an interview. This letter should describe why you're the best person for the job and point to relevant experience you might have mentioned in your CV. Often the 'letter' is an email with your CV attached. If you do get an interview, it means they liked what they saw in the letter and want to see if you'll be a good 'fit' for the job. Interviews are also a chance for you to see if this is the kind of place you'd like to work. For more tips on application letters, you can talk to careers counsellors at school or university, or check job sites that offer sound advice.

TYPES OF WORK

Once your CV is in order, you can start thinking about what type of work you want. You might want to consider how long you want to work for and whether you want to sample a career while you're away. Some of the jobs you do while you're travelling might not end up on your CV, but will get you the very necessary cash to stay on the move. Other jobs can be a way into an industry or even be something that will have an interviewer saying 'Ah, I see you've worked in an art gallery in New York, that's going to come in handy in curating.' If you're looking to build your career, an internship (see below) might be just the ticket. Otherwise you might want the low commitment of fruit picking, labouring work or even occasionally strutting onto a film set (see p125).

TEACHING ENGLISH

If you're reading this, you're probably one of the 345 million people in the world who have English as their first language. Did you know that English ranks third, after Mandarin Chinese and Spanish? You've probably been taking your mother tongue for granted, but it's actually complicated (ever tried explaining the difference between 'there', 'their' and 'they're' to a classroom full of non-English-speakers?) and very difficult to learn, particularly if you have a non-Germanic language background (those that aren't based on Latin, such as English, Italian or Spanish). Fortunately, this means that English-language teaching is always in demand.

Not only is it portable (you might need a textbook and a few hand-outs, but these can just be PDFs on a USB drive), but English-teaching is needed everywhere. Even in English-speaking countries new arrivals, including everyone from refugees to businesspeople, are keen to learn the lingo. Plus you'll get to meet local people and give them a skill that they'll have all their lives. This is a sure-fire way to make friends.

WHY GO TEFL?

This US-based site (www.whygo.com) has info, articles and blogs on TEFL courses and jobs around the world. It's a good read if you're interested in becoming a teacher and want the benefit of other people's experiences and opinions.

What to Expect?

Your teaching experience will depend on your class. You could be teaching one-on-one with a wealthy kid in Tokyo or you could be standing in front of a class of adults in a Brazilian village. Teaching one student can be easy and you'll get to know a single student better than a whole class, while a class has more difficult dynamics – who's getting on with whom, who's throwing paper planes at you and a hundred other challenges.

The good news is that teaching can pay very well, depending on where you are. A school in the United Arab Emirates (UAE), for example, pays US$4100 a month tax free, while one in Kazakhstan doles out US$5000 a month (before tax). Teaching English in Japan or Korea pays around US$2000 per month, though the same job in South America may offer a simple allowance of US$2000 for the entire year. Schools usually help out with your accommodation (either subsidising or helping find cheap local apartments) and flight costs so your expenses will be limited while you're teaching, though it could be tough to save up for a huge trip after teaching. Most schools are fairly clear on rates of pay and conditions on their websites.

Most schools will keep you pretty busy with four- or five-day weeks, plus there may be opportunities for extra tutoring. Preparing lessons is more time-consuming than you think though, and you should allow at least as much time to prepare a class as you'll be teaching. If you're marking written assignments (which is rare if you're doing a speaking-only class), this will also take up time. In a good school you may already have a curriculum to teach, complete with detailed lesson plans and exercises; in a bad one you may find yourself with a pile of faded Charles Dickens' books and a blackboard.

Outside the school, you'll often have a support network of other teachers to go out with or team up with for weekend escapes. Many schools will employ you for a year, so once you're finished it might be a good time to explore the rest of the country as you'll have developed better language skills yourself.

What You'll Need

There are several qualifications in teaching English that will help your job search. In the US, Canada and Australia, the qualification is called Teaching English as a Second Language (TESL), while in the UK it's called Teaching English as a Foreign Language (TEFL; pronounced 'teffle' by those in the know). In the UK, Ireland and New Zealand, courses can also be called Teaching English for Speakers of Other Languages (TESOL). Courses vary in length and the clout they carry with employers.

Not surprisingly, the most respected courses come from the UK, as many people still see it as the cradle of the English language. The Certificate in English Language Teaching to Adults (CELTA) is a widely respected qualification administered by the University of Cambridge (www.cambridgeenglish.org). There's an explosion of bogus places with similar names, so check for centres that offer the real deal on the University of Cambridge website. Another well-regarded course is Certificate in Teaching English to Speakers of Other Languages (CertTESOL) offered by **Trinity College London** (www.trinitycollege.com). Good courses usually take three to four months full-time and can be done part-time over a year.

Elsewhere in the world, there are local organisations (see the Directories chapter relevant to you in Part Four) and good web resources which offer their own version of these courses. Some courses even come with a job offer at the end, because they have links to schools around the world.

Here are a few global providers:

- **Cactus Language** (www.cactuslanguage.com) Offers language courses worldwide; also has an admissions service for internationally recognised TEFL certificate courses.
- **ICAL TEFL** (www.icaltefl.com) Online courses (120/150 hour options) include video lessons.
- **International House London** (www.ihlondon.com) Offers good 'distance education' modules to prepare you for CELTA courses.
- **International Teacher Training Organisation** (ITTO; www.teflcertificatecourses.com) A network of teacher-training groups that offer online training and placement after successful completion.
- **i-to-i (www.i-to-i.com)** Online TEFL courses that use video and audio; popular with volunteers; has a placement programme.
- **TEFL Online (www.teflonline.com)** A solid online provider with video-based courses.

Of course, you'll also need to sort out a visa, though many schools will organise this for you. Some schools will also ask for either general teaching experience or up to 200 hours of English-teaching experience.

Finding Work Teaching English

Many travellers find work through an established school, which will sort out most of the details for you. Schools prefer a TEFL/TESL qualification and some may even be looking for university graduates.

Here are some schools and organisations offering work:

- **Berlitz (www.berlitz.com)** A huge international employer with more that 400 schools worldwide. Teacher-training available.
- **Cactus Language** (www.cactuslanguage.com) Offers jobs and subsidised courses.
- **China TEFL Network** (www.chinatefl.com) Agency that links Chinese schools with foreign teachers.
- **ECC (http://recruiting.ecc.co.jp)** A Japanese agency that requires university graduation but no formal TEFL/TESOL qualifications. Requires a minimum one-year commitment. They also offer training.
- **English First (EF; www.englishfirst.com)** An international school offering work in China, Indonesia and Russia.
- **Japan Exchange and Teaching Programme (JET; www.jetprogramme.org/en)** One of the best opportunities in Japan. Recruits university graduates.
- **Marcus Evans Linguarama (www.linguarama.com)** Language schools in Western Europe.
- **YBM ECC (www.ybmecc.co.kr)** Runs a series of schools across Korea with placements of one year for university graduates.

If you have an ESL (English as a Second Language) teaching qualification and you're confident about finding work yourself, there's no shortage of places that have listings.

TOP WEBSITES FOR TEACHING JOBS

- **Ajarn** (www.ajarn.com) A site with jobs in Thailand.
- **Dave's ESL Cafe** (www.eslcafe.com) Dave Sperling's long-running ESL site has jobs listings, teaching advice and teachers' forums.
- **EL Gazette** (www.elgazette.com) Online TEFL magazine with teaching news and job listings.
- **O-Hayo Sensei** (www.ohayosensei.com) Bimonthly newsletter for foreign teachers in Japan, with extensive job listings.
- **Teachers of English to Speakers of Other Languages** (TESOL; www.tesol.org) International association that offers resources and preparation courses.
- **TEFL.net** (www.tefl.net) An international TEFL site with listings of jobs and courses and a forum for teachers.
- **TEFL.com** (www.tefl.com) An established jobs site with TEFL job listings worldwide.
- **TESall.com** (www.tesall.com) A large bulletin board of jobs plus advice and resources.

TOURISM & HOSPITALITY

Work in the tourism and hospitality industry covers a realm of jobs, ranging from being a walking guide in a national park or a ski-lift operator to waiting on tables in a Michelin-starred restaurant or serving drinks at a local pub. Some require skills and education, others the gift of the gab and a conscientious spirit.

Not all jobs in the hospitality are that glamorous (try being the only sober person in a bar full of drunks), but you can always find

MY FIRST ENGLISH PATIENTS

It started abruptly. While working at a crappy job in Adelaide, I occasionally surfed teacher websites, more out of curiosity than actual intent. Then there was an interesting job ad for a small school in central Japan, so I shot off an application. Eighteen days later I landed in Nagoya International Airport, pondering the question, 'Do I even like kids?'

No, it turned out to be more like a passion and I spent a year there teaching kindergarten and primary-school kids. Teaching, I quickly discovered, was a great skill to combine with travel; it allowed me to keep my expenses way down while getting a really rich experience of the culture. And no classroom was the same. In Japan the well-built classrooms were warm enough for me to teach wearing shorts and a T-shirt, unusual in such a formal country. In China, my classroom was only a few degrees above freezing level and my teaching attire was more like snow gear. In Russia I taught summer school and had no classroom at all, instead teaching the kids in the open air.

There was no shortage of challenges. For China, the oddity came in the first lesson, where my school wanted me to randomly assign 'English names' to each of my new students. It's remarkable how quickly you run out of names when required to produce them on the spot – my classes had far too many Johns, Bobs and Maggies that year. In Japan I somehow always seemed to find myself at the local karaoke bar at 3am with locals pleading me to butcher yet another Billy Joel classic.

Adam Stanford

10 GREAT REASONS TO TEACH ENGLISH

1. START AT ANY TIME

It takes a month and £1000/US$2000/A$2250 to qualify. Unqualified travellers sometimes pick up teaching work, but the pay is lower, the opportunities fewer and the teaching worse. If you want to dip a toe in the water before you decide, enrol in a weekend teaching course.

2. GO ANYWHERE

You can go to almost any place where people don't speak English. Fancy learning to tango in Buenos Aires, going diving in Thailand? Register on the job websites, start looking, say your goodbyes and pack!

3. LEARN A LANGUAGE

Learning another language is much easier when you live in that country, but easier still when you are teaching English to speakers of that language. If you teach at an institute, you may well be offered free local-language classes yourself.

4. EXPAND YOUR ADDRESS BOOK

Teaching English is a great way to make local friends, get social invitations, learn about your host culture and practice their language. Even if the language is too difficult to learn completely, you will earn yourself Brownie points for trying.

5. ENJOY THE REWARDS

It is nice to know that you have helped someone develop a skill they may use and benefit from forever. Learning English, the global language for business, is seen in so many countries as being the passport to a new and better life.

6. MEET OTHER TEACHERS

Unless you are in the middle of nowhere, there will likely be other English teachers from all over the world who can help you settle. If teaching English is a big life change for you, their often similar stories will inspire you and remind you why you're doing it.

7. BE THE ONLY ONE

If you are in the middle of nowhere, with no colleagues around, you will probably feel like a local celebrity! You will have the pleasure of knowing your experience is unique, and you can pat yourself on the back for your sense of adventure.

8. DEVELOP CONFIDENCE

Teaching in front of a class can stretch your confidence and transferable skills. See yourself as a comic, actor, world leader? Classes can be as interesting as you make them, so your creative juices can be employed to the full to help the students learn.

9. FALL IN LOVE...

You might meet the love of your life while you're living and working abroad.

10. CHANGE YOUR LIFE

The whole experience can help you reassess what you want in life and give you the fresh outlook to go get it. Indeed, the memories will leave a smile on your face when you remember them one day as you sit in that great waiting room for the sky.

work wherever people are raising a glass, enjoying food or pursuing outdoor activities. And some of the destinations that offer these jobs certainly tick the glamour box, such as resorts on exotic Caribbean islands, villages in the French Alps or bars in the sunny Greek islands. Holiday havens are a good place to look for work, particularly as they are more often looking for English speakers.

What to Expect?

Jobs in hospitality are typically busy and social. If you don't like talking to people and the idea of reciting a menu to a lunch-time crowd isn't your thing, hospitality may not be for you. This type of job will give you more confidence though, as you learn to chat with regulars and develop skills in cheerful conversation.

If you're working as waiting staff, shifts get busiest around meal times and in the evenings, with weekends flat out for both. Short shifts are usually four hours and can run as long as eight or 10 hours with a lunch and dinner break. This will eat into your social life, as most of the nights people want to go out will be the nights you'll be called in to work (practice saying 'No, I can't tonight. I'm working.' because you'll need it). Pay for this type of work is generally the bottom of the scale, though tips can supplement your take-home wage, especially in the US where tipping can be a competitive sport. Some jobs, especially in UK pubs, might be the live-in variety, where you'll get a small salary but your room and board will be covered – though you might be over pub grub after a while. A shorter-term option is to look for work at an event which will usually only last for a day or a week.

Working on the tourism end of things, there is plenty of variance. If you're guiding on a mountain, you'll be tied up most days, but have your evenings free. If you're driving transfer buses between a resort and the airport, or working in a ski chalet, you may have your days free and evenings (and very early mornings) booked up. If you're backpacking, you may also be able to find work in your hostel which will often involve doing a shift on the front desk, helping change sheets, general cleaning and possibly some cooking. Hostel jobs are often in exchange for accommodation so the pay package won't be brilliant, but you will get an instant peer group and the perks of the hostel such as free internet or a better room.

Your fellow tourism and hospitality workers are usually a cheery bunch who are in the job for a good time, not a long time, so you'll have plenty of friends at the ready when you have your time off.

What You'll Need

If you're planning on working in the outdoors, having the proper kit is essential, whether mountain apparel for a ski season, or sturdy hiking boots if leading alpine walks in the summer. Or, you may also need 'black and whites', the uniform of waiting staff around the world. This usually consists of a white (sometimes black in swanky places) dress shirt and a good pair of dress trousers or a skirt.

Experience and accreditation is crucial if you're going to be doing any guiding or instructing, and it certainly won't hurt that you've worked in a bar at home or done some catering work when looking for waiting jobs. If you're switched on, many companies will be happy to train you for the role. Often hospitality staff work their way up a ladder and get better paid as they work in more prestigious places, so a more sophisticated restaurant or stylish bar will take more experienced staff. Start at more basic places if you have no experience.

Doing a course in bartending or hospitality will come in handy, especially for making tricky cocktails, and in some cases a course can be a requirement. In Australia, for example, many employers require you to complete a Responsible Service of Alcohol (RSA) course, a six-hour session about when to stop serving customers who have had a little too much.

Here are a few providers of hospitality courses:

- **Australian Department of Education and Training** (www.myskills.gov.au) This government-run site provides a list of certified training centres across Australia for certificates such as the Responsible Service of Alcohol (RSA).
- **Nationwide Training Company** (NTC; www.nationwidetrainingcompany.com) UK organisation offering hospitality courses.
- **Restaurant & Catering Australia** (www.restaurantcater.asn.au) Australian professional association with lists of course providers.

You can also get work as an instructor in the tourism industry if you've got some training – see 'Professional Accreditation: from Mountains to Oceans' (see p155) for more information on courses that can get you trained up as an outdoor activities instructor.

Finding Tourism & Hospitality Work

Much of the work in this sector is seasonal, so depending on where you're travelling you'll want to start looking for jobs before the high season kicks off. Christmas is another peak time for bartenders, waiting staff and hotel workers.

The easiest way to find work in hospitality may be to look up from your breakfast plate to see a local café's wanted ad. Signs in windows are universal, though it's equally popular to walk into a restaurant with your CV and ask to speak to the manager – avoid meal times to get their full attention. For activity-

YOUR FIRST RESORT

Like the sound of a quick slalom down the slopes before the dinner shift, or taking a lunch-time dip in the resort's lagoon?

Or perhaps you'd prefer mixing drinks to the sound of waves swishing in the background? Resort jobs can get you to some of the oddest locations on someone else's dime. You could be a rock-climbing instructor, mixing cocktails or looking after a family chalet, and while the work will be demanding you'll still get to enjoy a bit of the lush life.

Here are a few sites that can get you resort-side before you can say 'Pass me a piña colada':

- **Club Med Jobs** (www.clubmedjobs.com) With more than 120 holiday villages around the world this organisation takes on thousands of resort staff ranging from hospitality to outdoor instructors.
- **Cool Works** (www.coolworks.com) Lists seasonal, resort and sporting jobs worldwide.
- **Leisure Opportunities** (www.leisureopportunities.co.uk) Good for leisure jobs in the UK and Europe.
- **Natives** (www.natives.co.uk) Online recruitment agency with listings of ski and resort work year-round.
- **Resort Jobs** (www.resortjobs.com) An AboutJobs.com subsite listing resort opportunities worldwide.
- **SeasonWorkers** (www.seasonworkers.com) Great advice on seasonal jobs, including a useful forum and jobs board.
- **Snow Season Central** (www.snowseasoncentral.com) It provides a guide to working in a USA-based ski resort for a winter season, as well as a jobs board.

based roles in tourism, such as guiding or instructing, check out the local hotspots for these activities and talk to locals about good operators who may need positions filled. Taking a day-trip with an activity operator may be something you'd already planned to do as part of your trip, so use your time on it to show your stuff and express your interest in working in the industry. For all tourism and hospitality work, you can also try word of mouth by asking travellers who've found work or by checking a hostel noticeboard. Hostels themselves often employ staff, so you can ask if there's work when you check in.

The following agencies specialise in hospitality jobs:

• Alseasons (www.alseasonsagency.com) Recruitment agency in Australia that provides work for working holiday-makers at certain times of year.

• Berkeley Scott (www.berkeley-scott.co.uk) A UK recruitment agency for temporary hospitality, leisure and office jobs.

• Caterer (www.caterer.com) Huge catering website with worldwide jobs.

• Helpx (www.helpx.net) Lists host families, farms, hotels, B&Bs and even sailing boats in Europe, Australasia and North America that provide free accommodation and food in exchange for unpaid labour.

• Natives (www.natives.co.uk) Summer and winter resort jobs and various tips.

• Season Workers (www.seasonworkers.com) Best for ski-resort work and summer jobs, though it also features English-teaching jobs and courses.

• Sonicjobs (www.sonicjobs.co.uk) London-based, this website and app will link you up with employers.

• Wine and Hospitality Jobs (www.wineandhospitalityjobs.com) Large US hospitality recruitment site.

Finally, special events can be a good source of work. You could find yourself staffing a vegan burger van at a music festival or passing around the champagne at the races. You'll need to contact the event organisers themselves at least three months in advance to lock in a job at most big events.

EXTRA, EXTRA!

If you want to give acting a try and work near celebrities, being an extra could be for you. Pay isn't great but you will be fed, get to wear a costume and maybe even get to pause Netflix to show everyone your scene. Some agencies ask for 'headshots' (portrait pictures of you) and acting classes, while others just need to fill another suit of armour in a massive battle sequence. You should be wary of casting calls for dancers (which can turn out to be exotic), but if you register with a reputable agency you can expect to get paid to stand around. Some agencies may charge a monthly fee, but beware of agencies that want to charge you to get some modelling shots of you (which will often cost a lot more). Start your web search here:

• Backstage (www.backstage.com) A US-based site that posts casting calls and features more tips on getting into 'serious' acting.

• Stagepool (www.stagepool.eu) A German-based agency that charges around €10 for registration and promises jobs on the continent.

• Uni-versal Extras (www.universalextras.co.uk) This site specialises in finding work for students as an extra in TV and film productions across the UK and Ireland. It costs £25 to join for two years (free for students).

INTERNSHIPS & WORK PLACEMENTS

So you're serious about going overseas and working in a job that will help your future career? Depending on where you go, these roles are variously called internships (North America), work placements (UK and Europe) or work experience (Australia and New Zealand). Whatever you dub them, internships can be a great way for students and graduates to break into an industry and employers are always impressed by overseas work experience. Internships are often confused with volunteering, but internships are more tightly tied up with careers, while volunteering (which can also lead to a career) primarily aims to help the country you're visiting.

What to Expect?

Completing an internship is the best way to get an idea of what an industry is really like from the inside. Management, finance, commerce, law and publishing are just some of the industries that have internship programmes, though you can ask any organisation if they take interns. Few organisations will turn down free labour, especially if you have some skills. Most organisations, though not all, will pay you a small salary or allowance, and the more selective ones may even pay for your travel costs and accommodation.

You'll actually be doing work that you'd do if you had a full-time position. Some of your co-workers might not have the right idea of what an intern does and may ask you to get the coffee, do the photocopying or even wash their cars. It's important to set some ground rules and ask about what the job entails when you're being interviewed for an internship. You can expect to be doing a certain amount of chores (so some photocopying might be okay), but you should also look to do a few higher-level tasks (such as helping out with a marketing plan at a publishing company) and possibly even completing a research paper or report about your time with the organisation.

The length of the job varies depending on the organisation. In North America summer internship lasts for two months, while in Europe paid interns are called *stagiaires*, with programmes lasting up to five months. Longer positions may even run for a year. There's a chance that your internship may lead to an ongoing job, but if it doesn't you're always free to keep on travelling.

What You'll Need

Like with most jobs you'll need a visa, but your employer will usually sort this out for you by acting as a sponsor (you'll still have some paperwork to fill out though). If your employer can't help out with a visa, there's a large industry around setting up visas for interns, but if you stick with reputable outfits such as **British Universities North America Club** (BUNAC; www.bunac.org), you can usually get a visa for a small fee. Most agencies will ask for an application fee, which will be used to cover your paperwork and possibly pay for your fare, so you'll need to have some savings behind you.

Obviously, if you're studying in a country with a language other than English, you'll need to speak that language and probably be able to read and write it. While English may be the global language of business, you'll find that local business likes to speak its own language, and you'll miss out on a lot of office gossip if you don't have the linguistic skills. Some programmes require you to be a university student and you'll apply for internships within your field of study. Others will put you through a rigorous selection programme of testing or video-conferencing interviews, but it's worth it.

Finding Internships & Work Placements

If you like the direct approach, many companies or organisations advertise on their sites for interns. Try Googling a couple of multinational organisations in your industry and look into their jobs pages. This can be a bit hit-and-miss, plus you may not have the support services of an agency behind you.

Here are a few examples of larger organisations that offer internships:

- **Apple** (www.apple.com/jobs/us/students.html) Aim big! This tech giant is consistently one of the top rated companies for interns.
- **Council of Europe** (http://hub.coe.int) Dig down to Traineeship Opportunities to get the dirt on working in European politics for this large organisation.
- **Deloitte** (www.deloitte.com) Offers graduate and student placements in finance and business industries across the globe.
- **Disney** (https://jobs.disneycareers.com/professional-internships) Offers paid internships for graduates. As they say, 'Every story has a beginning...'
- **European Commission** (http://ec.europa.eu/stages) For European nationals, with a few additional 'stages' for non-Europeans, to intern in various government organisations; you need to be a university student with skills in at least one language other than English.
- **European Parliament** (www.europarl.europa.eu/portal/en) Look for 'Traineeships' on this site that has opportunities for EU students in journalism and languages, with paid and unpaid options.
- **Facebook** (www.facebook.com/careers/university) Although getting a placement is competitive, an internship with this social media giant could jumpstart your career.
- **Google** (www.google.com/about/careers/students) Find out about internships at one of

MY FIRST RADIO CLASH

I was doing a study-abroad programme at the Hebrew University and managed to arrange a casual internship with JPost Radio, the internet-radio component of the Jerusalem Post newspaper. It didn't take long to realise that I was happier in the newsroom than I was slogging through essays on the 1948 Arab-Israeli War, so after a couple of months I dropped out of the university and took on a full-time journalist's workload for a weekly bus pass and the odd free lunch.

In the Middle East you're always thrown in the deep end and this was no exception. Mornings, I might be interviewing protestors outside the Prime Minister's house. Afternoons would be spent at funerals, in hospitals, and once at the scene of a suicide bombing. At night, when I wasn't waiting tables at a Jerusalem bar, I'd pursue my own stories, recording interviews with Palestinian musicians and teenage refuseniks.

It was dynamic, challenging, emotionally exhausting work for anyone, let alone a 19-year-old fresh out of school. But the team of reporters were incredibly supportive, pushing me to develop my skills and to cover things most journalists never have the chance to see.

Miriam Raphael

the web's biggest players, with offices in dozens of countries.

• **Guggenheim Museum** (www.guggenheim.org) Navigate your way to 'Education/Internships' to get experience at one of these museums in Venice, New York, Bilbao (Spain) or Berlin.

• **IBM** (www.ibm.com) Search for 'internships' on this massive site to find several information technology internships and graduate opportunities.

• **PricewaterhouseCoopers** (PwC; www.pwc.com) This leading management consultancy offers summer and long-term internships at its offices around the world, with pre-university options as well as graduate programmes.

Several good websites can point you in the right direction for other internship opportunities, including **Peterson's** (www.petersons.com/blog) and **Vault** (www.vault.com), the latter of which lists and ranks companies offering internships.

By far the best way to organise an internship is to go through an agency that will organise visas and check that your potential employer is on the level. Some of these organisations charge registration or application fees – some only charge on a successful placement, others will ask for a small fee upfront. These organisations can take a lot of the headaches out of finding a placement, but if you're looking at a small or unknown organisation, do your research and look around for good word of mouth on the web.

The US is definitely the place for internships, with several opportunities open to international applicants. Here are a few websites with placements in the US:

• **Camp Counsellors USA** (CCUSA; www.ccusa.com) Primarily about camp staff (see p139), but also has a good traineeship programme that helps with placement paperwork.

• **Cultural Vistas** (www.culturalvistas.org) Does work placements in the US with a focus on getting visas.

• **InterExchange** (www.interexchange.org) Sponsors training placements with prearranged placements or support if you want to find your own.

• **Internship Programs** (www.internshipprograms.com) US internship search engine that requires (free) registration.

• **Internships.com** (www.internships.com) Publishes guides to US internships, broken down by city or subject.

Look in the Directories chapter for opportunities only available to people from your country, but here are a few that are open to all:

• **Australian Internships** (www.internships.com.au) A good gateway to Australian internships for international visitors.

• **Intern Abroad** (www.goabroad.com/intern-abroad) Part of the larger Go Abroad group with intern positions worldwide.

• **Intern Jobs** (www.internjobs.com) Member of the AboutJobs.com group, with a huge database of internships worldwide and registration so they match you to internships.

• **International Association for Students of Economics and Management** (AIESEC; www.aiesec.org) The world's largest student organisation does graduate internships with online registration (for a fee).

• **International Association for the Exchange of Students for Technical Experience** (IAESTE; www.iaeste.org) Provides engineering and industrial placements overseas for some 300,000 students in more than 80 countries.

• **IST Plus** (www.istplus.com) Offers internships in the US, Australia, New Zealand, Singapore, Thailand and China for postsecondary students.

• **Kiwi Internships** (www.kiwi-internships.com) Organises custom-made internships and work-experience programmes in New Zealand with an environmental focus.

- **KPMG** (www.kpmgcareers.com) Head for your local site in order to find vacation, cadetship and work-placement opportunities at this accounting firm.
- **Monash Professional Pathways** (www.monashprofessional.edu.au) This university site offers job training and facilitates internships in Australia.
- **Mountbatten Program** (www.mountbatten.org) Has live, work and study programs in New York, London and Bangkok.
- **Office of the United Nations High Commissioner for Human Rights** (OHCHR; www.ohchr.org) Head for About Us/Work & Study Opportunities/Internship Programme if you've got a degree that relates to human rights and fluency in a second language.

Finally, a lot of job websites also list internships and work placements. Try searching the local branches of international job sites, especially of countries you're planning on visiting.

TEMPING

The term 'temp' was first used in the 1930s to mean 'temporary worker'. Today temps represent more than 10% of the total workforce. Some workplaces are so dependent on temps that they almost couldn't run without them. If you're looking for work as a temp, you're bound to find a job if you have the right skills. Most big companies use temp agencies to fill short- to medium-term vacancies while staff are off sick, on maternity leave, or taking a holiday. Temp agencies are also used when a company is having a busy period such as Christmas, or when they're launching a new product line.

What to Expect?

Mostly you'll be working in an office from nine to five doing basic tasks such as replying to emails, answering phones, filing or data entry. Simply put, it's often not very exciting, but you can rely on a pay cheque at the end of the week. Money generally starts at £8 an hour in the UK, US$10 an hour in America and A$22 an hour in Australia, with higher rates for legal staff or other specialised skills such as experience with accounting software, web-publishing skills or touch-typing. The IT industry usually commands higher salaries, particularly if you have programming skills, though even working on a help desk can pay well.

You'll be employed directly by an agency which will pay you a week in arrears, so don't count on the first pay cheque to pay the rent. You may also have to invoice the temp agency or fill out a timesheet. Placements can be very brief (a day), or an ongoing role that you could stay in for years. Your fellow temps will often be travellers but could also be locals working their way through university or paying the rent while they do another 'side project' (aspiring actors and artists often take temp jobs to finance themselves in between their other work).

Some travellers alternate between temp contracts and travelling, particularly in places such as London or Sydney, where you'll find plenty of work. While many people find temp work a little dull, the ability to quit at short notice ('Sorry I won't be in today – I'm in Amsterdam') does suit the travel lifestyle. While some travellers find it difficult to break the mould of being 'just a temp', others have turned a temp job into a career. You may also get some useful training in a temp job which will help you get a better job next time around.

What You'll Need

You'll need an up-to-date CV to start looking for temp work, and having at least one set of business clothes will be useful for interviews. Getting through your first week with one outfit is difficult, so your first pay cheque will be spent on expanding wardrobe options.

Any skills you can bring to an agency will help them find you a better temp job, so typing courses, software training and general communication courses will all work to your advantage. Bring along copies of qualifications you have as temp agencies may ask to see them. Having a few referees at home could also be useful.

Finding Temp Work

The best place to start looking for work is a temp agency. Most big cities have scores of them and some specialise in certain industries, such as IT, accounting, law, medicine or general office administration. Most temp agencies advertise in local newspapers, though you can often find them with a simple internet search. When you sign up with a temp agency they may get you to complete tests to gauge your typing speed, ability with various software packages, spelling and grammar, and resistance to boring, repetitive tasks. An agency will often interview you before they start to send you out to interviews with employers.

These global companies will get your temp job hunt started:

- **Adecco** (www.adecco.com) This international recruitment agency has more than 5000 offices in 62 countries and specialises in temp and permanent jobs in business, education, engineering, health and construction.
- **Drake International** (www.drakeintl.com) Drake has offices in the UK, USA, Canada, Australia, New Zealand, South Africa, Hong Kong, Singapore and the Philippines and covers most professions.
- **Hays** (www.hays.com) This leading recruitment agency specialises in office, IT, education, engineering and construction jobs and has offices worldwide. You can register and do a virtual interview over the web.
- **Kelly Services** (www.kellyservices.com) Has offices worldwide. There are temp and permanent office, technical, engineering, IT and education jobs around the world.
- **Reed** (www.reedglobal.com) Another multinational recruitment agency, with hundreds of offices in the UK, Europe, Canada, South Africa, Australia and New Zealand. Reed specialises in temporary and permanent office, engineering and construction jobs.

FREELANCING

Some people will tell you freelancing is just a fancy word for unemployment, because you're spending a lot of time looking for work. Occasionally you'll be lucky enough to score a longer contract which will give you some security. Or you may have plenty of contacts at home who can send work your way if needed. Freelancing is common in journalism, design, web development and translating, so if you have the skills to pay the bills, this may be for you.

What to Expect?

When you're a freelancer there's no such thing as a sick day. If you don't work, you don't get paid. It can be difficult for your bank account, with the balance often being on a bit of a rollercoaster ride. The upside is that you can choose the jobs you want to work on and say no to the ones that look dull (then later say yes to them when you need the money).

Depending on the industry, you'll generally work to deadlines set by clients and have to work hard to meet their needs if you want to work for them again. Clients are the best and the worst part of the job, so you should only pitch for jobs that involve working with the good people.

Rates of pay are always difficult to work out, as you'll often be pitching and including a price estimate in your pitch or quote. Most freelancers start out charging low rates so they can develop a portfolio of their work. The only problem is that it can be hard to get a client to pay you more if they're used to the 'bargain' rates. Start out with a realistic price, ask colleagues what they'd charge or look at professional associations for some rough indications. Work out an hourly rate, then roughly calculate how long a project will take, to give a rough quote. In journalism there are usually per-word rates for articles, but you can expect more for photographs.

What You'll Need

If you have skills (bring along any qualifications and portfolios you might have to prove it) in any of the big freelance areas, you're halfway there. You can do the work, but how do you find work? Getting some business cards will come in handy, though these days you might need to think about getting a website to market your work (especially if you're a web designer). You'll need an email address that you can check on the road so potential clients can contact you while you're away (or even before you get there). Even if you're a little shy, you'll need to be able to 'sell yourself' by talking about jobs you've done in the past and what you can do on this job.

Fields of Freelance Fit for Travel

Journalism is the most obvious freelance gig, especially if you've got a few stories from your recent travels that could make feature stories. Joining one of the following associations also

HAVING A LAUGH: ONE PERSON'S BEST JOBS ABROAD

- **Artist's model** (Hong Kong) I was in a pool changing my pose every three minutes. The teacher was explaining to the students how best to draw the monstrosity in front of them.
- **Smurf** (Noumea, New Caledonia) I helped sand down the boat for a friend of the hostel owner. It was blue and after a day, so was I. Walking home, a boy yelled out *Schtroumpf!*, which I learnt later means 'smurf'.
- **Salesperson** (Russia) On the Trans-Siberian, Chinese vendors were selling clothes, cameras and such from the windows to Russians on the platform. A guy in my compartment sold my shoes without asking, and smiled as he gave me the roubles.
- **Pan pipist (Austria)** Miming to a CD of Andean music, wearing a poncho and breaking out in hoots in time with my fellow performers.
- **Ladder holder** (Venice, Italy) For a week, I held the ladder while he painted a hotel. Passers-by ribbed me in Italian. The word *pazzo* (fool) was often uttered.
- **Dead body (Japan)** Lying under playground equipment with a head covered in fake blood, I practised zazen meditation and realised I'd never be a star on Japanese TV.
- **Santa, Lagos (Nigeria)** A new friend got me a job as a Santa for his company's Christmas party. They only paid me in beer, but the thrills on the kids' faces with my real white beard were worth the effort.
- **Medical experiment** (Australia) Signed up as a subject in a drug test for treatment for a socially communicable disease. Clean bed for a week, no need to keep food in my backpack in case of dormitory thieves. Came out with a wad of dollars and slightly green nipples.

JumpingGiant, traveller

means you'll get a press card in the country you're visiting and helps open doors to all sorts of events.

- **Media, Entertainment & Arts Alliance** (www.meaa.org) Australia's professional organisation for journalists, actors, cartoonists and entertainers.
- **National Union of Journalists – UK** (NUJ; www.nuj.org.uk) UK union for journos.
- **National Writers Union** (www.nwu.org) US union for writers and journalists.

Translating is another skill you can use almost anywhere, with translation into English becoming more important as businesses look to global markets. Teaching is also a skill you can freelance almost anywhere in the world with (see p118).

As a freelancer, you'll technically need a work permit though if you're working for clients back home then this may not be needed (it's a grey area). You'll still have to pay tax on these earnings as your friendly neighbourhood tax agent has an international reach.

Finding Freelance Work

You'll need to go out and get work, because work rarely calls up asking for you. In journalism you'll need to pitch your story to the travel editor of a relevant section of a newspaper or magazine, and if you're a web developer you'll need to be able to meet clients, assess their tech needs and then give them a quote of how long it will take to do the job.

Finding markets for journalism can be as simple as flipping through a local newsstand or writing down a few email addresses in a library. If you have any contacts back home, you can email them stories so you might like to write down a few editors' email addresses before you go. Lonely Planet's *How To Be A Travel Writer* can be a useful resource – it contains good advice on how to write an article as well as how to pitch it.

Finding work in areas such as IT can involve looking for tenders or ads for upcoming projects, which you can do with a good base of local contacts. Many web designers and IT professionals fund their travels by registering with temp agencies who can hook them up with longer-term contracts. You can take your name off the books to go travelling and then sign back on when you're ready to return (or when the money runs out).

Here are a few useful resources for journalists and other freelancers looking for work:

- **All Graphic Design** (www.allgraphicdesign.com) Useful resources for freelance designers.
- **Aquarius** (https://aquarius.net) Long-running agency with translating jobs worldwide.
- **Authentic Jobs** (www.authenticjobs.com) A high-quality job board mainly for web designers and developers and focused on the US, but with other openings available also.
- **The Freelancer by Contently** (www.contently.net) A resource site for freelancers in the media, which allows you to quickly build an online portfolio.
- **Freelance** (www.freelance.com/en) This French-based site mainly focuses on freelance IT professionals but it covers other employment areas as well.
- **Freelancers.net** (www.freelancers.net) A site with international listings for IT professionals.
- **Freelance Writing** (www.freelancewriting.com) Resource for information and opportunities for freelance writing.
- **ProZ.com** (www.proz.com) Site with extensive jobs message board for freelance translators.
- **Translation Directory** (www.translationdirectory.com) Portal for freelance translators with jobs and dictionaries.

WORKING ON A CRUISESHIP

Most travellers plug into the cruise scene by working for the mix of free transport, free accommodation and tax-free salaries. With bigger ships having a small army of 1000-plus staff, there's bound to be a vacancy. Some of the best gigs on a cruise ship are as entertainers with a packed bill every night featuring singers, musicians and dancers. If you have stage fright, there are plenty of other jobs as a cruise ship is like a town that needs gym instructors, sales assistants, waiting staff, cooks, cleaners, masseurs and admin staff. Staff are drawn from around the world, so you'll be part of a multicultural crew who'll be good friends to travel with afterwards.

What to Expect?

Top jobs pay anything from £25,000/US$40,000/A$45,000 per annum upwards, but most jobs pay as little as £12,000/US$24,000/A$35,000. If you're in hospitality your income will be at the bottom end, but it is often supplemented by tips. The work itself is demanding with 50-hour weeks common and cruise guests who assume you're always on call. You'll generally sign on for a season which usually lasts five to six months, though it's possible to sign on again for another season once you've finished.

What You'll Need

Whatever job you try out for, you'll need a passport that will be valid while you're working aboard a ship. Some international outfits might require a police check, just so they know you'll be trustworthy once you're on the high seas. Others require you to complete a medical check-up once they've decided you're right for the job.

Any experience you can bring to a job will be useful, even if you're just going for hospitality or retail positions. Obviously, jobs as entertainers will require some experience on stage and a few headshots will come in handy, but if you're looking at a job as a masseur, gym instructor or medical staff, a qualification is a must.

Finding Work on a Cruiseship

If you're looking for more information on working for cruise ships, check these links:

- **All Cruise Jobs** (www.allcruisejobs.com) A jobs board with global reach.
- **Cruise Ship Jobs** (www.cruiseshipjob.com) Site with a jobs board and profiles of the major cruise companies and their ships.
- **Viking** (www.vikingrecruitment.com) Has a jobs board and useful information.

FRUIT PICKING & FARM WORK

Rolling up your sleeves on a farm is a good option if you want to see the countryside and dodge the big city. Work is usually seasonal and extremely casual, so if you're looking for a no-strings-attached gig, this might be for you. There's no need for previous experience so it's a job that almost anyone can fall into. Any place that has agriculture usually needs hands to pick the crops, so you can expect to find work reasonably easily.

What to Expect?

The expression 'back-breaking labour' was probably coined by someone who had spent an afternoon pulling turnips from the dry ground. Picking fruit and vegetables is hard work and you'll need to be fit to do it. Chances are you'll be doing the same repetitive tasks so you will get bored and working with a phone full of music will make it more bearable. Fruit ripens fast so farmers are keen to get it to market quickly. This means that you'll be required to work hard, with very early starts (some travellers have reported 5am) and often six days a week. However, you won't be working for long as the average fruit-picking season lasts for only six weeks.

You can expect to meet plenty of other travellers who'll be doing this job to make some cash. Many travellers enjoy the social life with a real 'work hard, party harder' feel. Some just enjoy the break from the city. Better jobs will pay by the hour, but many pay based on how much you pick or harvest. About half of fruit-picking jobs involve climbing ladders, though grapes and other low fruit are okay if you suffer from vertigo. Some farms will include a bunkhouse with your own shower block, others will let you camp on their property for free. When a farm wants to charge you rent or other costs, work out if you'll be able to make enough money to make it worth your while – while there are only a few crooked farmers, you might not make much money if you have to travel to a distant place to work for a few weeks. If you're interested in farmstays, including Willing Workers on Organic Farms (or WWOOFing), check the Accommodation chapter (see p103).

As well as picking fruit, there are jobs for packing fruit, driving tractors, crushing grapes and a hundred other tasks. If you play your cards right a farmer may even need you in the off-season to help out with fencing, trimming trees, crop-dusting or other maintenance tasks.

HARVEST SEASONS

UK

- **apples and pears** – August to October
- **hops** – August to October
- **soft fruit** – June to October
- **vegetables** – May to October

France

- **apples and pears** – July to October
- **grapes** – September to October
- **olives** – November to December
- **soft fruit** – May to September
- **vegetables** – July to October

Southern Mediterranean

- **apples and pears** – June to October
- **grapes** – June to October
- **olives** – November to April
- **oranges** – November to April

Australia

- **apples and pears** – January to September
- **bananas** – July to August
- **grapes** – January to March
- **soft fruit** – August to December
- **vegetables** – year-round

New Zealand

- **apples** – January to May
- **grapes** – January to April
- **kiwi fruit** – May to July
- **soft fruit** – November to December
- **vegetables** – July to October

What You'll Need

You won't need any special skills to pick fruit, but if you have some good, sturdy shoes and sun-protecting clothing, it will help. A tent can be handy on some properties – check for second-hand camping gear on hostel noticeboards or local camping stores rather than lugging it from home.

Finding Fruit-Picking & Farm Work

Harvesting usually kicks off when the crop is ripe, with most small scale farmers advertising jobs locally in advance (or simply by word of mouth). Some larger operations even advertise in hostels and backpacker magazines to find

READY STEADY CREW: FROM SMALL SAILING YACHTS TO SUPERYACHTS

Crewing on a sailing yacht can be a good way to work your route, with short-term openings (often voluntary, or even sharing costs) to cover a particular journey.

SMALL YACHTS

This could take you from Dubrovnik to Venice, or even from Monaco to St Kitts. You'll have to be in shape and most skippers require sailing experience, particularly if an ocean crossing is involved. You'll also need a passport with at least a year left on it to sail into most countries. Meeting your skipper beforehand is a good idea to get a sense of what it would be like to be around them all the time. It's also crucial to inspect the boat and have confidence that it's seaworthy for the journey ahead. Make sure that you're comfortable and have enough money put back to get a ticket home if things don't work out. With the right skipper, though, you can learn new skills and have a blast.

Begin your job search with these sites:

- **Crew Seekers International** (www.crewseekers.net) Looks for crew (including cooks and waiting staff) across the world.
- **Sailnet** (www.sailnet.com) Check their 'Classifieds' for jobs or leave your own post to find a yacht where you want to go.
- **Sunsail** (www.sunsail.com) Employs around 1700 assorted staff on its yachts and beach resorts around the world. There are opportunities for qualified sailors, sailing instructors and general resort support staff.

SUPERYACHTS

Crewing on a superyacht is another kettle of fish, with positions being fairly well paid, including regular weeks off and often flights to/from home included in the package. However, schedules can change at the whim of the owner. Positions range from deckhands, cleaners and general kitchen staff up to chefs, senior engineers and captains, the latter of whom take home salaries in the hundreds of thousands. You are expected to work extremely hard and be happy about it, and you always need to be impeccably well presented. Some superyachts are occupied by guests only a few weeks a year, but they are often crewed regardless for upkeep and to get the vessel in position for the next all-important arrival. Other superyachts are chartered when the owner isn't aboard, which is harder work due to a constant stream of new guests each week (all with sky high expectations). It is a window into another world, which can be both good and bad, and it will take you to some incredible places.

Here are some agencies who provide crews for superyachts:

- **JF Recruiting** (www.jf-recruiting.com) This yacht crew agency posts 3000 positions annually.
- **Marine Resources** (www.marineresources.co.uk) An international recruiter for the industry.
- **Viking** (wwww.vikingrecruitment.com) A British company with a global reach.
- **yaCrew** (www.yacrew.com) This site provides details on job openings and training courses.

travellers. Check the Harvest Seasons table (p134) to get an idea of when you could pick fruit in a few destinations.

If you want to get really organised here are a few websites that advertise fruit-picking jobs:

- **Anywork Anywhere** (www.anyworkanywhere.com) A worldwide job board with fruit picking at its core.
- **Appellation Contrôlée** (APCON; www.apcon.nl) Popular Dutch organisation that places workers on the grape harvest in France.
- **Fruitful Jobs** (www.fruitfuljobs.com) This is a recruitment service for UK soft-fruit industry.
- **JobSearch Australia** (https://jobsearch.gov.au/harvest) Government website which tells you what's growing where and when.
- **Picking Jobs** (www.pickingjobs.com) Global site specialising in fruit picking around the world, including the US, Canada, Australia, New Zealand, Japan and much of Europe.
- **Seasonal Work** (www.seasonalwork.co.nz) New Zealand's first stop for fruit-picking jobs.
- **Willing Workers on Organic Farms** (WWOOF; www.wwoof.net) Join this international group to work (for six hours a day) on organic farms almost anywhere in the world.

CONSTRUCTION WORK

The construction industry relies on contractors, so short-term building work is easy to find in most countries. It can also pay well, particularly if you have experience working with heavy machinery. There are openings around the world for labourers, steelworkers, heavy-vehicle drivers, electricians, plumbers, bricklayers, roofers and carpenters.

What to Expect?

The average hourly wage for a general construction worker is £10.74/US$15.36/A$24.45.

What You'll Need

You'll need to be physically fit, and if you want to do anything more than being a general labourer, you'll also need some building-related qualifications and skills (the more you have, the higher your pay package).

Finding Construction Work

Going through an established recruitment agency will get you most jobs, though (as with hospitality) word of mouth can also get you a start. Construction is a heavily unionised industry so joining a local union can be a good way to start your job search. Building work can range from completely unskilled jobs such as labouring, to highly skilled jobs such as plumbing or structural engineering. As well as big construction sites, many small businesses take on unskilled labourers for short-term projects such as site clearing.

Useful resources for anyone thinking about building or construction work include:

- **Construction Jobs** (https://constructionjobs.com) US site with lots of job listings, with registration and CV posting.
- **Constructor** (www.constructor.co.uk) Good construction and civil-engineering site with lots of UK jobs.
- **Randstand** (www.randstad.com) A recruitment company with offices in 39 countries offering permanent and temporary work in construction, trades and mining and other industries.

AU PAIRS & NANNIES

Looking after someone else's children is the closest you can get to becoming a part of a family. Not only will you live in their home, but you'll get to go on family outings and develop real relationships with local people. Although the terms 'au pair' and 'nanny' are often interchanged, they are, in fact, two very different roles.

Au pairs are part of an internationally recognised cultural exchange programme, where individuals are offered the opportunity to live, work and travel with a host family in a country different to their own. Nannies, on the other hand, are childcare professionals with credentials or extensive experience in the field – they can be live in or live out. While au pairs may be expected to help with various housework, nannies tend to stick to only child-related housework.

What to Expect?

Depending on the age of the children you're caring for, this could involve anything from changing dirty nappies (diapers) and cleaning to helping with homework and the school run. Often this job will mean living in with a family, though some nannies do live elsewhere and come in while the parents are at work. If you're living in, you'll have free accommodation, but some families will want you to be always on call. You should discuss this with a potential employer and ask about having regular days off (usually weekends, which will be good for sightseeing). Many parents will want to spend time with their kids when they get home, so you may have your evenings free. If it's not made clear in the job description, you should have a conversation with your potential family about the amount of time you'll be expected to work and what kind of chores you'll be doing.

In a live-in job you can expect to work a minimum of 25 hours a week, though some families may ask for two nights per week of baby-sitting, which pays a little more. Most positions will be for a limited time period, usually a year, so you should allow for some travel after your trip.

Au pairs in Europe may even be encouraged to attend language classes, which brings another great dimension to the job. If you land one of these positions you'll get time off for classes, as well as a small contribution to the cost.

According to the **British Au Pair Agencies Association** (www.bapaa.org.uk), you should generally start at around £70-£85 a week plus board for 25 hours a week, though with more qualifications or additional hours you can expect more. The average weekly salary for live-out nannies in the UK ranges from £436 in Wales to £617 in London. This drops by a third to a quarter if you are living with the family. In the US, au pairs working five days a week for 45 hours can expect to start on US$195 per week, but again, more qualifications will increase the salary. Au pair salaries in Australia range from A$180-220 per week.

Work

It's worth bearing in mind that 'au pair' means 'on an equal footing', so you should be treated like a member of the family rather than a slave. You should talk to your family about what the job will entail, ideally at an interview, and work out if this is the right fit for you.

Generally, your duties should be based around the children, with a few extra helping-out tasks such as cleaning or shopping to be negotiated with your family. Some tasks you will do could include:

- Waking the children and getting them dressed.
- Preparing breakfast.
- Clearing up the children's rooms.
- Washing dishes or loading and unloading the dishwasher.
- Tidying away toys from every corner of the house.
- Collecting the children from school.

- Grocery-shopping.
- Playing with the children.
- Helping to prepare the children's meals.
- Bathing the children and putting them to bed.
- Sweeping up and vacuuming.
- Ironing the children's clothes.
- Accompanying the family on outings or holidays.

Generally, families are pretty reasonable, but if yours starts expecting you to cook for dinner parties or wash the car you need to have a conversation. Worst case, you should think about leaving.

NANNY SCAM

Web scams continue to sucker potential nannies and families out of a lot of cash. The most common scam involves the audacious perpetrator sending their chosen nanny a fat advance, then announcing (before the money has cleared) that there has been a family tragedy and the job is no longer available. They then ask the nanny to wire the advance back to them. By the time the nanny realises that the advance was a fraudulent one, their cash is long gone.

Another scam involves the family asking the nanny to send money to their lawyer to help with a domestic worker visa. Needless to say, no visa is procured and the nanny never hears from them again.

Using an agency avoids these problems though the odd scammer has tried to use a nanny agency as well – good agencies even list the names of scammers. You should beware of anyone who offers a too-good-to-be-true deal, and never send money in advance.

What You'll Need

You'll need to sort out a visa before you go, though many agencies will help you organise one. The US and UK have 'domestic employee' visas that you can apply for if you're 18 to 25, single, with no kids of your own. Generally the visas will require a commitment of two months to a year from both the family and you.

Generally, you'll need to pay for travel to your host so choosing a country that's cheaply accessible is a good idea. Even for au pair work, experience in working with children is crucial (higher-end agencies ask for 200 hours of documented experience, which can include baby-sitting) and you'll need to supply character references (usually from people who'll say you're trustworthy and responsible). Agencies will also require medical checks and a police record check. To work as a nanny you'll need to have evidence of experience and/or qualifications (in the UK nannies can register with the Ofsted Childcare Register).

Finding Au Pair or Nanny Work

The best way to find work is through an agency that will look after paperwork and vet families that seem difficult. You might also have some success looking on noticeboards in hostels or on job websites. You could also try childcare centres, particularly in Australia where nannies are less common.

Signing up with an agency takes a lot of hassle out of looking for work. Some agencies charge a fee, but ideally only when they place you with a family. This means you can register with several agencies and only pay the one that finds you work. Several agencies allow you to register online and create a profile detailing your experience and what you will and won't do.

Some good places to start include:

- **AIFS** (www.aifs.com.au/aupair-australia) A site to find work as an au pair in Australia.
- **Almondbury Au Pair & Nanny Agency** (www.aupair-agency.com) This site places people in many countries around the world.
- **Au Pair Association** (www.iapa.org) This international organisation has good links to member agencies in most European countries and the US.
- **Au Pair in America** (www.aupairamerica.co.uk) A British-based organisation that finds work in the US.
- **Au Pair World** (www.aupair-world.net) A global organisation that requires registration and lets you search for families and post your CV online.
- **Childcare International** (www.childint.co.uk) This resource lists placements in America, Australia, Canada, China, New Zealand and throughout Europe.
- **Go Au Pair** (www.goaupair.com) A good organisation for finding au pair work in the US and abroad.
- **Great Au Pair** (www.greataupair.com) Places nannies worldwide with online interviews where you can chat to families before you start.
- **Just Au Pairs** (www.justaupairs.co.uk) Places people in Europe and the US.
- **Scotia Personnel** (www.scotia-personnel-ltd.com) This is a Canadian agency that arranges au pair jobs throughout Europe and Australia, as well as some summer-camp work in Italy or the UK.
- **The French American Center** (http://www.frenchamericancenter.com/english/aupair.asp) Arranges au pair placements for North Americans in France which can include French language lessons.
- **Union Française des Associations Au Pair** (UFAAP; www.ufaap.org) Includes several French organisations and a search-by-region function for work anywhere in France.

CAMP COUNSELLORS

Summer camp is as American as apple pie, with over 7000 overnight camps and 5000 day camps entertaining children from six to 16 for periods between one and eight weeks over summer. More than 11 million attend these camps each year, which means there is no shortage of need for camp counsellors.

What to Expect?

You can expect to be very busy as you'll be both supervising the kids and getting them into hiking, water sports, basketball, horseback riding, crafts, music and several other activities. The days are long, but it can be surprisingly fun, plus there are a few weeks to sightsee when camp finishes.

In Europe there's a job called 'camp courier' which often involves working with children, but frequently with a whole family too. You'll generally be working closely with guests, doing everything from cleaning their tents to acting as a guide to the local area. You'll be on call during the day or the evening in case guests need help, and you get additional training in first aid for emergencies.

Most camps will ask you to pay for flights, application fees, insurance and other costs, or they will be deducted from your salary, so do the sums before you sign up to see which deals work out best. If you have specialist skills, such as working with special-needs children or teaching an activity, you might qualify as a specialist counsellor with a higher wage.

Finding Camp Counsellor Work

The best time to look for camp jobs is autumn though camps recruit year-round. Although camps are most popular in the US, it's also possible to find jobs elsewhere, with the UK offering some good opportunities. Here are a few organisations to kick-start your job search:

- **Acorn Adventure** (www.acornadventure.co.uk) A UK adventure-holiday company with 300 jobs across Europe; includes a training course and activity-training options.
- **American Camp Association** (www.acacamps.org) Useful for finding camps in specific states.
- **Barracudas** (www.barracudas.co.uk) A UK outfit specialising in day camps, with teaching and training qualifications an advantage.
- **British Universities North America Club** (BUNAC; www.bunac.org) A UK-based organisation that runs nine- to 12-week camps in the US.
- **Camp America** (https://campamerica.com.au) A huge organisation that looks for Aussies and Kiwis to work on camps.
- **CCUSA** (www.ccusa.com) Offers camp jobs in the US and Canada.
- **Club Med** (www.clubmedjobs.com) This global hotel consortium takes camp counsellors and others to look after kids.
- **Kingswood Group** (www.kingswood.co.uk) Does camps in the UK with a need for activity instructors and general staff.
- **PGL** (www.pgl.co.uk) UK provider of camps that offer some outdoor training for instructors; jobs run from one to six weeks.
- **Village Camps** (www.villagecamps.com) Has jobs for camp staff (including hospitality and counsellors) across Europe.
- **Xplore** (www.xplorerecruitment.com) A UK outfit that runs summer programmes.

TREE PLANTING IN CANADA

Fruit picking is one thing, planting up to 4000 trees a day in the rugged wilderness of Canada is another.

Thought to be one of the world's toughest jobs, tree planting will burn through more calories a day than running a marathon – besides the never-ending digging, you'll be lugging 25kg bags of saplings and covering around 20km per day. And then there are the bugs...

Pay is typically per tree planted, so the faster you are the more you can earn. An average planter beds in around 1600 trees a day, which would equate to around C$175 (US$133). Be one of the better ones, and you can reap almost C$450 (US$343). Work typically runs on rotations, such as four days on, one day off.

While there is great competition among planters to be the top earner, there is also incredible camaraderie. Crews live in remote camps with access to civilisation only in the case of emergency. Sleeping is done in a tent, and basic food is provided. Before you head out into the wilds you'll need to spend between C$500-1000 (US$380-760) to kit yourself with shovels, planting bags, camping equipment and such. You'll also need to have a criminal background check and visa.

Planting generally runs from early May to August, so it's a great way to bulk up your funds over a few months, experience some remote parts of Canada, and then have the rest of the year to travel. The website Replant (www.replant.ca) provides great information on the industry, and includes a forum for questions. The book *Step By Step: A Tree Planter's Handbook* by Jonathan Clark is also a valuable resource.

VOLUNTEERING

'Think globally, act locally' was a phrase coined in 1972 by René Dubos, an adviser to the UN Conference on the Human Environment. Although the phrase initially referred to looking after our environment, it touched a global nerve and came to mean acting locally in any worthwhile capacity. Buying coloured wristbands and donating money via text message from the comfort of your lounge room to send abroad is one thing. Actually giving up your time and money (most volunteer programmes are far from free), and going to another part of the world to contribute your knowledge, skills or labour is quite another. But this is exactly what an increasing number of people around the globe are choosing to do with their holidays, during gap years, on career breaks, or upon retirement. Almost anyone can volunteer: if you're aged between 18 and 75 you should be able to find a placement.

However, the more popular international volunteering becomes, the more difficult it is to pinpoint where to go, what to do and which organisation you want to volunteer with. For starters, the sheer number of volunteering opportunities today can be overwhelming. Then there's the problem that not all volunteering is good volunteering. There are plenty of volunteer organisations that are not meeting or responding to local needs, not working in proper partnership with host communities and certainly not working towards sustainable solutions. And, let's face it, no-one wants to become that volunteer who has just built a bridge where no bridge was needed.

Volunteering abroad should be the best thing that you've ever done, but the onus is on you to act responsibly, to do the research and to find a volunteer programme that works both for you and for the host community. If you want some help navigating your way through the process, pick up Lonely Planet's *Volunteer: A Traveller's Guide to Making a Difference Around the World.*

AREAS OF VOLUNTEERING

What tasks you perform as an international volunteer depends both on what you want to do, and on what is needed by the community or environment where you're going.

Within this framework you've got a number of broad choices, the first of which is whether you want to work with people (usually called 'development volunteering') or with the environment and animals (referred to as 'conservation and wildlife volunteering').

Once you've made that basic choice, decide whether you consider yourself a skilled or unskilled volunteer. Skilled volunteers are often people such as teachers, accountants, civil engineers or nurses who work in their professions abroad.

DEVELOPMENT VOLUNTEERING

There are nine main areas within the development volunteering sector:

- **Emergency and relief** An option for highly skilled and experienced volunteers only, this is where doctors, nurses, midwives, psychologists and so on, respond to humanitarian crises, conflicts, wars and natural disasters abroad.
- **Working with children** Typically, work in this area might include volunteering as a sports coach, working in an orphanage or with street children. Having a clean criminal record is a requirement in these fields.

• **Education and training** Most volunteer placements in this category are teaching English.
• **Business administration and office work** You might work for a local Non-Governmental Organisation (NGO) writing fundraising proposals, managing a project or volunteering in their marketing, PR or finance departments. The aim is usually to train local people in the skills you possess so that they can become self-sufficient.
• **Building and construction** Good old-fashioned manual labour often plays a big part in volunteering overseas. There is also a need for skilled volunteers in this area to work.
• **Health and nutrition** Health professionals are generally required in this area, but non-medical volunteers can often help with the promotion of health and hygiene issues in a local community.
• **Community development** This covers a wide variety of community and social programmes.
• **Staff volunteering** Some volunteer organisations, particularly those aimed at the youth market, need in-country volunteer staff to help them manage and organise their overseas programmes.
• **Agriculture and farming** This is almost exclusively for skilled volunteers. Communities often need horticulturalists, foresters, agronomists and agriculturists.

CONSERVATION & WILDLIFE VOLUNTEERING

The majority of opportunities involve short-term stints working on long-term projects alongside scientists or other experts. Volunteering in conservation could involve clearing or constructing trails in African national parks, studying flora and fauna in a cloud-forest reserve in Ecuador, or monitoring climate change in the Arctic. If you choose to work with animals you might

ETHICAL VOLUNTEERING: FIVE QUESTIONS TO ASK

1. How do I know if the host community or country will really benefit from my volunteering? This is a crucial question. There should only ever be one reason for a volunteer programme to exist, and that is to meet the needs of a local community. Just as importantly, all volunteer programmes should do this in a sustainable way.

2. If I only have a short amount of time to give, will I be able to make a difference? The answer very much depends on the aims and objectives of your project. The shorter the time you have, the more specific your project needs to be.

3. Am I actually doing more good by volunteering than just donating my money? The two short answers to this question are 'yes' and 'no'. All organisations working overseas need money to implement their programmes. However, sending yourself, as opposed to just sending your money, means you are making a very special contribution. How valuable either contribution is depends on the effectiveness of the volunteer programme itself.

4. Will my volunteering take a paid job away from a local person? It is crucial that it doesn't, and you need to ask this question of your sending agency or local organisation (if you are finding your own placement) before you sign up.

5. Does the organisation work with a local partner organisation? If a volunteer programme is to be of any real value to a local community it should work in collaboration with, rather than be imposed on, that community.

© Brendan Delzin / Shutterstock

A leatherback turtle on a nesting beach at sunset in Costa Rica

do anything from helping monitor sea turtle populations in Costa Rica to analysing the migration of grey whales in Canada to working in a home for neglected or orphaned wild animals in Namibia.

ORGANISED VOLUNTEER PROGRAMMES

These are highly organised volunteer experiences, where almost everything is arranged for you: your volunteer placement; international flights; board and lodging; travel insurance; visas; orientation courses; in-country support and transport. Volunteers can work on either development or conservation and wildlife projects. They often work in teams, but individual placements are also common. The cost of volunteering through one of these organisations can seem high, although their 'all-inclusive' nature means that everything is covered in the cost (bar pocket money). Other benefits tend to include pre-departure training and briefing and a higher standard of in-country support.

WHAT TO EXPECT?

For some volunteers there can be too much structure, too much 'hand-holding', as these programmes are designed to take care of everything. You'll usually have to make a solid time commitment (between three months and 27 months), in which the organisation will have a definite idea of the tasks you'll be completing, so think carefully about the commitment you want to make.

Although you'll be paying for this trip, you won't be treated like a hotel guest. Accommodation won't be fancy, as you'll often be living in a developing community. A room of your own and breakfast in bed are unlikely. You'll probably live with other volunteers, who will give you support and be your travel companions when you want a diversion, though homestays with locals will give you a chance to rub shoulders with your community.

WHAT YOU'LL NEED

If you meet the skills criteria for the placement you are after, you'll also need a clean criminal records check if your volunteering will involve time with children or vulnerable adults. Visas, all other logistical details and lodging will be sorted by the organisation after you've paid up front (see Paying to Volunteer? box opposite), so you'll just need some spending money.

FINDING ORGANISED VOLUNTEER PROGRAMMES

Here are a few organisations that offer organised volunteer placements:

- **AVI** (www.avi.org.au) The best known of Australia's volunteer programmes, AVI is a not-for-profit organisation committed to achieving economic and social development outcomes across Asia, the Pacific and Africa. Most placements are six to 18 months long.
- **International Citizen Service** (www.volunteerics.org) Funded by the UK Government, it offers teams of 18-25 year olds the opportunity to volunteer for three months on projects in developing nations.
- **International Federation of the Red Cross Red Crescent Societies** (www.ifrc.org) Works in disaster management – preparedness, risk reduction, response, recovery and resilience – in health, water and sanitation, livelihoods, support to migrants and refugees, shelter, social inclusion and many other humanitarian services.
- **Médecins Sans Frontières** (www.msf.org) MSF is one of the best-recognised international voluntary medical relief organisations. It delivers emergency aid to people affected by armed conflict, epidemics and natural or man-made disasters.
- **Peace Corps** (www.peacecorps.gov) An independent federal agency of the US Government that has sent more than 220,000 Americans on 27-month volunteer assignments around the world.
- **Projects Abroad** (www.projects-abroad.co.uk) It has a huge variety of projects available: animal care, archaeology, business, care, conservation, culture and community, journalism, language courses, law and human rights, medicine and healthcare, sports, teaching, veterinary medicine. Placements range from two weeks to 12 months.
- **Scope Global** (www.volunteering.scopeglobal.com) The delivery partner of the Australian Volunteers for International Development (AVID) programme, its programmes enable positive change by building the capacity of people and organisations in developing countries. Placements are usually 12 months long.
- **Volunteer Service Abroad** (www.vsa.org.nz) New Zealand's oldest and most experienced volunteer agency works in the field of international development and is always on the lookout for people with the diverse skills needed by its partner organisations overseas, from beekeeping to nursing.
- **VSO (www.vsointernational.org)** An international development charity that works to alleviate poverty in the developing world by recruiting professional volunteers. One- to two-year placements are available.

STRUCTURED & SELF-FUNDING VOLUNTEER PROGRAMMES

Some charities and sending agencies offer a structured volunteer programme but might require you to find your own accommodation or book your own flights. Basically, not everything is organised for you, and this is reflected in the fee.

In terms of independence, the next rung on the ladder is self-funding volunteering programmes. An agency will match you with an overseas placement but you're pretty much on your own from then on. You pay all your own costs, organise all the practical details (eg flights, visas and accommodation) and receive very little additional support.

WHAT TO EXPECT?

There is support from your agency but much less hand-holding than with an organised volunteer programme – both in your home country prior to departure and once you're abroad. This does give you more freedom, such as the ability to create or tailor your placement to better suit your own interests and skills. But it can end up with you being bored or frustrated if things don't go to plan.

WHAT YOU'LL NEED

As with fully organised options, you'll need the skills required for the role, and likely a squeaky clean criminal record too. Visas (it's ok to volunteer on a tourism visa), flights and lodging will most likely need to be sorted (and paid for) by you. You'll also require funds to sort out the placement fee (around £1000/US$1200/A$500), as well as for all your meals, transport and day-to-day spending.

FINDING STRUCTURED & SELF-FUNDING VOLUNTEER PROGRAMMES

Listed below are a few organisations that can offer either structured or self-funding volunteer placements:

• **Association Iko Poran** (www.ikoporan.org) Based in Rio de Janeiro, it tackles specific challenges identified by local councils. It now operates in 11 countries, covering parts of South America, Africa and Asia. Placements are

PAYING TO VOLUNTEER?

It often comes as a surprise to would-be volunteers that giving up their time isn't enough. In the majority of cases, you also need to pay to volunteer. There are five main reasons for this:

1. There are significant administrative costs involved in maintaining a well-managed volunteer programme and in finding you a volunteer placement. As such, it is normal for a fee to be charged.
2. The host programme incurs costs by using volunteers. Volunteers have to be looked after, possibly trained and certainly supervised. Then there's the question of who is going to pay for board and lodging, in-country transport and any other ancillary costs.
3. Hosting volunteers is often a way for local projects to earn an additional source of income. In many cases, part of your fee will help fund the project you're working on.
4. The cost of volunteering varies considerably. It usually depends on the volunteering experience you want and how long you're going for. If you want an all-inclusive, bells-and-whistles organised volunteer programme, you might pay between £3250 and £4500 (US$4000 to US$5500; A$5275 to A$7250; NZ$5600 to NZ$7725) for a three-month placement.
5. At the other extreme, you may sign up with a charity, NGO or sending agency that charges you a placement fee but then expects you to be completely self-funding. In the UK or US, if this is the case, you might be charged £1000 (US$1200) in fees and have to pay all other costs, such as international flights, accommodation and food. In Australia and New Zealand, a prospective volunteer may be asked to pay between A$300 and A$500 (NZ$320 and NZ$530) in partially refundable fees, or as a deposit to reserve a place on a programme.

incredibly diverse and developed according to volunteers' abilities and interests.

- **Blue Ventures** (www.blueventures.org) Operating in Madagascar, Belize and Timor-Leste, it runs projects and expeditions to research and conserve global marine life. Volunteers carry out research with scientists.
- **Casa Guatemala** (www.casa-guatemala.org) It runs a children's village on the banks of the Rio Dulce in Guatemala City, where it cares for 250 orphaned, abandoned or poverty-stricken children from the surrounding villages.
- **Conservation Volunteers Australia** (www.conservationvolunteers.org) From wildlife surveys to tree planting, CVA's work aims to protect, preserve and restore the unique and beautiful Australian environment.
- **Earthwatch Institute** (www.earthwatch.org) The US branch of this global conservation charity places volunteers on scientific research expeditions in over 50 countries. Projects range from studying climate change in the Arctic to protecting turtle hatchlings.
- **Elephant-Human Relations Aid** (www.desertelephant.org) This Namibia-based organisation works to reduce conflicts between elephants and humans. One week of your two-week placement is spent constructing elephant-proof walls and locals' water sources, the other is spent tracking, identifying and monitoring the movements of desert-adapted elephant herds.
- **Engineers Without Borders Australia** (www.ewb.org.au) EWB Australia may be the ideal opportunity for engineers with a global conscience. Volunteers work to respond to humanitarian challenges in the areas of water, sanitation and hygiene, clean energy, appropriate housing and digital access.
- **Habitat for Humanity International** (www.habitat.org) This non-denominational Christian housing charity is dedicated to eliminating poverty housing around the globe and works in around 100 countries. Volunteers are sent overseas to work in teams alongside the local community to build improved accommodation.
- **Himalayan Light Foundation** (www.hlf.org.np) Working in the Himalaya and South Asia, this small, grassroots organisation works to improve the quality of life in remote villages by introducing environmentally friendly, renewable-energy technologies.
- **Orangutan Foundation** (www.orangutan.org.uk) This charity actively conserves the orangutan and its Indonesian rainforest habitat. Volunteer placements are generally construction based.
- **Volunteer Action for Peace** (www.vap.org.uk) Working across all continents, VAP's short-term international work camps bring together groups of international volunteers from many different backgrounds to undertake unskilled tasks that would otherwise be impossible without paid labour.

DO-IT-YOURSELF VOLUNTEER PLACEMENTS

If you don't fancy any of these options, you can tee up a volunteer placement directly with a grassroots NGO or locally run programme. There are two main ways of doing this: you can either organise a placement using one of the many online databases of worldwide volunteering opportunities; or arrange a volunteer placement once you arrive in a country.

Many prospective volunteers make a hasty decision to go it alone without properly thinking through the demands and challenges. Reflecting upfront on your strengths and weaknesses, your preferred ways of working and your skills and values will help you decide whether a do-it-yourself placement is right for you.

FANCY A DIG?

If you see yourself as the next Indiana Jones or Lara Croft, archaeology is probably not for you – volunteers are more likely to be digging out fire pits than unearthing buried treasure. It's painstakingly slow and laborious work, which requires patience and commitment. But if you're still keen, you don't need to be a scientist or historian to take part. Volunteers typically cover their own expenses and camp or stay in local guesthouses.
The Council for British Archaeology (http://new.archaeologyuk.org) and the Archaeological Institute of America (www.archaeological.org) both publish opportunities on their websites.

WHAT TO EXPECT?

Going it alone places special demands on the volunteer. No matter how much research you've done, there'll be an element of the unknown. You will have to assume complete responsibility for yourself and your actions, as you will have no support network to fall back on. In addition, you will often be out of your comfort zone.

With some grassroots organisations you may not need to pay any placement fee; for others you will be expected to make a donation or fundraise. Most local charities and grassroots NGOs are small scale, and this means you can often define your own role, matching your aptitudes and objectives to a project's needs. The ability to extend your placement once you are there is another benefit. The length of your placement is also more flexible in most cases.

Volunteering independently means that you'll probably have to organise your own accommodation and entertainment, and you may be the only volunteer in an entire community.

IS INTERNATIONAL VOLUNTEERING THE NEW COLONIALISM?

This question gets asked a lot, and the short answers are: 'yes', 'no', 'sometimes' and 'maybe'. International volunteering is part of a long tradition of people from the West setting off to help or change the countries of the Global South (aka the developing world). Where once these people were missionaries and soldiers, colonialists and explorers – now they are international volunteers.

If volunteers travel in the belief that they have little to learn and a lot to give, then they do risk being little more than 'New Age colonialists'. No-one becomes an international volunteer for purely altruistic reasons: they also do it because it is exciting, because they might learn something, because they want to meet new people who live differently and because, maybe, they might have something to offer. By acknowledging why you volunteer, you are telling our hosts that they are people you can learn from and with, not that they should be the grateful recipients of your altruism. You ask them to be your teachers, instead of forcing them to be your students.

So, whether international volunteering is the new colonialism or not is, in large part, down to the attitudes of you, the volunteer, and the organisation you go with. If you don't want to be a 21st-century colonialist, rule out organisations that suggest you'll be 'saving the world' or give a patronising image of the developing world. Then question yourself. Why you want to volunteer and what you have to learn from those you visit? Avoiding being patronising will take effort and research, and will require getting rid of many of the usual preconceptions about the developing world.

Dr Kate Simpson

There's no denying it, however, organising your own placement can be time-consuming. And as local organisations or projects will not have been vetted by a third party, you may end up with something that doesn't match your expectations. You'll only really find out how the local project is run, whether it is meeting genuine needs, what you'll be doing and whether you can make a valuable contribution once you are in situ.

WHAT YOU'LL NEED

Key attributes, which will help in facing the kind of unpredictable situations that can crop up when you're volunteering independently, include self-reliance, maturity, patience, communication and interpersonal skills, sensitivity to cross-cultural issues and a good sense of humour.

Sorting your tourism visa, flights and lodging will all need to be taken care of by you, as will all the costs associated with your placement: meals, transport and day-to-day costs.

FINDING A DO-IT-YOURSELF VOLUNTEER PLACEMENT

The following organisations provide the contact details of grassroots organisations and projects that accept volunteers directly:

- **Friends of the Earth** (www.foe.org)
- **Idealist** (www.idealist.org)
- **International Volunteer Programs Association** (www.volunteerinternational.org)
- **True Travellers Society** (www.truetravellers.org)
- **Volunteer South America** (www.volunteersouthamerica.net)
- **Volunteer Latin America** (www.volunteerlatinamerica.com)
- **Volunteering Australia** (www.volunteeringaustralia.org)

COURSES

Wherever you go, you'll always take your head with you, so doing a little study can make a great souvenir. It can also allow you to acquire skills that may lead to another career.

There are millions of courses you could try: mastering Arabic in Morocco, for instance, or practicing yoga in a Goan ashram, studying art history in Florence, acquiring your Yachtmaster qualifications or getting qualified to become a ski instructor. Because courses are usually in small groups, you will also meet other travellers interested in similar subjects, some of whom may become friends and perhaps future travel partners.

LANGUAGES

A big buzzword in language learning is 'immersion'. This means putting yourself in a situation where you'll be saying goodbye to your mother tongue and fully embracing the local language. This way you'll be learning all the time, not just in classes. Going to a weekly class is a good start, but 'living in' a language is hard to beat. Everyday you'll have a chance to practice and see how the language relates to a culture, plus you'll pick up all the informal aspects that they won't teach you in class.

If you already know a little bit of a language, going overseas to do a course will help make you fluent and introduce you to locals. Most courses offer advanced options and some may even team them with cultural studies such as dance or cookery. It's not a bad idea to get a head start before your trip by taking a short course at your local community college or polytechnic – it will come in handy no matter where you travel.

GENERAL LANGUAGE ORGANISATIONS

There are several groups that offer language programmes, which are great chances to learn and travel. Shop around as prices vary, but here are a few places to start:

- **AmeriSpan** (www.amerispan.com) Began with Latin American programmes and now does language immersion for Spanish, Italian, German, French, Portuguese, Arabic, Japanese, Chinese and Russian.
- **Bridge Education Group** (www.bridge.edu) Offers in-country opportunities (as well as US-based courses) to learn Spanish in Brazil, Argentina or Chile.
- **Cactus** (www.cactuslanguage.com) Offers tailor-made language holidays worldwide, combining courses with activities ranging from salsa dancing to diving and gastronomy. Languages include most Western European languages, Chinese, Japanese, Greek, Russian and Turkish.
- **CESA Languages Abroad** (www.cesalanguages.com) These are in-country courses in Chinese, Japanese, Latin-American Spanish, Arabic, Russian and most Western European languages.
- **EF (www.ef.com)** Provides courses in Chinese, French, German, Italian, Russian and Spanish, sometimes teamed with Teaching English as a Foreign Language (TEFL) courses and/or au pair placements.
- **Language Courses Abroad** (www.languagesabroad.co.uk) Offers language courses and work-experience programmes in Chinese, Arabic, Japanese, Russian and several other European languages. Also has homestay options and courses in cookery or dance.
- **LSI** (www.lsi.edu) Language courses and work-experience in Chinese, French, German, Italian, Japanese, Russian and Spanish.
- **OISE** (www.oise.com) Offers intensive language training, teaching, and can include homestays for young learners in Heidelberg (Germany) and Paris (France).

ARABIC

- **Arabic Language Institute** (www.alif-fes.com) In Fes (Morocco), this organisation offers Arabic instruction in three- and six-week segments.
- **University of Jordan Language Center** (www.ju.edu.jo) In the Jordanian capital of Amman, there are regular courses on offer.

CHINESE

- **Bridge School** (www.bridgeschoolchina.com) Based in Běijīng, it offers group and one-on-one classes. Has scheduled classes you can join at various language levels. Also offers cultural courses from cooking to mahjong.
- **Culture Yard** (www.cultureyard.net) Also based in Běijīng, this cultural centre offers a six-week course, but you can tailor courses to suit your needs. Its 'Survival Chinese' course is ideal for tourists.
- **Omeida Chinese Academy** (www.omeidachinese.com) Located in Yángshuò, this school offers two- to 48-week Chinese-language classes (15 hours per week).
- **Taipei Language Institute** (TLI; www.tli.com.tw) With five centres in Taiwan, you can transfer between them to see more of the country while you study; also has centres in mainland China, Japan and USA.

FRENCH

- **Elfe** (www.elfe-paris.com/en) Set in a mansion near the Arc de Triomphe, courses can include culture classes.

• **France Langue** (www.france-langue.com) Runs courses in Nice, Paris, Bordeaux and Biarritz, as well as the island of Martinique in the French Caribbean.
• **EC** (www.ecfrench.com) Runs courses in Montréal, Canada.

GERMAN

• **Actilingua Academy** (www.actilingua.com) Situated in central Vienna. Courses for beginners start once a month, while intermediate-level courses start weekly.
• **Colón Language Center** (www.colon.de) This long-standing Hamburg school starts with beginners' courses and ranges to advanced.
• **GLS** (www.german-courses.com) Runs regular courses in Berlin.
• **Goethe Institut** (www.goethe.de/en) This worldwide organisation promotes German language and culture. Its institutes can be found across Germany.

GREEK

• **The Athens Centre** (www.athenscentre.gr) One of the leading places to study Greek, with regular classes and a summer school.

ITALIAN

• **Istituto Italiano, Centro di Lingua e Cultura** (www.istitutoitaliano.com) Ten minutes' walk from the Colosseum in Rome, beginners' courses here start monthly and other courses each Monday.
• **Linguaviva** (www.linguaviva.it) Classes are held in Milan, in a beautiful Art Nouveau building in the centre of town, and in Florence, in a 19th-century building close to the main railway station. Most courses start weekly. You can also study cookery, art, design and photography along with your language course.

JAPANESE

• **KCP International** (www.kcpinternational.com) Japanese tuition and cultural immersion for students with some Japanese language already. Students live in dorms or homestays and take part in weekly cultural excursions.

RUSSIAN

• **Liden & Denz Intercultural Institute of Languages** (www.lidenz.ru) Situated in the heart of beautiful St Petersburg; most courses start twice a month. There is also a school in Moscow, Riga and Irkutsk.

SPANISH & LATIN AMERICAN SPANISH

Latin American Spanish has evolved so far from its European parent that the language you learn in Mexico will be very different to the language of Spain, and vice versa. Studying one will help you with the other, but find out which one you're learning in advance by asking if it's Castillian Spanish or Latin American Spanish.
• **Academia Tica** (www.academiatica.com) One of Costa Rica's oldest schools; they offer courses for various levels.
• **ABCHumboldt** (www.abchumboldt.com) Overlooking Barcelona (Spain), this school has excellent beginner's classes.
• **don Quijote** (www.donquijote.org) This well-regarded international organisation offers courses in both Spain and Latin America, with homestays and student flats.
• **Estudio Internacional Sampere** (www.sampere.com) This large school offers courses in several spots in Spain, Ecuador and Cuba.
• **Excel Language Center** (http://excelspanishperu.info) Courses at Cusco, near Match Picchu.
• **Latin Immersion** (www.latinimmersion.com) Based in Chile, with schools in Peru, Costa Rica, Ecuador, Mexico and Argentina.

• **Malaca Instituto** (www.malacainstituto.com) An upmarket option in Spain that can include cooking and dance courses.
• **Spanish Abroad** (www.spanishabroad.com) Offers programmes with language schools across Latin America and Spain, including specialised classes for professionals and cultural add-ons.

CULTURE

Whether it's learning to whip up a green curry or perfecting the art of the flamenco, embracing aspects of your destination that you can continue to enjoy at home means that your travelling experience never really ends. These are just a few ideas and you can usually find more in a guidebook.

ART & CRAFT

• **Art History Abroad** (www.arthistoryabroad.com) Runs four- or six-week trips to Italy that look at the masterpieces of European art.
• **Art Workshops in Guatemala** (www.artguat.org) An art programme that includes backstrap-weaving, beading, painting and Mayan culture lessons.
• **Dedalo Center for Contemporary Art** (www.centrodedalo.it) An international association running residential courses in print making.
• **China Culture Center** (www.chinaculturecenter.org) Běijīng-based organisation with classes in Chinese opera, calligraphy, mah jong and more.
• **Istituto di Moda Burgo** (www.imb.it) Fashion and design school in Italy's fashion capital of Milan.
• **Scuola Orafa Ambrosiana** (http://scuolaorafa.com) Famous goldsmith school teaching jewellery-making in central Milan (Italy).
• **The Verrocchio Arts Centre** (www.verrocchio.co.uk) A residential art school in Tuscany offering varied fine-art courses.

COOKING

• **Apicius** (http://apicius.it) Florence's first-rate cooking school with everything you need to know about pasta, wine and more.
• **Casa Luna Cooking School** (http://casalunabali.com) Lessons in making Balinese grub worthy of paradise.
• **Chiang Mai Thai Cookery School** (www.thaicookeryschool.com) Great school for Thai curries and other dishes.
• **Mexican Home Cooking School** (www.mexicanhomecooking.com) Hands-on courses that can have you cooking up colonial cuisine in Tlaxcala (Mexico) and can include accommodation.
• **Rhode School of Cuisine** (http://www.rhodeschoolofcuisine.co.uk) Courses in Tuscany (Italy), Marrakech (Morocco) and Surrey (UK).
• **Small House Chiang Mai Thai Cooking School** (www.chiangmaithaicooking.com) Courses include transport, a visit to a local market, and span northern Thai dishes. The small two- to four-person classes are intimate and the experience feels more local than touristy.
• **Tasting Places** (www.tastingplaces.com) Cookery holidays in UK, France, Italy, Thailand, Spain, Greece and China.

FILM

• **The Film School** (www.filmschool.org.nz) A New Zealand school that has a good international reputation in TV and film. Unique for its visiting tutor programme, where tutors come into the school direct from the film industry.
• **New York Film Academy** (www.nyfa.edu) Has short practical courses on screenwriting, acting, film-making, editing and production.
• **Sydney Film Base** (www.sydneyfilmbase.com.au) Offers three-month-long short courses for would-be directors.

FURTHER EDUCATION

If you didn't get enough of school at home, what about an exchange programme?

It might sound crazy to go across the world to study, but some travellers look at international study as a way of expanding their CV and getting experience of the wider world. Some qualifications seem to be worth more than others, so with experience at a prestigious British school or an Ivy League qualification in the US you could be flooded with job offers when you get home. Other courses may not fit within your home country's educational system, so check before you go if a course will be accredited in your country.

Exchanges are offered by secondary and tertiary schools and often last for a year. Some involve staying with host families while others involve dormitories or finding your own digs. Some programmes have selection criteria and look for 'future leaders', while other (generally self-funding) programmes have few requirements.

Here are a few organisations for exchange, though you might find your university, college or school has regular programmes:

- **AFS** (www.afs.org) An international organisation that offers high-school and university exchanges.
- **American Institute For Foreign Study** (AIFS; www.aifsabroad.com) All-inclusive university study programmes for Americans.
- **DAAD German Academic Exchange Service** (www.daad.de/en) University study in Germany.
- **IAESTE** (www.iaeste.org) Offers opportunities to secondary students interested in technical work.
- **StudyAbroad** (www.studyabroad.com) An international directory of study opportunities at high-school and university level.

MUSIC & DANCE

- **Càlédöñiâ Languages Abroad** (www.caledonialanguages.co.uk) Offers holidays with dance programmes, language and culture in Latin America and Europe.
- **Carmen de las Cuevas** (www.carmencuevas.com) Based in Granada (Spain), this school teaches flamenco dance and music, which can be combined with Spanish.
- **Kala Academy Goa** (http://kalaacademygoa.co.in) Goa's most prestigious cultural group offers courses in traditional Indian dance and singing.
- **Kusun Study Tour to Ghana** (www.ghanadrumschool.com) Play with Ghana's virtuoso drummers, dancers and singers in these limited tours.

YOGA & WELLNESS

- **Morarji Desai National Institute of Yoga** (www.yogamdniy.nic.in) This Delhi (India) centre offers pranayama and hatha yoga along with meditation.
- **Purple Valley Yoga** (www.yogagoa.com) This long-established school in Goa (India) offers drop-in classes and longer programmes in Ashtanga, hatha and pranayama yoga, as well as meditation.
- **Thai Massage School of Chiang Mai** (www.tmcschool.com) Northeast of Chiang Mai (Thailand), this well-known school offers a government-licensed massage curriculum. There are three foundation levels and an intensive teacher-training programme.

SPORTS & OUTDOORS

If you want to pick up a new sporting skill, try some of these schools on for size.

DIVING

- **Apnea Total** (www.apneatotal.com) The capable, outgoing and enthusiastic staff has earned several awards in the free-diving world, and possesses a special knack for easing newbies into this awe-inspiring sport. Located in Ko Tao (Thailand).

• **Belize Diving Services** (www.belizedivingservices.com) Professional and highly recommended for PADI-certification courses – it offers immersions around the local reefs of Caye Caulker (Belize), as well as offshore dives and the Blue Hole.

• **Byron Bay Dive Centre** (www.byronbaydivecentre.com.au) Based in Byron Bay (Australia), it offers introductory, freediving and Professional Association of Diving Instructors (PADI) courses.

• **Manta Dive (www.manta-dive.com)** The biggest and still one of the best dive schools on Gili Trawangan (Indonesia). It is also has special kids programmes.

• **Scuba Iguana** (www.scubaiguana.com) Run by two of the most experienced divers in the Galápagos (Ecuador), Scuba Iguana runs courses of all levels.

KITESURFING & WINDSURFING

• **ION Club** (www.ion-club.net/en) This worldwide surfing organisation operates intensive kitesurfing and windsurfing courses from its schools in Le Morne (Mauritius), Dakhla (Western Sahara/Morocco), Sal (Cape Verde), Safaga (Egypt) and Tarifa and the Canary Islands (Spain).

• **Kitesurfing Lanka** (www.kitesurfinglanka.com) This kitesurfing camp in Sri Lanka is almost 275km north of Colombo. Its sandy peninsula has consistent winds and warm waters.

• **Yoaneye Kite Centre** (www.yoaneye.com) This IKO-affiliated centre offers kitesurfing classes for beginners and more experienced kitesurfers at Le Morne Peninsula (Mauritius).

MOUNTAIN BIKING

• **Bike Addict** (www.bike-addict-megeve.com) This Megève-based operation in the French Alps is run by a seasoned downhill competitor and incurable bike nut who provides lessons and excursions for families, hardened cyclists and everyone in between.

• **Endless Biking** (www.endlessbiking.com) Located in the mountain biking mecca of the North Shore (Vancouver, Canada), the friendly folks here provide lessons for newbies and expert advice to all other levels.

• **Moab Mountain Bike Instruction** (http://mmtbi.com) This certified bike skills instruction company in Moab, Utah (USA) offers co-ed camps, women's skills camps and private tuition.

ROCK-CLIMBING

• **Hot Rock Climbing School** (www.railayadventure.com) This longstanding school operates in perhaps the best area for beginners in the world – Railay (Thailand).

• **Plas y Brenin** (www.pyb.co.uk) A mountaineering centre based in Wales, which offers lessons in various areas of the UK.

• **Vertical Adventures** (www.vertical-adventures.com) Top-rated climbing school in Joshua Tree National Park (California, USA) that gets you on to the rock walls during beginners courses or helps you fine-tune your skills during more advanced sessions.

SAILING

• **Modern Sailing School & Club** (www.modernsailing.com) Based in Sausalito, California (USA), this school offers beginner courses and advanced American Sailing Association (ASA) certifications.

• **Sunsail** (www.sunsail.co.uk) This global operation offers Royal Yachting Association

(RYA) accredited courses in the UK, Croatia, Greece, British Virgin Islands and Australia.

SNOWSPORTS

- **Breckenridge** (www.breckenridge.com) This resort's groomed runs and energetic instructors make it a great place to start on skis.
- **ESF** (www.esf2alpes.com) With more than 250 skilled instructors, this ski school at Les Deux Alpes (France) can organise lessons for all levels.
- **Levitunturi** (www.levi.fi) You'll find plenty of chilled runs for beginners here, plus two snow parks with half-pipes and a superpipe for snowboarders.

SURFING

- **Mario Surf School** (www.mariosurfschool.com) Offers excellent lessons for all levels in the Todos Santos and Pescadero areas of southern Baja California (Mexico).
- **Merrick's Learn to Surf** (www.learntosurf.com.au) Merrick's is one of the most popular surf schools on the Sunshine Coast (Australia), offering super-fun, two-hour group lessons twice daily, as well as providing the option of private tutorials.
- **Pro Surf School** (www.prosurfschool.com) Right along Kuta Beach in Bali (Indonesia), this well-regarded school has been getting beginners standing for years.
- **Surf Goddess** (www.surfgoddessretreats.com) Surf holidays for women that include lessons, yoga, meals and lodging in a posh guesthouse in the backstreets of Seminyak, Bali (Indonesia).
- **Uncle Bryan's Sunset Surratt Surf Academy** (www.surfnorthshore.com) Uncle Bryan, born and raised on the North Shore of O'ahu (Hawaii, USA), has been coaching pro surfers there for decades. He and his staff teach all levels from beginner to advanced.

Surf's up in New South Wales, Australia

PROFESSIONAL ACCREDITATION: FROM MOUNTAINS TO OCEANS

If just learning an outdoor skill isn't enough for you, you could always do an instructor course, which may give you the qualifications to work your way around the world.

CLIMBING & MOUNTAINEERING

• **International School of Mountaineering** (www.alpin-ism.com) Based in Leysin (Switzerland), this school is operated by experienced instructors holding IFMGA credentials.

• **Plas y Brenin** (www.pyb.co.uk) This mountaineering centre in Wales (UK) runs an intensive four-month Fast Track Adventure Pro course that helps you to make the leap from student to teacher. It includes courses in climbing, hiking, mountain biking and paddling, with one-to-one mentoring sessions. You are free to choose a speciality.

DIVING

• **Padi** (www.padi.com) This international organisation has literally set the standard for diving accreditation, with countless schools running its programmes. PADI-rated Assistant Instructors and Open Water Scuba Instructors are the most sought-after positions in the global diving industry.

SAILING

• **Spinnaker Sailing** (www.spinnakersailing.com) Operating out of San Francisco Bay, this long-standing company offers courses towards American Sailing Association (ASA) certificates, from beginner (ASA 101) to advanced (ASA 107).

• **UKSA** (https://uksa.org) Based on the Isle of Wight (UK), it offers a 14-week course (58 days afloat) to obtain a RYA Yachtmaster Offshore certificate, which is recognised around the world, and will allow employment as a sailing instructor, or as skipper on charters, yacht deliveries and flotillas.

SNOWSPORTS

• **Australian Professional Snowsport Instructors** (APSI; www.apsi.net.au) Offers courses in snowboarding, Nordic and downhill.

• **British Association of Snowsport Instructors** (BASI; www.basi.org.uk) Offers coaching courses around Europe in adaptive, alpine, Nordic, telemark and snowboard disciplines. BASI credentials travel extremely well. Its website is a good place to look for global job postings.

• **Canadian Ski Instructors' Alliance** (CSIA; www.snowpro.com) Professional development through four levels of alpine skiing, plus Snow Park credentials.

• **New Zealand Snowsports Instructors Alliance** (NZSIA; www.nzsia.org) It's respected credentials incorporate skiing, snowboarding, telemarking and adaptive divisions.

• **Professional Ski Instructors of America & the American Association of Snowboard Instructors** (PSIA-AASI; www.thesnowpros.org) They run accreditation courses in multiple disciplines. US-based jobs are posted on its website.

WILDLIFE GUIDING

• **Bushwise Field Guides** (www.bushwise.co.za) After finishing its 23-week Level 1 FGASA Professional Field Guide Course in Limpopo province (South Africa), all graduates are eligible for a six-month work placement as a safari guide in the field. Topics covered include guiding principles, biomes, animal behaviour, climate and hospitality.

• **Southern African Wildlife College** (www.wildlifecollege.org.za) A course in bush skills and conservation in South Africa.

Opposite, clockwise from top left: Florence's Campanile, Italy; Turquoise Bay in Western Australia; the Taj Mahal, Agra, India; Peru's Cordillera Huayhuash mountain range

WHERE TO GO?

PART THREE CONTENTS

ROUND-THE -WORLD

Think you can take on those slowcoaches from The Amazing Race? In this jet age, Phileas Fogg's 80-day circumnavigation is looking pretty slow, so your version of the trip around the world will be much faster. Chances are you'll be switching between planes, trains, automobiles, camels and tuk-tuks to get around the world any way you can. For more information on globetrotting, go to Transport Options (p90), particularly the section on getting a round-the-world (RTW) ticket. If you're going around the world you'll be hopscotching through countries and skipping over borders, so this chapter will tell you a little more about factors that affect planning such as climate and hassle-free border crossing.

PLANNING YOUR ROUTE

The most exciting part of any trip is when you spread out the maps, break the spines of those guidebooks and start planning your global adventure. Using a RTW ticket or linking flights from budget and major airlines are both good ways to touch down on several continents, but how will you work out your route? With RTW tickets you'll need to lock in your destinations before you head off around the world...even if you're going to be flexible about timing.

CREATING AN ITINERARY

Personal decisions should always come first when you're planning your route. Start with a list of your 'must-sees' then prioritise 'would-like-to-sees' and 'would-like-but-can-drops', down to 'really-don't-cares' and 'not-in-a-million-years'. You can get a better idea of your priorities (including big festivals and the best weather) by checking the destination chapters in Part Three. You might also like to think about balancing your trip so there's some downtime between journeys.

From here you'll need to search for a RTW ticket (or group of tickets) that covers all your 'must-sees' and work out how many of your other priorities you can conceivably take in. You might have to drop a few of your choices or take side trips via an add-on flight or overland trip. If you have a RTW ticket that drops you in Sydney, for example, you could get a budget flight to Darwin before heading south to see Uluru, then loop back to Sydney via the wineries around Adelaide. Try to work out how long you want to stay in each place including side trips, so you can look at getting visas (see p26) for the right length of time.

Sounds too complicated? A travel agent can take some of the grunt work out by helping to sort out a RTW ticket for you.

The basic RTW loop generally includes London–Singapore–Sydney–Los Angeles (LA). However, more complex (and pricier) routes could look like this:

- Singapore–Sydney–Christchurch–Wellington–Auckland–Rarotonga–Papeete (Tahiti)–LA–London
- LA–New York–London–Cape Town–Johannesburg–Perth–Melbourne–Brisbane
- London–Helsinki–Bangkok–Singapore–Cairns–Sydney–Auckland–Santiago–Lima–Buenos Aires–London

You might also like to plan a few 'surface sectors' by going overland to explore places in depth. It can be the legendary road trip, a camel ride or a long hike. We've listed some popular surface sectors here.

- **Africa** Nairobi (Kenya) and Johannesburg (South Africa); Johannesburg and Cape Town (South Africa)
- **Asia** Bangkok (Thailand) and Singapore; Bangkok and Bali (Indonesia); Beijing and Hong Kong (China)
- **Australia and New Zealand** Sydney and Melbourne (Australia); Perth and Brisbane (Australia); Cairns and Sydney or Melbourne (Australia); Adelaide and Darwin (Australia); Auckland and Christchurch (New Zealand)
- **The Indian Subcontinent** Delhi and Mumbai (India); Delhi and Kathmandu (Nepal)
- **North America** LA and New York (USA); San Francisco and LA (USA); Vancouver and Toronto (Canada)
- **South America** Rio de Janeiro (Brazil) and Buenos Aires (Argentina); Quito (Ecuador) and La Paz (Bolivia); Lima (Peru) and Santiago (Chile)

CLIMATE

Hitting your destination at its sweetest time means working out the weather and making sure you get there in the right season. The temperate zone of each hemisphere has different seasons, with the northern hemisphere's enjoying spring from March to May, summer from June to August, with autumn running September to November and winter sinking in from December until February. In the southern hemisphere's temperate zone, summer runs from December to February, autumn runs from March to June, winter from June to August and spring from September to December.

Not surprisingly, many travellers opt for summer and spring, when the days are long and the temperatures warm in many destinations, so each hemisphere is popular during these seasons. Days get longer in summer the closer you get to the poles, so places in northern Scandinavia experience the 'midnight sun' where the sun is partying for most if not all of the night. This is balanced in the depths of winter with the 'midday dark', when Scandinavians look to sunbeds to supplement their lack of solar rays.

As well as checking the When to Go sections of the destination chapters, you can look up some of these sites that give average temperatures in several world destinations:

- **Weather Underground** (WU; wunderground.com) Includes excellent weather maps and active storm tracking.
- **World Climate Guide** (www.worldclimateguide.co.uk)
- **World Travel Guide** (www.worldtravelguide.net/destinations) Useful descriptions of seasons and advice on what to wear.
- **Yahoo Weather** (www.yahoo.com/news/weather/)
- **YR** (www.yr.no) Norwegian site with a global reach on weather

Wet, Dry & Hurricane Seasons

Different regions experience very different weather systems. The simplest pair are the Arctic (in the extreme north of the world) and Antarctic (in the south) regions which both suffer long winters and very short summers.

At the other end of the extreme are the tropics, the broad band that surrounds the equator (roughly between the latitudes of 23°30'N and 23°30'S, if you want to get technical) and includes Africa, India, South America as well as southern parts of the

ROUND-THE-WORLD

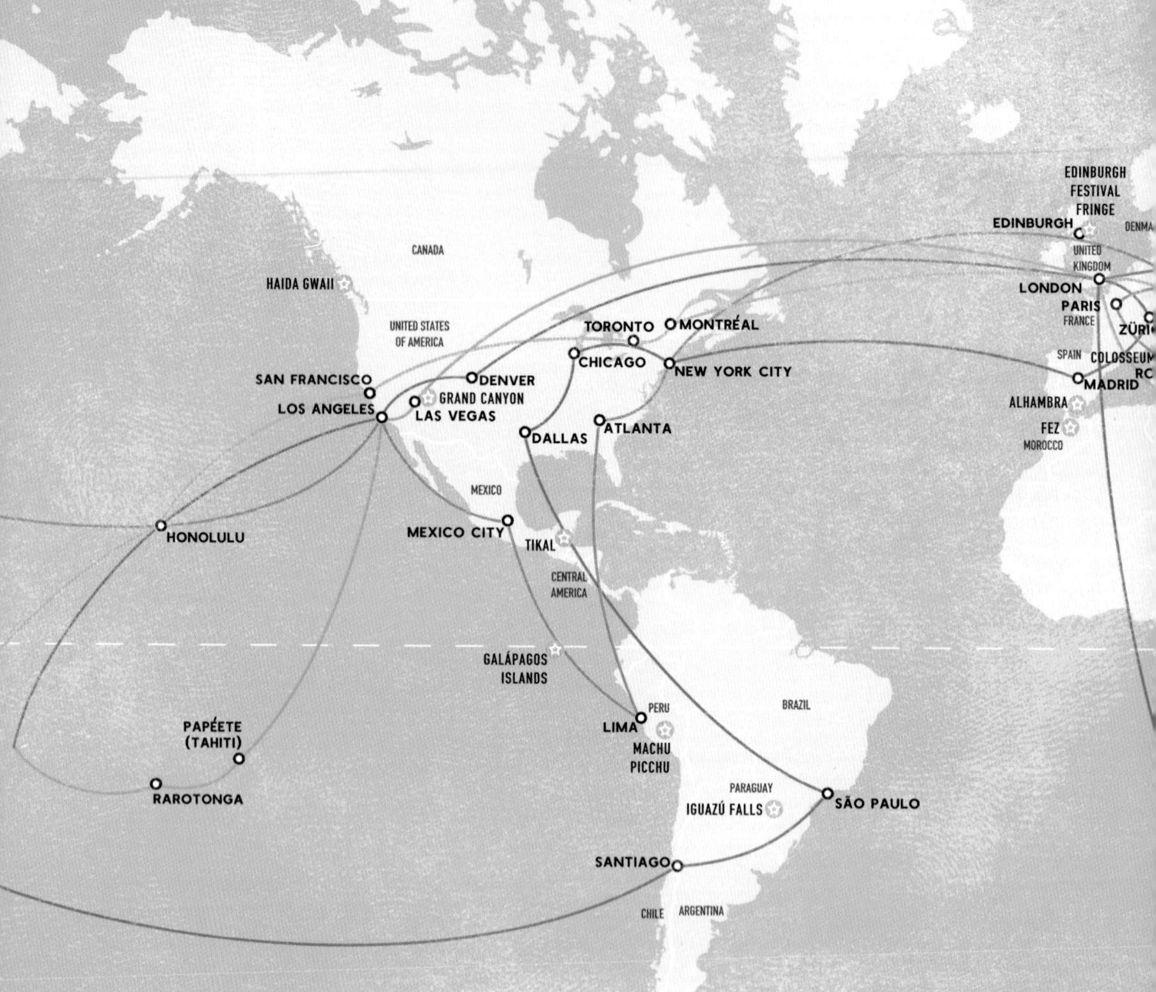

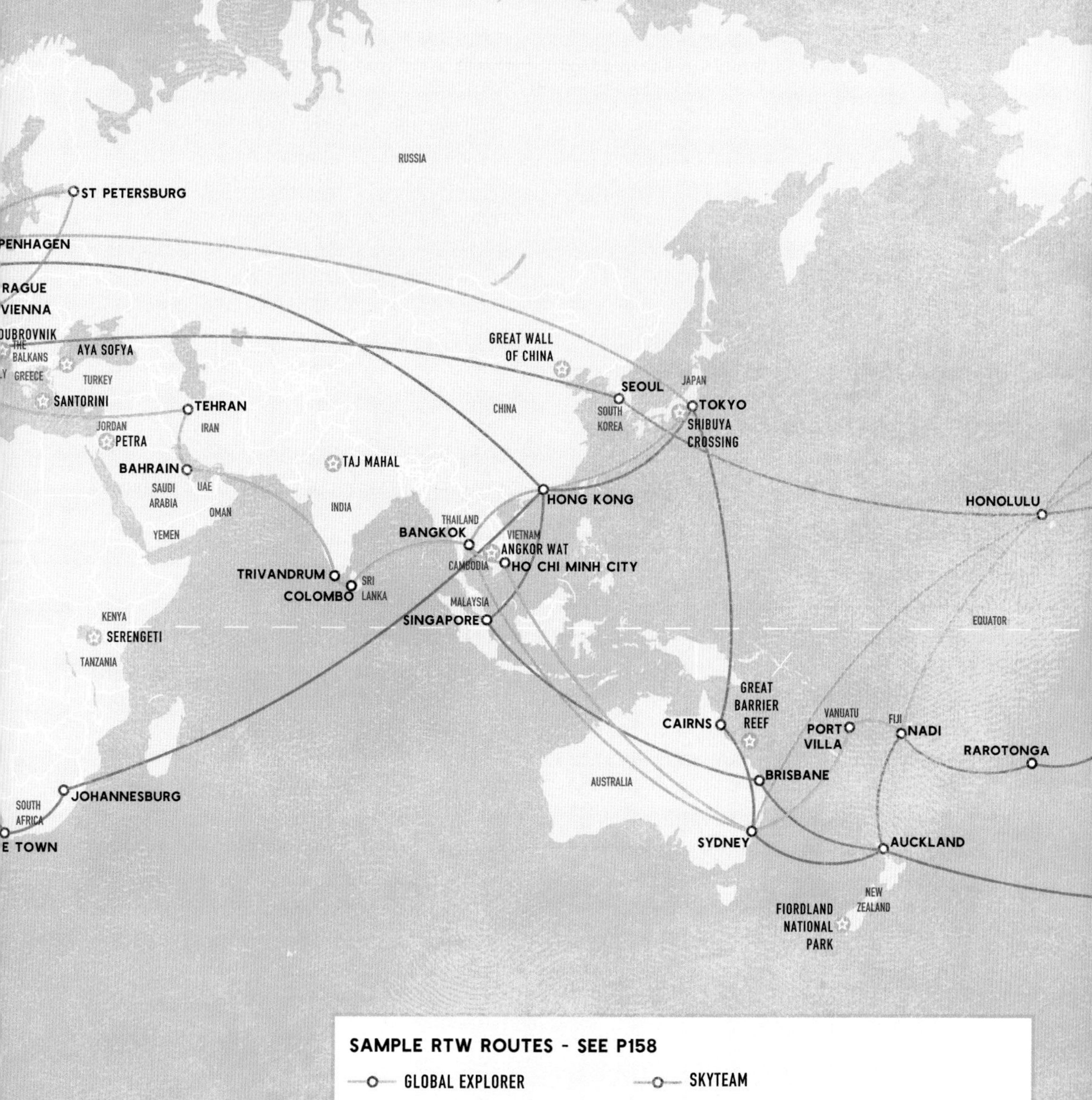
RUSSIA
ST PETERSBURG
PENHAGEN
RAGUE
VIENNA
DUBROVNIK
THE BALKANS
AYA SOFYA
GREECE
TURKEY
SANTORINI
TEHRAN
IRAN
JORDAN
PETRA
BAHRAIN
SAUDI ARABIA
UAE
OMAN
YEMEN
TAJ MAHAL
INDIA
TRIVANDRUM
COLOMBO
SRI LANKA
KENYA
SERENGETI
TANZANIA
JOHANNESBURG
SOUTH AFRICA
E TOWN
GREAT WALL OF CHINA
CHINA
SEOUL
SOUTH KOREA
JAPAN
TOKYO
SHIBUYA CROSSING
HONG KONG
THAILAND
BANGKOK
VIETNAM
ANGKOR WAT
CAMBODIA
HO CHI MINH CITY
MALAYSIA
SINGAPORE
EQUATOR
HONOLULU
GREAT BARRIER REEF
CAIRNS
VANUATU
PORT VILLA
FIJI
NADI
RAROTONGA
BRISBANE
AUSTRALIA
SYDNEY
AUCKLAND
NEW ZEALAND
FIORDLAND NATIONAL PARK
SAMPLE RTW ROUTES - SEE P158
GLOBAL EXPLORER
GREAT ESCAPADE
ONEWORLD EXPLORER
SKYTEAM
STAR ALLIANCE
HIGHLIGHTS

US, northern areas of Australia and much of Southeast Asia. Travel in the tropics is ruled by the rain belt which rages through the southern hemisphere from October to March, creating the wet season. Expect rain almost every day with brief intense showers in the afternoon. It's still hot though, and some tourists call this 'the green season' because plant life loves the mix of rain and heat (and so do mosquitoes). At the same time the northern hemisphere experiences the dry season, when there isn't so much rain and it can be a good time to travel. The northern hemisphere gets its dose of the wet season from April to September, when it's better than travelling in the southern hemisphere's dry season.

Between the tropics and the Arctic is the northern temperate zone and to the south of the tropics lies the southern temperate zone. These typically have four seasons each year though they can both be struck by unpredictable weather.

Another season that will affect your travel plans is the hurricane season, when there are... well, hurricanes. The Atlantic hurricane season stirs in the Atlantic Ocean during the northern-hemisphere summer and autumn and affects countries around the North Atlantic Ocean, Caribbean Sea and Gulf of Mexico. The Pacific hurricane works its way around the Pacific Ocean (including the southwest coast of the US and Mexico) from May to November. Hurricane season doesn't mean there will be a violent storm rolling through the area at these times – in fact, many nations never see hurricanes during this season. See Health & Safety (p39) for local travel advisories on the situation.

BORDER CROSSINGS & CUSTOMS

Even with all the bureaucracy of customs regulations, crossing borders should be relatively simple, so long as you're doing the right thing. Most countries have limits on how much alcohol and other goods you can bring in (see p63) and quarantine laws about not taking out animal products or local art treasures. In certain parts of Africa and the Middle East you may only take out small amounts of local money unless you enjoy filling out lengthy declaration forms. Obviously, drugs and firearms are off limits when leaving or entering a country.

Provided you've got all that sorted, the process should be a matter of a customs official looking at your passport and possibly stamping it on entry and exit. You may be asked a few questions on entry, such as where you'll be staying, but leaving a country is usually fairly straightforward. One notable exception is Israel. If you get your passport stamped in Israel, it may prevent you from entering Lebanon and countries on the Arabian Peninsula. The alternative is to ask customs officials to stamp a separate piece of paper that they'll attach to your passport. There have been similar issues with Cuban stamps in passports when travelling through the US in the past, and Cuban authorities have happily stamped a separate piece of paper. After a thawing of relations under the Obama administration, things have cooled under Trump, so best to check the latest situation before handing over your passport for a stamp in Cuba. Closed borders are typical when diplomatic relations break down between countries, so check travel advisories for the latest.

EUROPE

With more than 40 countries packed into this continent, each European culture has become dynamic and unique to distinguish itself from its neighbour. The European Union (EU) has thrown a lasso around many of them to create a powerful trading bloc that is unified in name but diverse in its traditions. Many travellers come to the area to explore the 'living museums' of fairy-tale Prague or classic Athens and Rome, while others come for the party life of smoky Amsterdam, hedonistic Ibiza or techno-pulsing Berlin. With budget flights and reliable public transport, it's possible to hopscotch between countries so quickly that they blur into one another. Slow down to spot the differences between Slovenia and Slovakia, or Latvia and Lithuania.

You've probably heard of the big-name destinations – London, Paris, Rome, Barcelona – but swilling a pint in a corner pub, devouring your éclair in a café, refuelling with coffee in a little-known piazza or tasting tapas after a night of drinking will really let you feel like these 'brand names' are your own. Always popular, Europe has a particularly busy calendar from June to August, and if you don't like the crowds try out some of our Roads Less Travelled ideas.

ITINERARIES

Getting around in Europe is relatively easy as most countries have good public transport. If you'll be travelling around by train, consider buying the **European Rail Timetable** (www.europeanrailtimetable.eu) and getting a **Eurail pass** (see p96). Get on the bus with **Eurolines** (www.eurolines.de/en), which runs coaches to most Western European capitals. Look out for deals from budget airlines.

EUROPEAN VACATION

You'll see most of Western Europe on this tour. Touch down in **London** and settle in by hitting the legendary museums, markets and nightlife. Then you can hop over to **Dublin** to embrace the Irish spirit, sample pubs and enjoy traditional craic (good times), double back to London and catch the Eurostar across to **Paris** for Seine strolls, Eiffel Tower views and Mona Lisa at the Louvre. You can head north to **Antwerp**, Belgium's capital of cool, for café-filled cobbled lanes, its riverside fortress and some amazing beer, then on to the charismatic canals of **Amsterdam**. Keep cruising along the Rhine and spend a few days exploring history and cool parties in **Berlin**. **Vienna** beckons with its classical music riches, then head west to **Zürich** and the **Alps** for awesome hiking (or skiing if in season). Take espresso and gelato in equal measure while wandering the canals of **Venice**, before kicking on to **Florence** with all its historic charm. The Eternal City, **Rome**, is next with the Colosseum and the Vatican – spend a day exploring each. Ferry across to **Athens** and then explore an island such as **Rhodes**. Head back to the south of France and Mediterranean towns like **Nice** to relax. Continue on to **Barcelona's** bonanza of Gaudí architecture before heading to the Moorish towns of the south such as **Granada** with its epic Alhambra. Finish up with laid-back **Lisbon**, savouring a *pastel de nata* (or three), and toasting the continent with a glass of local port.

MEDITERRANEAN MEANDER

This itinerary takes in some of Europe's classic sites. Hop across the channel from **London**

EUROPE

GREENLAND SEA
Faxaflói
REYKJAVÍK
ICELAND
NORWEGIAN SEA
FAEROE ISLANDS (DENMARK)
TRONDHEIM
SHETLAND ISLANDS (UK)
SOGNE - FJORDEN
NORWAY
BERGEN
OSLO
SCOTLAND
NORTHERN IRELAND
EDINBURGH
BELFAST
NORTH SEA
DENMARK
COPENHAGEN
IRELAND
DUBLIN
Irish Sea
UNITED KINGDOM
WALES
ENGLAND
THE NETHERLANDS
HAMBURG
LONDON
AMSTERDAM
SOUTHBANK
ANTWERP
BERLIN
ATLANTIC OCEAN
BELGIUM
GERMANY
LUXEMBOURG
PRAGUE
PARIS
LUXEMBOURG
HIGHLIGHT
EUROPEAN VACATION
MEDITERRANEAN MEANDER
NORTHERN LIGHTS
AIR
TRAIN
BOAT
FRANCE
ZÜRICH
BERN
AUSTRI
Bay of Biscay
SWITZERLAND
SLOVENI
SAN SEBASTIÁN
BAYONN
VENICE
NICE
PORTUGAL
ANDORRA
MARSEILLE
FLORENCE
MADRID
ITALY
LISBON
CORSICA (FRANCE)
SPAIN
BARCELONA
ROME
THE ALGARVE
VALENCIA
CÓRDOBA
BALEARIC ISLANDS (SPAIN)
COLOSSEUM
SEVILLE
FARO
ALHAMBRA
SARDINIA (ITALY)
TARIFA
GRANADA
MÁLAGA
MADEIRA (PORTUGAL)
TYRRHENIA SEA
MEDITERRANEAN SEA
CANARY ISLANDS (SPAIN)
MOROCCO
ALGERIA
TUNISIA
MALT

NORDKAPP
BARENTS SEA
White Sea
ROVANIEMI
GULF OF BOTHNIA
FINLAND
TAMPERE
EDEN
HELSINKI
RUSSIA
STOCKHOLM
TALLINN
ESTONIA
RIGA
LATVIA
BALTIC SEA
LITHUANIA
KALININGRAD (RUSSIA)
VILNIUS
KAZAKHSTAN
BELARUS
POLAND
WARSAW
CH
UBLIC
UKRAINE
SLOVAKIA
BRATISLAVA
NA
BUDAPEST
MOLDOVA
Sea of Azov
HUNGARY
CASPIAN SEA
JANA
AGREB
TURKMENISTAN
CROATIA
ROMANIA
GEORGIA
NIA &
CEGOVINA
BELGRADE
BUCHAREST
BLACK SEA
AZERBAIJAN
EVO
SERBIA
ARMENIA
NTENEGRO
PRISHTINA
BULGARIA
SOFIA
PODGORICA
KOSOVO
AYA SOFYA
OVNIK
SKOPJE
TIRANA
MACEDONIA
THRACE (TURKEY)
ANKARA
ALBANIA
DISI
TURKEY
AEGEAN SEA
GREECE
IRAN
ATHENS
NIAN
SEA
CYCLADES ISLANDS
SYRIA
IRAQ
RHODES
SANTORINI
CYPRUS
LEBANON
MEDITERRANEAN SEA

Fado musicians play into the night in Lisbon's old Alfama district

A gondolier guides his vessel past Basilica di San Marco in Venice

The Alhambra fortified palace complex, built by the Moors, in Granada, southern Spain

Lights on one of Amsterdam's many arched bridges illuminate a city canal in front of the Astoria building

and take in the poetry of **Paris** before heading southwest to picturesque **Bayonne**. Cross over into Spain's Basque country with a visit to **San Sebastián**, where grand architecture and a packed cultural calendar are framed by golden beaches and lush hillsides. Next, travel south to **Madrid**, a city that lives like no other.

Catch a train from there to Portugal's lovely capital of **Lisbon** and continue south to the old town of **Faro** and the beaches of the Algarve. Make your way east to **Seville's** intoxicating mix of resplendent Mudéjar palaces, baroque churches and winding medieval lanes, before checking out the kitesurfing haven of **Tarifa** and the art scene in **Málaga**. From there continue on to **Granada** for the Alhambra fortress, **Córdoba** for the mesmerising multiarched Mezquita and **Valencia** for its futuristic Ciudad de las Artes y las Ciencias. Next is **Barcelona's** bounty of culture before cutting back into France for seaside stops at **Marseille** and **Nice** before stepping into Italy. No Italian tour would be complete without a visit to **Venice**, **Florence** and **Rome**.

Next is Greece or Croatia (or both depending on your timing). Reach Greece by boat from **Brindisi** (Italy), check out the ruins of **Athens** and spend the last leg relaxing in the Greek islands, or instead cruise from **Bari** (Italy) to **Dubrovnik** (Croatia). With extra time, you could link Greece and Croatia with a remarkable road trip through Albania and Montenegro.

NORTHERN LIGHTS

If flying into Europe from North America, try to arrange a stopover in **Iceland** for a few days of exploring. Failing that, there are often cheap return flights from **London**. From London zip over to **Amsterdam** by plane or the Eurostar to check out its famed *bruin cafés* (traditional Dutch pubs), then strike out for Scandinavia and Finland on this arctic adventure. Head to **Hamburg** (Germany) to see a big port town at work, then ferry across to the capital of Scandi cool, **Copenhagen** (Denmark).

Continue north to **Stockholm** (Sweden) to cruise the city's Gamla Stan (Old Town) on a series of islands before veering west to **Oslo** (Norway) to explore its Viking Ship Museum. Take the train to the coast at **Bergen** and then wind your way northwards to **Trondheim** and the spectacular Arctic Circle. Bus north to **Nordkapp**, Europe's most northerly point before returning south through **Rovaniemi** (Finland), where there are husky rides and snowball fights to be had. Continue south through **Tampere**, which has been dubbed the 'Manchester of Finland' for its wild nightlife and post-industrial cityscape. Finally, snuggle up in **Helsinki**, the country's austere capital, before catching a flight out.

WHAT TO DO?

HIGHLIGHTS

- Walking the Southbank from the London Eye to Tower Bridge, taking in the best of **London** (UK), old and new: Big Ben, St Paul's Cathedral, the Tate Modern, Shard and Borough Market.
- Standing on Charles Bridge in **Prague** (Czech Republic), looking up to the castle's glorious old-world architecture and exploring enigmatic neighbourhoods.
- Romancing **Paris** (France) amid the Gothic cathedrals, winding streets, sophisticated cafés and foot bridges over the Seine.
- Pinching yourself on the island of **Santorini** (Greece), where villages topping lava-layered cliffs look like a sprinkling of icing sugar.
- Fancying yourself as a medieval noble in **Florence** (Italy) while you stroll by merchant stalls on the Ponte Vecchio en route to the famed Uffizi Gallery.

Clouds gather over the jagged Sassolungo mountain range in the Italian Dolomites

• Checking in on La Sagrada Família in **Barcelona** (Spain) – fanciful and profound, this marvel of Gaudí has been a work in progress since 1882.
• Gliding past **Sognefjorden** (Norway), Europe's longest, deepest and most impressive fjord.
• Following the **Berlin Wall Trail** as it traces between East and West in Germany's remarkable and energising capital.
• Crossing bridge after beautiful bridge in Eastern Europe's most stunning city, **Budapest** (Hungary).
• Sailing into **Dubrovnik** (Croatia) and seeing the crystal waters of the Adriatic lapping at the ancient walled city.

GET ACTIVE

Europeans love their mountains, whether hiking up or skiing down, and most are also huge fans of the bicycle, either for getting around town or exploring on weekends.

Walking & Mountaineering

From country strolls in Ireland to mountaineering in Italy's Dolomites, Europe has unlimited options to get out there and wander. The Alps offer the greatest variety for mountaineers, while trekkers may opt for Spain's national parks or France's rolling countryside (try the Pyrenees for remote villages). Alternatively, escape the crowds by heading to the Carpathian Mountains (Romania), the High Tatras mountains (Slovakia), Sardinia (Italy) and Bulgaria.

For long-distance walkers there are transcontinental routes, known as Gran Recorrido (GR) in Spain and France. The most popular is the Camino de Santiago pilgrim's route, which starts in France and ends in Santiago de Compostela (Spain). Northern Italy's Cinque Terra is a shorter (but more dramatic) walk through five coastal towns in a region known for its history, food and wine.

Via Ferrata is a high-adrenalin cross between walking and mountaineering, popular in southern France, Switzerland and Italy. You're roped up to climb using steel rungs and pre-attached cables.

Cycling & Mountain Biking

Europe is a cyclist's paradise. Cities such as Amsterdam, Copenhagen and Berlin are flat enough for anyone to ride around, and London has vastly improved its cycle routes. The proliferation of bike share schemes also make it easier than ever to get a hold of two wheels.

Mountain-bikers can pump their calf muscles through the Alps and pannier-laden tourists breeze their way through southern France. Among the best cycling regions (with huge cycle-path networks) are the Netherlands, the Belgian Ardennes, Scandinavia, the west of Ireland, the upper reaches of the Danube in southern Germany, and Provence and the Dordogne (France).

As foot passengers you won't be charged extra for taking a bike on most ferries and trains – just look for the bike symbol on the timetable. This makes cycling an attractive option in Europe's pricier regions such as Scandinavia and some of central Europe, where transport and accommodation costs can easily be cut with two wheels and a tent.

© gorillaimages / Shutterstock

Downhill skiing in the shadow of the Matterhorn in the Swiss Alps

Snowsports

With climate change, the ski season is less predictable than usual, meaning seasons can run short, start late or provide endless bounties of the white stuff for months on end. January and February are the sure-fire bets, and are unsurprisingly the busiest months. The French Alps are the best and most popular ski destination in Europe. Well-known resorts include Chamonix (France), Interlaken (Switzerland) and Val d'Aosta (Italy). The highest resorts, such as Zermatt and Sass-Fee in Switzerland and Val d'Isere and Tignes in France, are your best options late in the season. The best skiing in the Pyrenees can be found at Soldeu-El Tarter and Pas de la Casa-Grau Roig in eastern Andorra. These are among the most affordable ski resorts in Europe in terms of equipment hire, lift passes, accommodation and après-ski. There are cheaper (though more limited) options opening up in Bulgaria, Romania, Slovakia, the Czech Republic and Poland. One of the most attractive Alpine resorts for snowboarders is the Stubai Glacier, which is south of Innsbruck in Austria.

Cross-country skiing is very popular in Scandinavia and the Alps, while snowshoeing (a great alternative to winter walking) is also possible – these activities are more popular from February to April.

Water Sports & Diving

There are some good surf breaks on the Atlantic coasts of southern France, Portugal and Spain. There are good waves in the UK's Cornwall, such as in Newquay. Tarifa (Spain) is one of the best kitesurfing and windsurfing locations in Europe.

Canoeing and kayaking is possible on rivers and lakes across Europe and sea kayaking around the Greek islands and Scandinavia is popular. More extreme whitewater rafting can be found in the Alps, Norway, the Pyrenees, Slovenia and Turkey.

Great sailing locations include the Greek and Balearic Islands, Croatia, southern France, Ireland and Turkey. Look out for crewing opportunities along the Côte d'Azur (France) and Europe's wealthier sailing centres.

There are dive centres all around the Mediterranean. Croatia, Malta and the Balearic Islands are particularly recommended along with Turkey and Greece if you want to dive among antiquities.

FESTIVALS

Europe likes to party whenever it can, but many events warm themselves up around the good weather, so June to August are busy. Here are a few favourites:

- **Kiruna Snöfestivalen** (Sweden; www.snofestivalen.com) This Lapland snow festival in late January is based around a snow-sculpting competition.
- **Venice Carnevale** (Italy) Held in the 10 days leading up to Ash Wednesday (January/February). Venetians don masks and costumes for a continuous street party.
- **St Patrick's Day** (Ireland; www.stpatricksday.ie) March's excuse for multiple drinks, parades and revelry, all in the name of Ireland's patron saint.
- **Las Fallas** (Spain) Week-long party in Valencia held in mid-March with all-night drinking, dancing and fireworks.
- **Budapest Spring Festival** (Hungary; https://btf.hu) This two-week festival in March/April is one of Europe's top classical-music events.
- **Semana Santa** (Spain; www.semana-santa.org) There are parades of penitents and holy icons in Spain, notably in Seville, during Easter week.
- **Beer Festival** (Czech Republic; www.ceskypivnifestival.cz/en) This Prague beer festival offers food, music and some 70 Czech beers from mid- to late May.
- **Karneval der Kulturen** (www.karneval-berlin.de) This joyous street carnival celebrates Berlin's multicultural tapestry with parties and a parade of flamboyantly costumed dancers, DJs and artists in late May or June.
- **Roskilde** (Denmark; www.roskilde-festival.dk) Grungy Danish music festival with alternate vibe, held in June or July.
- **Hellenic Festival** (Greece; www.greekfestival.gr) Ancient venues host music, dance, theatre and much more at Athens' annual cultural shindig, which runs from mid-June to August.
- **Bastille Day** (France) 14 July is a national holiday and celebrations take place across the country but the biggest celebration is in Paris (check out the fireworks at the Eiffel Tower).
- **Baltica International Folk Festival** (Estonia, Latvia and Lithuania) Week-long celebration of Baltic music, dance and parades, held in mid-July.
- **Exit Festival** (Serbia; www.exitfest.org/en) Europe's hippest music festival with stages in a hilltop fortress overlooking the Danube River, held during July.
- **Castle Party** (Poland; http://castleparty.com) July's annual Goth music festival in a spooky old castle.

• **Il Palio** (Italy) An extraordinary horse race held in the main piazza of Siena on 2 July and 16 August. Get to it if you can.
• **Festival of Avignon** (France) Held between early July and early August featuring some 300 shows of music, drama and dance. There's also a fringe festival.
• **Edinburgh Festival Fringe** (Scotland; www.edfringe.com) Heckle the world's best comedy and stroke your chin at intriguing arts every August.
• **Tomatina** (Spain; http://latomatina.info/en) Every August, the little town of Buñol breaks out into a massive food fight with overripe tomatoes as weapons.
• **Zurich Street Parade** (Switzerland; www.streetparade.com) This techno celebration held alongside Lake Zurich in mid-August has established itself as one of Europe's largest and wildest street parties.
• **Notting Hill Carnival** (London) London's African-Caribbean community takes to the street in August for one of the world's largest street parties.
• **Oktoberfest** (Germany) Starting mid-September in Munich and finishing a week into October, this beer festival has no equal.
• **Belfast International Arts Festival** (Northern Ireland; www.belfastinternationalartsfestival.com) Held in a wide cache of venues, this event celebrates the intellectual and the creative without excessive hype.
• **Guy Fawkes Night** (UK; www.lewesbonfirecelebrations.com) Bonfires and fireworks erupt across Britain on 5 November, but there's nowhere better to experience it than in Lewes.
• **Hogmanay** (Scotland; www.edinburghshogmanay.com) Sing out the old year with Scotland's biggest knees-up replete with whisky, haggis and dancing.

MARIJUANA & HASHISH

Despite what you may have heard, cannabis is not technically legal in the Netherlands. The purchase and possession of small amounts (5g) of 'soft drugs' (ie marijuana, hashish, space cakes and mushroom-based truffles) is allowed and users won't be prosecuted for smoking or carrying this amount (although authorities do have the right to confiscate it, but this is rare). This means that coffeeshops selling it are actually conducting an illegal business – but again, this is tolerated to a certain extent.

NIGHTLIFE

There are never enough nights to enjoy Europe's energy after dark, so you'll have to be selective.
• **Amsterdam** (Netherlands) Amsterdam is one of the wildest nightlife cities in Europe and the world. Beyond the Red Light District and hotspots around Leidseplein and Rembrandtplein, the clubbing scene is also rapidly expanding thanks to 24-hour-licensed venues. Yet you can easily avoid a hardcore party scene: Amsterdam remains a *café* (pub) society where the pursuit of pleasure centres on cosiness and charm.
• **Barcelona** (Spain) A nightlife-lovers' town, with an enticing spread of candlelit wine bars, old-school taverns, stylish lounges and kaleidoscopic nightclubs where the party continues until daybreak.
• **Belgrade** (Serbia) Quiet cafes morph into drinking dens at night; clubs get thumping in the early hours. In spring and summer, action spills out on to the terraces and pavements, not to mention Belgrade's (in)famous barge nightclubs.

Crowds gather in a Munich marquee to celebrate German beer at the Bavarian capital's famed Oktoberfest

- **Berlin** (Germany) From cocktail lairs and concept bars, craft beer pubs to rooftop lounges, the next thirst parlour is usually within stumbling distance. Since the 1990s, Berlin's club culture has taken on near-mythical status, and is in a constant state of creative flux.
- **Ibiza** (Spain) It is one of the world's most famed nightlife destinations, hosting legendary megaclubs such as Pacha, Amnesia and Privilege. The globe's top DJs spin their magic here in summer, and the clubbing industry is very much the engine of the Ibizan economy.
- **London** (UK) The pub is at the heart of London life and is one of the capital's great social levellers. Virtually every Londoner has a 'local' and looking for your own is a fun part of any visit to the capital. When it comes to clubbing, London is up there with the best of them.
- **Madrid** (Spain) Nights in the Spanish capital are the stuff of legend. They're invariably long and loud most nights of the week, rising to a deafening crescendo as the weekend nears. And what Ernest Hemingway wrote of the city in the 1930s remains true to this day: 'Nobody goes to bed in Madrid until they have killed the night.'

ROADS LESS TRAVELLED

There are still pockets of Europe where you won't be pushed aside by tour groups, and even just visiting in winter can help beat the crowds. If you steer clear of Prague, Eastern Europe still feels undiscovered – try sailing down the Dalmatian coast (Croatia), hitting the Albanian Riviera or making the pilgrimage to Rila Monastery (Bulgaria).

If your wallet can handle it, Scandinavia has rugged wilderness such as Norway's spectacular fjords, or sophisticated cities including Copenhagen. Billed as the 'next big thing', the Baltics are ideal for finding your own haunts such as medieval Estonia and historic Lithuania.

WORKING

If you've got yourself a visa that allows you to work, or have an EU passport, then getting a job in Europe is usually straightforward. If you don't have either then most countries will make you jump through some seriously difficult hoops to get work legally.

Jobs in hospitality, temping, nannying, au pair work and seasonal fruit picking are all popular with travellers though there are limitless possibilities. The Jobs section (p115) provides various resources – organised by field of work – which will help you find work in Europe.

A SUMMER STUDYING IN SPAIN

In one fleeting summer my world changed: my host family's mother became my Spanish mom, I walked to school with a newfound curiosity, and I achieved my dream of becoming fluent in Spanish. And I surprised myself, not because I fell in love with Spain, but because my new perspectives breathed life into everything mundane.

Kait Reynolds

WHEN TO GO?

Summer is definitely the most enjoyable and beautiful time to hit Europe. Bright sunshine turns the Eiffel Tower and Paris into a set from a romance film, lazy warmth grips Rome and the Med, and England shines in every shade of green. Unfortunately this isn't a secret, so you won't be travelling alone. Even Europeans know how good it is and many take extended summer holidays in August in big cities such as Paris and Barcelona. Others shut up shop to head off to their holiday houses.

Winters in southern Europe are mild so Andalucía (Spain), the Greek islands, Malta, the Canary Islands and Cyprus are good places to get a winter tan, but in Scandinavia and northern UK you can expect very short grey days, often with snow. Spring and autumn may be a little wetter, but they can be good times to visit out of season.

WHAT TO EXPECT?

Europe can be broadly split into western and eastern halves separated by a line that once marked the so-called 'iron curtain'. The western zone is more heavily touristed, has better infrastructure, is chock-a-block with iconic monuments and – to most outsiders – more familiar. Travelling in this area is, invariably, comfortable and easy. The east is grittier, more community-focused, less affluent, but more inclined to grow on you. Travel in the east requires a little more effort, preplanning and spontaneity. However, when it comes down to the nitty-gritty (depth of food, architecture and culture) there's nothing between them.

LOCALS & OTHER TRAVELLERS

The people of Europe are a diverse bunch, as are those who've now made it their home. It makes for a cultural extravaganza in many places you'd wouldn't necessarily expect it – think it's just English spoken in England? Not a chance – there are actually 300 different languages currently spoken in the streets and schools of London today.

Given there are so many cultures spread across the continent, it's worth doing some

SAMPLE COSTS

	United Kingdom (Pound, £)	France (Euro, €)	Finland (Euro, €)	Czech Republic (Czech Crown, Kč)
Hostel: dorm bed	£15-30 (€16.50-33)	€18-30	€25-35	Kč300-400 (€12-16)
Midrange hotel: double room	£65-200 (€72-222)	€90-190	€80-130	Kč2600-3600 (€100-140)
Street snack	Cheese toastie £5-7 (€5.50-7.75)	Savoury crepe €5-7	*Lihapiirakka* €3-7	*Klobásy* Kč50-75 (€1.90-3)
Budget meal	£7-11 (€7.75-€12.20)	€10-15	€8-15	Kč120-150 (€4.70-5.85)
Midrange restaurant: main	£10-20 (€11-22)	€12-30	€17-27	Kč200-500 (€8-20)
Cappuccino	£2.40-3.50 (€2.65-3.90)	€2-5.50	€2.50-4	Kč40-60 (€1.50-2.35)
1.5L bottle of water	£0.75-2 (€0.83-2.22)	€1-1.50	€1.50-3	Kč10-25) (€0.40-1)
1L Petrol (gas)	£1.30 (€1.44)	€1.47	€1.50	Kč31 (€1.20)

research before you arrive in each country so that you may better understand the cultural and religious nuances. As with travelling anywhere, the overriding rule is to respect the people you're visiting. A church or mosque frequently visited by tourists could also be a weekly place of worship, and a photo opportunity in a market could block a thoroughfare as well as offend locals. Common sense and taking your cues from the locals are definitely the way to go.

Tourist crowds from across the world tend to hit popular spots such as Paris and London. The UK has long been a second home for many Antipodeans and Canadians, who use it as a base to work in before exploring continental Europe and the rest of the world. The support network in London is so good that you might want to head for other parts of the UK where you'll feel less surrounded by people from your homeland. You'll also meet intrepid Americans, though with limited work visas they may be on shorter trips and want to zip around Europe in

A traditional fisherman's lunch in Ibzia's Cala Mastella

a hurry.

If you're backpacking and looking for other people to travel with, there are plenty of hang-outs in London, Barcelona, Amsterdam, Berlin and Prague, with hostels always the top spots to hook up with other travellers.

FOOD

Table for one? Europe will tuck a napkin into your shirt and have you savouring its celebrated regional grub before you know it. Italian and French cuisine have already conquered the world, but tasting a rich tomato sauce slapped on a pizza crust in Naples, where the famous pie was born, or slurping down bouillabaisse in Marseille, are quintessential food experiences.

Spain and Portugal are catching up on the culinary giants with tapas, cured *jamón* (ham) and juicy sardines grilled to deliciousness. And new Nordic cuisine has captured the attention of the world's food lovers over the past decade or so. The eating scene in the UK has also transformed itself. No longer a culinary joke, the London of today is a global dining destination. Some travellers may complain that Scandinavians are a little too fond of pickled herrings, and that vegetarians options still have a way to go in Eastern Europe, but you'll never go hungry.

There's no shortage of beverages either, with trendy independent cafes preparing artisan coffees everywhere from Bucharest to Reykjavik. On the evening beverage front, there is quality behind every bar: Britain's returned to drinking real ale, absinthe is popular in France, Switzerland and the Czech Republic, and Italy's and France's best wines are there for the sipping. Scotland's distilleries make whisky so good that it's mystically called *uisce beatha* (the breath of life). Whatever you do don't try to outdrink locals on *ouzo* (Greece), *raki* (Turkey) or *Jägermeister* (Germany) – all powerful spirits that will make you thankful for Europe's excellent coffee the next morning.

LANGUAGE

English is a widely understood second language in much of Europe. In Scandinavia and the Netherlands most people will be happy to speak English, but elsewhere you'll get better results if you kick off a conversation in the local language. Learning a few basic words in French, German and Spanish is ideal for travellers around the Continent.

Never expect someone to understand English, or show frustration if they don't – the name of the game is patience and understanding. Speaking English louder or losing your temper over miscommunications are only going to make you look stupid. In parts of Eastern Europe you'll definitely need a phrasebook (or translation app such as iTranslate Voice) as English is uncommon.

COMMUNICATION

Europe is plugged in to new technology. Most of Europe uses the GSM 900 mobile network, which is good news for Australians and New Zealanders who also use this network (meaning you may be able to use your phone in Europe – check with your mobile company if they offer global roaming), but not for North Americans. GSM 1900/900 phones work in some countries, but you may be better off to rent or buy a pay-as-you-go phone.

Internet cafés are less common than in the past, but Wi-Fi has proliferated in many hotels and cafés.

HEALTH

All up, Europe is in pretty good shape. There are few required shots or vaccinations.

HIV and sexually transmitted diseases (STDs) are on the rise in Europe (use a condom) and a typhoid vaccination is also recommended for some southeastern countries. Tuberculosis is becoming more common, especially in the east, and there's the odd case of rabies. Tick-borne encephalitis (TBE) can occur in most forest and rural areas of Europe, especially in Austria, Germany, Hungary and the Czech Republic. Consider a vaccination against this disease if you're in the woods between May and September or if you are doing some extensive hiking.

Consult the Health & Safety chapter and seek professional medical advice for more travel-health information.

ISSUES

Tourist visas are generally not needed in Europe, with most nations signed up to the Schengen Agreement. This piece of diplomatic

EPIPHANY AT NOTRE DAME

After graduating from college, I lived in Paris for three months before beginning a one-year teaching fellowship in Greece. Footloose and purposeless, I was trying to figure out what to do with the rest of my life.

One afternoon I wandered into Notre Dame. At first I was overwhelmed by the vast stony hush, towering limestone arches and columns, and ethereal stained-glass windows. Then I saw a stone basin of water with a sign in seven languages: "In the name of the father and the son and the Holy Spirit." Illustrations showed a hand dipping into the water, then touching a forehead. Hesitantly I touched my hand to the cool, still water. As I brought wet fingers to my head, chills ran through my body and tears streamed into my eyes. Somehow that simple act had forged a palpable connection with the past: the fervent flow of pilgrims to the very stone on which I stood, the fervent procession of hands to water and fingers to forehead, all sharing this basin, this gesture.

I felt an electric sense of the history that flows within us and around us and beyond us – and I felt suffused with a new sense of purpose too. What would I do with my life? I would dip my fingers into the prayer water of human experience, all around the world. I would become a fervent pilgrim-writer, and I would bear witness to the sacred places, creations, and encounters, the history and humanity, that connect us all.

Don George

genius allows US, Australian, New Zealand and Canadian citizens to skip over most of Western Europe and Scandinavia's borders with ease (providing they hold a valid passport) for a period of up to 90 days. EU citizens will usually get no more than a bored eye from local customs officials and a wave through. It's not yet known how Great Britain and Northern Ireland's departure from the EU will affect its citizens ability to move throughout Europe, though it's unlikely it will be any more restrictive than that faced by Antipodeans or travellers from North America.

Citizens of the USA, Canada, Australia, New Zealand and the UK need only a valid passport to enter nearly all the other countries in Europe. At the time of writing, there were still a few exceptions where obtaining visas prior to travel are needed: Russia (apply at least a month in advance), Turkey (apply for an e-visa) and Belarus (only required if staying longer than five days).

Border guards, police officers, train conductors and other low-level bureaucrats in some parts of Eastern Europe may ask travellers for a bribe to oil their creaking bureaucratic machines, but more common occurrences in popular tourist destinations are rip-offs, scams and petty thefts. Tourist areas and routes are often targeted, so in these areas in particular you should keep your wits about you. Be sure to know where your money, passport and credit cards are, and you should be okay. See Health & Safety for more tips.

Another issue to stay on top of in some areas is political instability and terrorism. Staying away from the Iraqi and Syrian borders in Turkey is advised due to continued flare ups. Check travel advisories for more information. In parts of Croatia, Bosnia and Hercegovina and around Kosovo unexploded land mines remain a problem. Sarajevo's **Mine Action Centre** (www.bhmac.org) has valuable mine-awareness information.

URBAN MYTHS – STENDHAL SYNDROME

Here's one we're still not sure about. In 1817 French writer Marie-Henri Beyle (better known by his pen name Stendhal) visited Florence and was so overwhelmed by all the art and beauty he saw that he became physically sick. Yet it wasn't until 1989 that his sudden affliction was given a name. Psychiatrist Dr Graziella Magherini, having spent 20 years observing racing heart rates, nausea and dizziness in patients at her hospital in Florence following their visits to the Uffizi Gallery and other sights, coined the condition as 'Stendhal Syndrome' in her book *La sindrome di Stendhal*.There have been no fatalities or trips to emergency wards as a result of the syndrome, and it is not yet listed as a recognised condition in the Diagnostic and Statistical Manual of Mental Disorders, but if you start to feel overwhelmed by the art, take a seat and drink some fluids.

GETTING THERE

Air travel is surprisingly affordable in Europe thanks to the competition of several budget carriers, but rail and ferry transport are also superefficient.

AIR

Most travellers begin by flying into one of London's airports (Heathrow, London City and Gatwick are closest to the centre, but Luton, Stansted and Southend are also options). There are also direct international flights to many other big-name cities in Europe. Most countries in Europe have their own national airline, but here are some of the bigger ones.

• **Air France** (www.airfrance.com)
• **British Airways** (www.britishairways.com)
• **KLM** (www.klm.com)
• **Lufthansa** (www.lufthansa.com)
• **Swiss International Air Lines** (www.swiss.com)

Flexible 'open-jaw' tickets (flying into one city and out of another) are a good option if you're planning to do some overland travel while in Europe. Budget airlines also mean that it's cheaper to hop between European destinations.

There are just over a hundred budget carriers jetting around Europe and beyond, but here are a few of the more popular ones:

• **Aer Lingus** (www.aerlingus.com) A low-cost carrier flying from Dublin, Shannon and Cork to destinations throughout Europe.
• **BMI Regional** (www.bmiregional.com) UK-based airline with cheap flights to Europe.
• **EasyJet** (www.easyjet.com) Another good budget outfit flying out of the UK with destinations around Europe.
• **Eurowings** (www.eurowings.com) Headquartered in Düsseldorf and owned by Lufthansa, it serves almost 80 destinations.
• **FlyBe** (www.flybe.com) Based in the UK, it flies to 81 airports in Europe.
• **Helvetic** (www.helvetic.com) Flies to Eastern European destinations from its hub in Zürich.
• **Jet2** (www.jet2.com) Based in Leeds (UK), flies to 58 destinations in Europe.
• **Norwegian Air Shuttle** (www.norwegian.com) Flies to over 150 destinations in Europe, North America and Asia, often direct from London.
• **Ryanair** (www.ryanair.com) Flying from London's Stansted to dozens of European destinations.
• **Tui** (www.tui.co.uk) The world's largest charter airline, Tui covers many European destinations, and a limited selection from the Mexico, Caribbean, Africa and Asia.
• **Vueling** (www.vueling.com) With bases in Barcelona and Rome, it flies across Europe.
• **Wizz Air** (www.wizzair.com) Central European budget operator that connects Budapest, Katowice and Warsaw with the rest of Europe.
• **Wow Air** (http://wowair.co.uk) Offers cheap tickets to Reykjavík (Iceland) and North America from various airports.

SEA & OVERLAND

There are numerous sea-travel options for crossing from the UK into France, Belgium, the Netherlands and Scandinavia. Calais in France is one of Europe's busiest ports and a main gateway into the continent. If you're not sure which ferry service is available where, **Ferry Lines** (www.ferrylines.com) can give you an overview of Europe.

The most popular route is between the UK and the Continent. Here's a handy list of the passenger ferries that provide routes from the UK:

• **Brittany Ferries** (www.brittanyferries.com) Connects Britain and Ireland, Spain and France.
• **DFDS Seaways** (www.dfdsseaways.co.uk) Sails between the UK and Scandinavia.
• **P&O Ferries** (www.poferries.com) Plies the waters between Britain, France, the Netherlands and Spain.
• **Stena Line** (www.stenaline.com) Links Britain and Ireland, Scandinavia and the Netherlands.

For a swifter trip, catch the **Eurostar** train (www.eurostar.com) from London directly to the heart of Paris, Brussels or Amsterdam. It is also possible to travel into Europe from Central and Eastern Asia, although it takes at least eight days to do so. Railway routes include the Trans-Siberian, Trans-Mongolian, Trans-Manchurian and Trans-Kazakhstan. For more information see the chapter on Russia, Central Asia and the Caucasus (p324). Many visitors to Europe purchase a **Eurail Pass** (www.eurail.com), which is a budget train ticket that allows you several trips over a limited time period. This is only an option for non-Europeans, however.

SPECIALIST TOUR OPERATORS

There are hundreds of tour operators running specialist activity and sightseeing tours in Europe. A few European specialists include:

- **Busabout** (www.busabout.com) Aimed at backpackers, this hop-on/hop-off tour operator offers maximum flexibility.
- **Contiki Holidays** (www.contiki.com) Offers group trips across Europe for between three and 48 days for 18-35 year olds.
- **Exodus Travels** (www.exodus.co.uk) Adventure holidays for small groups that embrace culture, local traditions, cuisines and the environment.
- **Intrepid** (www.intrepidtravel.com) A longstanding tour operator that uses knowledgeable local guides for small group trips to 40 European countries. For travellers of all ages.
- **Radical Travel** (www.radicaltravel.com) Parent company for Shamrocker Irish Adventures, Haggis Adventures (Scotland) and Highland Explorer Tours (Scotland), which organise group tours in their respective regions.
- **Responsible Travel** (www.responsibletravel.com) This eco-conscious, culturally-sensitive company can hook you up with small group trips across Europe.
- **Topdeck Travel** (www.topdeck.travel) Runs double-decker adventures for '18 to 30 somethings', plus a few short trips to festivals.

BEYOND EUROPE

Classic overland routes from Europe include journeys across Russia on the Trans-Siberian Railway, from Gibraltar to Morocco and on to the rest of Africa, or from Denmark and Iceland on to Greenland. Access to Iran for the gateway to Central Asia is best via Turkey, Azerbaijan or Armenia (Iraq and Syria continue to be off limits).

FURTHER INFORMATION

WEBSITES

- **Atlas Obscura** (www.atlasobscura.com) Crowd-sourced travel guide to offbeat attractions around Europe and elsewhere.
- **BUG** (www.bugeurope.com) The Backpacker's Ulimate Guide is a good resource with country-by-country transport advice and hostel reviews.
- **Discover Europe** (www.visiteurope.com) With information about travel in 33 member countries.
- **Europa** (http://europa.eu) The gateway site for the European Union.
- **Go Scandinavia** (www.goscandinavia.com) Combined tourist-board website for the four mainland Nordic countries.
- **Hidden Europe** (www.hiddeneurope.co.uk) Fascinating magazine and online dispatches from all the continent's corners.
- **Lonely Planet** (www.lonelyplanet.com) Up-to-date travel information and articles written by our travel writers and Lonely Planet Locals who live in each city.
- **Money Saving Expert** (www.moneysavingexpert.com) Tips on the UK's best travel deals, money exchange and more.
- **Sleeping in Airports** (www.sleepinginairports.net) A funny and useful resource for backpackers flying stand-by.
- **Spotted by Locals** (www.spottedbylocals.com) Insider tips for cities across Europe.

• **The Man in Seat 61**... (www.seat61.com) A personal site that covers transport in Europe (including itineraries to get you anywhere) and beyond.

BOOKS

• **Almost French** Live the romantic (and not so romantic) life of a young woman in France. By Sarah Turnbull.
• **Bury Me Standing** A deeply moving account by Isabel Fonseca of the Roma people trying to retain their rich culture in post-communist, nationalist Eastern Europe.
• **Europe: A History A sweeping overview of Europe's history** by Professor Norman Davies.
• **In Europe: Travels through the Twentieth Century** A fascinating account of Geert Mak's travels.
• **Neither Here Nor There** Wander the continent with US best-selling author Bill Bryson for comedic company. His *Notes from a Small Island* is also fantastic.
• **On the Shores of the Mediterranean** Lap up the sun, sand and strife with travel-writing veteran Eric Newby.
• **The Sun Also Rises** A classic Ernest Hemmingway novel about the lives of American expatriates in Europe during the 1920s.
• **Through the Embers of Chaos: Balkan Journeys** Dervla Murphy details a sobering bicycle ride through the Balkans.
• **Venice** Jan Morris gets under the skin of this enigmatic Italian city.

FILMS

• **A Room with a View** (1985) This classic adaptation provides some stunning visuals of Florence.
• **Cinema Paradiso** (1988) Tells the heart-warming tale of one boy's cinematic love affair in rural Italy.
• **Before Sunrise** (1995) The classic Eurail love story where an American falls for a French girl and they spend the night in Vienna.
• **Notting Hill** (1999) American movie star meets west London travel book seller – romance and calamity ensues.
• **Amelie** (2001) With a knowing smile and skimming of a stone, Amelie orchestrates life around here in Montmartre, Paris.
• **l'Auberge espagnole** (2002) A slightly uptight French guy shares a pan-European student house in wild Barcelona.
• **The Bourne Identity** (2002) The first in the series, and a thrilling introduction to the streets of Paris.
• **Vicky Christina Barcelona** (2008) Woody Allen rom-com makes use of a beautiful Barcelona backdrop.
• **The Girl with the Dragon Tattoo** (2009) Dark and atmospheric murder mystery set in and around the islands of Stockholm in Sweden.
• **Star Wars: The Last Jedi** (2017) Skellig Michael starred at the end of *Star Wars: The Force Returns*, and Ireland again – this time the Wild Atlantic Way – plays host for this instalment.

AUSTRALIA, NEW ZEALAND & THE PACIFIC

Beach and bush to culture and cosmopolitan cities of wonder – is there anything Australasia doesn't offer? If you're up for awesome mountain experiences, engaging Māori interactions and spooky rafting through caves, New Zealand can deliver. Australia can serve up expanses of outback and Uluru, incredible Aboriginal culture, the Great Barrier Reef, beaches, world-class cuisine and two of the planet's top cities: Sydney and Melbourne. If you really want to get away from it all, find your very own Pacific paradise lost in a dazzling sea fringed with coral.

There are well-worn flight paths between this region and the world, so in Australia and New Zealand locals certainly won't be surprised by the sight of you. If you're backpacking, there are definitely hubs of action: Byron Bay, Sydney and Cairns in Australia; and Rotorua, Auckland and Queenstown in New Zealand. These places will have plenty geared towards your budget and there'll be ample short-term jobs if you need to top up the budget. That said, all these destinations have rather chic sides too, and if you have more money in your wallet you'll have abundant options to happily part with it (such as having brunch at Tea Leaf in Byron Bay).

If you want some truly intrepid travel, head for the Aussie outback or discover the Pacific. In the vast ocean you'll choose between Polynesia (from the Greek for 'many islands'), Melanesia ('black islands') and Micronesia ('small islands'), with a heady cocktail of cultures to keep you guessing. Pack some flexibility and cultural sensitivity with the sun lotion as Islanders come from very different backgrounds. Wherever you choose to go, Australasia won't let you down.

ITINERARIES

Most travellers opt for the big sites of Australia and New Zealand by arriving through Sydney or Auckland. Try wandering out into the Pacific if you want to dodge other travellers.

OZ–NZ: THE WORKS

Start out in **Sydney** then meander north to **Byron Bay** and onto **Cairns**, then double back to **Townsville**. Head west into the Red Centre for destinations including **Alice Springs** and **Uluru**. Dogleg north for **Darwin** then go west for a pretty pit stop at **Kununurra** or the getaway mecca of **Broome**. Sweep out to **Ningaloo Reef** or down to **Monkey Mia** before heading further down to **Perth**. Prepare for one sunburnt arm if you're driving across the **Nullarbor Plain** to **Adelaide**. If you have time, do a side trip up to the winelands of **Barossa Valley** or the ochre-coloured **Flinders Ranges**.

Crack on to **Melbourne** via the spectacular **Great Ocean Road**. Consider a trip south to **Tasmania** – best done by ferry – if you have a bit of time up your sleeve. Back in Melbourne, take the coastal route north via **Wilsons Promontory**, through coastal spots such as **Narooma** or bushy **Jervis Bay**. Detour to **Canberra** before hitting the wonder that is Sydney again.

From here it's a plane ride over to New Zealand's **Auckland**, where you can take time out snorkelling around **Goat Island**, then rip over to the **Bay of Islands** to see where the Treaty of Waitangi was signed. Double back south and make for the forests of the **Coromandel Peninsula** before hitting **Rotorua**. Head west for **Waitomo** with its impressive caves, then dawdle your way to **Wellington** taking in **Lake Taupo** or the Art Deco town of **Napier**. From the New Zealand capital catch a ferry across to **Blenheim**, then wander around the stunning bays of **Abel Tasman National Park**. Ease down the west coast with stops for the layered rocks of **Punakaiki** and the jade polishing in **Hokitikia** before getting your pick of **Franz Josef and Fox Glaciers**, magnificent trips if you don't mind the cold. Depending on your budget, you can continue down to **Queenstown** (the world's outdoor adrenaline capital), or double back to fly out of **Wellington**.

COMPREHENSIVE KIWI

See New Zealand top to bottom, by starting in **Auckland** and heading up to the **Bay of Islands** to juggle surfboards, kayaks and scuba gear in this outdoorsy spot. Return to Auckland then make for **Rotorua** for volcanic bubble and gush before heading further to **Lake Taupo**. It's time for café culture in **Wellington** or beeline for the Beehive (national parliament).

From here catch the ferry across the Cook Strait to the South Island and some whale watching in **Kaikoura**. Cathedrals are the go in **Christchurch**, but for more fauna make for **Otago Peninsula**. Head back into town at **Dunedin** before taking the side road down to the magic of **Milford Sound** then looping back to the outdoor adventure capital of **Queenstown**. Either head north for **Franz Josef and Fox Glaciers** or fly out of here.

ALL OVER AUSTRALIA

Make the east-coast run from **Sydney** first by taking in renaissance **Newcastle**, surf-haven **Byron Bay** and on to **Brisbane** and whale watching in **Hervey Bay**. If your budget can stretch, head for the blissful **Whitsundays** and on to tropical **Cairns**.

Fly back to Sydney and, if needed, work a little to power the next leg. Head south for summer by taking on the outback with a trip out via country-music capital **Tamworth** and onto the deserty mining outpost of **Broken Hill**. You could head southwest to **Adelaide** if you like a long drive or take the trip down to artsy **Melbourne** with a stop for a paddle-boat ride in **Mildura**.

After you've sipped all the flat whites you can handle in Melbourne, head west to **Adelaide** and soak up the key wine regions: the **Barossa and Clare Valleys**. Head north into the Red Centre by taking the Ghan railway all the way to **Uluru** and **Alice Springs**. Finish up in **Darwin** and fly back to **Sydney** or out to Southeast Asia.

PAN-PACIFIC CHAMPIONSHIP

Start your race in **Sydney**, with side trips to the **Blue Mountains** for treks, views and waterfalls, or up to the **Hunter Valley** for a wine tasting or two. From here hop on a plane across to **Auckland** to start experiencing Polynesian culture. Explore the North Island (**Rotorua**, **Taupo**, even **Wellington**) before shipping out to **Rarotonga** for classic coconut tree-lined lagoons.

When you've had all the sun you can stand, hop over to **Pape'ete**, the vibrant capital of

AUSTRALIA–NEW ZEALAND–THE PACIFIC

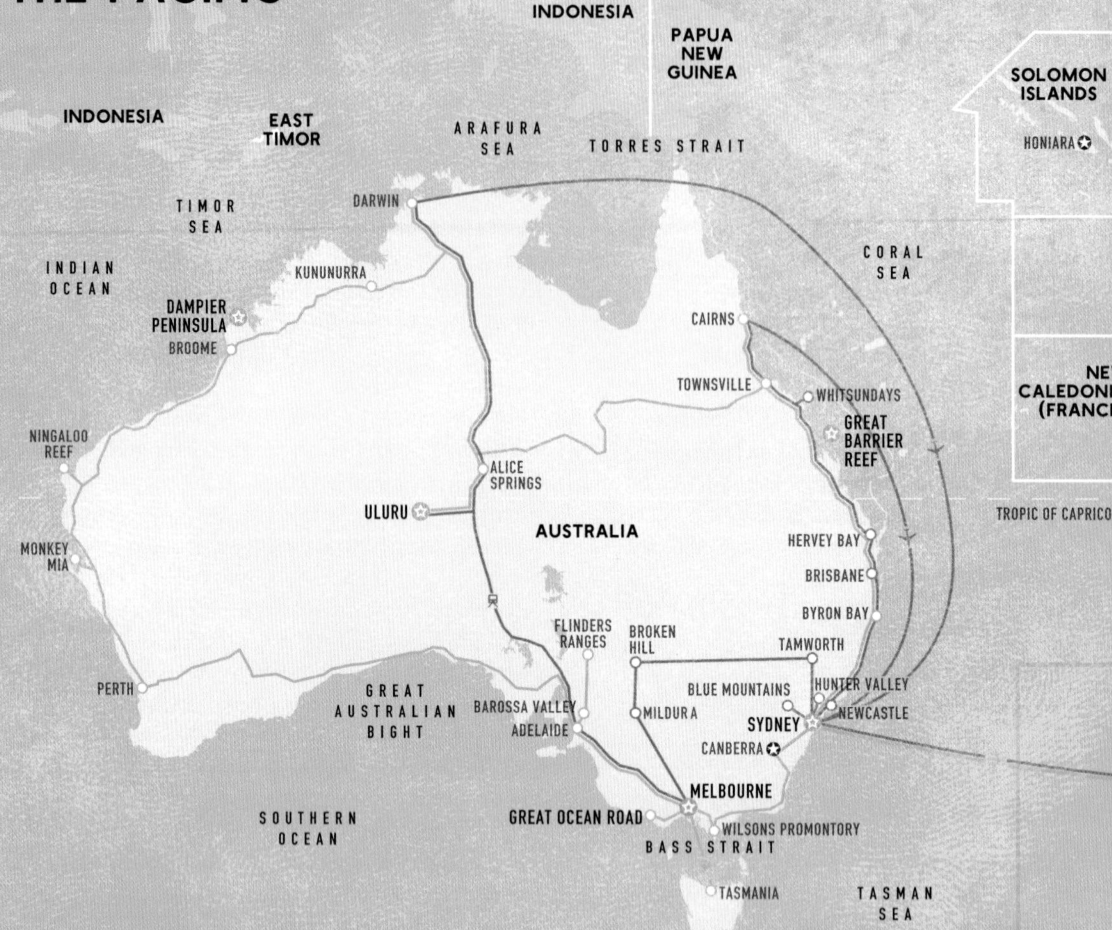

HIGHLIGHTS
OZ–NZ: THE WORKS
COMPREHENSIVE KIWI
ALL OVER AUSTRALIA
PAN-PACIFIC CHAMPIONSHIP
AIR
TRAIN
BOAT

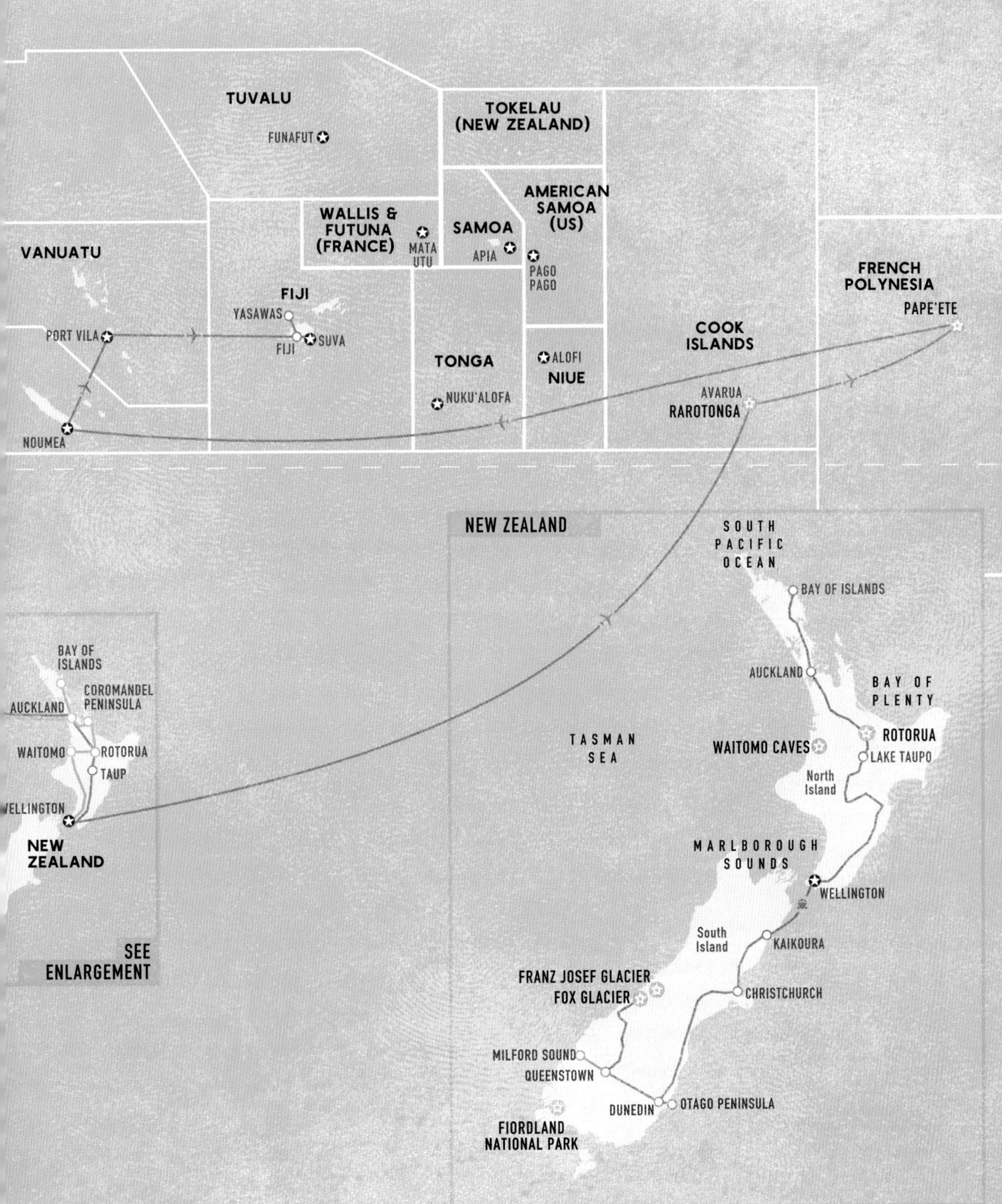

TUVALU
FUNAFUT
TOKELAU (NEW ZEALAND)
AMERICAN SAMOA (US)
WALLIS & FUTUNA (FRANCE)
MATA UTU
SAMOA
APIA
PAGO PAGO
VANUATU
FIJI
YASAWAS
PORT VILA
FIJI
SUVA
FRENCH POLYNESIA
PAPE'ETE
COOK ISLANDS
TONGA
ALOFI
NIUE
NUKU'ALOFA
AVARUA
RAROTONGA
NOUMEA
NEW ZEALAND
SOUTH PACIFIC OCEAN
BAY OF ISLANDS
AUCKLAND
BAY OF PLENTY
ROTORUA
TASMAN SEA
WAITOMO CAVES
LAKE TAUPO
North Island
MARLBOROUGH SOUNDS
WELLINGTON
South Island
KAIKOURA
FRANZ JOSEF GLACIER
FOX GLACIER
CHRISTCHURCH
MILFORD SOUND
QUEENSTOWN
DUNEDIN
OTAGO PENINSULA
FIORDLAND NATIONAL PARK
BAY OF ISLANDS
COROMANDEL PENINSULA
AUCKLAND
WAITOMO
ROTORUA
TAUP
WELLINGTON
NEW ZEALAND
SEE ENLARGEMENT

© NurIsmailPhotography / Getty Images

The snow-covered summit of Aoraki/Mt Cook rises 3724m over New Zealand's South Island

© Justin Foulkes / Lonely Planet

Mapping a road trip through the North Island, New Zealand

© Matt Munro / Lonely Planet

A diver prepares for another plunge to the Great Barrier Reef

Sandy beaches reach along the coast towards the headland in Byron Bay, New South Wales, Australia

French Polynesia via **Avarua**. Next make the trip over to **Noumea** in New Caledonia, then onto **Port Vila** in Vanuatu. Make for Fiji, a regional hub that will allow you to catch a boat out to the **Yasawas** or head home.

WHAT TO DO?

HIGHLIGHTS

- Riding the ferries, walking the streets, eating the food and soaking up the soul of beach-blessed and icon-endowed **Sydney** (Australia).
- Diving the polychromatic coral of the **Great Barrier Reef** (Australia) that sparkles with rare fish.
- Staying in **Melbourne** (Australia) long enough to realise that its coffee isn't the only thing that's addictive – its people, culture, cuisine, parks and spirit will grip you.
- Striking out from **Broome** to the far-flung **Dampier Peninsula** (Australia) where extraordinary cliffs, Indigenous cultural experiences and outdoor adventures await.
- Honouring the Australian outback's spiritual red heart at **Uluru**.
- Embracing M□ori culture around **Rotorua** (New Zealand) – attend a h□ngi (a traditional feast cooked in the ground), attempt a *haka* (war dance) and soak in percolating mud pools.
- Playing it cool at **Franz Josef and Fox Glaciers** (New Zealand) as ice floes tumble before you.
- Blackwater rafting through eerie glow-worm-lit **Waitomo Caves** (New Zealand).
- Biting into **Rarotonga** (Cook Islands), a chilled-out slice of heaven just a plane hop from New Zealand.
- Fusing cosmopolitan French chic and Pacific paradise beach-bumming at **Pape'ete** (Tahiti).

GET ACTIVE

Australasia is one massive playground. If you're not busy bungee jumping in New Zealand, you'll be bush walking or surfing Australia's sweetest swells. National parks are the best places to find activities.

Surfing

Awesome beach breaks make surfers travel here from across the globe. Best of all, anywhere there's a swell, a surf school will be there renting out all the gear and giving a few hours' instruction to get you up on a board.

Surf culture is deeply rooted in Australia, with classic breaks all along the coast at Bells Beach (Victoria), Byron Bay (New South Wales), Margaret River (Western Australia) and Fleurieu (South Australia). The Pacific islands have great surfing destinations such as American Samoa, the Cook Islands, Guam, Tonga, French Polynesia and Fiji.

New Zealand surfers wear wetsuits all year round, particularly so on the South Island, but if you don't mind zipping up there's always somewhere to bust out the board. There are awesome breaks at Ragland (including the famous Waikato break), Marlborough Sounds and even around Wellington.

Kitesurfing & Windsurfing

Blustery Geraldton (Western Australia), Newcastle (Australia), Melbourne (Australia) and the Bay of Islands (New Zealand) are all great kitesurfing and windsurfing spots.

Extreme Sports

New Zealand shreds the biscuit and washes it down with a draught of pure adrenaline when it comes to fear-enhanced activities (Australia tries to keep up). New Zealand is famous for bungee jumping in Queenstown, Hanmer Springs, Taupo and Auckland, and jet-boating at Queenstown and the Bay of Islands, but there's also zorbing (the Kiwi-invented sport

A surfer makes a bolt for the breakers off the coast of New Zealand

of rolling down a slope in a giant transparent ball) and blowkarting (another New Zealand innovation that has you 'sailing' on land in a custom-built cart). In Australia bungee jumping is popular on the Gold Coast which, along with Byron Bay and Townsville, also makes an awesome spot for parachuting. Then there's paragliding on thermal winds at spots such as Rainbow Beach (Australia), Bright (Australia) and Taupo (New Zealand). Thrill-seekers in New Zealand have been known to go river sledging in the waters around Queenstown and Wanaka. Then there's cave rafting, riding a tube through the dark caverns around Waitomo, Westport and Greymouth.

Diving & Snorkelling

Divers are in for a real treat in the Pacific Ocean with its clear waters, unique marine life, impressive wrecks and heaps of places to grab a snorkel and explore. Most travellers float over Queensland's Great Barrier Reef, but there are impressive dives at South Australia's shipwreck-strewn Kangaroo Island, and at Esperance, Rottnest Island, Ningaloo Reef and Carnarvon, all in Western Australia. There are plenty of places where you can learn to dive and rent gear, so beginners won't miss the fun. New Zealand's best aqua action is around Bay of Islands Maritime Park, Hauraki Gulf Maritime Park, Great Barrier Island, Goat Island or Marlborough Sounds.

Diving among the Pacific islands' stunning coral, jaw-dropping drop-offs and the undersea museum of WWII wrecks make it a highlight for divers the world over. Operators vary greatly in this area – from a bloke with a boat to fully qualified PADI masters – so check the credentials before you climb aboard. Rarotonga (Cook Islands), French Polynesia, Tonga and

New Caledonia are all popular spots for diving. Don't forget tiny islands such as the Federated States of Micronesia, Guam and the Marshall Islands, which are less crowded and have coral-encrusted wrecks.

Cycling & Mountain Biking

Spin two wheels through Australasia and you'll see the region at a good pace. The light traffic and good bike tracks make for enjoyable riding throughout. Smaller Pacific islands can be crossed without changing gears, never mind hiring a car. Coastal routes – the east coast in Australia and around the North Island in New Zealand – can be scenic pedalling for beginners. The more adventurous take on longer trips, such as New Zealand's Otago Central Rail Trail (following an old rail line through the gold region), and the experienced can try heading out from Alice Springs along the Todd River. If all that sounds a bit tame you can hurtle down rough roads on a mountain bike – many wilderness areas have good trails, including Australia's Blue and Snowy Mountains and New Zealand's Queen Charlotte Track.

© Matt Munro / Lonely Planet

Nitmiluk National Park's Katherine Gorge in the north of Australia

Both Australia and New Zealand offer plenty of camp sites or other cheap accommodation. Renting bicycles is affordable, though it's also cheap to buy a bike when you arrive if you plan on doing a lot of cycling. While laws in the Pacific are pretty forgiving, Australia and New Zealand both slap fines on cyclists for not wearing helmets and for riding under the influence of alcohol.

Kayaking, Rafting & Other Water Sports

Surrounded by expanses of ocean and often blessed with calm conditions, the Pacific islands are a great spot for sea kayaking. Countries such as Fiji, Tonga, New Caledonia and Samoa rent out kayaks and sometimes offer multiday trips. Papua New Guinea's turbulent mountain rivers offer some extreme kayaking opportunities.

Australia's best whitewater rafting trips are probably on the upper Murray and Nymboida Rivers in New South Wales and Tully River in Queensland. There's great canoeing in Katherine Gorge in Nitmiluk National Park (Northern Territory), the Ord and Blackwood Rivers (Western Australia), Murray River National Park (South Australia) and the Franklin River (Tasmania).

New Zealand's best rafting takes place on Rangitata River, but the Shotover and Kawarau Rivers are both strong contenders for the title. Sea kayaking at the Bay of Islands, Marlborough Sound, Abel Tasman National Park, Milford Sound and Coromandel offers slower-paced enjoyment.

Or you can slow it down on a cruise yacht. Sailing cities such as Auckland (the so-called

City of Sails), Sydney and Hobart, as well as Vava'u (Tonga) and Fiji, are all good places to get shanghaied as a crew member. There are also sailing cruises from spots which take in impressive vistas, including Cairns (Queensland), the Bay of Islands (New Zealand) and Dunedin (New Zealand).

Trekking & Mountaineering
Whether it's bush walking (in Australia) or tramping (in New Zealand), it's easy to explore the wilderness on foot and the pair of countries offer plenty of opportunities.

Tasmania (Australia) boasts the magnificent Overland Track (plus plenty of other walks in Cradle Mountain–Lake St Clair National Park), while South Australia has the impressive Mawson Trail in the Flinders Ranges. The Blue and Snowy Mountains both have well-trafficked trails, but less-beaten tracks include Western Australia's Bibbulmun Track and central Australia's challenging Larapinta Trail.

Many of these regions also offer fantastic rock climbing; don't forget to check out Mt Arapiles and the high country around Mt Buffalo (Victoria), Warrumbungle National Park (New South Wales), the Hazards (Tasmania) and Karijini National Park (Western Australia). The best places for caving in New Zealand are around Auckland, Wellington and Waitomo (which offers a spectacular 100m abseil into the Lost World cave).

New Zealand is crisscrossed with thousands of kilometres of marked tracks, many serviced by well-maintained huts. The South Island has wonderful walking trails through majestic national parks, including the Abel Tasman Coastal, Heaphy, Milford and Kepler Tracks. The North Island offers the Tongariro Northern Circuit and Whanganui Journey. The walking season follows the good weather from January to March, but tracks are useable any time from April to November. Mt Cook has New Zealand's most outstanding mountaineering and climbing areas; others are Mt Aspiring National Park, Lake Taupo and Fjordland.

Papua New Guinea also has a network of trails (including the infamous Kokoda Trail) that take several days to complete, but most of the Pacific islands are too small to offer really challenging walks.

Snowsports
From June to November, New Zealand boasts some of the best downhill skiing and snowboarding in the southern hemisphere, particularly on the South Island around Queenstown, Wanaka and Arthur's Pass. The North Island, while home to fewer slopes, does offer the chance to blaze down volcanoes – both Mt Ruapehu and Mt Taranaki are popular resorts. Australia has a brief season from mid-June to early September, but slopes are limited to the resorts of Thredbo and Perisher in New South Wales' Snowy Mountains and those of Falls Creek, Mt Hotham and Mt Buller in Victoria.

WILDLIFE
Outside Africa there are few places where the wildlife is as unique and as accessible as in Australasia. For instance, Australia's Kangaroo Island, more than a third of which is a national park, is crawling with wallabies, koalas, echidnas, bandicoots and, you guessed it, roos. Migrating whales pass Australia's southern shores between May and November. Popular whale-watching spots include Warrnambool (Victoria), Head of Bight (South Australia), Albany (Western Australia), and Hervey Bay and Fraser Island in Queensland. Dolphins are ubiquitous and can be seen year-round along the Australian

east coast (Jervis Bay, Port Stephens, Byron Bay) and Western Australia (Bunbury, Rockingham, Esperance, Monkey Mia).

Kaikoura on New Zealand's South Island is the centre for marine mammal watching, with dolphins and seals swimming year-round, while sperm whales are visible from October to August. Whakatane, Paihia and Tau are other good spots to see dolphins in New Zealand. Look out for kiwis, the cute flightless national bird, at sanctuaries and parks across the country.

FESTIVALS

There's no shortage of festivals, sporting events and general partying in Australasia. Here's just a sample of what you can get up to:

- **Festival of Sydney** (Australia; www.sydneyfestival.org.au) The metropolis' high-art showcase, with open-air concerts, street theatre and fireworks in January.
- **Bread & Circus** – World Buskers Festival (New Zealand; www.breadandcircus.co.nz) See the streets of Christchurch alive in January as international performers have their eyes on the trophy.
- **MONA FOMA** (Australia; www.mofo.net.au) In Hobart, this festival of music and art in January is as edgy, progressive and unexpected as the MONA museum itself.
- **Adelaide Fringe** (Australia; www.adelaidefringe.com.au) Hyperactive comedy, music and circus acts spill from the Garden of Unearthly Delights in the parklands. This month-long fringe in February/March is second only to Edinburgh's version.
- **Marlborough Wine Festival** (New Zealand; www.wine-marlborough-festival.co.nz) A chance to gobble great quantities of gourmet food and booze in mid-February in Blenheim.
- **Sydney Gay & Lesbian Mardi Gras** (Australia; www.mardigras.org.au) A two-week cultural and entertainment festival celebrating all things queer. It culminates in the world-famous massive parade and party on the first Saturday in March.
- **Perth Festival** (Australia; www.perthfestival.com.au) Held over 25 days in February/March, it spans theatre, classical music, jazz, visual arts, dance, film and literature.
- **Te Matatini National Kapa Haka Festival** (New Zealand; www.tematatini.co.nz) This engrossing Māori *haka* (war dance) competition happens in early March/late February in odd-numbered years.
- **Pasifika Festival** (New Zealand; www.aucklandnz.com/pasifika-festival) An explosion of Polynesian partying, from traditional dancing to hip-hop, on the streets of Auckland in March.
- **Naghol** (Vanuatu) From April to July, unbelievable 'land-diving' rituals take place to ensure a good yam harvest. Local men strap their ankles to vines and plummet from 30m towers – their heads must touch the ground!
- **Queenstown Winter Festival** (New Zealand; www.winterfestival.co.nz) This southern snow-fest is a four-day party in late June/early July, with fireworks, live music, comedy, a community carnival, and wacky ski and snowboard activities.
- **Heiva i Tahiti** (French Polynesia) Approaching its 140th year, this three-week festival in Pape'ete each July is worth travelling for – dancers and singers perform alongside parades and sports comps.
- **Henley-on-Todd Regatta** (Australia; www.henleyontodd.com.au) Alice Spring's unusual boat race 'run' on a dry river bed in August/September.
- **Brisbane Festival** (Australia; www.brisbanefestival.com.au) One of Australia's largest and most diverse arts festivals. It runs for 22 days in September and features an

impressive line-up of concerts, plays, dance performances and fringe events.

- **Rise of the Palolo** (Samoa & Fiji) In October and November, a week after the full moon, *palolo* (coral worms) rise from the reef at midnight and are promptly netted. Join in on the feast of the 'Pacific's caviar'.
- **Melbourne Festival** (Australia; www.melbournefestival.com.au) From early October to November, some of the best of opera, theatre, dance and visual arts from around Australia and the world are on show.
- **Hawaiki Nui Va'a** (French Polynesia; www.airtahitinui.com) Massive canoe race between the islands of Huahine, Rai'atea, Taha'a and Bora Bora in October/November.

Christian festivals are a big deal in the south Pacific, so if you're around for Christmas or Easter, prepare for much merriment.

NIGHTLIFE

There's no shortage of places for a night out in Australasia. Melbourne's drinking scene is easily the best in Australia and as good as any in the world. There's a huge diversity of venues, ranging from hip basement dives hidden down laneways to sophisticated cocktail bars perched on rooftops. Sydney has long had a pub culture, but a recent relaxation in NSW licensing laws has seen a blooming of numerous small wine bars and hole-in-the-wall cocktail lounges.

Auckland's Karangahape Rd (aka K Rd) and Ponsonby are the epicentres of nightlife on the weekends, but you can seek out a few other places in Britomart or the Viaduct. Live music has always been big in Wellington, and you can find no shortage of backpacker drinks specials in Rotorua, Taupo and Queenstown.

Nightlife in the Pacific is typically a relaxed affair, with a beer or cocktail to celebrate the setting sun.

Night falls over Sydney Harbour and its famous bridge

ROADS LESS TRAVELLED

Luckily, there's plenty of Australasia to go round so if you're looking to get away from it all, there's always somewhere. In Australia you can head over to Perth, the western capital that isn't visited because of its isolation. For accessible outback drives, head for Broken Hill – its streets are named after minerals and you'll find characters in every pub. Or make a beeline for Coober Pedy, South Australia's underground opal capital.

In New Zealand you can find plenty of space on the South Island, from the hippy hang-out of Golden Bay to the wildlife wonders of Otago Peninsula. There are even spectacular places that weren't used as sets for *Lord of the Rings*, including Doubtful Sound and the bird haven of Stewart Island.

Your best bet for escapes, though, is the Pacific islands; from far-flung Easter Island to the Cook Islands, there's a hidden paradise waiting to be discovered.

WORKING

Getting a job can be a great way to extend your stay. If you're lucky enough to get a working holiday visa, you can easily and legally find work in Australia and/or New Zealand. Many travellers use Australia and New Zealand as a place to work and jobs don't have to be a drudge – there are opportunities in ski resorts (you can sample the slopes on your day off) and in the outback on a cattle or sheep station as a jackeroo or jillaroo. In French Polynesia you could mix drinks poolside at a resort. You might not find a career, but the skills and experiences you'll acquire will be some of the best souvenirs.

Employment prospects in Australasia are usually good, with plenty of casual work on offer, including fruit picking and work in the hospitality industry. Hostels are often good places to start your job hunt, with many travellers finding other jobs on notice boards. If you have some basic computer skills, temping in office jobs is another option (see p129); several temp agencies find employment specifically for working-visa holders. While the working holiday visa prevents you from working in your professional field (though this is difficult to police), you can gain good career-building experience by volunteering.

Employment in the Pacific is trickier. You could try working in a resort – many recruit activities trainers and hospitality staff from Australia, New Zealand, the UK and the US.

WHEN TO GO?

When isn't a good time to go to Australasia? Southern Australia and New Zealand's South Island are not at their best in winter, but temperatures still compare very favourably with the UK or North America. Overall, spring (September to October) and autumn (April to May) are probably the best times to travel – the weather is reasonably mild everywhere and spring brings out the outback's wild flowers. Some parts of the outback will be extremely hot from November to February, so you may want to plan around these unbearable temperatures.

The wet seasons in far-northern Queensland, around Darwin (November to December and April to May) and Papua New Guinea (December to March) can make travel difficult, with dirt roads often closed in Papua New Guinea. Heading into the Pacific during shoulder seasons (October and May) will reward you with smaller crowds and lower prices. Christmas is difficult everywhere, with many expat islanders returning home – flights can be booked out months in advance.

WHAT TO EXPECT?

LOCALS & OTHER TRAVELLERS

If you're backpacking, you certainly won't be lonely in most parts of Australasia, as wandering Canadians, backpacking South Africans and working-holiday Brits have established a trail across the region.

Australians and New Zealanders are a diverse group, with backgrounds spanning much of the globe. Starting at home are Australia's Aboriginal peoples and Torres Strait Islanders, who number almost 700,000 – their culture is enduring throughout the country. In New Zealand, where Polynesian migration is common, the indigenous Māori population tops 600,000 and its beliefs and traditions remain accessible and engaging. The rest of Australians and New Zealanders are either descendants of early European arrivals, more

SAMPLE COSTS

	Australia (Australian dollar, A$)	New Zealand (New Zealand dollar, NZ$)	Fiji (Fijian dollar, F$)	Cook Islands (New Zealand dollar, NZ$)
Hostel: dorm bed	A$28-40	NZ$25-40 (A$22.50-36)	F$40-80 (with breakfast) (A$25-50)	NZ$25-35 (A$22.50-31.50)
Midrange hotel: double room	A$130-250	NZ$110-200 (A$99-180)	F$140-300 (A$90-195)	NZ$125-250 (A$112-225)
Street snack	Kebab A$8-10	Meat pie NZ$5-6 (A$4.50-5.40)	Samosa F$10-12 (A$6.50-7.75)	*Ika mata* NZ$8-10 (A$7.25-9)
Budget meal	A$12-20	NZ$12-25 (A$10.80-22.50)	F$15-20 (A$9.75-13)	NZ$10-15 (A$9-13.50)
Midrange restaurant: main	A$15-30	NZ$15-32 (A$13.50-29)	F$10-30 (A$6.50-19.50)	NZ$20-35 (A$18-31.50)
Cappuccino	$A3.50-5	NZ$4-5 (A$3.60-4.50)	F$6.50 (A$4.20)	NZ$2-2.50 (A$1.80-2.25)
1.5L Bottle of water	A$3-4	NZ$3.50-4.50 (A$3.15-4.05)	F$3.50 (A$2.25)	NZ$4.50 (A$4.05)
1L Petrol (gas)	A$1.45	NZ$2.10 (A$1.90)	F$2.08 (A$1.32)	NZ$2.26 (A$2.03)

recent immigrants from the Asia Pacific region or products of multicultural societies, with many citizens coming from Europe and the Middle East during the post-WWII wave of immigration. Australia and New Zealand have a sporting and cultural rivalry, but both are famously laid-back and share a mutual love of the beach and the outdoors.

Diversity is the only rule among Pacific islanders. Although Christianity was brought to many of the islands during the period of colonisation (and is still widely practiced in many areas), many islanders still embrace traditional beliefs and practices alongside their Christian faith. For instance, many visitors correctly sense that below the surface of the outwardly friendly and casual Samoan people lies a complex code of traditional etiquette. There, the demanding *Fa'a Samoa* (Samoan Way) is rigorously upheld.

Fresh seafood is in plentiful supply throughout Oceania

In Tonga, a largely homogenous, church- and family-oriented society, people are open and extremely hospitable, but due to cultural nuances visitors can often feel a bit at arm's length. In the Solomon Islands, islanders' obligations to their clan and village bigman (chief) are eternal and enduring. While in Fiji, its population of all backgrounds goes to great lengths to make you feel welcome. But not wishing to disappoint, a Fijian 'yes' might mean 'maybe' or 'no', which can be disconcerting if not confusing.

FOOD

An abundance of fresh seafood and produce means that Australasia can boast some truly spectacular eating. New Zealand is known for its organic produce and dairy goods, as well as some incredibly fine wines. Some visitors base itineraries around wine regions such as Marlborough, Hawkes Bay or the aptly named Bay of Plenty. Australia has good grapes in the Barossa, Clare, Yarra and Hunter Valleys (and beyond), and the country's reputation for beer is borne out by thirst-quenching ales from a multitude of world-class craft breweries.

Dining in Sydney and Melbourne serves up some of the world's best, with Greek, Vietnamese, Italian and Thai cuisine all filling plates. Auckland is similarly cosmopolitan, including the flavours of the Pacific, making it one of the best places to sample Polynesian food. Many of the Pacific islands are moving away from traditional foods as arable land disappears and globalisation sees the rise of tinned food. Still, you can find Māori *hāngi*, which is mutton, pork or lamb baked underground – ideally using volcanic heat!

LANGUAGE

English is spoken throughout Australasia, though sometimes with impenetrably thick accents. Both Australians and New Zealanders notoriously abbreviate many words, so you can expect to eat *brekky* (breakfast) after a night of slapping *mozzies* (mosquitoes) and downing *tinnies* (cans of beer). Fortunately, in both countries you can get out of most scrapes by calling someone '*mate*' (friend or buddy).

For insider's slang and indigenous languages, Lonely Planet's *Australian Language & Culture* guide should have you bunging another shrimp on the barbie in no time.

New Zealand has two official languages: English and Māori, which are both taught in schools, so even *Pakehas* (non-Māori New Zealanders) use a little Māori in their daily conversation. You'll probably only need English, though learning Māori will make your trip more interesting and you'll undoubtedly win bonus points with Kiwis you meet along the way.

The South Pacific has a fascinating mass of languages, but most islanders also speak either French or English. Unless you're having an extended stay, you probably won't need to learn any more of the Pacific languages than those covered in Lonely Planet's *South Pacific Phrasebook* (which also covers Māori).

URBAN MYTHS – DROP BEARS

There's nothing Australasians love more than to pull your leg, especially about the dangerous (and entirely made-up) predators of their countries. When the coals of a barbecue begin to fade, a crazed uncle will usually warn younger kids about the dangers of drop bears. The fictional beastie is (depending on the insanity of the storyteller) either a rare carnivorous koala, a genetically modified or nuclear-mutated marsupial or a very lost polar bear. Allegedly the drop bear will pounce from gumtrees that people camp under, though the danger of falling branches is the real threat. Drop bears make a cameo on *Family Guy*, when Peter is pounced on by one after he pokes a crocodile. Bunyips and yowies (southern hemisphere Bigfoot) are other Australian inventions used to scare tourists and explain bumps in the night.

COMMUNICATION

Broadband and Wi-Fi, pay-as-you-go mobile phones and cheap phonecards are widely available in Australia and New Zealand's bigger cities. Travellers with smartphones, tablets and laptops usually have no problems uploading photos and videos even in internet cafés.

Wi-Fi in South Pacific accommodation is commonplace these days, especially if you're paying for more than budget digs. You'll also

CORAL ISLAND CASTAWAY

Sitting under the whispering casuarina trees in the dunes above Shark Bay, I lingered after dusk. The noddies were there, as always, flying in close pairs as they skipped across the reef flat. Then other birds appeared amongst them, soaring and pirouetting through the smouldering embers of sunset. I felt my pulse quicken as first a dozen, then a hundred, then thousands of them gathered in the skies above Heron Island. After months of ocean wandering, the wedge-tailed shearwaters had converged en masse to breed on this speck of land. As darkness fell, the magic began: the nocturnal song of the shearwater – a crooning, wailing chorus – ebbing and flowing across the island. I walked slowly into the forest and crouched a few feet from a pair already consumed by courtship. They sat facing each other, preening, rattling bills and uttering that haunting song. The birds seemed oblivious to me. I spent the entire night watching them until, a couple of hours before dawn, they began to make their way towards the dunes. The whoops and yelps of their chorus reached a crescendo, and then they launched themselves off the dune crests. By sunrise, most had vanished.

The Take Away

On the night the shearwaters arrived, I had been living on Heron in Australia's Great Barrier Reef for over a month – a voluntary castaway, studying the island's wildlife. It evokes a time when my clock reset to simple cues like day, night, tide and rhythms of wildlife. It taught me to slow down, pause and look a little while longer.

William Gray – taken from Lonely Planet's *The Best Moment of Your Life*

find Wi-Fi hot spots in major tourist and urban centres, and busy internet cafes. Some of the more remote islands may not have any internet at all; others may surprise you with fast connections. In the Solomon Islands and Easter Island, however, connections are still slow.

HEALTH

Despite exaggerated reports of sharks, snakes, and other scary critters, Australia and New Zealand are generally very safe and free of health risks. A few cases of mosquito-borne diseases (such as dengue fever, Ross River fever, malaria and Murray Valley encephalitis) have been reported in northern Australia. You can get amoebic meningitis from bathing in New Zealand's geothermal pools, and a few unclean lakes and rivers have been known to transmit giardia. Parts of the Pacific are prone to mosquito-borne diseases, so check with a doctor for vaccinations beforehand and take precautions when visiting.

The weather poses the greatest risk to health in the region. The sun can be fierce, especially if you're not used to it, so heat exhaustion, dehydration and sunburn pose a constant threat. Most Aussies pack sunscreen and a bottle of water with them before facing summer days, and sun hats are compulsory. Skin cancer is an all-too-real threat, and you can burn in as little as six minutes in some places. In New Zealand, exposure and hypothermia are dangers for unprepared trekkers at high altitude.

For more travel-health information consult the Health & Safety chapter and seek professional medical advice.

ISSUES

Australasia remains a relatively safe destination. In Australia and New Zealand there are few health risks (and world-class medical facilities if something does happen) and serious crime is limited. If you're unlucky, the worst you'll encounter is a swiped purse in a market or a less-than-scrupulous hostel owner overcharging you.

In the Pacific there are some hot points to be aware of. Papua New Guinea has a notorious reputation, though the dangers are largely overhyped. Outside Port Moresby, Lae and Mt Hagen, things are much more relaxed. Tribal fighting is still an issue in Hela and the Southern Highlands but rarely involves outsiders or foreign travellers. In Timor-Leste foreigners have been imprisoned for carrying small amounts of drugs or being in vehicles with others carrying drugs, so be aware of what is legal as well as who you're travelling with. There are frequent reports of foreign women being sexually assaulted in Dili – this often happens during the day and in public areas so travel with others if possible.

On the health front, there is a risk of the zika virus in some areas of the Pacific, and there have been recent outbreaks of dengue fever. The latter is a virus spread by the bite of a day-biting mosquito. It causes a feverish illness with headache and severe muscle pains similar to those experienced with a bad, prolonged attack of flu. Another name for the disease is 'break-bone fever' and that's what it feels like. Danger signs include vomiting, blood in the vomit and a blotchy rash. There is no preventive vaccine, and mosquito bites should be avoided whenever possible. Medical facilities in the region are modest at best and limited in scope. On remote islands there may trained nurses only.

Up-to-date health warnings and advice can be found on government travel advisory services, such as that provided by the British Foreign & Commonwealth Office (see Is Your Destination Safe? on p40 for details).

GETTING THERE

AIR

Flying is definitely the most popular way into the region. With a round-the-world (RTW) ticket you can grab a couple of stopovers, particularly in the South Pacific, which is otherwise very costly to reach. Some basic return fares will offer stopovers in South America, the Middle East and, more commonly, Asia. More than one stopover is possible with some airlines, and some offer more open-jaw ticket options and general flexibility on this route than on others.

The main international hubs are Sydney, Melbourne, Perth and Auckland, though some airlines offer connections into Brisbane, Darwin, Wellington, Hobart, Cairns, Canberra and Adelaide. In the South Pacific, Nadi (Fiji), Pape'ete (French Polynesia) and Apia (Samoa) are regular stopovers for jets coming from the US (Air New Zealand flights from Los Angeles stop in a number of South Pacific islands), but many South Pacific destinations are serviced via Sydney or Auckland.

Most major airlines (Qantas, Etihad, Qatar, British Airways, Singapore Airlines, Cathay Pacific, Emirates, Malaysian Airlines, Royal Brunei, Korean Airlines, Thai Airways and Air New Zealand) fly into the area, but the region is opening up more with budget carriers Jetstar and Tiger Air. It's worth shopping around and even planning on buying a budget flight to Asia while you're in Australia or New Zealand.

SEA & OVERLAND

After a real challenge? Heading to Australasia by land should give you plenty of kicks. From Europe you'll pass through the Middle East and Southeast Asia on what was once called the 'hippie trail', partly because of the easy narcotics that were said to be available to travellers in the 1960s. There are no ferries linking Southeast Asia to Australia, so crewing a yacht or hitching a ride on a cargo boat are the only options.

Coming from the US can be a great tour through Pacific life as you island-hop your way from Hawaii or Easter Island. Boat transport between islands is often by small operators and can be difficult to coordinate, but relax and have another daiquiri and the boats will come.

SPECIALIST TOUR OPERATORS

- **AAT Kings** (www.aatkings.com) Run myriad guided tours that last up to 22 days, some of which are small group luxury tours. It covers Australia and New Zealand.
- **Adventure Tours Australia** (www.adventuretours.com.au) Two- to 24-day tours taking in Uluru, Alice Springs, Darwin and Kakadu in the Northern Territory, and Adelaide, Barossa Valley and Kangaroo Island in South Australia.
- **Nullarbor Traveller** (www.thetraveller.net.au) Small company running relaxed minibus trips across the Nullarbor Plain between South Australia and Western Australia.
- **Red Carpet Tours** (www.redcarpet-tours.com) New Zealand tours with a *Lord of the Rings/ Hobbit* focus ranging from six to 14 days around all of Middle Earth.
- **World Expeditions** (www.worldexpeditions.com.au) Operate small group tours across Australia, New Zealand and the South Pacific.

BEYOND AUSTRALIA, NEW ZEALAND & THE PACIFIC

Leaving already? Flights to Asia are particularly cheap with budget airlines, and flights to Africa, South America and North America from Australia and New Zealand are all reasonably priced. But check to see if it's cheaper to use a RTW ticket from your home country to travel on to these countries. You can also extend Pacific island-hopping from major destinations such as New Caledonia, Samoa and Fiji to Hawaii or Easter Island, which also make great gateways into North or South America. Again, a RTW ticket is handy for this, but you can organise individual hops.

With a one-way ticket to Australia you can go on some brilliant overland trips to get back home. You could head to Timor-Leste and fly to Indonesia (there are no ferries linking the two countries) to follow the old 'hippie trail'. Or head north to China and take the Trans-Mongolian railway from Beijing to Moscow. With a few stops in the Pacific, you can take a wandering route to North or South America.

FURTHER INFORMATION

WEBSITES

For the lowdown on specific countries, check out Destinations on Lonely Planet's website (lonelyplanet.com). These websites will help you with planning:

- **Australia Online** (www.australiaonline.com.au) Information on accommodation, tours and activities.
- **BUG** (www.bugpacific.com; www.bugaustralia.com) Two sites from backpacking pros that cover Australia, New Zealand and the Pacific.
- **Bureau of Meteorology** (www.bom.gov.au) Nationwide weather forecasts.
- **Department of Conservation** (www.doc.govt.nz) New Zealand Department of Conservation site with news and information about parks and conservation.
- **Destination New Zealand** (www.destination-nz.com) Event listings and info from NZ history to fashion.
- **Fiji Visitors Bureau** (www.fiji.travel) Fiji's official tourist site.
- **Go to New Zealand** (www.gotonewzealand.co.nz) Details on everything from studying in the country to internships, au pair work and immigration.
- **Imagina Isla de Pascua** (https://imaginaisladepascua.com/en/) Helpful Easter Island information, though we're told to take the historical accuracy of some sections with a grain of salt.
- **Pacific Regional Environment Programme** (www.sprep.org) Detailed information on environmental issues in the Pacific.
- **Parks Australia** (www.environment.gov.au/topics/national-parks) Australia's national parks and reserves.
- **Papua New Guinea Tourism Promotion Authority** (www.papuanewguinea.travel) Official website of PNG's peak tourism body. Has good links.
- **Solomon Islands Visitor Bureau** (www.visitsolomons.com.sb) Official tourism site with oodles of information about activities, accommodation and services.
- **South Pacific Islands Tourism Organisation** (www.spto.org) Useful directory with info on South Pacific countries.
- **Study in Australia** (www.studyinaustralia.gov.au) A government site with the lowdown on courses and universities.
- **Tahiti Tourisme** (www.tahiti-tourisme.com) Official tourism website.
- **Tahiti Traveler** (www.thetahititraveler.com) Range of info, from history to local sights.
- **Te Ara** (www.teara.govt.nz) Online encyclopedia of NZ.
- **Tourism Australia** (www.australia.com) Glossy main government tourism site with visitor info.
- **Tourism New Zealand** (www.newzealand.com) Comprehensive official tourism site.

BOOKS

- **Sean & David's Long Drive** Sean Condon's tale of two ill-equipped urban Australians faced with the vastness of their own country.
- **Crossing the Line** Kim McGrath explores Australia's involvement in the Timor Sea.
- **Down Under/In a Sunburnt Country** Bill Bryson, America's funniest traveller, hilariously carves up Australia.
- **Getting Stoned with Savages** J Maarten Troost's humorous South Pacific travelogue.
- **Kava in the Blood: A Personal & Political Memoir from the Heart of Fiji** Diplomat Peter Thomson's engaging memoir of Fiji's cultures and coups.
- **The Luminaries** Eleanor Catton's Man Booker Prize winner: crime and intrigue on New Zealand's West Coast goldfields.
- **The Narrow Road to the Deep North** Richard Flangan writes of the Hobart to the Thai-Burma Death Railway.
- **The Other Side of the Frontier** A fascinating and frightening Aboriginal view of Australia's colonisation by Henry Reynold.
- **The Wish Child** Catherine Chidgey's harrowing, heartbreaking WWII novel; NZ Book Awards winner.
- **Where We Once Belonged** A gripping account of a Samoan girl's rite of passage. By Sia Fiegel.
- **Tu** Written by Patricia Grace, it follows a Maori battalion in WWII.

FILMS

- **Mutiny on the Bounty** (1962) Trevor Howard played Bligh and Marlon Brando was Christian. Filmed on Tahiti and Bora Bora.
- **The Piano** (1993) A piano and its owners arrive on a mid-19th-century West Coast beach in New Zealand.
- **Cast Away** (2000) Tom Hanks is all washed up on a desert island. Shot in Fiji.
- **Whale Rider** (2002) A young girl asserts her identity among the male-dominated Maori.
- **The Disappearing Tuvalu** (2005) A documentary exploring the Pacific's inconvenient truth about rising water levels flooding islands.
- **Sione's Wedding** (2006) Four Samoans living in Auckland try to sort out their friend's hilariously messed-up wedding.
- **Ten Canoes** (2006) A stunning retelling of an Aboriginal legend in the remote Arnhem Land.
- **Australia** (2008) Director Baz Luhrmann's big-budget homecoming about the romance between a stockman and a female aristocrat.
- **Boy** (2010) Taika Waititi's bittersweet coming-of-age drama set in the Bay of Plenty, New Zealand.
- **Beatriz's War** (2013) A Timorese film following the life of a young resistance fighter whose husband mysteriously reappears 16 years after a massacre.
- **Tanna** (2015) Romeo and Juliet tale set on Tanna island, Vanuatu.

NORTHEAST ASIA

China is vast. Off-the-scale massive. With its riveting jumble of wildly differing dialects and climatic and topographical extremes, it's like several different countries rolled into one. Yet, it is but one piece of the fascinating Northeast Asia puzzle. There are of course the wonders of Japan, South Korea, Mongolia and more.

In China take your pick from the tossed-salad ethnic mix of the southwest, the yak-butter-illuminated temples of Xiàhé, a journey along the dusty Silk Road, spending the night at Everest Base Camp in Tibet or getting into your glad rags for a night on the Shànghǎi tiles.

You'll find that Japan is a truly timeless place where ancient traditions are fused with modern life as if it were the most natural thing in the world. Its cultural surprises run from anime to Zen, and you'll have the chance to bunk down on a tatami mat in a *ryokan* (traditional Japanese inn) or to go a night without sleep while at a karaoke bar in Toyko. There are also some incredible mountains for you to ski or board in perfect powder.

South Korea's snow season delights are no longer a secret after the successful 2018 Olympic Winter Games in PyeongChang, and the country's rich landscape and relics of its 5000 years of history and culture are easily explored on superb public transport. Ultra-modern and dynamic Seoul may have its fashion and technology on full display, but it's also deeply traditional, and manages to mash up palaces, temples, cutting-edge design and mountain trails, all to a nonstop K-Pop beat.

Rugged Mongolia is another kettle of fish, a place of pure adventure where travellers can experience nomadic culture and vast, untouched landscapes. Mongolians have been traversing their country on horseback for thousands of years. You should do the same. Or better yet, ride a two-humped camel into the Gobi Desert in search of dinosaur bone yards.

ITINERARIES

If you're serious about exploring the region, you'll definitely wander through China. Well-known gateways such as Hong Kong and Tokyo are getting strong competition from Běijīng, Shànghǎi and even Macau, as more tourists want to discover their own routes.

THE WHOLE SHEBANG

Here's a route that will give you a little of everything Northeast Asia has to offer, but hurry up as you can't stay anywhere too long! Kick off in **Tokyo**, drift south to check out traditional **Kyoto**. Now ferry from western **Honshu** to **Busan** in South Korea where there are enough palaces, temples and nightlife to keep you busy for a week. Call into **Seoul** to get a feel for the capital, then from Incheon ferry to **Tiānjīn**, an old town in China worth exploring for its antiques. From here slide over to **Běijīng** to wonder at the Forbidden City and see a section of the Great Wall. Wander over to **Xī'ān** to see the terracotta warriors before heading north to **Ulaanbaatar** for some horse trekking in Mongolia. Backtrack to **Běijīng** to fly out or onto **Shànghǎi**, the artsy, cosmopolitan second-largest city of China.

SWINGING IN THE SOUTH

Spend a few days shopping in **Hong Kong** before hopping over to casino capital **Macau.** With your winnings, hit the mainland in **Guǎngzhōu,** where you could spend a few nights in the city before heading on to **Guìlín** with its stark karst scenery. A boat trip around **Yángshuò** is the serenest way to view the limestone peaks from their best vantage points. You can check out two of the country's most spectacular natural features – **Huángguǒshù Falls** and **Zhījīn Cave** – in **Guìzhōu** or press on to **Kūnmíng** (where you can also branch south into Vietnam). From here stop in at **Lìjiāng,** a maze of cobbled streets and gushing canals that's one of the most visited spots in **Yúnnán.** Take time out for a few treks in the verdant **Xīshuāngbǎnnà** region before heading up to **Shànghǎi** for your last leg.

FROM BĚIJĪNG TO BUDDHA

Touch down in **Běijīng,** where you can soak up the atmosphere of China's capital. From here catch a train out to **Xī'ān** to meet the terracotta warriors before railing it south to **Chéngdū** for panda action. Next take the spectacular 43-hour train route to **Lhasa,** the centre of the Tibetan Buddhist world for over a millennium. From there you can venture overland across the Himalaya to **Kathmandu** in Nepal.

SEWING UP THE SILK ROAD

Follow the Silk Road from **Běijīng** by stopping in at **Xī'ān** to gawk at the terracotta warriors, then stop at the end-of-the-world fort at **Jiāyùguān** before calling in at the cave grottos of **Dūnhuáng.** Next stop is the Martian-like deserts of **Xīnjiāng.** Stop off at China's Death Valley, **Turpan** – at 154m below sea level, it's the world's third lowest depression. Take the train to medieval **Kashgar,** a Central Asian city of Turkic-speaking Uighurs that buzzes with the world's greatest bazaar. From here exciting options include heading over the **Irkeshtam** or **Torugart** mountain passes into Central Asia or down the **Karakoram Highway** to Pakistan.

WILD WILD EAST

From **Tokyo** start off with a few warm-up strolls, such as **Kamikōchi,** an excellent base for hikes up the 3180m **Yari-ga-take.** Now you're ready to take on China. Fly over to **Kūnmíng** and make for **Tiger Leaping Gorge,** one of the world's deepest gorges complete with dramatic cliffs and waterfalls. There are other hikes around **Yúnnán i**ncluding the spectacular rice terraces of **Yuányáng,** so take your time before heading west to Tibet, where the altitude change will mean you'll have to take it easy for a couple of days around **Lhasa** before a *kora* (pilgrimage circuit of a holy site) around **Drepung Monastery.** Not exhausted yet? Make the impressive four- to five-day hike from **Ganden Monastery** to **Samye Monastery** with the aid of some good guides. If you've still got some energy fly to **Xī'ān** and take on **Huá Shān,** one of five sacred Taoist mountains. From Huá Shān head to **Běijīng** for a lie-down.

WHAT TO DO?

HIGHLIGHTS

- Selecting the **Great Wall** (China) according to taste: perfectly chiselled, dilapidated, stripped of its bricks, overrun with saplings, coiling splendidly into the hills or returning to dust.
- Attempting a Tibetan *kora* (pilgrimage) around holy **Mt Kailash** (China), Asia's most sacred mountain that is worshipped by more than a billion Buddhists and Hindus.
- Riding the hair-raising Peak Tram above the financial heart of **Hong Kong** (China) for superlative views of the city and the

NORTHEAST ASIA

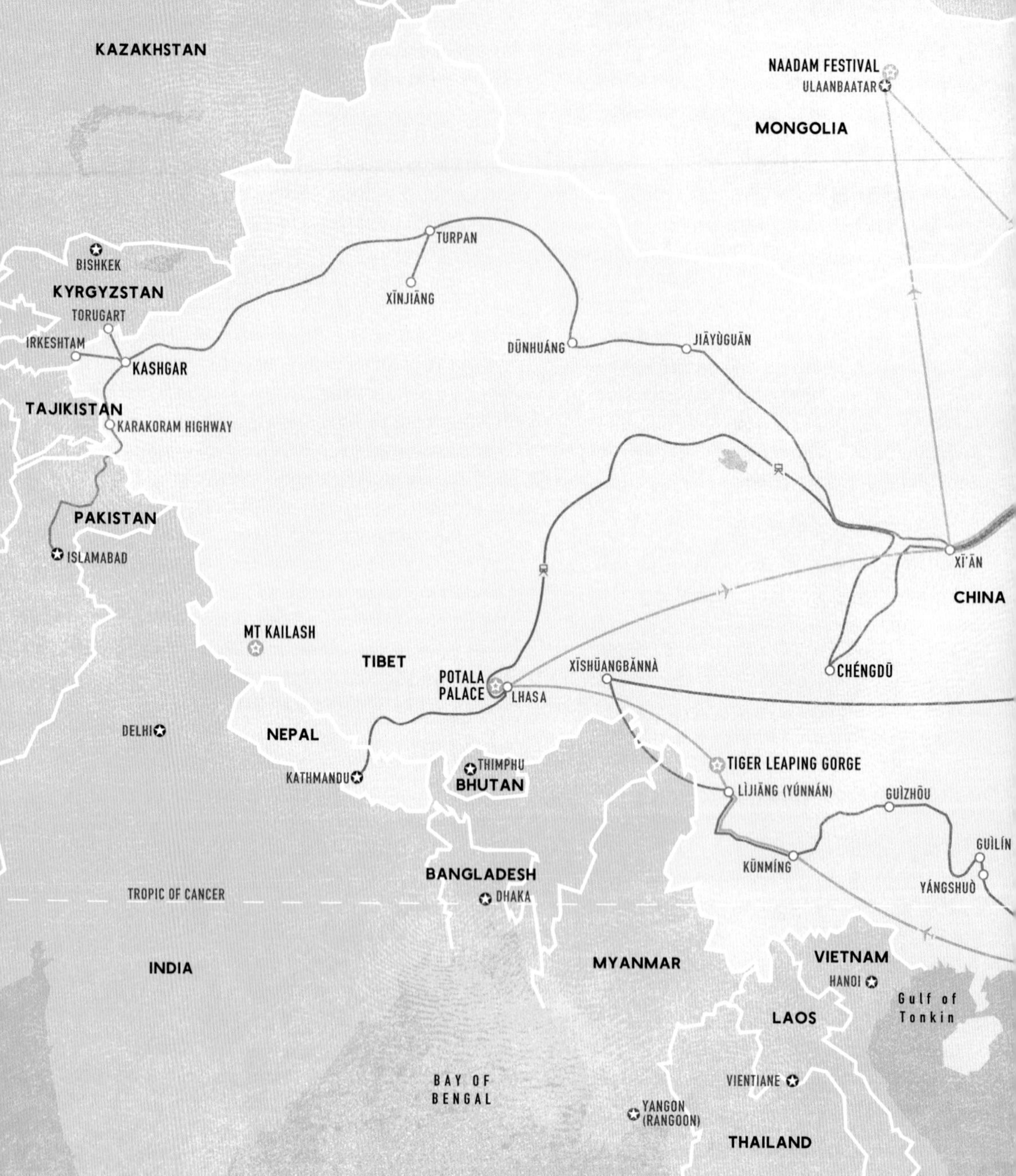

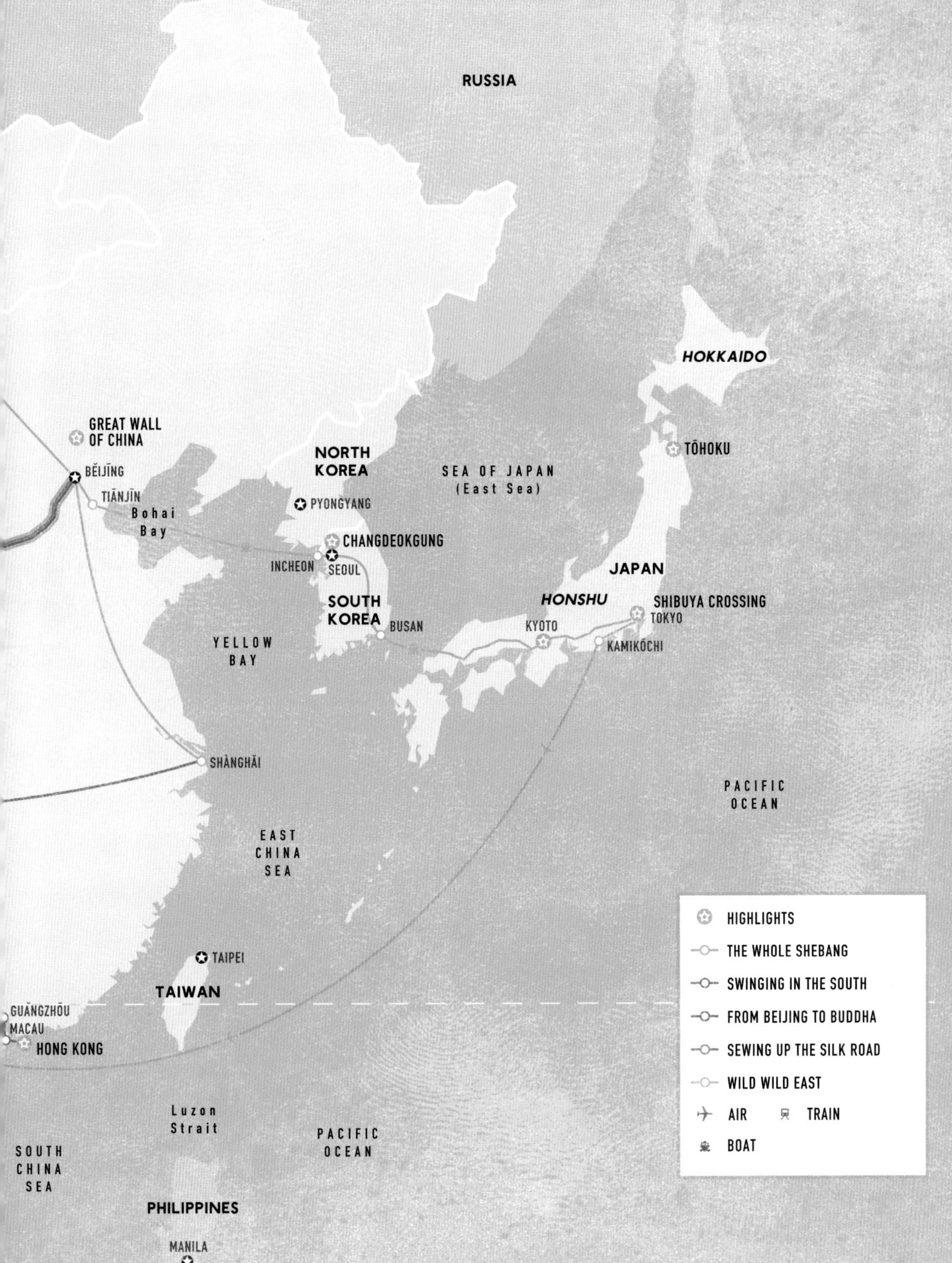

RUSSIA
HOKKAIDO
GREAT WALL
OF CHINA
NORTH
KOREA
TŌHOKU
BĚIJĪNG
SEA OF JAPAN
(East Sea)
TIĀNJĪN
PYONGYANG
Bohai
Bay
CHANGDEOKGUNG
INCHEON
SEOUL
JAPAN
HONSHU
SHIBUYA CROSSING
SOUTH
KOREA
TOKYO
BUSAN
KYOTO
YELLOW
BAY
KAMIKŌCHI
SHÀNGHĂI
PACIFIC
OCEAN
EAST
CHINA
SEA
HIGHLIGHTS
THE WHOLE SHEBANG
SWINGING IN THE SOUTH
FROM BEIJING TO BUDDHA
SEWING UP THE SILK ROAD
WILD WILD EAST
AIR
TRAIN
BOAT
TAIPEI
TAIWAN
GUĂNGZHŌU
MACAU
HONG KONG
Luzon
Strait
PACIFIC
OCEAN
SOUTH
CHINA
SEA
PHILIPPINES
MANILA

Drawing the bow during a traditional archery festival in Ulaanbaatar

The Great Wall of China meanders its way across the landscape

Potala Palace in Lhasa, Tibet, is the historical winter palace of the Dalai Lama and sits at an altitude of 3700m

mountainous countryside beyond.

- Visiting Lhasa's iconic **Potala Palace** (China), the former home of the Dalai Lamas, is a spiralling descent past gold-tombed chapels, opulent reception rooms and huge prayer halls into the bowels of a medieval castle.
- Bathing in volcanic bubbles at a traditional *onsen* (hot spring) in **Tōhoku** (Japan).
- Exploring some of the monumental temples in **Kyoto** (Japan), the imperial capital of Japan for a thousand years.
- Asserting your inner warrior with horse racing, wrestling or archery at **Naadam Festival** (Mongolia).
- Chasing **Tiger Leaping Gorge** (China) from the depths of the Jinsha River to the peaks of Haba Shan.
- Viewing the 'secret garden' of Huwon under moonlight within **Changdeokgung** (South Korea), the 'Palace of Illustrious Virtue'.
- Haggling yourself hoarse at **Kashgar** (China), a Central Asian city with the world's wildest market.

GET ACTIVE

Japan, South Korea, China and Mongolia love their outdoors, and there is certainly no shortage of activities available that allow you to embrace the wilderness.

Trekking & Mountaineering

Scaling sacred mountains provides both a spiritual and health high in Northeast Asia. The trek up Mt Fuji (3776m) is the must-do overnight pilgrimage. Treks up one of China's sacred mountains – Éméi Shān, Huángshān or Tài Shān – wind up thousands of stone steps to a network of Buddhist monasteries linked by mountain paths. With thousands of Chinese on the roads, you won't be a lonely pilgrim.

Elsewhere there's classic, accessible walking, particularly in the mountains of Japan, South Korea and Taiwan. Many routes have camp sites and mountain huts. You can also try these: Japanese Alps on Honshū and in the heart of Hokkaidō; Songnisan and Seoraksan National Parks in South Korea and Yangmingshan National Park in Taiwan.

The most exciting vertical terrain lies in the huge Himalayan peaks of western China and Tibet. The remote mountains of western Sìchuān offer challenging treks and horse treks, but lodges or trekking agencies are difficult to find. Other spectacular hikes include the alpine valleys of Jiǔzhàigōu (Sìchuān), Tiger Leaping Gorge and the jungles of Xīshuāngbǎnnà (both in Yúnnán).

Cycling & Mountain Biking

Biking is the way to explore China – it's environmentally sound and plenty of locals will pass you cheerfully chiming their bells. Hángzhōu has the world's largest bicycle-share network; however, its success (and foreigner-friendly ease of use) has only been fitfully replicated elsewhere in China. Generally, the best places to try are youth hostels, which rent out bicycles – as do many hotels. Cycling around the wondrous peaks of Yángshuò is one of China's real highlights, while the physically demanding run from Lhasa to Kathmandu is one of the world's great mountain biking routes.

The mountains of Japan, South Korea and Taiwan also offer numerous mountain bike trails. Japan's back roads, especially in the coastal regions, are particularly popular with cycling tourists.

Snowsports

South Korea's winter exploits were on display at PyeongChang in 2018, and there are more options than ever for snowsports. Japan has more than 300 resorts for skiing and boarding, most of which get some great powder from December to April. In Japan powder hounds head for Niseko, Shiga Kōgen or Nozawa Onsen (which offers skiing and some warming hot springs afterwards). Cross-country skiing is also very popular and often cheaper. Skiing in China hasn't been anything to write home about, but the facilities for (and the legacy from) the 2022 Olympic Winter Games may change the face of snowsports in the country.

Other Activities

There's good scuba diving around the Japanese islands of Okinawa and Yaeyama; Jejudo in South Korea (a volcanic island and home of female pearl divers); and Kenting and the Penghu Islands in Taiwan (the cheapest place to learn).

Saddle up for horse riding across the steppes of Mongolia, plus there are cheap multiday horse treks around Sōngpān (China). Camel rides are popular in inner Mongolia and the deserts around Dūnhuáng (China).

WILDLIFE

The animal celebrities of the region are definitely the pandas, who have turned China's Wòlóng Nature Reserve into their dressing room and stage. While receiving less press, the threatened snow leopard must be the most longed-for species in the region (if not the world) – it prowls parts of the Tibetan Plateau and Mongolia.

China's other wildlife is less spectacular, unless you're heading into the northwest to spot reindeer, moose or the rare Manchurian tiger. You'll be able to see the odd small mammal such as squirrels and badgers in wilderness areas, with monkeys very common – especially macaques who are known to intimidate hikers into handing over their picnics at Éméi Shān in China.

Sneaky macaques even found their way over to Japan, where they hang around areas such as Honshū, Shikoku and Kyūshū. You may even spot Japan's only carnivores – two species of bear, though hopefully not while camping. Korea's hikers have been known to spot the Siberian tiger, though it's more common to see chipmunks and squirrels.

FESTIVALS

The region's fascinating festivals are a varied and unusual mix:

- **Tsagaan Sar** (White Month; Mongolia) The Lunar New Year is celebrated with merriment at some point between late January and early March. It's a great time to meet Mongolians and, if you're lucky, get invited to a family celebration.
- **Chinese New Year** (China, Korea and Taiwan) Usually falling in January or February, this huge festival is the reason fireworks were invented, plus there's traditional culture and merriment.
- **Sapporo Snow Festival** (Japan; www.snowfes.com/english) Held in February. Expect ice sculptures and illumination of the park's winter landscapes.
- **Losar** (China) A colourful new-year festival. Tibetan opera is performed and the streets are thronged with Tibetans in their finest cloaks. It takes place during the first week of the first lunar month (February/March).
- **Water-Splashing Festival** (China) Held at Xīshuāngbǎnnà in Yúnnán around mid-April, this is a giant water fight in the name of washing away the dirt of the old year.
- **Sanja Matsuri** (Japan) The grandest Tokyo

festival of all, this three-day event, held over the third weekend of May, attracts around 1.5 million spectators to Asakusa. The highlight is the rowdy parade of mikoshi (portable shrines) carried by men and women in traditional dress.

- **Lotus Lantern Festival** (South Korea; www.llf.or.kr/eng) The weekend preceding Buddha's birthday, Seoul celebrates with a huge daytime street festival and evening lantern parade – the largest in South Korea.
- **Dragon Boat Festival** (Hong Kong) Thousands of the world's strongest dragonboaters meet in Hong Kong in June for three days of intense racing and partying at Victoria Harbour.
- **Naadam** (Mongolia) Showcases Mongolia's nomadic roots (horse racing, archery and wrestling) across the country on 11 and 12 July.
- **Gion Matsuri** (Japan) Commemorating a 9th-century request to the gods for an end to the plague sweeping Kyoto; an incredible parade of massive human-dragged floats on 17 July.
- **Boryeong Mud Festival** (South Korea; www.mudfestival.or.kr) Head to Daecheon Beach in July to wallow in mud pools and take part in stacks of muddy fun and games.
- **O-Bon** (Japan) The Buddhist Festival of the Dead taking place in July and August with dazzling lanterns hung everywhere.
- **Birthday of Confucius** (China) Celebrated on 28 September with a giant festival in Qufu (Shandong province), where the great sage was born and died.

NIGHTLIFE

Any Japanese city of reasonable size will have a *hankagai*, a lively commercial and entertainment district. Famous ones include: Tokyo's Kabukichō, Osaka's Dōtombori and Sapporo's Susukino. Such districts are stocked, often several storeys high, with a medley of drinking options that include *izakaya* (traditional

LIGHTENING THE LOAD

Bzzzzzd...

My heart pounds with the stroke of the blade.

Bzzzzzzd...

It's a sunny day in May and I can see the Himalayas towering in front of me.

Schwomp.

Brown locks pass through my fingers and onto the floor. I'm in a quaint Buddhist community, spending time to get to know 'the real me' and... apparently, to shave my head. Traveling solo throughout Asia has indeed become my medium of self-discovery.

It's amazing what a year-long journey after quitting your job can bring you. In my case, a complete and utter shedding.

To shave my head had been a secret desire for years, but it was always a wild wish, something I couldn't possibly do. Fear, a constant companion, had long inhibited risks and often actions – walking away from the life I knew inspired me to start standing up to them. With practice, it became easier to confront my other worries, like the judgment of others.

With each challenge, encounter and emotional bump in the road, I let go mentally and spiritually, trusting more in myself and the world. And now I'm letting go physically. This is the most powerful I have ever felt.

The Take Away

Traveling is empowering. It strengthens your courage muscle, while at the same time softening your ego. You learn to surrender to happenstance and learn from little moments of connection. When I began 'the shave' I was in sync with what my heart most desired from this journey – another layer of letting go.

Ashley Garver – taken from Lonely Planet's *The Best Moment of Your Life*

pubs), cocktail bars, Western-style pubs, jazz cafes, karaoke parlours, nightclubs and more – all awash in the neon lights that form Japan's urban signature.

In China, there are plenty of bars in larger cities. Chinese drink more than any other Asian country (or even Britain), though most of it is done at meals and is an important part of many business deals. Beer and the face-numbingly strong *báijiǔ* (a white spirit) are the most common tipples. Whiskey, red wine and cocktails are status symbols; microbreweries are on the rise. Běijīng and Shànghǎi have the most club options, with home-grown electronic music on the rise.

Koreans also know how to drink. Most restaurants are social affairs, with many doubling as bars as a night's drinking of beer, *soju* (local vodka), *makgeolli* (fermented rice wine) or whiskey-by-the-bottle progresses.

© Matt Munro / Lonely Planet

All is serene in Kabira Bay among the islands of Okinawa, Japan

Seoul has world-class club nights.

ROADS LESS TRAVELLED

To escape the throngs, seek out the pockets of China where there are fewer tourists, such as traditional villages including Chuāndǐxià just outside Běijīng, or head for Ānhuī province which has several tranquil spots including Hóngcūn and Xīdì – even quieter are the villages of Nánpíng, Guānlù, Bìshān and Yúliáng. Countries off the backpacker trail, such as Taiwan and South Korea, are good places to score some tranquillity.

WORKING

Go east! China's economic growth has brought with it more opportunities in all fields, though teaching English is a great option. You'll need a working visa and some Mandarin would be useful, though you can also improve your chances by studying a TEFL/TESOL course. Start your job search at **ChinaJob.com** (www.chinajob.com). For English-teaching jobs, try **Dave's ESL Cafe** (http://eslcafe.com). Japan is also looking for English-language teachers, and having a university degree will get you ahead of the crowd. It can be expensive to set up in Japan, but once you're earning yen it can be reasonably affordable. The Japan Exchange and Teaching Programme (JET, see p120) is a good place to start. Besides freelancing, bartending, hostessing and even modelling are all possibilities in Japan, Korea and Taiwan. Taiwan offers several good language opportunities, which you can start to explore at **English in Taiwan** (www.englishintaiwan.com).

WHEN TO GO?

Stretching from sub-Siberian Mongolia down past the Tropic of Cancer, Northeast Asia straddles varied climates, though you'll find more extreme weather in the north and south. The northern hemisphere enjoys summer from June to September, though the humidity can be unpleasant in high summer. That's also when Japan, southeast China and South Korea are hit by the odd typhoon. Taking on the Silk Road during the sizzling temperatures of August is really only for heat freaks.

Spring and autumn (when the foliage is spectacular and skies are clear) are the best times to travel in China, though you have to be prepared for any weather at this time. In Mongolia and north of the Great Wall of China it gets incredibly cold in winter, while the central Yangzi River valley experiences fiercely hot temperatures during long, hot summers – the only time it's unlikely to rain in central China. Summer is also the best time to visit Tibet, the mountains of western Sìchuān and Mongolia, though the days can be hot in the Gobi Desert. South China is sweet year-round, though some travellers opt for winter because temperatures are cool but not prohibitively cold and the crowds of tourists are absent.

Japan has the most diverse climate in the region (thanks to the length of the archipelago and high mountains down its spine), which means it can be snowing in northern Hokkaidō and positively balmy in southern, subtropical Okinawa. Western Japan receives a large amount of precipitation in winter, while the Pacific side is cold but less snowy. If you're travelling in summer or winter, try to focus on coastal and southern areas, which are more temperate than inland.

WHAT TO EXPECT?

LOCALS & OTHER TRAVELLERS

Within each nation the peoples are diverse, with complex etiquette and religious beliefs. While greeting is handled differently in most places, handshakes are generally best – never go for cheek kissing or hugging, which is considered alarming in places such as Japan and China. Hand shaking is also the quick method of apology in Mongolia if you accidentally touch shoes with someone else. Some travellers struggle with what they perceive as a lack of directness, or that people often tell them what they think they want to hear. Others, particularly in China, find the lack of warmth (and absence of smiles) from locals hard to deal with, but in China these acts are more reserved for family and it shouldn't be construed as rudeness. As China was closed to foreigners until the late 1970s, many older people have a curious or suspicious attitude to travellers, especially in remote areas. You may here yourself being called *lǎowài*, which means 'outsider' or 'foreigner'.

Another key they to keep in mind while travelling across the region is to avoid making someone feel like they are losing face by forcing them to back down in front of others. Be patient, be kind and forgiving. Lastly, a smile always goes a long way to diffusing any awkward situation or cultural gaffe.

Even when travelling in China – a country of 1.4 billion people – you'll not be alone.

China's blisteringly hot economy between 1990 and 2010 brought tens of thousands of Westerners to the country, with large expat communities forming in Guǎngzhōu, Shànghǎi and Běijīng. The business hub of Hong Kong, a British Colony until 1997, has long had a sizeable population of expats – some 60,000 Americans and 30,000 Britons now call it home. Outside of these cities, the backpacker hubs of China's south around Yángshuò and in Yúnnán, and popular tourist areas such as Xī'ān and Chéngdū (pandas), you may still be a novelty.

Travellers are much more common in Japan,

South Korea and Taiwan, where locals are used to seeing tourists. Seoul and Tokyo have large English-speaking expat communities.

FOOD

If you're used to Chinese takeaways or sushi at home, then Northeast Asia will blow your taste buds away. The fiery flavours of China's Sìchuān cuisine leave many grabbing for a jug of water, Peking duck is justifiably famous but the authentic wood-fired flavour only tastes this good in Běijīng, and Hong Kong's celebrated dim sum or *yum cha* (Chinese snacks taken with tea) just keep coming on trolleys heavy with goodies you'd never see in Chinatown back home.

Japanese restaurants often specialise in one dish, so you'll be able to discover your favourite *yakitori* (skewers of grilled meat and vegetables) or *sushi-ya* (top-shelf tuna or squid sushi). Korean cuisine is all about seafood and pickled vegetables. The kapow of *kimchi* (pickled cabbage) is a flavour you won't forget in a hurry.

LANGUAGE

You can get by with English in major areas of Japan, South Korea, Taiwan and Hong Kong, but in mainland China it's mostly a language for students and businesspeople. China is a tongue-tangling mix of languages and dialects. Mandarin (Putonghua) is the official language, though Cantonese is dominant in the south and in Hong Kong. Then there are at least half a dozen other Chinese languages, as well as minority languages, ranging from Turkic to Thai. Are you confused yet?

Much like after the World Cup in Japan and South Korea, there has been an ever increasing number of signs with English letters accompanying local script in China post-Běijīng Olympics, but you'll definitely need to understand a few characters in Mandarin to get around. Many travellers take a course before they go or have an audio lesson on their iPhone, but look for courses that include a written booklet as well. Local script is included in Lonely Planet guidebooks to the region.

By contrast, the Japanese and Korean languages are fairly uniform across their respective countries, with only a few obscure dialects in rural areas. Korea has adopted a new method of Romanising the Korean language and introduced a few new spellings. You may see some old spellings knocking around.

COMMUNICATION

Unless you're in Mongolia or rural China, you're likely to get good mobile-phone coverage, internet access and Wi-Fi.

HEALTH

China is a reasonably healthy country to travel in, but becoming ill in some way is not unusual. Outside of the major cities, medical care is often inadequate, and food and waterborne diseases are common. Malaria is still present in some parts of the country; altitude sickness can be a problem, particularly in Tibet.

Mongolia's dry, cold climate and sparse human habitation means there are few of the infectious diseases that plague tropical countries in Asia. Health care is readily available in Ulaanbaatar, with private hospitals and modern facilities (though check with your embassy about which are most recommended). Health services in the countryside are generally poor but are improving.

Japan and Korea enjoy a high level of medical services, though unfortunately most hospitals and clinics do not have doctors and nurses who speak English (university hospitals are your

THE LONE LASS IN CHINA: 10 FACTS

• **She is a rock star.** Self-conscious? You're out of luck. In China, you will be photographed, sketched, and sniffed at by children. If the attention gets old, simply imagine that you're a celebrity. A rock star. And you're simply huge in China.

• **She can skip the gym for a while.** Because a few weeks of squatting over hole-in-the-floor toilets will give you the thighs of a James Bond vixen. Just remember: a successful vixen always carries her own toilet paper.

• **She only thought she was jaded.** Even everyday life in China is foreign enough to fascinate: pharmacy employees starting their day with a dance; t'ai chi with swords and fans; that lane-by-lane dance you do to cross the enormous road; 'Edelweiss' in Chinese; wrigglies on sticks...

• **She's grateful that she packed some good novels.** Because the bookshops in Chinese airports are all business, featuring such titles as *Forty-Nine Habits Related to Success and Failure*, *Do Business So Simple*, and the enchantingly cryptic *Things That Build Up the Relation and Do Correctly*.

• **She is at peace with the background music.** Copious, lusty, soulful spitting abounds; embrace cultural difference and get used to it. The ubiquitous guttural '*chhh*' and the heartfelt '*ptoo!*' that follows it... Really, it's no worse than blowing your nose. Just don't look too closely.

• **She can enjoy interplanetary travel without leaving Earth.** Shànghǎi is Jupiter and Saturn and the setting of every science-fiction story ever written – all cones and improbable spheres, extreme planes and swooping roofs. It's the 24th century as imagined by the 12th – baffling, strange and very beautiful.

• **She enjoys a good foot rub.** Also blissful ignorance. If there's a red light outside the foot-massage place, do know that feet are not the only body parts massaged there. Though truth be told, one might not realise this until much later, long after one has received a rather decent and well-priced foot rub.

• **She writes left-handed and amazes many.** Chinese children are made to write with their right hand in school, so if you're a lefty, you qualify as a sort of medical oddity; folks will gather round, enthralled. Just smile, keep writing and imagine yourself all doll-like and inscrutable.

• **She knows when to proffer an orange.** Carry snacks to share with the locals who will offer you food, hand you their babies (but beware those bare bottoms!), and approach you with awkward but genuine curiosity. Enjoy these encounters; all you need is an open mind...and a bag of oranges.

• **She makes a little Mandarin go a very long way.** *Mei guanxi* means 'no problem, it doesn't matter, no worries' and it's not a bad mantra for your trip. Taxi driver lost? Camera stolen? Charged three times as much as the locals? *Mei guanxi.* Eventually, you'll even begin to believe it!

Pirate_Jenny, Traveller

A view of Tokyo station at twilight

best bet in this regard). Larger cities, especially Tokyo and Seoul, are likely to have clinics that have doctors who speak English (but they will be pricey). In Hong Kong and Taiwan, finding English-speaking doctors is less of an issue.

Dengue fever and Japanese encephalitis occasionally occur in Taiwan and are present in rural China, which is also a huge reservoir of hepatitis B and various forms of flu. Schistosomiasis (bilharziasis) and typhoid are present in the central Yangzi River basin.

You may have the odd out-of-stomach experience when trying new food in China and Mongolia, though travellers rarely have problems in Japan or Korea. Consult the Health & Safety chapter and seek professional medical advice for more travel-health information.

ISSUES

Independent travel is forbidden in Tibet, so you'll need to organise your travel through a tour company. It should be able to organise the needed Tibet Tourism Bureau (TTB) permit and the paperwork required for travel beyond Lhasa (up to 14 days is required to obtain the TTB permit). A hard-to-get Chinese visa is also required prior to departure.

China's economic progress has come at considerable cost, with pollution of air and water at levels that can cause discomfort for some travellers. The World Health Organisation (WHO) ranks six of China's cities within the world's 30 most polluted (only India fares worse).

GETTING THERE

AIR

Most big airlines offer direct flights into Northeast Asian hubs, including Běijīng, Shànghǎi, Hong Kong, Seoul, Taipei, Tokyo and Osaka.

Major local players include:

- **Air China** (www.airchina.com)
- **ANA** (www.ana.co.jp/en)
- **Asiana Airlines** (https://flyasiana.com)
- **China Airlines** (www.china-airlines.com)
- **China Eastern** (http://ph.ceair.com/en)
- **China Southern** (http://www.csair.com/en)
- **Cathay Pacific** (www.cathaypacific.com)
- **Hainan Airlines** (www.hainanairlines.com)
- **Japan Airlines** (JAL; www.jal.com)
- **EVA Air** (www.evaair.com)
- **Korean Air** (www.koreanair.com)
- **Malaysia Airlines** (www.malaysiaairlines.com)
- **Singapore Airlines** (www.singaporeair.com)
- **Thai Airways International** (www.thaiairways.com)

These budget carriers might be an option:

- **Air Asia** (www.airasia.com)
- **Ch.Com – Spring Airlines** (https://en.ch.com)
- **Eastar Jet** (www.eastarjet.com)
- **Hong Kong Express Airways** (www.hkexpress.com)
- **JEJU Air** (www.jejuair.net)

SAMPLE COSTS

	China (yuán, ¥)	Hong Kong (Hong Kong dollar, HK$)	Japan (yen, ¥)	South Korea (Korean won, ₩)
Hostel: dorm bed	¥40–60 (US$5.85-8.75)	HK$180–500 (US$23-64)	¥3000 (US$27)	₩20,000 (US$18)
Midrange hotel: double room	¥200–600 (US$29-87)	HK$900–1900 (US$115-242)	¥6000-25,000 (US$55-225)	₩40,000-250,000 (US$36-220)
Street snack	*Jiānbing* ¥5-7 (US$0.75-1)	Bowl of wontons HK$30-60 (US$3.75-7.50)	*Onigiri* ¥200-600 (US$1.80-5.50)	*Haemul pajeon* ₩6000 (US$5)
Budget meal	¥10-60 (US$1.50-8.75)	HK$60-150 (US$7.50-19)	¥800-1000 (US$7.25-9)	₩7000-10,000 (US$6-9)
Midrange restaurant: main	¥40-160 (US$5.85-23.40)	HK$100-250 (US$12.75-32)	¥1000-5000 (US$9-45)	₩12,000–25,000 (US$10.50-22)
Cappuccino	¥20-35 (US$2.90-5.10)	HK$30-40 (US$3.75-5)	¥300-500 (US$2.75-4.50)	₩4000–5500 (US$3.50-5)
1.5L Bottle of water	¥4-8 (US$0.60-1.20)	HK$15-25 (US$1.90-3.20)	¥150-250 (US$1.35-2.25)	₩1500–2250 (US$1.35-2)
1L Petrol (gas)	¥7 (US$1.02)	HK$15.50 (US$1.97)	¥140 (US$1.26)	₩1600 (US$1.42)

- **Jetstar** (www.jetstar.com)
- **Jin Air** (www.jinair.com)
- **Peach** (www.flypeach.com/pc/en)
- **Scoot** (www.flyscoot.com)
- **Skymark Airlines** (www.skymark.co.jp/en)
- **Solaseed Air** (http://www.solaseedair.jp/eng)
- **Star Flyer** (www.starflyer.jp/en)
- **Vanilla Air** (www.vanilla-air.com/en)

It's no problem getting open-jaw tickets into the region, plus Běijīng, Hong Kong and Tokyo crop up on most RTW tickets. Stopovers to the latter two, plus Osaka and occasionally Seoul, are possible on some tickets into Sydney (Australia) with carriers such as Japan Airlines and Korea Air.

Northeast Asian routes are highly competitive and there's usually a wide choice of fares. British Airways, Air China, Cathay Pacific, Gulf Air, Emirates and Air Astana often turn out cheap deals.

SEA & OVERLAND

Although there's plenty of sea transport between the countries in Northeast Asia, there are only three sea links out of the region, namely the ferries from Vladivostok (the terminus of the Trans-Siberian railway) to Fushiki in Japan and Sokcho in South Korea, or the much shorter run from Korsakov (Sakhalin Island, Russia) to Wakkanai (Hokkaidō, Japan).

You can cross overland from China to Vietnam, Laos, Nepal, Pakistan, Kyrgyzstan, Kazakhstan and Mongolia. Train routes lead in from Mongolia, Kazakhstan and Vietnam. There are some fantastically scenic high road passes to Pakistan and Kyrgyzstan in the far west. You're not able cross into Afghanistan, Bhutan or India by land.

SPECIALIST TOUR OPERATORS

- **Khampa Caravan** (www.khampacaravan.com) Runs overland trips from Yúnnán to places including Tibet. The company emphasises sustainable tourism and supporting local communities.
- **Koryo Group** (www.koryogroup.com) North Korea and Mongolia specialists.
- **Nomadic Expeditions** (www.nomadicexpeditions.com) Mongolia specialists offering palaeontology trips, camel trekking and more. Known for its sustainable practices, it also has an office in Ulaanbaatar.
- **Panoramic Journeys** (www.panoramicjourneys.com) UK-based specialist in Mongolia. Tailor-made and standard tours to off-the-beaten-path destinations. Excellent sustainable development philosophy.
- **Wild China** (www.wildchina.com) Professionally-run adventurous trips to China's most interesting regions.

BEYOND NORTHEAST ASIA

The Far East is much easier to get to nowadays than when Marco Polo dragged himself over from Europe. Flights out of the region's hubs can take you anywhere in the world reasonably cheaply. Heading overland on the Trans-Mongolian or Trans-Siberian railways will take you on one of the world's great train journeys.

Then there's the mind-blowing possibility of crossing into Nepal from Tibet and following the old overland 'hippie trail' from Kathmandu back through Iran and the Middle East. Travellers are also hopping across the border into Vietnam, Laos or Myanmar and heading on to Australasia. Circle Pacific airfares (see p91) will let you explore the great ocean's islands and it won't cost the earth.

FURTHER INFORMATION

WEBSITES

- **Chinasmack** (www.chinasmack.com) Human-interest stories and videos of China.
- **Discover Hong Kong** (www.discoverhongkong.com) Hong Kong's tourist association website.
- **Everyday Korea** (www.everydaykorea.com) Info on a whole range of Korean topics.
- **Far West China** (www.farwestchina.com) Indispensable resource for Silk Roaders.
- **Gaijin Pot** (www.gaijinpot.com) Jobs in Japan and general travel tips.
- **HyperDia** (www.hyperdia.com) Comprehensive train schedules and fares.
- **Japan National Tourism Organization** (www.jnto.go.jp) Official tourist site with planning tools and events calendar.
- **Korea Tourism Organization** (english.visitkorea.or.kr) Stacks of Korean travel information and links.
- **Life in Korea** (www.lifeinkorea.com) A busy but brilliant guide to living and travelling in Korea.
- **Outdoor Japan** (www.outdoorjapan.com) An

overview of outdoor activities in Japan.

- **Popupchinese** (www.popupchinese.com) Excellent podcasts (great for learning Chinese).
- **Tokyo Cheapo** (https://tokyocheapo.com) Budget saving tips for Tokyo and travel in Japan.

BOOKS

- **A Geek in Korea** Fully illustrated, Daniel Tudor's book ranges from religion and traditional martial arts to K-Pop, Samsung and the hallyu pop-culture wave.
- **Country Driving: A Chinese Road Trip** Peter Hessler's amusing and insightful journey at the wheel around the highways and byways of China.
- **Ghengis Khan and the Making of the Modern World** Jack Weatherford's groundbreaking book on the Mongol empire.
- **Memoirs of a Geisha** Arthur Golden's modern classic that looks into the life of one of Japan's oddest professions.
- **Mörön to Mörön** Tom Doig writes about the wacky adventures of two Aussies making their way across Mongolia on pushbikes.
- **Riding the Iron Rooster** Travel veteran Paul Theroux rides China's trains to meet its characters and conductors.
- **Sky Shamans of Mongolia** Kevin Turner's eye-opening and well-researched account by a practising shaman describing his encounters with a Mongolian counterpart.
- **The Book of Tokyo: A City in Short Fiction** Edited by Michael Emmerich, Jim Hinks and Masashi Matsuie, it features 10 stories by contemporary Japanese writers set in the capital.
- **The Secret Lives of the Dalai Lama** Alexander Norman's engaging overview of Tibetan history, full of unexpectedly juicy detail.
- **Trespassers on the Roof of the World** Peter Hopkirk recreates European explorers' early attempts to enter forbidden Tibet.

FILMS

- **Eat Drink Man Woman** (1994) Taiwanese-born Ang Lee's early drama is a must-see for those interested in Taiwanese culture.
- **Kundun** (1997) Martin Scorsese's beautifully shot depiction of the life of the Dalai Lama.
- **Crouching Tiger, Hidden Dragon** (2000) Multi-award winning film set in 18th century Qing Dynasty China.
- **Hero** (2002) A blockbuster where a single man takes on three assassins who are scheming to kill one of China's greatest warlords.
- **Lost in Translation** (2003) Two Americans find themselves isolated in contemporary Tokyo and form a possibly creepy bond.
- **Kung Fu Hustle** (2004) A beat-'em-up parody of martial-arts movies set in the gangster world of 1930s Shànghǎi.
- **Lust, Caution** (2007) Director Ang Lee tells an espionage tale set in WWII Shànghǎi.
- **47 Ronin** (2013) Based in historical truth, this is the story of a band of samurai who seek revenge on a ruthless shogun for the death and dishonour of their master.

Songzanlin Temple in Zhongdian city, Yunnan province, China

© saiko3p / Shutterstock

A traditional Chinese junk in Victoria Harbour provides sightseers with a different perspective of Hong Kong's tremendous cityscape

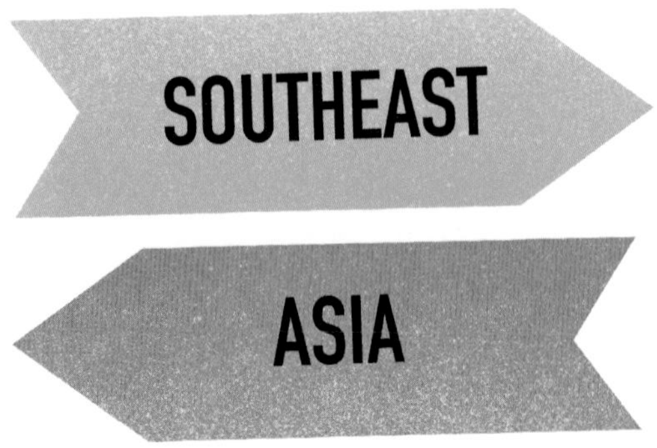

SOUTHEAST ASIA

Ringing rickshaw bells, chanting monks, cheap T-shirts and streetside coconut curries – Southeast Asia's urban realm can be a jumble of convenience and inefficiency, spirituality, consumerism and unforgettable cuisine. Megacities such as Thailand's Bangkok and Malaysia's Kuala Lumpur exist alongside the postcolonial capitals of Vientiane (Laos), Hanoi (Vietnam) and Phnom Penh (Cambodia).

Yet most visitors to Southeast Asia come for the wow-worthy beaches and a shot of exotic culture. There is certainly no shortage of either. Wildlife and history also have their pull, with jungle safaris and thousands of ancient temples such as Angkor Wat (Cambodia) or Borobudur (Indonesia).

While there are loads of other travellers, you don't have to travel far to find 'undiscovered' Southeast Asia. The beaten path isn't very wide. Within the confines of even the most touristy towns are streets where only the locals go.

Wherever you decide to travel, you will join an illustrious list of Southeast Asian pilgrims, ranging from Indian merchants to Chinese mandarins, and European colonisers to modern globetrotters.

ITINERARIES

Most trips start from Bangkok, because the metropolis is central and usually has cheap inbound flights, but you can customise these trips to your own plans. Spend a few more days on the beach, go wild in the club scene or take a few extra days for a riverboat cruise – the choice is yours.

BEACH BUMMING

Get to **Bangkok**. Enjoy the temples, cuisine, floating market and river taxis, then head south to do some beach bumming in the **Gulf of Thailand**. From the mainland town of **Surat Thani** you can choose between boats to resorty **Ko Samui**, hammock-friendly **Ko Pha-Ngan** or dive-paradise **Ko Tao**. After you've had your fill, step over to the Andaman beaches in upscale **Phuket**, where there's the rock-climbing haven **Krabi** and navel-gazing retreat **Ko Lanta**. If you're after a secluded spot, try **Ko Tarutao National Marine Park**.

When you're done with Thailand, traverse the border into Malaysia at **Satun** and beeline for family-friendly **Pulau Langkawi** or continue by boat to **Georgetown**, a spicy port city. Bus from **Butterworth** to **Kota Bharu**, the gateway to the jungle islands of **Pulau Perhentian**. Chase the coastline south to **Mersing** and pop into beach villages such as those on **Pulau Tioman** before taking a sand-shaking shower and hitting the town in **Singapore**. Next fly to Bali. **Kuta** is the sun-worshipping temple of the backpacker trail, while **Nusa Lembongan** is perfect for surfers. Those with more sybaritic desires can settle into **Seminyak**. Next are the quiet sands of **Lombok**, then ferry to **Gili Islands** for snorkelling among the brilliant reefs or catch the curl with surfing **Sumbawa**. Head back to **Jakarta** before you get sunstroke and fly out.

SOUTHEAST ASIA'S GREATEST HITS

Fly from **Bangkok** over to **Siem Reap** for a spin of Angkor's top temples. Take the bus or riverboat south to **Phnom Penh**, the colonial capital that still has a faded charm. Then journey east to **Ho Chi Minh City**, Vietnam at its most dizzying, where high-octane commerce and culture mix with pulsating energy. Navigate your way north to the leafy boulevards and lakes of **Hanoi** before skipping the tracks over to **Luang Prabang**, Laos' temple epicentre. Fast-forward to **Chiang Mai** in Thailand, a cool pocket in the tropics, where you can hit pause for a while before heading back to **Bangkok**. From here you can choose the Myanmar playlist: the ruins of **Bagan**, the floating gardens and island monasteries of **Inle Lake**, and mysterious **Mandalay**; or fly straight to **Kuala Lumpur** (Malaysia).

Malaysia is at your fingertips, so decide if you'd like to take a bus to the hill station of Tanah Rata in the **Cameron Highlands** or head further on to the historic port of **Melaka** then on to **Jerantut**, where long-tail boats dip into the rainforests of **Taman Negara**. Rewind to **Kuala Lumpur** and fly on to **Borneo** through **Bandar Seri Begawan**, Brunei's capital, or skip to up-tempo **Singapore** which pulses to Indian, Malay and Chinese beats. Tune into Javanese heritage in **Yogyakarta** and go slack-jawed at **Borobudur**, the giant stupa that tops travellers' must-see charts. Next it's **Gunung Bromo**, an active volcano, before jetting to **Denpasar** to chill out in **Bali** or soak up the sun in **Kuta**. Mix it up with Balinese culture in **Ubud**. Head back to Denpasar then fly to the stunning landscape of **Flores** before touring **Komodo**, the stomping ground of the namesake mini-Godzilla.

Reverse to Denpasar, then get into the rhythms of Sulawesi's capital **Makassar** before getting down to **Dili** in Timor-Leste and on to Australia or Papua New Guinea. Alternatively, swing back to **Singapore** and take off to your next destination.

CULTURE VULTURE'S CHALLENGE

Begin in **Singapore** with a scramble through Little India, Chinatown, Malay-based Kampung Glam and the colonial area of Clarke Quay. This should whet your appetite for a deeper look into Asia's different cultures. Wing your way over to **Angkor Wat** (via Siem Reap) to admire the ancient temples, then head up to Vietnam's **Hoi An**, a living museum of a trading town turned colony.

Contrast this with a trip to **Vientiane** (Laos) to see traditional wood houses with colonial mansions and modern concrete monstrosities. Head up to **Chiang Mai**, famed for its moated old city that held off Burmese invaders more than 700 years ago. From here choose a responsible, socially conscious operator to visit remote Hill Tribe communities. Now head to **Bangkok** and hop on a cheap flight over to **Yogyakarta**, the base for heading onto **Borobudur**, a Buddhist monument in the middle of the world's largest Islamic population. By now, you've earned a break so unwind in **Bali** before heading on via **Jakarta** or **Dili**.

MEKONG RIVER EXPEDITION

The Mekong River is known as the Father of Waters and it works hard throughout this region as a highway, marketplace and habitat. Swim upstream from Vietnam's flat delta to Thailand's hilly interior with a start in bustling **Ho Chi Minh City**. Catch a bus to **My Tho**, the gateway to the **Mekong Delta**. Charter a boat to rural **Ben Tre** and bus to the floating markets of **Can Tho**. Take a bus to **Rach Gia**, the jumping-off point to tranquil **Phu Quoc Island**, a good detour if you need to chillax.

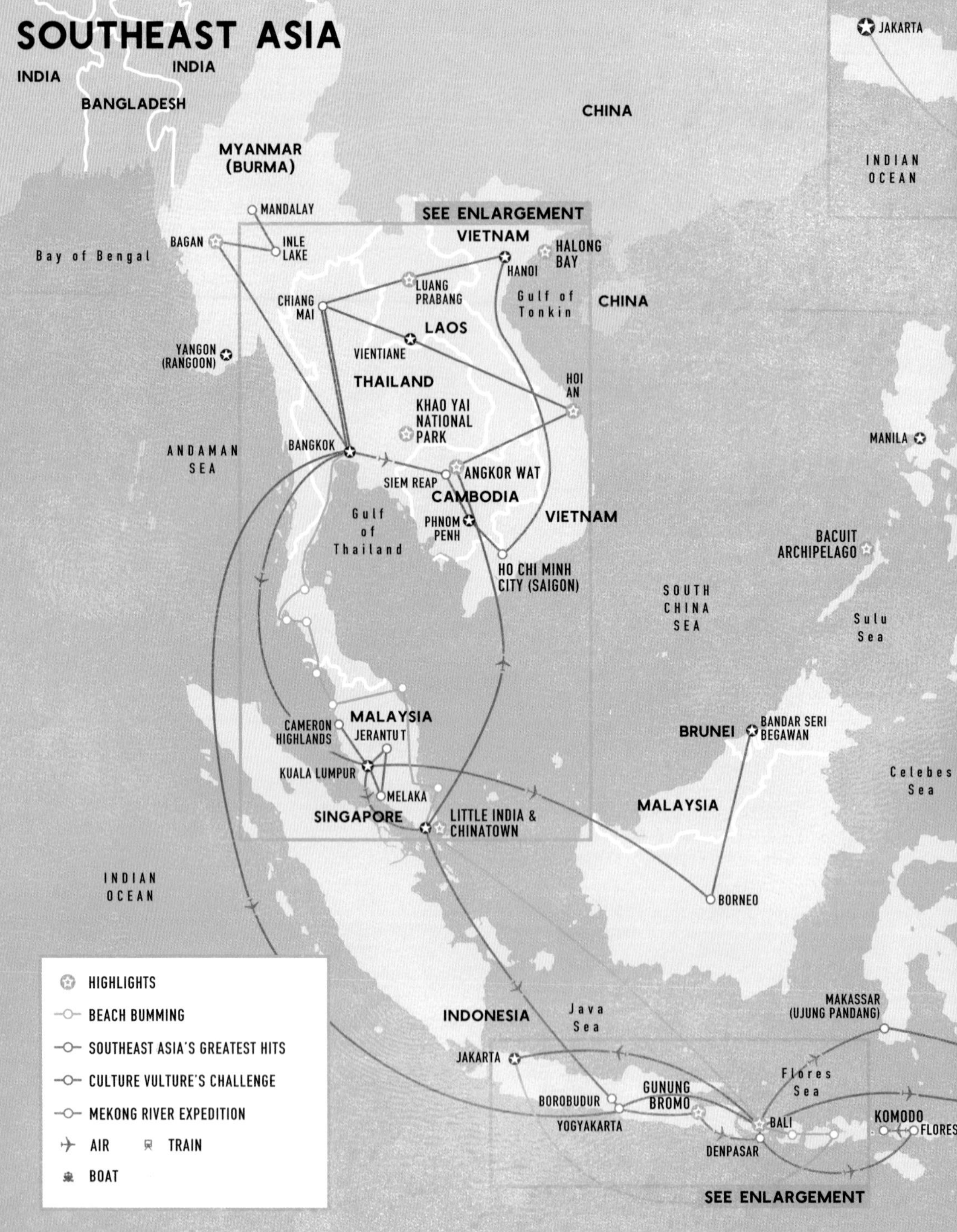
SOUTHEAST ASIA
INDIA
INDIA
BANGLADESH
CHINA
MYANMAR (BURMA)
MANDALAY
SEE ENLARGEMENT
VIETNAM
HALONG BAY
BAGAN
INLE LAKE
Bay of Bengal
HANOI
LUANG PRABANG
CHIANG MAI
Gulf of Tonkin
CHINA
LAOS
YANGON (RANGOON)
VIENTIANE
THAILAND
HOI AN
KHAO YAI NATIONAL PARK
ANDAMAN SEA
BANGKOK
ANGKOR WAT
SIEM REAP
CAMBODIA
Gulf of Thailand
PHNOM PENH
VIETNAM
HO CHI MINH CITY (SAIGON)
SOUTH CHINA SEA
MALAYSIA
CAMERON HIGHLANDS
JERANTUT
KUALA LUMPUR
MELAKA
SINGAPORE
LITTLE INDIA & CHINATOWN
BRUNEI
BANDAR SERI BEGAWAN
MALAYSIA
BORNEO
INDIAN OCEAN
JAKARTA
INDIAN OCEAN
MANILA
BACUIT ARCHIPELAGO
Sulu Sea
Celebes Sea
INDONESIA
Java Sea
MAKASSAR (UJUNG PANDANG)
JAKARTA
BOROBUDUR
GUNUNG BROMO
Flores Sea
YOGYAKARTA
BALI
DENPASAR
KOMODO
FLORES
SEE ENLARGEMENT
HIGHLIGHTS
BEACH BUMMING
SOUTHEAST ASIA'S GREATEST HITS
CULTURE VULTURE'S CHALLENGE
MEKONG RIVER EXPEDITION
AIR
TRAIN
BOAT

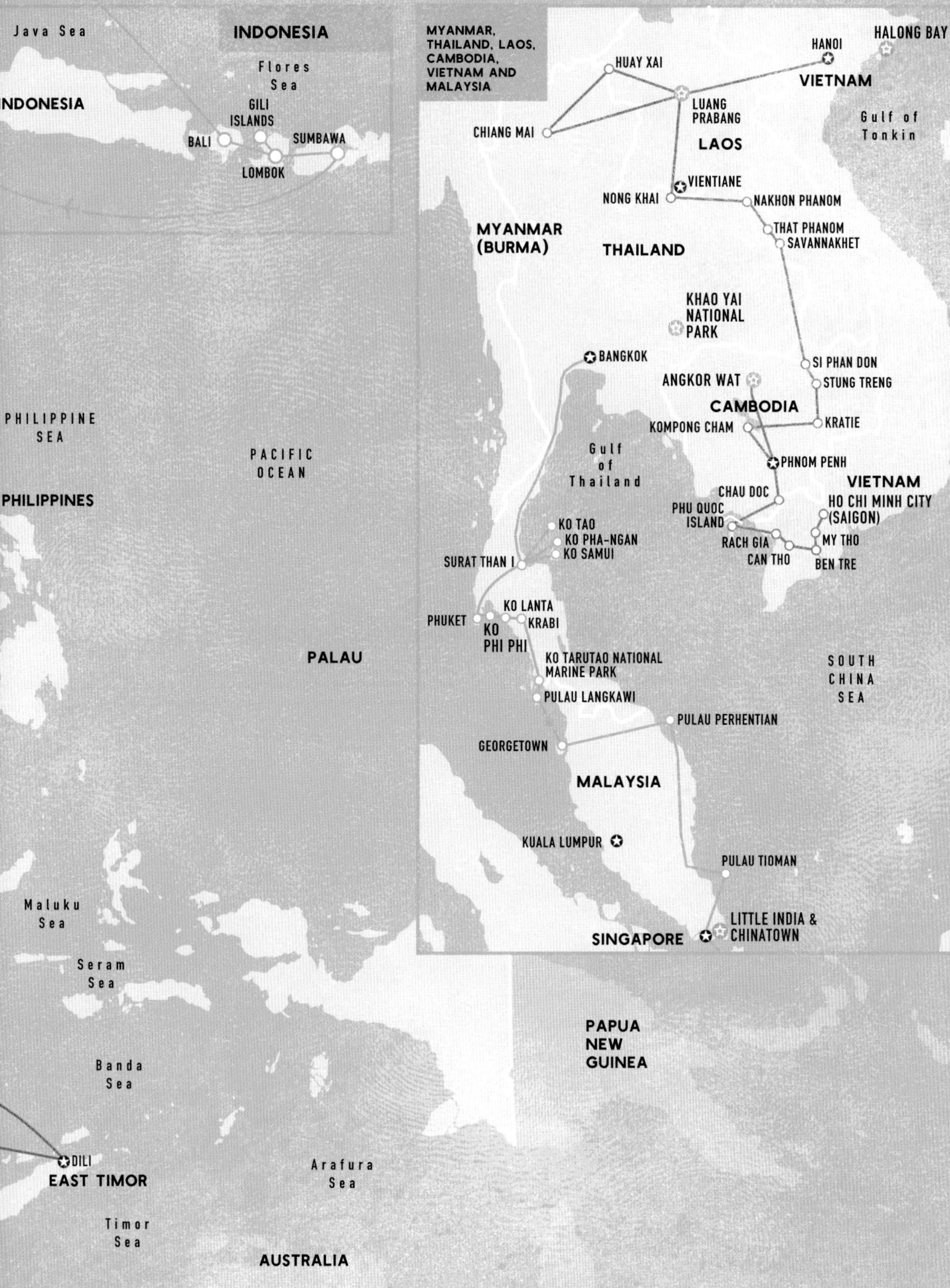
Java Sea
INDONESIA
Flores Sea
INDONESIA
GILI ISLANDS
BALI
SUMBAWA
LOMBOK
MYANMAR, THAILAND, LAOS, CAMBODIA, VIETNAM AND MALAYSIA
HUAY XAI
HANOI
HALONG BAY
VIETNAM
LUANG PRABANG
Gulf of Tonkin
CHIANG MAI
LAOS
VIENTIANE
NONG KHAI
NAKHON PHANOM
MYANMAR (BURMA)
THAT PHANOM
SAVANNAKHET
THAILAND
KHAO YAI NATIONAL PARK
BANGKOK
SI PHAN DON
ANGKOR WAT
STUNG TRENG
CAMBODIA
PHILIPPINE SEA
KOMPONG CHAM
KRATIE
PACIFIC OCEAN
Gulf of Thailand
PHNOM PENH
VIETNAM
PHILIPPINES
CHAU DOC
HO CHI MINH CITY (SAIGON)
PHU QUOC ISLAND
RACH GIA
MY THO
CAN THO
BEN TRE
KO TAO
KO PHA-NGAN
KO SAMUI
SURAT THANI
KO LANTA
PHUKET
KRABI
KO PHI PHI
PALAU
KO TARUTAO NATIONAL MARINE PARK
SOUTH CHINA SEA
PULAU LANGKAWI
PULAU PERHENTIAN
GEORGETOWN
MALAYSIA
KUALA LUMPUR
PULAU TIOMAN
Maluku Sea
LITTLE INDIA & CHINATOWN
SINGAPORE
Seram Sea
PAPUA NEW GUINEA
Banda Sea
DILI
EAST TIMOR
Arafura Sea
Timor Sea
AUSTRALIA

Keeping the stupa spotless at Wat Xieng Thong's Red Chapel in Laos

A Vietnamese tricycle-taxi driver awaits his next fare

Above: the forest-covered islets of Halong Bay, north Vietnam. Opposite: Mt Merapi viewed from the Buddhist temple of Borobudur in Java, Indonesia

Back on the mainland, catch a bus to **Chau Doc**, before floating into Cambodia at the Kaam Samnor–Vinh Xuong border crossing, all the way to the faded gentility of **Phnom Penh**. You could side-trip to **Angkor Wat** from here or stick with the river by bussing to **Kompong Cham** and speedboat to **Kratie**, home of the rare freshwater dolphin. Continue by boat north through the rocky rapids to **Stung Treng**, a transfer point into Laos via the Voen Kham border crossing and the 4000 river islands of **Si Phan Don**. Get a bus to **Savannakhet**, a border crossing into Thailand at Mukdahan.

Twist with the river's crook to the hamlets of **That Phanom** and **Nakhon Phanom** to charming **Nong Khai**, another crossing point into Laos at **Vientiane**. Hop on a bus to bewitching **Luang Prabang**. Stick with the watery route northwest to **Huay Xai** to bust another border into northern Thailand, then continue south to **Chiang Mai**. Many travellers head east to **Hanoi**, continuing this journey on to **Kūnmíng** in China's **Yúnnán province** (see p203).

WHAT TO DO?

HIGHLIGHTS

- Discovering your top temple at **Angkor Wat** (Cambodia), vestige of the mighty Khmer empire.
- Grazing on street snacks and hawker treats as you wind your way through Little India and Chinatown in **Singapore**.
- Watching the sun (and hot air balloons) rise over the plains of **Bagan** (Myanmar) and its thousands of ornate Buddhist temples.
- Cruising in the **Bacuit Archipelago** (Philippines), a surreal seascape of brooding limestone outcrops, dotted with hidden beaches and coral reefs perfect for diving.
- Witnessing Buddhist monks on their daily call to alms in the former royal capital of **Luang Prabang** (Laos), one of Southeast Asia's great temple cities.
- Kayaking beneath the towering limestone outcrops of **Halong Bay** (Vietnam) and into magical wave-carved grottoes and fascinating hidden lagoons.
- Playing in **Bali** (Indonesia) – its beaches, temples and unique Hindu culture are as ripe for surfing as they are for yoga, meditation and massage.
- Climbing the sacred peak of **Mt Kinabalu** (Malaysia), the abode of the spirits, to see a horizon that stretches as far as the Philippines.
- Wandering the beautiful old port town of **Hoi An**, Vietnam's most graceful outpost, with its traditional houses and family chapels lining the streets.
- Looking for elephants, monkeys, gibbons, hornbills, pythons, bears, a million bats and even a few wily tigers while trekking in **Khao Yai National Park** (Thailand).

GET ACTIVE

Most activities in Southeast Asia are all about the water or heading into the jungle to discover tough terrain or rare beasties. Whatever you choose to do, search for responsible operators who are qualified to work in sustainable, eco-friendly ways.

Diving, Rafting & Other Water Sports

Gin-clear waters and dazzling coral reefs make Southeast Asia a must for aquaholics. Thailand owns the diving crown, thanks to its accessibility and budget-friendly PADI-certificate courses, particularly on the east-coast island of Ko Tao. From Phuket, on the west coast, live-aboard trips go to the uninhabited Similan Islands. Indonesia gets second prize with Bali offering a variety of dives and live-aboard plunges around Komodo and Flores. If you're after a little fauna with your aqua, the seas around Sulawesi abound with sharks and turtles. The Philippines also has a wealth of underwater action around Alona Beach (Panglao Island, off the coast of Bohol), Puerto Princesa (Palawan), the island of Apo and the Bacuit Archipelago.

The rivers of Southeast Asia are curved and cut perfectly for whitewater rafting. Good spots include the following: Java's Suyugai Citarak (Citarak River), which borders Gunung Halimun National Park near Bogor; the Pai River in Thailand; the Chico or Cagayan Rivers in the Philippines; and in Bali. There's also kayaking and tubing on the rivers around Vang Vieng (Laos). For a change of pace, rafting trips on large bamboo 'house rafts' drift down a number of rivers in northern Thailand around Pai, Fang and Tha Ton.

Surfing

If you've ever seen a surf movie with thundering waves and drool-worthy breaks, it was probably filmed in Indonesia, one of the world's wildest surf destinations. Top spots include the Bukit Peninsula in Bali, Java's G-Land (Grajagan on the southeastern tip), Pulau Nias in northern Sumatra and the Nusa Tenggara islands. Windsurfing is possible in the southern resorts of Bali. Elsewhere, the breaks off Siargao Island (Philippines) reach Hawaiian heights between October and May. Kuta in Bali is a famous spot, but there's surf right along the south coast of the inner islands – from Sumatra through to Sumbawa, and Sumba across to Papua. Pulau Nias, off the coast of Sumatra, is another beloved place.

SOUTHEAST ASIA'S TOP BEACHES

- **Phu Quoc Island** (Vietnam) Vietnam's poster island, ringed by picture-perfect white crescents and sandy bays sheltered by rocky headlands.

- **Railay** (Thailand) Rock-climbers gravitate to the karst cliffs, but the sands between the outcrops are snippets of paradise.

- **Bohol** (Philippines) Natural and cultural wonders onshore, and a haven for sand and scuba addicts.

- **Pulau Tioman** (Malaysia) Hollywood's stand-in for Bali Ha'i is castaway perfection, with added dive appeal.

- **Ko Pha-Ngan** (Thailand) This backpacker legend rages during Full Moon parties, but its sun-kissed coves doze in between.

- **Lombok** (Indonesia) The other Kuta, with a string of perfect sands, and the iconic Gili Islands just offshore.

- **Koh Rong** (Cambodia) Good times rule at Cambodia's new favourite party islands, but you'll still find serene stretches of sand.

- **Mui Ne** (Vietnam) Squeaky sands, towering dunes and kitesurfing galore.

Trekking

Like the sound of scaling volcanoes or visiting minority hill-tribe villages? Then it could be that Southeast Asia is the place for you. In Indonesia, you can trek Sumatra's volcanic peaks in Berastagi. Java's volcanic peaks, such as Gunung Merapi, can be a taxing climb, while spectacular Gunung Bromo is more of a stroll. Gunung Batur and Gunung Agung volcanoes in Bali are popular day trips. To see the destruction wrought by Mt Taal, a tiny volcano that packs a punch, take a boat tour around the incongruously picturesque lake. The volcano that dominates Lombok, Gunung Rinjani (3726m), offers a strenuous but worthwhile three-day jaunt.

Too hot to handle? Indonesia is a world-renowned destination for cool jungle treks, thanks to its huge tracts of uninhabited rainforest, second in size to Brazil's. There are more adventurous jungle-trekking opportunities in Kalimantan and Papua (Irian Jaya). Despite intense logging in Malaysia, Taman Negara National Park is a primal delight with deep, dark jungles, canopy walks and lots of insects. Sabah's main event is a climb to the top of sacred Mt Kinabalu (4101m), which is half the height of Mt Everest.

In the mountainous regions of northern Thailand (Chiang Mai, Mae Hong Son and Chiang Rai), Laos (Luang Nam Tha) and Vietnam (Sapa), minority hill-tribe communities make rewarding trekking destinations when done in a responsible manor.

Rangda, the demon queen, as portrayed in traditional Balinese dance

Cycling & Motorbiking

Touring the region by bicycle is as challenging as it is rewarding, and it's becoming more popular. Many travellers choose to combine cycling with buses to skip some of the more tiresome stretches, or they take organised cycling tours. For long-distance touring, bring your own bike and gear, as bike shops aren't widespread or well stocked. In towns throughout the region, guesthouses rent out rickety bicycles for day trips.

Hands down, Vietnam is the most spectacular country in the region for cycle touring, as the north–south highway predominately hugs the coast. Cycling is a great way to take advantage of the terrain in northern Vietnam (around Sapa) and Laos, and traffic is pretty light. Malaysia and Thailand also have viable touring routes, especially along the peninsula and the relatively flat terrain of the Mekong River. In the Philippines, areas around Moalboal on Cebu, and Guimaras Island, are other popular options.

Experienced bush-bashing motorcyclists prize the rough roads of Cambodia, Laos and northern Thailand. You'll hear the put-put of a motorbike in most places you visit in the area, and many travellers hire a motorbike for excursions. Before hiring you'll need to give the bike a quick once-over (check tyre tread and obvious oil leaks), and pack some sunglasses in case goggles aren't supplied.

WILDLIFE

You'll definitely spot monkeys if you spend any time in Southeast Asia, usually cheekily swiping your lunch on hiking trails or around temples. In Sumatra and Kalimantan, look out for orang-utans, the only great ape species outside Africa. If you think you've seen birds, wait until you get to Thailand, which has more than 1000 different species. Then there are Borneo's rainforests that hide freakish fauna such as the hornbill, pygmy elephant and the extremely rare Bornean rhinoceros. Indonesia's east has the famous Komodo dragon and the cute Papuan tree kangaroo.

FESTIVALS

Religious festivals – Buddhist, Muslim and Christian – dominate the calendar in Southeast Asia. Here are a few highlights:

- **Black Nazarene Procession** (Philippines) Locals prance a life-size statue of Jesus through the streets of Manila's Quiapo district on 9 January.
- **Ati-Atihan** (Philippines) A three-day Mardi Gras celebrated on Panay in the third week of January.
- **Thaipusam** (Malaysia) Crowds converge at the Batu Caves north of KL for this dramatic Hindu festival involving body piercing. Falls between mid-January and mid-February.
- **Chinese New Year** Widely celebrated in January or February with fireworks and parades in Bangkok (Thailand), Kuala Lumpur (Malaysia), Singapore and other Chinese communities.
- **Tet** (Vietnam) Celebrates the lunar new year with large family gatherings and prolonged business closings.
- **Buddhist New Year** (Water Festival) In mid-April, Buddhist countries celebrate their lunar new year with symbolic water-throwing and religious observances. Celebrated with particular aplomb in Chiang Mai, Thailand, and in larger cities across Cambodia, Laos and Myanmar.
- **Bun Bang Fai** (Laos) May's rocket festival is an animist celebration with processions and firing of bamboo rockets to prompt rain. A similar festival is held in northern Thailand.
- **Tiet Doan Ngo** (Vietnam) Summer Solstice Day in June sees the burning of human effigies to satisfy the need for souls to serve in the army of the god of death.
- **Rainforest World Music Sarawak** (Malaysian Borneo) celebrates tribal music from around the world during this three-day music festival around July.
- **Singapore Grand Prix** (Singapore; www.singapore-f1-grand-prix.com) The only F1 full night race screams around Marina Bay. Off-track events include international music acts.
- **Ubud Writers & Readers Festival** (Indonesia) This festival in Bali brings together scores of writers and readers from around the world in a celebration of writing.
- **MassKara** (Philippines) Mischievous masked men stir the masses into a dancing frenzy on the streets of Bacolod, capital of Negros Occidental, during the weekend that falls closest to 19 October.
- **Bon Om Tuk** (Cambodia) The most important Khmer festival honours the wet season's end in early November.
- **Deepavali** Hindus across the region celebrate the festival of lights to mark the triumph of good over evil. Tiny oil lamps are ceremoniously

Revellers discover that there ain't no party like a Full Moon Party on Hat Rin Beach in Koh Pha-Ngan, Thailand

lit in Malaysia, Thailand and Bali, and Singapore's Little India hosts public festivities. Usually in November.

• **ZoukOut** (Singapore; www.zoukout.com) The state's biggest outdoor dance party, held over two nights in December on Siloso Beach, Sentosa. Expect A-list international DJs.

NIGHTLIFE

Southeast Asia is renowned for life after dark, and it's as varied as it can be fun. Here are some of the top sites.

• **Bali** (Indonesia) Sunset on the beach is popular, with a drink at a cafe with a sea view or from a beachside beer vendor. Later, the legendary nightlife action heats up around Kuta. Many spend the early evening at a hipster joint in Seminyak before working their way south to oblivion.

• **Bangkok** (Thailand) Bangkok's club scene is a fickle beast, and venues that were pulling in thousands a night just last year might be a vague memory this year. Clubs here also tend to heave on certain nights – Fridays and Saturdays, during a visit from a foreign DJ, or for a night dedicated to the music flavour of the month – then hibernate every other night.

• **Ko Pha-Ngan** (Thailand) Home of the very first Full Moon parties in Southeast Asia, it still pays a lunar tribute to the party gods with trance-like dancing, wild screaming and glow-in-the-dark body paint. For something mellower, the west coast has several excellent bars, where you can raise a loaded cocktail glass to a blood-orange sunset from a hilltop or over mangrove trees at the water's edge.

• **Kuala Lumpur** (Malaysia) Bubble tea, iced kopi-o, a frosty beer or a martini with a twist atop a helipad – Kuala Lumpur's cafes, teahouses and bars offer a multitude of ways to wet your whistle. There's no shortage of honest pubs, sophisticated speakeasies and other alcohol-fuelled venues where you can party the night away.

• **Nha Trang** (Vietnam) While no longer the hedonistic backpacker haven, it's now set with sleek skybars, smart lounges and boistrous beach parties that draw huge crowds of young Chinese, Korean and local tourists.

• **Phnom Penh** (Cambodia) PP has some great bars and clubs, so it's definitely worth one big night out here. There are lots of late-night spots clustered around the intersection of Sts 51 and 172, appropriately nicknamed 'Area 51'.

• **Singapore** From speakeasy cocktail bars to boutique beer stalls to artisan coffee roasters, Singapore is discovering the finer points of drinking. The clubbing scene is no less competent, with newcomers including a futuristic club in the clouds, a basement hot spot fit for the streets of Tokyo, and a techno refuge in Boat Quay.

ROADS LESS TRAVELLED

Believe it or not, there are still a few secret spots in Southeast Asia where you can find a beach to yourself. In Thailand, the underdeveloped beaches of Ko Tarutao National Marine Park won't be too crowded, and Koh Kong Island in Cambodia is a little further off the backpacker trail. You could try working your way up Vietnam's coast to find a spot where you can unfurl a towel without anyone else on the beach. Similarly, the Philippines can be too far for some travellers, so you can often find quieter pockets.

WORKING

Visas permitting, there are a few job opportunities for travellers in Southeast Asia, though local currency won't travel as well as what you might be paid at home.

Besides freelancing in your field, you can earn in the region by teaching English. The pay may not be rewarding but you will get to

FLYING FLIP-FLOPS & THE BIRKENSTOCK

With a whopping clank the Coke can flew skyward and into the darkness of the night. The crowds erupted and I ran gleefully, arms raised and one foot bare, to retrieve my weapon – a size 46 Birkenstock sandal.

An hour earlier, as I wandered the damp streets of Hanoi's Old Quarter, I stopped to watch an intriguing street game. Being played by kids, it involved flip-flops being hurled at the said can. Soon the rules became apparent: miss, and you walk to retrieve your sandal in disgrace, then stand 'trapped' behind the can (and its keeper); strike it, and you run wildly to get your footwear before the keeper can tag you with the can. Successful throws also free 'trapped' participants and bring adulation.

With a mix of excited and sceptical looks (from the children and their parents, respectively), I was encouraged to try. Eyes bulged and jaws dropped – clearly nobody had ever seen what an ultimate-playing Vancouverite could do with a Birk. Crowds soon grew and every time I stepped up, they all started chanting loudly. I don't know what it translated to, perhaps: 'He's big. He's crazy. He sure can throw!' And after each triumphant can battering a little boy would tug at my shirt sleeve, his face beaming, his thumb raised.

The Take Away

I guess I knew that laughter and sport were both international languages, but until that evening I never realised just how powerful they could be. Engaging with cultures, and sharing moments of commonality, is one of life's greatest rewards.

Thomas Mills – taken from Lonely Planet's *The Best Moment of Your Life*

interact with locals and make some friends. Bangkok, Ho Chi Minh City and Jakarta all have several language schools you can try.

If you've arranged work before leaving, you'll need to have organised the appropriate paperwork in your home country. Many visitors, however, just show up and organise work visas when they find work. Arrangements can be even more informal if you're working in a hostel, in a bar or as a dive instructor, although you'd definitely need a PADI certification for the latter.

Alternatively, you could consider volunteering to give something back to the region.

WHEN TO GO?

Most of Southeast Asia, with the exception of northern Myanmar, lies within the tropics. You can expect warm or downright hot weather, with high humidity in lowland areas.

Mainland Southeast Asia (Thailand, Laos, Myanmar, Cambodia and Vietnam) experiences a three-season climate – cool and dry from November to March (average temperature 25°C/77°F to 30°C/86°F), followed by hot and dry from March to May (average temperature 30°C/86°F to 35°C/95°F), and hot and rainy from June to October (average temperature 25°C/77°F to 30°C/86°F). Highland areas are significantly cooler than the lowlands; for example, Hanoi is 5°C/9°F to 10°C/18°F cooler than Bangkok.

Oceanic Southeast Asia (southern Thailand, Myanmar, Brunei, Indonesia, Malaysia and Singapore) experiences two monsoons annually: one from the northeast (usually between October and April) and one from the southwest (between May and September). Rain is usually heavier during the northeast monsoon. Often you'll find better weather simply by crossing from one side of the island or country to the other. Travel is limited only during the peaks of the rainy season.

WHAT TO EXPECT?

LOCALS & OTHER TRAVELLERS

You can expect to see plenty of travellers here as it's a convenient holiday spot for Australians and Asians, and Brits and Europeans (particularly Scandinavians, Dutch and Germans) use it as a round-the-world stopover. Many French travellers pay homage to the former colonies of Vietnam, Laos and Cambodia, while North Americans are discovering bigger destinations such as Thailand and Vietnam. Thailand's east-coast islands, especially Ko Tao and Ko Pha-Ngan, rank high with the 20-somethings, with Ko Pha-Ngan famous for trippy full-moon raves. Stunningly beautiful Phuket and Ko Samui attract older crowds (and larger wallets).

Locals are generally curious when it comes to travellers and you should expect plenty of questions. The questions aren't meant to be nosey, but they are measures for placing outsiders into their highly hierarchical society. Your status (your age, your marital status, number of children, your job and even your wealth) determines how much deference should be afforded to you. Also, chitchat is a well-practised art in the region and those who take the time to talk to you are extending their famed hospitality.

Unlike Western cultures which prize individuality, Asian cultures value homogeneity, and the group, particularly the family, is paramount. The concept of 'face' – avoiding embarrassment for yourself or the group – is a guiding principle in social interactions. This can translate into a host of baffling

SAMPLE COSTS

	Thailand (baht, B)	Singapore (Singapore dollar, S$)	Cambodia (US$ or riel, r)	Indonesia (rupiah, Rp)
Hostel: dorm bed	300-600B (US$9-18)	S$25–45 (US$18-23)	(US$4-10)	100,000-160,000Rp (US$6.82-10.90)
Midrange hotel: double room	1000-4000B (US$30-120)	S$150–300 (US$109-218)	(US$25-80)	300,000-1,500,000Rp (US$20.50-102)
Street snack	Pad Thai 35-50B (US$1-1.50)	Hawker noodles S$5-8 (US$3.63-5.80)	*Banh chev* 2000r (US$0.50)	*Piseng goreng* 1500Rp (US$0.10)
Budget meal	50-120B (US$1.50-3.60)	S$6-20 (US$4.36-14.52)	12,000-16,000r (US$3-4)	28,000-50,000Rp (US$1.90-3.41)
Midrange restaurant: main	150-350B (US$4.50-10.50)	S$10–30 (US$7.26-21.78)	(US$5-15)	50,000-250,000Rp (US$3.41-17)
Cappuccino	45-130B (US$1.35-3.90)	S$3-6 (US$2.18-4.36)	6000-12,000r (US$1.50-3)	25,000-45,000Rp (US$1.70-3.07)
1.5L Bottle of water	13-20B (US$0.39-0.60)	S$1-2.50 (US$0.73-1.82)	2000-6000r (US$0.50-1.50)	5500-10,000Rp (US$0.38-0.68)
1L Petrol (gas)	30B (US$0.90)	S$2.27 (US$1.65)	4000r (US$0.98)	8600Rp (US$0.58)

behaviours – sometimes locals will give incorrect information just to avoid admitting that they don't know something. Often the vaguer the answer, the closer you are treading to a face-saving game. Showing anger is a sure-fire way to make everyone lose face and should be avoided at all costs. A better tool is a smile, which can be used a gracious excuse for minor cultural gaffes (such as putting your feet on chairs/tables or facing the soles of your feet to someone). A smile will endear you to market sellers, children and even water buffalo, but path-blocking monkeys and stray dogs are immune.

To avoid offence (and potentially jail time) you should respect the government, religion, and monarchy. In Thailand, to openly express negative opinions (in talking, or even on social media) about the king will land you jail (yes, really). Any such sentiments should be kept to yourself, even if you think no-one around understands English.

Dress is an often overlooked cause of offence. Hot temperatures may make you feel like wearing beach attire, but in Southeast Asia exposing your body may cause offence. You should wear clothes that cover to your elbows and knees, or even further in Muslim countries, where female visitors should even consider covering their heads (especially in rural areas). Standards are relaxed on the beaches due to tourist inundation, but this stops short of any nudity. Men and women should pay special attention to the proper attire and behaviour required in the various temples and mosques across the region.

FOOD

Prepare for some lip-smacking goodness as Southeast Asia has some of the most exciting dining you'll find anywhere in the world. Rice and fish are the basics, but chillies pep up most meals. Feel their kick in *sambal* (fried chilli and prawn paste) from Indonesia and Malaysia, or Thailand's *naam phrik* (chilli paste). Hotheads should also look out for Indian-inspired curries that crept south with migration. Noodles are another big travelling food, originally coming from China but reinterpreted in Vietnam's signature dish, *pho* (noodle soup), and Malaysia's soupy *laksa* (noodles in spicy coconut soup). Eating the latter from the hawker stalls along Madras Lane in Kuala Lumpur was recently ranked as the second-best eating experience in the world in *Lonely Planet's Ultimate Eatlist*. Eating *som tum* (papaya salad) in Bangkok was ranked fifth.

With every country there's another 'must-try'. The Philippines has *adobo*, a stew that has Spanish influences but tastes of Filipino playfulness. The roadside favourite in Vietnam is the spring roll, stuffed with prawns, basil and mint. We could go on – green curries, chilli crab, banana pancakes and mango smoothies almost everywhere – if only our bellies and bursting belts would allow. There are a few culinary cautions to keep your adventures illness-free, but apart from these simple rules, eat up.

FAST FOOD OR FAMISH

When I began my five months of travel in Asia, I made an earnest pledge to try to avoid chain restaurants, which I saw as contributing to cultural homogenisation. Instead, I told myself, I would dine only in local establishments, exasperating waiters as I butcher their native language, struggling valiantly to pronounce dishes like *moo goo gai pan*. As many travellers like to point out, the word 'travel' is rooted in the French word travail. It's work. You get out of it what you put into it, and it shouldn't be too easy.

But after I'd walked several more blocks and still hadn't found a restaurant serving anything new, the promise of crispy fresh vegetables from a salad bar, something I hadn't come across in months on the road, seemed alluring. I headed for the Sizzler and put my cultural travels on hold.

Jim Benning

LANGUAGE

Southeast Asia has several different languages, including Thai, Bahasa (in Indonesia and Malaysia), Khmer (in Cambodia), Lao, Vietnamese and several hundred sub-dialects. That's the bad news. On the upside, in bigger, cosmopolitan cities (such as Bangkok, Singapore and Kuala Lumpur), you can get by with English. Rural areas of the region may present problems for English-only speakers and you'll probably need a phrasebook or translation app on your phone.

You'll definitely get more out of your trip if you learn a few words and locals will appreciate you making the effort. Try the Lonely Planet phrasebooks if you want to master the lingo. The *Southeast Asia Phrasebook* is tailored for trips that cover several countries in the region.

COMMUNICATION

Southeast Asia is incredibly well connected, with abundant Wi-Fi access, plentiful internet cafes, fast connections and low prices, though service dips outside of tourist resorts and cities. Internet connections normally mirror the destination's road network: well-sealed highways usually mean speedy travel through the information superhighway. 3G and even 4G mobile access is available in cities. Censorship of some websites is in effect across the region, particularly in Vietnam and Myanmar.

COSTS

The most stable currencies are the Thai baht, Singapore dollar, Malaysian ringgit, Indonesian rupiah and Philippine peso. The local currencies of Vietnam (dong), Cambodia (riel), Laos (kip) and Myanmar (kyat) are used for small purchases on the street, but US dollars act as the second currency and are required for larger purchases (lodging and transport).

The table on p233 is useful as a planning guide only. Please don't use it to haggle with hotel owners – they really don't like that.

HEALTH

Get your arm ready to be pin-cushioned, because the World Health Organization recommends quite a few jabs before any travel to Southeast Asia. Start planning for

A FAMILY AFFAIR: MEET FLEUR & CO.

Fleur Bainger, her husband and sons (aged one and three) flew the coop in Australia to travel through Singapore, Thailand, Italy, France, England, Croatia and Dubai.

How long are you going to be away for? My little family has set off for five months of adventures.

What inspired the trip? I had dreamt about an extended trip for years, and suddenly I realised we only had one year until our oldest child started school. It was time to act! Six weeks later, I'd booked our flights.

Was it easy to release yourself from life at home, whether work or other responsibilities? I'm a freelance writer and my husband is the stay-at-home parent, so it was relatively easy to organise.

What was your biggest worry prior to travelling? Paying for the trip! We got clever and rented out our house in Oz, and put insurances that don't cover you if you're not in your home country on hold. I also worked freelance as we travelled – all you need is a laptop and a net connection. I also worried the long trip would disrupt the kids' schedules – it did, and fatigue was an issue (for the parents!) in the early days, but they soon adapted and became pro travellers.

What has been the most joyous aspect? Being able to spend so much more time than usual with my children, watching them develop as a result of their experiences and the whole family being amazed by particular destinations.

How do you think it will change life for you and your kids once back home? I plan on remembering to slow down. Pausing to be with family is more fun and more important, and shared experiences and the memories of them are far more valuable.

© Matt Munro /Lonely Planet

A row of golden buddhas at Wat Pho Temple, Bangkok

© Matt Munro /Lonely Planet

A tuk tuk navigates through the famous Khao San Road, Bangkok

your vaccines eight weeks in advance and check with your travel clinic on current recommendations. At the time of writing the following made the list: diphtheria, tetanus, hepatitis A and B, measles, mumps, rubella and typhoid. Further vaccinations are recommended for travellers who plan to remain in the region for longer than a month. Mosquito-borne diseases such as dengue fever, Japanese B encephalitis and malaria can be a problem in certain rural areas.

Amoebic dysentery, giardiasis and traveller's diarrhoea often have the same initial symptoms – rushed trips to the bathroom. Rabies is a concern in the region as well.

An estimated 3.5 people are living with HIV in Southeast Asia, and it is one of the most common causes of death in people under the age of 50 in Thailand. The epidemic is worsening in Cambodia, Myanmar and Vietnam. Heterosexual sex is the primary method of transmission, and most of these countries have unregulated sex industries. Always practise safe sex. Consult the Health & Safety chapter and seek professional medical advice for more travel-health information.

ISSUES

Politics & Terrorism

Thailand was once known for its peacefulness but in 2004 there were politically motivated attacks by separatists in the far south around the Malaysian border. The area continues to simmer, and at the time of writing it was still the subject of various travel advisories. None of the destinations in Thailand featured in this book are within this area.

In 2014 the country was rocked by a military coup and large scale political unrest, and although things have been calmer on the larger political front since then, chances of large demonstrations still exist – as is the case in most of the world, it's best to give political gatherings a wide berth. Between 2014 and 2017 there have been various terrorist bombings, some of which were in Bangkok. Sadly, this risk now exists in most major cities, from Berlin to Boston, London to New York and Paris to Sydney. It's not a reason to stop travelling, but it's wise to be vigilant, whether at home or abroad.

Terrorism has also been an issue in Indonesia, most notably with the Bali bombing of 2002 and then subsequent smaller-scale attacks in Jakarta and around Surabaya in East Java. Areas around Timor-leste's border can be volatile, so again have a close look at government travel warnings.

Insurgents in the Philippines also mean travel to the Mindanao and Sulu archipelago is currently unsafe. The entire island of Boracay, one of Southeast Asia's top beach destinations (and party capitals), was closed by the country's government for six months in April 2018. The move wasn't made over terrorism, but rather overtourism – namely the environmental issues being caused by it. The plan was to rehabilitate the environment in the area and force the tourism industry to be more environmentally sustainable, particularly with its waste practices. How the island's tourism economy will bounce back is still unknown.

Drugs

It seems insane that some travellers would risk their futures by smuggling drugs into countries such as Singapore and Malaysia, where it's not just illegal but can carry the death penalty. The so-called Golden Triangle of opium production is cleaning up its act, but it's targeting travellers rather than growers and dealers. And that means marijuana too. 'Soft' drugs can carry hard penalties for possession, including jail terms in Thailand, and in Indonesia not reporting possession can be a chargeable offence. High-profile cases (Australians will know the Bali Nine and Schapelle Corby cases) have been harsh lessons for travellers who didn't know the laws of the countries they were visiting and assumed their own country would protect them. Simply put: they won't. Know the risks by heeding warnings in guidebooks and those posted by your government on its travel advisory pages.

GETTING THERE

Southeast Asia has long been a hub of world travel with two key ports (Bangkok and Singapore) that have made way to central airports in the jet age. Overland routes through the region were popularised during the flower-powered 1960s, but today many travellers use Asia as a stopover.

AIR

The major airports of Bangkok, Kuala Lumpur and Singapore are buzzing with aircraft, many refuelling on long-haul flights. Direct flights into these cities are frequent, so if you're flying on to Vietnam, Cambodia, the Philippines, Indonesia or Thailand it can be cheaper to catch a budget flight on from these hubs. Hong Kong is also a good entry point, with several budget carriers flying on from there.

Major local players include:

- **Cathay Pacific** (www.cathaypacific.com)
- **Garuda** (www.garuda-indonesia.com)
- **Malaysia Airlines** (www.malaysiaairlines.com)
- **Singapore Airlines** (www.singaporeair.com)
- **Thai Airways International** (www.thaiairways.com)
- **Vietnam Airlines** (www.vietnamairlines.com)

Budget options include:

- **Air Asia** (www.airasia.com)
- **Cebu Pacific** (www.cebupacificair.com)
- **Citilink** (www.citilink.co.id)
- **Firefly** (www.fireflyz.com.my)
- **Jetstar** (www.jetstar.com)
- **Lion Air** (www2.lionair.co.id)
- **Nok Air** (www.nokair.com)
- **Philippine Airlines** (www.philippineairlines.com)
- **Scoot** (www.flyscoot.com)
- **VietJet** (www.vietjetair.com)

SEA & OVERLAND

There are no regular scheduled ferry routes to Southeast Asia from India or China. One adventurous option is to book passage on one of the cargo ships plying routes around the Indian and Pacific Oceans. Some freighters have space for a few non-crew members, who have their own rooms but eat meals with the crew. Prices vary depending on your departure point, but costs start at around US$150 a day plus fees. There's always the chance, though, to pick up berths on yachts heading between Southeast Asia and Australia. The **Darwin to Ambon Yacht Race** (www.darwinambonrace.com.au) is a good place to start. Working your way overland to China through Vietnam is popular, and another route to try is across into India.

BEYOND SOUTHEAST ASIA

Travelling along the Mekong River, many travellers are heading north into China. Laos, Vietnam and, theoretically, Myanmar all have border crossings with China, though political differences can make this difficult, particularly in Myanmar, which can also serve as an excellent land-based route into India. Heading south you can hop across the Indonesian Archipelago into Timor-Leste, then into Australia's remote north or over to Papua New Guinea as an entry point into the Pacific isles.

FURTHER INFORMATION

WEBSITES

- **Bangkok Post** (www.bangkokpost.com) In-depth analysis of current events in Southeast Asia.
- **Cambodian Information Center** (www.cambodia.org) Comprehensive list of links on culture, government and current events.
- **ClickTheCity.com** (www.clickthecity.com) A great listings site for happenings in Manila and around the Philippines.
- **Ecology Asia** (www.ecologyasia.com) Profile of the region's flora, fauna and eco-organisations.
- **Ecotourism Laos** (www.ecotourismlaos.com) Provides information about the Lao environs, largely focusing on trekking and other ecotourism activities.
- **Experience Philippines** (www.experiencephilippines.org) Tourism authority site; good for planning.
- **Go-Myanmar.com** (www.go-myanmar.com) Plenty of up-to-date travel-related information and advice.
- **Inside Indonesia** (www.insideindonesia.org) News and thoughtful features.
- **Lao National Tourism Administration** (www.tourismlaos.org) Mostly up-to-date travel information from the government.
- **Malaysia Asia** (http://blog.malaysia-asia.my) Award-winning blog packed with local insider information.
- **Move to Cambodia** (www.movetocambodia.com) Insightful guide to living and working in Cambodia.
- **Myanmar Tourism Federation** (http://myanmar.travel) Inspirational pictures, good background information and travel tips.
- **Richard Barrow** (www.richardbarrow.com) Prolific blogger and tweeter focusing on Thai travel.
- **Tourism Malaysia** (www.tourism.gov.my) Official national tourist information site.
- **Tourism Authority of Thailand** (TAT; www.tourismthailand.org) National tourism department covering info and special events.
- **TravelFish** (www.travelfish.org) Popular travel site specialising in Southeast Asia.
- **VientianeTimes.com** (www.vientianetimes.

org.la) Not the official government mouthpiece that it first appears to be.

- **Your Singapore** (www.visitsingapore.com) Official tourism board website.

BOOKS

- **A Great Place to Have a War** Joshua Kurlantzick takes a fresh look at America's 'secret war' in Laos, why it transformed the nation and how it emboldened a fledgling CIA.
- **Burma's Spring** Rosalind Russell's lively memoir, with a broad cast of characters from girl-band singers and domestic workers to opposition politicians.
- **First They Killed My Father** (Luong Ung) A sometimes-harrowing tale of the Khmer Rouge coming to power as seen by an urban Cambodian family.
- **Into the Heart of Borneo** (Redmond O'Hanlon) A cheerfully ill-prepared naturalist treks through the jungle into the remote interior of the island.
- **Krakatoa – The Day the World Exploded** Simon Winchester melds history, geology and politics, all centred on the 1883 eruption.
- **Playing with Water – Passion and Solitude on a Philippine Island** James Hamilton-Paterson's timeless account of life on a remote islet sheds much light on Philippine culture.
- **Tales from a Broad** A woman's tale of charming her way around Singapore's expat community with more than a dash of sass. By Fran Lebowitz.
- **The Beach** Alex Garland's legendary tale about a backpacker utopia in southern Thailand.
- **The Quiet American** Graham Greene writes of the battle for 'hearts and minds' in the lead-up to Vietnam's conflict.
- **The Sympathizer** Superbly written spy novel by Viet Thanh Nguyen, which deals with the aftermath of the American War; 2016 Pulitzer Prize–winner.
- **This Earth of Mankind** (Pramoedya Ananta Toer) The controversial (it was banned) recapturing of 100 years of Indonesia's colonial period.

SWAP SHOPS

Book swaps are common on the Southeast Asian trail, so you'll rarely be without the printed word. At hostels and shops you can usually bring a book in and trade it for another. While the range may not be great, you'll definitely be able to read something.

FILMS

- **Apocalypse Now** (1979) Set in Vietnam, filmed in the Philippines, this psychological thriller is the ultimate anti-war film.
- **Mekong Full Moon Party** (2002) A comedy-drama which takes a critical look at Thailand's spiritual faith being challenged by modern technological scepticism.
- **The Act of Killing** (2012) Oscar-nominated documentary about anti-communist purges in 1960s Indonesia.
- **Ilo Ilo** (2013) Moving meditation on middle-class family life in Singapore, with an international cast.
- **Cemetery of Splendour** (2015) The living world and the spirit world collide in northern Thailand when soldiers succumb to a weird sleeping illness.
- **Interchange** (2016) A film noir–style supernatural thriller set in KL.

THE INDIAN SUBCONTINENT

Epic, squalid, triumphant and disastrous, the Indian subcontinent provides one of the world's most powerful travel experiences. This is the home to some of the highest, wettest, most remote and most crowded places on the planet. The range of experiences is breathtaking and intimidating – tiger-hiding jungles abutted by impenetrable concrete megalopolises, Himalayan passes climbing into ever-thinning air, starving orphans in the streets trodden over by billionaires in Prada. It's intense.

India has long been the region's tourism epicentre, though Nepal and Sri Lanka are welcoming back more and more travellers following their respective troubles, the Gorkha earthquake of 2015 and the Sri Lankan civil war (1983-2009). Meanwhile Pakistan has fallen off the radar due to security issues, Bangladesh has yet to find its tourism feet and Bhutan's pricy policy of 'tour-only' tourism is keeping numbers of visitors down in the spectacular Himalayan Buddhist kingdom. Meanwhile India continues to tear along frenetically. It's still cheap – the cost of food, transport and admission to many sights is rock bottom – and economic growth has changed the face of the region. Now you will find startlingly cutting-edge art and music scenes in the cities to contrast your temple visits and chai-sipping stints. But the quintessential subcontinental experience remains unchanged: a spiritual journey through mountains, rainforests, deserts and choked cities that culminates in jarring self-discovery.

The subcontinent is not for everyone. In most of the region, the crush of humanity and poverty is overwhelming. This, combined with the endless scams and the notorious bouts of Delhi belly, is enough to send unprepared travellers packing within days. In addition, there are safety and security issues across the region, particularly for women travellers, which means you should keep a high level of vigilance at all times.

But if you're up for it, the bustle and energy are addictive and the journey mind-blowing. After you've spent time on the subcontinent, other regions feel like they have the sound turned down and the lights dimmed. In the end, no-one goes away unchanged.

ITINERARIES

Most trips start from one of India's urban centres, but you can pick up the trail anywhere along the way.

EAST, NORTH OR WEST FROM DELHI

The following itineraries cram some must-have North India experiences into a packed trip. Start off contemplating the atmospheric Old City of **Delhi** and its many monuments before training off to **Agra** to witness India's signature memorial, the **Taj Mahal**. Make a detour to the ghostly abandoned city of **Fatehpur Sikri**, then head to **Khajuraho** for a peek at its risqué, erotic temples. Next, go farther east to the spiritual centre of **Varanasi**. From here you can make your way to **Kolkata** and then hop over to **Dhaka** in Bangladesh.

Heading west will take your through the colourful wonders of **Rajasthan**. From **Delhi**, take the train to the 'Pink City' of **Jaipur**, from where you can hit **Amber Fort** and **Ranthambore National Park** – probably your best chance to see a tiger in the wild. Bus over to **Pushkar** and **Udaipur** for temples, palaces and lakeside relaxation. Next stop is the 'Blue City' of **Jodhpur** and its unfathomable fortress, then on through the desert (perhaps by camel) to the ancient fortress of **Jaisalmer**, the 'Golden City'. Alternatively, you can head northwest from Delhi for a truly auriferous site, the Golden Temple in **Amritsar**.

Once you're back in Delhi, it's easy to catch a cheap flight up to **Kathmandu**, Nepal, to begin your trekking adventure.

A SOUTHERN EXCURSION

Mumbai is the easiest starting point for exploring India's steamy southern tip. Kick off in its cosmopolitan restaurants, nightspots and shops, then sashay south by rail to the lazy palm-fringed beaches of **Goa**. Head inland to historical, ruined **Hampi** and chill in **Bengaluru**. Next, cruise south to **Kerala** and spend endless days on its languorous backwaters. Move over to French-flavoured **Puducherry** before catching a train to **Chennai**. Fill up on *idli* (spongy, round fermented rice cake) and finish up with a flight to **Colombo**, the starting point for your Sri Lankan holiday.

THE CORNERS

Feeling particularly intrepid, flush with cash and OK with paperwork? Head for the corners: the area's northeast, northwest, southeast and southwest. India's northeastern states, such as the incredible mountain state of **Sikkim**, rarely see foreign travellers and provide amazing cultural diversity. The northeast also holds the mysterious neighbouring **Kingdom of Bhutan**. Note that travel permits are required for Sikkim and other areas of the northeast (apply at least three months in advance), and a visit to Bhutan must be made in conjunction with an official tour company.

In the northwest the main draw is **Ladakh** – its spectacularly jagged, arid mountains enfold this magical Buddhist ex-kingdom. It's a haven for adventurers, with everything from alpine mountaineering and mountain biking to river rafting and yoga on tap. After flying into **Leh** you'll need some days to acclimatise, but lucky for you the old town is dotted with stupas and crumbling mudbrick houses, and the whole scene is dominated by a dagger of steep rocky ridge topped by an imposing Tibetan-style palace and fort.

With some more permits you can almost completely escape the travel crush with several lazy days on India's **Andaman Islands**. A flight from **Chennai** gets you there in hours.

Finally, if luxurious beach resorts are your style, jump off India's southwest coast and kick back in the **Maldives**.

WHAT TO DO?

HIGHLIGHTS

- Exploring the endless sands of Rajasthan by camel, starting from the honey-coloured fort at **Jaisalmer** (India).
- Basking in the shade of the gem-encrusted **Taj Mahal** in Agra (India), the ultimate monument to love.
- Stirring your soul with a gentle boat ride along the sacred ghat-lined Ganges in **Varanasi** (India).
- Diving into **Mumbai**, India's wild and wonderful melting pot.
- Kicking back on a languid boat cruise through

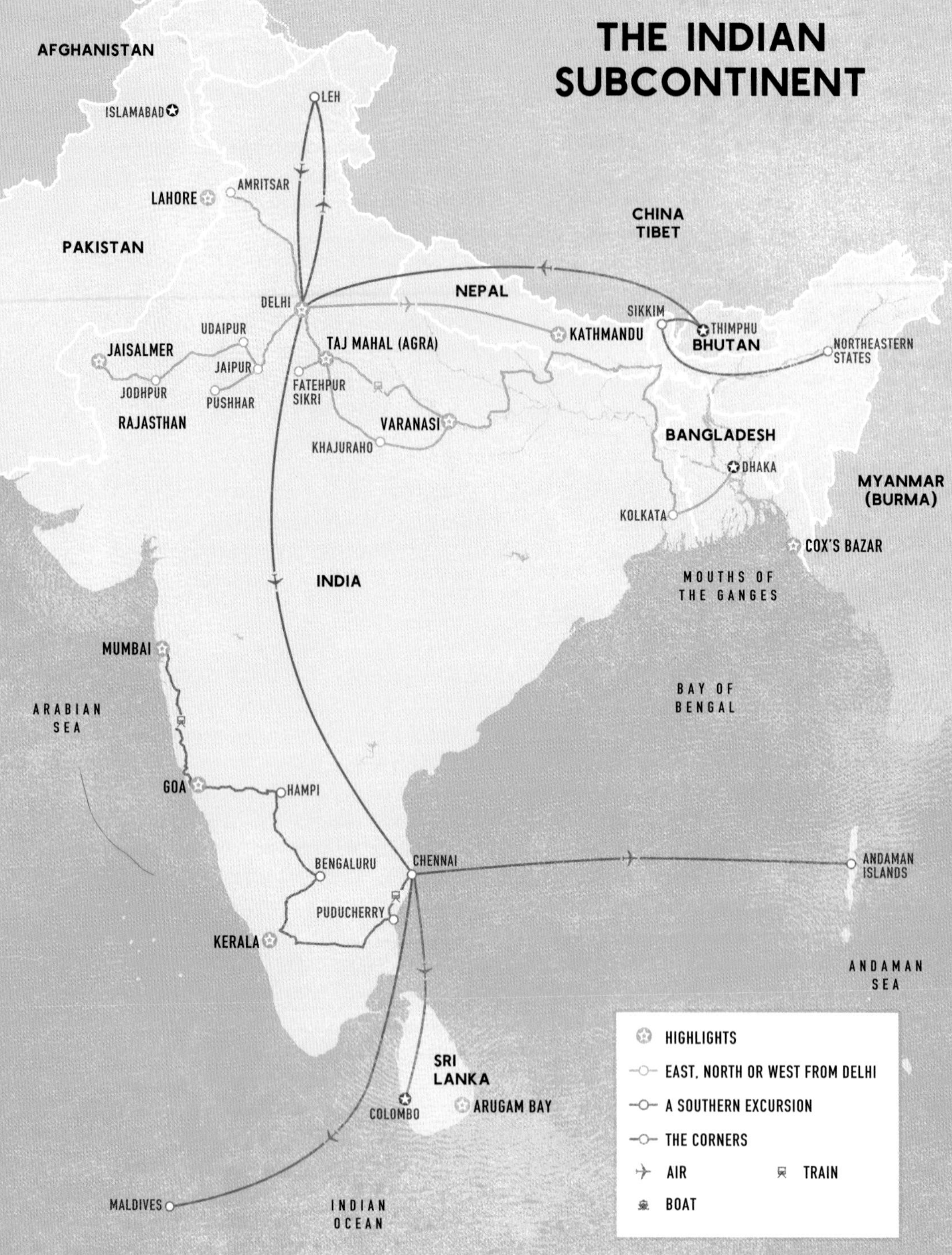
THE INDIAN SUBCONTINENT
AFGHANISTAN
ISLAMABAD
PAKISTAN
LAHORE
AMRITSAR
LEH
CHINA
TIBET
NEPAL
DELHI
KATHMANDU
SIKKIM
THIMPHU
BHUTAN
NORTHEASTERN STATES
UDAIPUR
JAISALMER
JAIPUR
JODHPUR
PUSHHAR
RAJASTHAN
TAJ MAHAL (AGRA)
FATEHPUR SIKRI
VARANASI
KHAJURAHO
BANGLADESH
DHAKA
KOLKATA
MYANMAR (BURMA)
COX'S BAZAR
MOUTHS OF THE GANGES
INDIA
MUMBAI
ARABIAN SEA
BAY OF BENGAL
GOA
HAMPI
BENGALURU
CHENNAI
ANDAMAN ISLANDS
PUDUCHERRY
KERALA
ANDAMAN SEA
SRI LANKA
COLOMBO
ARUGAM BAY
MALDIVES
INDIAN OCEAN
HIGHLIGHTS
EAST, NORTH OR WEST FROM DELHI
A SOUTHERN EXCURSION
THE CORNERS
AIR
TRAIN
BOAT

A decorated gateway at the Amber Fort in Jaipur, India

Playing cricket at Oval Maidan next to Bombay High Court in Mumbai

India's Bandhavgarh National Park is famed for its Bengal tigers

Wish you were here: greetings from the Yamuna River en route to the Taj Mahal in Agra, India

the palm-fringed backwaters of **Kerala** (India).
• Soaking up the magical atmosphere of the Sikh's holiest of shrines, the Golden Temple in **Amritsar** (India).
• Lying on the sand by day and raving by night on the beaches of **Goa** (India).
• Exploring (and surfing) the laid-back beaches around **Cox's Bazar** (Bangladesh).
• Immersing yourself in the historic centre of old **Kathmandu** (Nepal), an open-air architectural museum of magnificent medieval temples, pagodas and shrines.
• Spotting leopards, treading the mangrove forests and catching the waves at **Arugam Bay** (Sri Lanka).
• Climbing the high path to Bhutan's iconic cliff-clinging monastery, **Taktshang Goemba**.

GET ACTIVE

Even the simplest task can be a major activity in North India, Nepal and Bhutan, where sheer mountain sides, winding paths and thin air demand fitness.

Trekking & Mountaineering

Compared with the Himalaya, other mountain ranges aren't even trying. The world's highest mountains stretch all the way across the subcontinent from southern China to Afghanistan. These snowy mountains and lofty valleys naturally offer some of the best trekking on the planet.

Traditionally, Nepal has been the easiest place to trek, with the legendary Annapurna Circuit and the Everest Base Camp treks being top draws. There are basic hotels and restaurants along the main trails and the permits and such are easily obtainable. All trekkers are required to register their trek by obtaining a **Trekking Information Management System** (TIMS; www.timsnepal.com) card. The card costs the equivalent of US$20 for individual trekkers or US$10 if you are part of a group. You need to show the TIMS card at the start of the Annapurna and Langtang treks. At the time of research, the local authorities in the Khumbu had introduced a US$17.75 'entry fee' to the Everest region, but this could change, so check before heading out to Lukla.

India is also well set up for Himalayan trekking. Sikkim has some of the best, though high-altitude treks require permits – these can be organised by your trekking agents (as you must be accompanied by a guide). Application is made in Gangtok, so if you join a tour in Yuksom or Utterey, allow at least a day (and pay suitable expenses) for your documents to be delivered to the capital and back. Himachal Pradesh and Uttarakhand offer treks to remote temples and holy lakes, but you may need a permit and guide, and most routes are camping-only.

If you can afford to pay Bhutan's mandatory set fee for an all-inclusive guided trip (US$200-250 per person per day, depending on season), you'll experience some fantastic trekking routes. Mountain trekking is currently not considered safe in Pakistan. Trekking is strictly low altitude in Sri Lanka.

Lastly, altitude sickness can strike the fittest of trekkers (and yet leave an out-of-shape smoker alone), so always be aware of the warning signs – headache, dizzeness, fatigue, nausea, lack of appetite, trouble sleeping and shortness of breath – not doing so can be fatal. For more information on trekking in any of these areas, consult the relevant Lonely Planet guidebook or trekking guide.

Rafting

The rivers that rush down from the Himalaya offer spectacular whitewater rafting. Nepal is the best place to organise a trip – dozens of rafting companies offer trips on the Trisuli River near Kathmandu and the Sun Kosi River in east Nepal.

In India, you can go rafting on the Teesta and Rangeet rivers in Sikkim and West Bengal, and the Beas, Ganges, Indus, Spiti and Kanskar rivers in Himachal Pradesh. Rafting is also possible in Bhutan, but it's not really advisable in Pakistan.

Cycling & Mountain Biking

The subcontinent provides opportunities to experience mountain biking in its most extreme form – but be sure to bring your own ride, as locally made bikes aren't up to the rugged terrain. Popular spots to indulge include the Kathmandu Valley in Nepal and Sikkim and Himachal Pradesh in India. There are also more challenging routes along the Thimphu and Paro Valleys in Bhutan, and when it is safe the Karakoram Highway in Pakistan can be a highlight.

Lowland cycling is also popular in central and southern India and Bangladesh, but you'll have to share the roads with wandering cows, speeding trucks and drivers with seeming death wishes. Expect punctures, long days under the beating sun and endless questions from locals about your flashy foreign bike. On the upside, almost everyone will offer to help with minor fixes, and you'll have plenty of cyclist company everywhere.

Read up on bicycle touring before you travel: Rob Van Der Plas' *Bicycle Touring Manual*, Stephen Lord's *Adventure Cycle-Touring Handbook* and Laura Stone's *Himalaya by Bike* are good places to start.

Diving, Snorkelling & Water Sports

Sri Lanka, traditionally beach central, offers everything from waterskiing to parasailing. Surfers will find decent breaks on the east coast between April and October and from November to April on the south and west coasts. Arugam Bay is the pick for the east, while Midigama and Weligama are great shouts on the south coast. Hikkaduwa is the west coast's best break. Sri Lanka is a good place to learn because of its consistent surf year-round, but it must be said that the quality of waves is far lower than in nearby Maldives and Indonesia.

South India's surf scene is booming. Hit the waves with surf schools in Kerala, Goa, Tamil Nadu, Puducherry (Pondicherry) and the Andaman Islands.

For some decent scuba diving and snorkelling your options are Sri Lanka (at Hikkaduwa and Unawatuna), on the touristy Maldives, or on India's Andaman Islands.

Other Activities

Adventure sports are incredibly cheap in India, but tread carefully, as safety standards aren't always up to scratch. Himachal Pradesh, Goa and Maharashtra are the main centres for paragliding and hang gliding, but there have been some tragic mishaps over the years.

Indian skiing has a better record and prices are possibly the lowest in the world. The main resorts are Solang Nullah in Himachal Pradesh. The ski season runs from January to March, with equipment available for hire from just ₹500 (£5.60/US$7/A$10).

Spectator sports are a popular diversion across the subcontinent, and there are countless opportunities to cheer on the local team. The most popular sports are cricket, which is a national obsession, football (soccer), field hockey and the bizarre traditional sport of *kabaddi* (which consists of teams of seven players trying to evade an opposition 'raider', who has to keep chanting '*kabaddi*' without drawing breath).

WILDLIFE

Lovers of rare animals and plants will be thrilled by the opportunities India's national-park system affords, from one-horned rhinos in the northeast to snow leopards in the Himalaya.

The huge draws are tigers and elephants. The opportunities to see tigers are the tiger reserves of Sunderbans, Bandhavgarh, Mudumalai and Tadoba-Andhari, and the national parks of Ranthambore, Kanha, Bandipur and Pench. Wild elephants can be seen in Kerala's wildlife sanctuaries of Periyar and Wayanad and many of the national parks in Assam. For rhinos, head to Royal Chitwan National Park in Nepal or Kaziranga National Park in India. Conventional leopards can be seen in many national parks in Sri Lanka.

Other animals that you might encounter include Asiatic lions, bears, crocodiles and numerous species of deer and birds. Monkeys are ubiquitous – so be wary of carrying bananas anywhere!

Some parks still offer safaris on elephant back, but we don't recommend these as there is now overwhelming evidence available to suggest that such activities are actually harmful for the elephants. The animals involved also often undergo brutal and systematic abuse in order to 'learn' how to accept riders.

A few parks can be explored by boat, including Sunderbans Tiger Reserve in West Bengal. Most parks have cheap government-run or private accommodation.

FESTIVALS

From the raucous exuberance of Holi to the anarchy of the Pushkar camel fair, festivals on the subcontinent are spectacular. Following is just a smattering of what's on offer.

- **Holi** (India) One of North India's most ecstatic festivals; Hindus celebrate the beginning of spring according to the lunar calendar, in February or March, by throwing coloured water and *gulal* (powder) at anyone within range. Bonfires the night before symbolise the demise of demoness Holika.
- **Losar** (Tibetan Buddhist areas) Buddhists celebrate the Tibetan new year in February/March with masked dances and processions.
- **Shivaratri** (India and Nepal) Hindus fast in February/March in honour of the cosmic dance performed by the god Shiva. Sadhus (holy men) make pilgrimages to Nepal and bathe in the Bagmati River in Kathmandu.
- **Punakha Drubchen** (Bhutan) This unique three-day event, whose highlight is a dramatic re-creation of a 17th-century battle, features hundreds of costumed warriors. A three-day *tsechu* then follows. It's held in February/March.
- **Rath Yatra** (India) Held in June/July, it's when Hindus commemorate the journey of Krishna from Gokul to Mathura with processions of gigantic temple 'chariots' pulled by thousands of eager devotees. The most famous procession takes place at Puri in Orissa.
- **Esala Perahera** (Sri Lanka) Kandy holds this huge and important pageant, with 10 days of candlelight processions and elephants lit up like giant birthday cakes. It's held in July/August.
- **Kataragama** (Sri Lanka) Hindu pilgrims visit the shrine at Kataragama and put themselves through the whole gamut of ritual masochism. It's held in July/August.
- **Onam** (India) In August or September, Onam is Kerala's biggest cultural celebration, when the entire state celebrates the golden age of mythical King Mahabali for 10 days.

• **Ganesh Chaturthi** (India and Nepal) Each August or September Hindus celebrate the 10-day Ganesh Chaturthi, the celebration of the birth of the much-loved elephant-headed god, with verve, particularly in Mumbai, Hyderabad and Chennai.
• **Durga Puja** (West Bengal, Northeast India and Bangladesh) Held in October, this is when Hindus make thousands of colourful statues of the goddess Durga and ritually immerse them in rivers and streams. At the same time, Nepal celebrates the Dasain festival with animal sacrifices, and central parts of India hold the Dussehra festival to celebrate the defeat of the demon king Ravana.
• **Diwali** (India and Nepal) During October/November, Hindus across the subcontinent light oil lamps and let off firecrackers for five days to show the god Rama the way home from his period in exile. The festival is known as Deepavali in some parts of India and Tihar in Nepal.

Buddhist monks celebrate the Tsechu festival in Thimphu, Bhutan

• **Pushkar Camel Fair** (India) One of the most famous events on the backpacker circuit, Pushkar's annual market day is now a chaotic free-for-all. You don't have to be in the market for a camel, as racing events and associated merrymaking make for a fantastic time. It's held in November.
• **Eid al-Fitr** (Pakistan, Bangladesh) In Muslim areas, people fast during the holy month of Ramadan and many shops and restaurants stay closed. The fast is broken on the feast of Eid al-Fitr. The festival moves with the lunar calendar, advancing 10 or 11 days each year.
• **Tsechu** (Bhutan) In spring and autumn, Buddhist monasteries across Bhutan hold five days of masked dances in honour of Guru Rinpoche.
• **Kumbh Mela** (India) Every three years, the world's largest festival (think tens of millions attending) takes place at either Allahabad, Haridwar, Nasik or Ujjain to commemorate an ancient battle between gods and demons.

NIGHTLIFE

The unquestionable capital of nightlife is Mumbai. Whatever your tipple and whatever your taste, you'll find it here, from dive bar to sky bar. The Colaba neighbourhood is rich in unpretentious pub-like joints (but also has some very classy places), while the neighbourhoods of Bandra, Juhu and Andheri are home turf for the film and model set. Some of the most intriguing new places are opening in midtown areas like Lower Parel, where a craft-beer revolution has taken hold. Dress codes often apply, so don't rock up in shorts and sandals.

The Indian university town of Bengaluru now has rock-steady reputation for nightlife and wide choice of chic watering holes makes it the place to indulge in a spirited session of pub-hopping in what's the original beer town of India. Many microbreweries have sprung up in the past few years, producing quality ales.

The rest of the region packs up much earlier. While you'll be able to grab a late-night beer almost anywhere travellers frequent, you won't get much in the way of nightlife. The use of alcohol is frowned upon in Pakistan, Bangladesh and Bhutan, and relatively rare in Sri Lanka and Nepal.

ROADS LESS TRAVELLED

Wanna really get away? Try Bangladesh. Chances are, once you're outside Dhaka you'll be the only foreigner. You'll be able to explore temples, beaches and archaeological sites in peace and you'll get to see the magnificent Sunderbans Tiger Reserve in a way almost no-one does. Check the news and exercise caution when visiting Bangladesh, as periodic political violence – usually centred on election periods – can mar the travel experience.

India's northeast, comprised of Assam, Sikkim and the surrounding states, offers opportunities for wildlife-watching and ruin-exploring without the tourist crush as well. Sadly, several other spectacular regions, including Pakistan's mountainous north and Kashmir, are too dangerous for many travellers.

OTHER ACTIVITIES

India is the source of many 'alternative' therapies. Yoga was invented here around 500 BC, and Siddhartha Gautama (the Buddha) achieved enlightenment near Bodhgaya at the same time.

The best place to study yoga is Rishikesh, India. Most ashrams expect you to follow strict rules regarding silence, diet and behaviour. Those in search of inner peace can study Buddhist meditation in Bodhgaya and Dharamsala in India and Kathmandu in Nepal. For a total-immersion experience, consider staying at a famous ashram, such as **Aurobindo** (www.aurosociety.org) near Puducherry.

A word of warning: not all subcontinental spiritual experiences are entirely wholesome. Every year, Lonely Planet receives dozens of complaints about thefts, scams and overzealous proselytising at ashrams and retreats. Do your homework before signing up for anything.

WORKING

If you're looking to pay your way, you're out of luck: you can't compete with the throngs of workers who need the employment more than you do. Even teaching English, the staple of the pay-your-own-way rover, is a tough gig to come by. This is because most secondary schools in the area teach English as a required subject. A few organisations offer (poorly) paid teaching gigs, but do your homework as several of these are dodgy.

Volunteering is a different story. India, Nepal and Sri Lanka have hundreds of humanitarian and conservation projects that need teachers, researchers, health-care staff and other support workers. Some accept direct applications, but most get their staff through various international volunteering organisations.

WHEN TO GO?

Peak season is between November and February, when views are clearest and the weather is relatively cool and dry. From February, the heat begins to build up. Travel can become unbearable until the monsoon arrives in June.

Some high-altitude areas – including Ladakh, Spiti and Lahaul in India – are accessible by road only from June to September.

WHAT TO EXPECT?

LOCALS & OTHER TRAVELLERS

India tosses up the unexpected. This can be challenging, particularly for the first-time visitor: the poverty is confronting, Indian bureaucracy can be exasperating and the crush of humanity may turn the simplest task into a frazzling epic. Even veteran travellers find their nerves frayed at some point.

One of the most common trigger points is constantly being within shouting distance of touts, hawkers and con merchants, who hang around the main travellers' haunts. As some of the most visible people you'll meet, they can tend to dominate parts of your day if you let them. In these situations it's best to keep your sense of humour and don't fall for the bait. Offer a smile and a bit of a chuckle – it tends to disarm them – and then just keep on walking. If you do the opposite and stop to protest, or make a scene, the aggravation only gets worse.

Expect prices to often be elevated for foreigners, but you can usually bargain down – keeping in mind that you'll be unimaginably rich in the eyes of many people you meet. Of course, there are some real *badmashes* (scoundrels). Theft is a risk in some areas – often through the use of drugged food and drink on trains. In all areas keep a low profile during public demonstrations and flash points of religious conflict.

Yet this is all part of the ride. With an ability to inspire, frustrate, thrill and confound all at once, adopting a 'go with the flow' attitude is wise if you wish to retain your sanity. Love it or loathe it – and most travellers see-saw between the two – to embrace India's unpredictability is to embrace its soul.

While some of the same challenges are faced in Nepal, Bangladesh and Sri Lanka, they are generally much less intense. Bhutan in comparison is a walk in the park – it's almost completely devoid of the scams, begging and theft that affects its neighbours.

As for your fellow travellers, well, you'll probably never meet such a broad selection of intellectuals, freaks, do-gooders, adventurers, enlightenment seekers, beach bums, drug fiends, obsessive trekkers and bar-stool philosophers. Enjoy.

BAKSHEESH PLEASE

Don't be surprised by regular demands for *baksheesh* (tips) in India, Nepal and Bangladesh, whether from someone in need in the street, from a porter in your hotel or from a bureaucrat who stamps your passport. It can feel like a gift, tip or bribe depending on the circumstances, but in the case of the latter it can open doors and make problems go away. In the case of the former, it's not really seen as begging; it's part of accepted local morality that rich people give some of their income to those less fortunate.

Don't feel persecuted – well-to-do locals also pay *baksheesh* on a regular basis. Always be conscious of the expectations that will be placed on the next foreigner in light of the amount you give and don't feel embarrassed about not giving *baksheesh* to someone who rendered absolutely no service at all.

FOOD

The food of this region is some of the best in the world. It's impossible to do the vast array of regional cuisines justice in a short space.

India provides the region's most famous cuisine, and the offerings in the surrounding countries resemble Indian food. Roughly speaking, the north emphasises breads such as *naan* and *roti*, and the high Muslim population ensures the ready availability of meat dishes such as goat, lamb and chicken. Fiery chillies, rich creams and hearty potatoes add heft to meals. In the south, rice is the staple carb, and fish and vegetables are the order of the day. Coconut milk and curry leaves add to the spicy mix.

Bangladeshi food tends to be less diverse, with fewer spices. Nepal's traditional offerings are even less diverse, with the main staple being *daal bhaat tarkari* – literally lentil soup, rice and curried vegetables. It's a tried and true fuel to keep you trekking, all day, every day (and it's usually the only thing available on the walking circuits). Kathmandu and Pokhara, however, are crammed with Indian, Chinese and European restaurants. Sri Lankan food is fresh and tasty, with emphasis on roasted spices and simmered curries.

Fresh juices and lovely yoghurt *lassis* are available almost everywhere you can go in the region, but stay clear of anything made from unboiled or untreated water. For drinking water, use a purifier if possible, and if you can't then stick with bottled water at all times. Also make sure that all fruits and vegetables have been peeled and that hot food has been thoroughly and freshly cooked.

LANGUAGE

English is widely spoken, but each region has its own dialects and languages. In India, Hindi is an official language, but 80% of the population speaks something else. Urdu is spoken by the northern and western Muslim population (especially in Pakistan), and Tamil and Sinhalese are the official languages of Sri Lanka. Bengali is spoken in Bangladesh, Nepali in Nepal and Dzongka (related to Tibetan) in Bhutan. Lonely Planet's *Hindu, Urdu & Bengali Prasebook* and *Nepali Phrasebook* will help you get your tongue around most of the local languages.

INDIAN MYTHS DEBUNKED

There's good news and bad news.
Bad news first: many of the myths are true. Yes, hotel owners may spike your drinks. Yes, children may fling shit at you in order to distract you from your bags or pockets. Yes, you can be thrown in jail for your entire life if you hit a cow in Nepal.
Some stuff, however, is just plain ridiculous. Take, for example, the paranoia-inducing legend that bottled-water sellers will replace the good stuff with tap water by drilling a hole in the bottom of the bottle. The claim is that the unsuspecting customer is tricked by the unbroken bottle-cap seal, so the vendor gets away with it. Nice story – but it makes no sense. You would have to miss the fact that (if this story were true) the seller would be draining away perfectly good bottled water, which they could simply sell in the first place for the same price – without going to all the trouble of drilling.
There are several more insidious myths that need debunking. You will not wake up in a bathtub full of ice to find your kidneys missing. You will not get attacked by tigers or elephants in the streets. Practising yoga in an ashram will not enable you to live to more than 200 years old. And you will not have to share a train carriage with goats, cows or chickens (that is, unless one of your fellow passengers has bribed the conductor).

COMMUNICATION

GSM and 3G network coverage tends to be decent in urban centres throughout the region, but in rural areas of India and Nepal it may be unreliable. Almost every hotel, restaurant and cafe in larger towns offer free Wi-Fi and connections are pretty good. You can even get (paid) Wi-Fi in places along the Everest Base Camp trek. Internet cafes are available in smaller towns.

HEALTH

No matter how careful you are, chances are you'll develop a case of the runs. Most bugs are short-lived, and you should avoid taking blockers such as Imodium unless you have a long bus trip in store. If things stay dodgy for more than two days, see a doctor.

Before you go, get advice on vaccinations, as you'll need plenty. Antimalarial medication is sensible if you're travelling in lowland areas. Other health problems can include cholera, dysentery, giardiasis and, in some areas, altitude sickness.

ISSUES

The most irritating aspect of your stay will most likely be the endless array of scammers, touts and con artists who will desperately try to part you from your money. The unfortunate truth is that almost all the rumours are true, from gem scammers who sell you worthless 'jewellery' to shady hotel restaurateurs who drug clients. Get educated at www.lonelyplanet.com/thorntree, where you'll find the advice you need to stay relaxed and secure.

Cases of sexual assault against female travellers have sadly been on the rise in India, and most governments advise that women should not travel alone. Caution should still be exercised even if travelling in groups.

Periodic violence dots the region. India and Pakistan continue to squabble over Kashmir, so it's still a no-go zone, and Pakistan itself is no longer considered safe for travel due to a high level of terrorism and the threat of kidnapping. India's northeastern states of Assam, Nagaland and Manipur have also experience political tension. Check the situation at travel advisory sites before setting off.

GETTING THERE

Most people fly into Mumbai, Delhi, Chennai or Kolkata. Trekkers in Nepal will generally make a beeline for Kathmandu. Bangladesh and Sri Lanka are connected with the major Indian cities by cheap flights. The majority of travellers to Bhutan arrive by air at Bhutan's only international airport in Paro, though some enter by road from India.

In India and Bangladesh, most independent travellers get around by rail, which is cheap and relatively efficient. Budget airlines will whisk you around for reasonable prices, and in the more mountainous regions (as well as in Nepal) you'll rely on buses.

AIR

A host of international airlines serve the region. Following are the local major players:

- **Air India** (www.airindia.com)
- **Biman Bangladesh Airlines** (www.biman-airlines.com)
- **Nepal Airlines** (www.nepalairlines.com.np)
- **SriLankan Airlines** (www.srilankan.com)

Budget options include:

- **GoAir** (www.goair.in)
- **IndiGo** (www.goindigo.in)
- **JetKonnect** (www.jetkonnect.co.in)
- **SpiceJet** (www.spicejet.com)

SAMPLE COSTS

	India (rupee, ₹)	Nepal (US$ or rupee, Rs)	Sri Lanka (US$ or rupee, Rs)	Bangladesh (taka, Tk)
Hostel: dorm bed	₹400-600 (US$5.70-8.50)	Rs 1130 (US$10)	Rs 1500-3000 (US$10-20)	Tk 250-1800 (US$3-21)
Midrange hotel: double room	₹1500-5000 (US$20-70)	Rs 2820-9025 (US$25-80)	Rs 3500-9000 (US$22-56)	Tk 1000-3000 (US$12-36)
Street snack	Samosa ₹7-10 (US$0.10-0.14)	*Momos* Rs 50-100 (US$0.45-0.90)	*Isso wade* Rs 25-50 (US$0.15-0.30)	*Bhelpuri* Tk 15-25 (US$0.18-0.30)
Budget meal	₹100-350 (US$1.40-5)	Rs 170-380 (US$1.50-3.36)	RS 200-500 (US$1.25-3.12)	Tk 80-150 (US$0.95-1.80)
Midrange restaurant: main	₹150-300 (US$2.13-4.25)	Rs 250-500 (US$2.21-4.42)	Rs 250-800 (US$1.56-5)	Tk 150-300 (US$1.80-3.60)
Cappuccino	₹50-150 (US$0.71-2.13)	Rs 150-250 (US$1.33-2.21)	Rs 300-500 (US$1.87-3.12)	Tk 25-50 (US$0.30-0.60)
1.5L Bottle of water	₹20-35 (US$0.28-0.50)	Rs 30-50 (US$0.27-0.45)	Rs 80-150 (US$0.50-0.94)	Tk 30-40 (US$0.35-0.50)
1L Petrol (gas)	₹75 (US$1.07)	Rs 106 (US$0.94)	Rs 128 (US$0.80)	Tk 90Rp (US$1.08)

SEA & OVERLAND

It's theoretically possible to travel overland from the subcontinent to Tibet, Afghanistan or Myanmar, but these journeys are either prohibitively expensive or perilous. International ferries are non-existent.

SPECIALIST TOUR OPERATORS

- **Asian Trekking** (www.asian-trekking.com) A large, well-organised and well-connected company that can organise logistically complicated treks and mountain climbs across the subcontinent.
- **Bhutan By Bike** (www.bhutanbybike.com) This tour company specialises in bike tours, from four-day jaunts to 10-day expeditions, and is able to customise tours.
- **Blue Sheep Journeys** (www.bluesheep.com.np) French-, German-, Spanish- and English-speaking agency, part of well-regarded Thamserkuu Trekking; tailored independent trekking experiences.

• **Himalayan Single Track** (www.himalayansingletrack.com) Offers an exciting and comprehensive array of mountain bike tours.
• **Jatrik** (www.jatrik.com) This is a boutique tour agency that organises cultural, literary, artistic, musical and special-interest tours to several festivals and events across rural Bangladesh.
• **Rainbow Photo Tours** (www.rainbowphototours.com) Photography enthusiasts should check out its expert-guided itineraries.
• **Sunbird Tours** (www.sunbirdtours.co.uk) An international birdwatching tour operator that includes Bhutan, India, Nepal and Sri Lanka in its extensive list of destinations.
• **Xplore Bhutan** (www.xplorebhutan.com) This adventure-tour company combines activities such as rafting and hiking with cultural tours.

Southern Asia's national parks are havens for big cats, including leopards

BEYOND THE INDIAN SUBCONTINENT

From India, you can catch relatively cheap flights to Singapore, Beijing, Hong Kong, Tokyo, the Middle East via Dubai, and Europe.

FURTHER INFORMATION

WEBSITES

• **Bangladesh Parjatan Corporation** (www.parjatan.gov.bd) The national tourism organisation website, with a wealth of information.
• **Bangladesh Railway** (www.railway.gov.bd) Timetables, train fares.
• **Incredible India** (www.incredibleindia.org) The official tourism site, with national travel-related information.
• **Inside Himalayas** (www.insidehimalayas.com) Online magazine and blog.
• **National Portal of Bhutan** (www.bhutan.gov.bt) Official government site.
• **Nepal Tourism Board** (www.welcomenepal.com) The official site: tourism news, a rundown of the country's sights and some glossy photos.
• **Sri Lanka Tourist Board** (http://srilanka.travel) The official tourism site, with tons of information.
• **Tourism Council of Bhutan** (www.tourism.gov.bt) Approved tour operators and travel regulations.
• **Visit Maldives** (www.visitmaldives.com) Official tourism site.
• **Visit Nepal** (www.visitnepal.com) Comprehensive private website with detailed travel tips.
• **Yamu** (www.yamu.lk) Sri Lanka-focused, it has excellent restaurant reviews, sights listings and more.

BOOKS

• **A Fine Balance** Rohinton Mistry's beautifully written, tragic tale set in Mumbai.

- **A Suitable Boy** More than 1300 pages of romance, heartbreak, family secrets and political intrigue from Vikram Seth.
- **Midnight's Children** Salman Rushdie's epic tale of a boy born at Indian independence.
- **Rabindranath Tagore: An Anthology** The masterworks of the greatest Bengali literary figure of all time.
- **Sam's Story** The simple, incisive tale of an illiterate village boy working in Colombo, by Elmo Jayawardena.
- **The Circle of Karma** Kunzang Choden tells the story of a young woman's journey across Bhutan to find her destiny.
- **The God of Small Things** Arundhati Roy writes a heartachingly beautiful story about a woman and her brother from Kerala.
- **While the Gods Were Sleeping** Elizabeth Enslin's part memoir, part-anthropological account of life in a Brahman family in Nepal.
- **White Tiger** Aravind Adiga's Booker-winning novel about class struggle in globalised India.

FILMS

- **Sholay** (1975) The most popular Bollywood film of all time. A cross between a spaghetti western, a buddy flick and a classic myth.
- **Gandhi** (1982) The masterwork that chronicles the great man's life and the struggles of Indian-Pakistani Independence and Partition.
- **Monsoon Wedding** (2001) A riotous and poignant affair directed by Mira Nair.
- **Devdas** (2002) A prodigal-son-gone-wrong tragedy, complete with betrayed love and hellfire. Actor Shahrukh Khan's masterwork.
- **Slumdog Millionaire** (2008) A runaway hit depicting the lives of the inhabitants of Mumbai's shantytowns and slums.
- **Everest** (2015) A gripping film about the deadly 1996 Everest expeditions, based on survivor Beck Weather's memoir.

DISCOVERING LIFE BESIDE THE GANGES

Not to sound overly melodramatic – I didn't think I was going to make it home. On my back as I checked into my flight was a bag full of 300 hypodermic needles. Two weeks before I'd learned that I'd need to inject myself in the stomach with blood thinner every 12 hours, like clockwork. Despite my overwhelming fear of death, I still knew I needed to go – I was a successful young geologist but wasn't happy with life, and I'd hoped this first solo adventure would be the kick in the backside my soul needed.

I landed in Varanasi, arguably the most overwhelming city in India. It's the most sacred place on earth for Hindus to die (liberating them from the cycle of birth, death and reincarnation), so the city welcomes countless Indian pilgrims who are nearing the end of their days. The sight of corpses is commonplace, and the first of many was carried past me within minutes of arrival. The streets were also heaving with life and poverty, and all the sights, sounds and smells that come along with it. The intensity of the situation was beyond anything that I had ever imagined, let alone ever experienced. Yet when I reached the western bank of the River Ganges, and looked down over all the funeral pyres to the grass-covered floodplains on the opposite bank, I felt such a sense of peace and calm.

Life and death was on full display, and at that moment I knew I'd not only love India, but my life too. My biggest realisation? The biggest tragedy wouldn't be dying – it would be not actually living. I was right. That scared young geologist didn't return home. I did. And I've never looked back.

Matt Phillips

Stilt fishermen can still be found practising their craft on the shoreline of some Sri Lankan beaches

USA, CANADA & THE CARIBBEAN

The great American experience is about so many things: bluegrass and beaches, snow-covered peaks and redwood forests, restaurant-loving cities, big open skies and – last but not least – road trips. There are some four million miles of highways in the USA that lead past red-rock deserts, below towering mountain peaks and through fertile wheat fields that roll off towards the horizon. Veer off the interstate and into a brimming metropolis whose name alone conjure a million different notions of culture, cuisine and entertainment.

Look more closely, and the American quilt unfurls in all its surprising variety: the eclectic music scene of Austin, the easy-going charms of antebellum Savannah, the eco-consciousness of free-spirited Portland, the magnificent waterfront of San Francisco and the captivating French Quarter of jazz-loving New Orleans. Each city adds its unique style to the grand patchwork that is America.

To the north is Canada, the globe's second-biggest country that not only stretches from sea to sea to sea, but also across six times zones. It has an endless variety of landscapes: sky-high mountains, glinting glaciers, spectral rainforests, outstretched prairies and remote beaches. These are the backdrop for plenty of awe-inspiring wildlife encounters from a big cast of local characters: bears, whales, elk and moose. The terrain also makes for a fantastic playground. Whether it's snowboarding Whistler's mountains, surfing Nova Scotia's swells or whitewater kayaking in the Northwest Territories, adventures abound. But Canada is more than just its great outdoors – its welcoming cities are a joy. No wonder three of them (Vancouver, Calgary and Toronto) were ranked in the world's top 10 most liveable cities at last count.

The Caribbean is a joyous mosaic of islands beckoning paradise-hunters, an explosion of colour, fringed by beaches and soaked in rum. It's a lively and intoxicating profusion of people and places spread over 7000 islands. But, for all they share, there's also much that makes them different.

Most visitors to the area spend some time in the USA, though Commonwealth ties and painless working holiday visa arrangements mean most Australians, Kiwis and Brits spend more time north of the border.

ITINERARIES

Hitting the trail in the States or Canada usually involves a car, but think outside the metal box and you might find yourself catching the train or even walking the trails of the Rockies or Appalachians. However you get there, it's a big region, so don't be shy of taking the odd flight to cover some country.

CANADIAN CROSSING

Hike, cycle and munch your way through **Vancouver**, where mountain trailheads brush shoulders with nude beaches and Chinatown. From Vancouver, head north along the stunning **Sea to Sky Hwy** to **Whistler** for year-round mountain sports. Stop for a tipple in the **Okanagan Valley**, one of Canada's best wine regions, before bunking down in **Kelowna** on the lip of a lake. If time allows, laze your way on Rte 6 southeast to **Nelson**, an artist hang-out with many a bong raised to dull the pain from biking/skiing/boarding wipeouts. Back north on the Trans-Canada Hwy, hike up massive snowcapped mountains in **Banff National Park**. For more winter wonderland, take the spellbinding **Icefields Parkway** north to **Jasper National Park**.

Warm up a little by heading out of the mountains into the plains of **Alberta** and **Saskatchewan**, where patchwork fields stretch off forever in every direction. **Saskatoon** breaks the monotony before **Winnipeg** with plenty of history, and a French quarter for good coffee and croissants. East of **Thunder Bay** in Ontario, the Trans-Canada Hwy skirts cliffs along **Lake Superior**. Skirt south to the car ferry 'short cut' to lake-studded **Bruce Peninsula** for top scuba and kayaking options. Snake south to the Canadian side at **Niagara Falls**, then plan on spending a couple of days in **Toronto** to enjoy the quintessential Canadian experiences of tower views, the **Hockey Hall of Fame** and full-moon canoe trips on the harbour. Detour north to **Algonquin Provincial Park**, Canada's wild side with wolves howling from hilltops over clear lakes.

Southeast in the capital **Ottawa**, snack on a famed Beaver Tail, and, during winter, skate with commuters on the frozen canal. Crack open the French phrasebook for **Québec** and plan a few days for **Montréal**, with partying and bagels that hold their own with New York City's. Watch out for freshwater whales in the **St Lawrence River**, which leads northeast to the province's cobblestone capital, **Québec City**.

WEST-COAST WANDERER

See the stars in **Los Angeles**, then take the fabled **Hwy 1**, built on fault lines and skirting rocky bluffs overlooking the Pacific. Stay a night in the college beach town of **Santa Barbara**, for beaches and a Spanish Moorish-styled courthouse.

Pitch your tent at cliff-clutching **Big Sur** for hiking or diving at the **Point Lobos State Reserve**, then bunk down at Steinbeck's Cannery Row in **Monterey**. Leave Hwy 1 to head off to **San Francisco** for boho by the bay, then rejoin Hwy 1 on the **Golden Gate Bridge**. Follow Hwy 1 to its end just south of the **Redwood National Park**, home to the famed big trees. Backtrack inland to get a glimpse of **Mt Shasta** on the way to Oregon. For more outdoorsy fun take in **Crater Lake National Park**, with drives along the country's deepest lake.

Back on the **Oregon Coast**, throw down your towel on the sand at places such as **Cannon Beach**. Save at least a day for the college town of Portland, with tasty beers and lively locals. Make for Washington and stop in the seaport town **Port Angeles** near glaciated Mt Olympus. In **Seattle** take the local caffeine high up the **Space Needle**, where grunge got going all those years ago. Cycle, kayak or sail around some of the 457 **San Juan Islands** before pulling into **Vancouver** and on into British Columbia's wilderness.

ROUTE 66 REVISITED

The Great Mother Road is a nostalgic drive through quintessential Americana. Only traces of the once-great highway remain, but this version is the United States drive-thru style. Start in **Chicago**, Illinois and head for **St Louis**, a legendary blues town. Stop for petrol (gas) in the cowtown-cum-metropolis **Kansas**, which contains a whole 13 miles of the original Route 66 before it cuts across to the true west of **Tulsa** and **Oklahoma City**.

Then the road grabs the panhandle of Texas,

USA, CANADA & THE CARIBBEAN

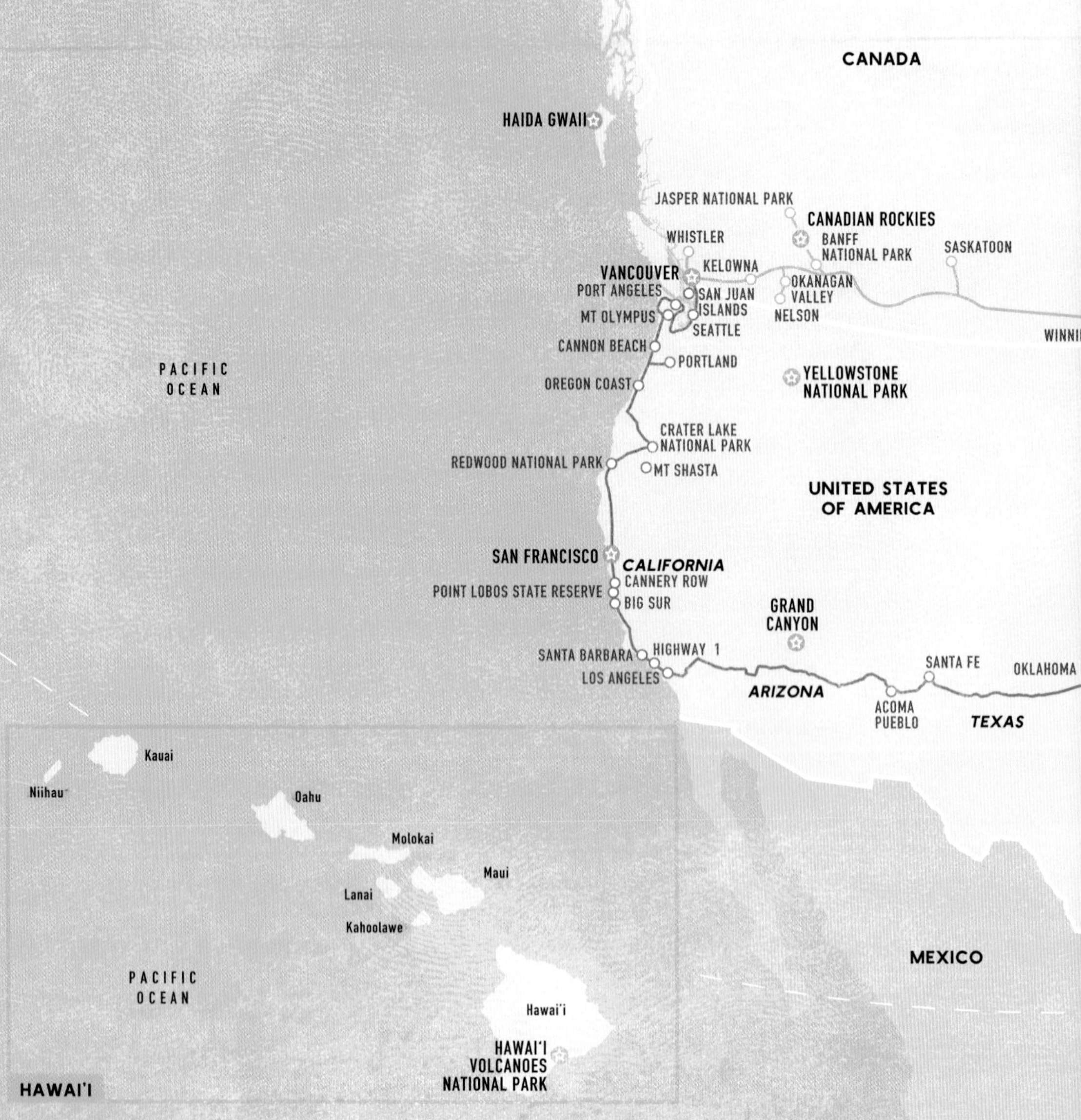

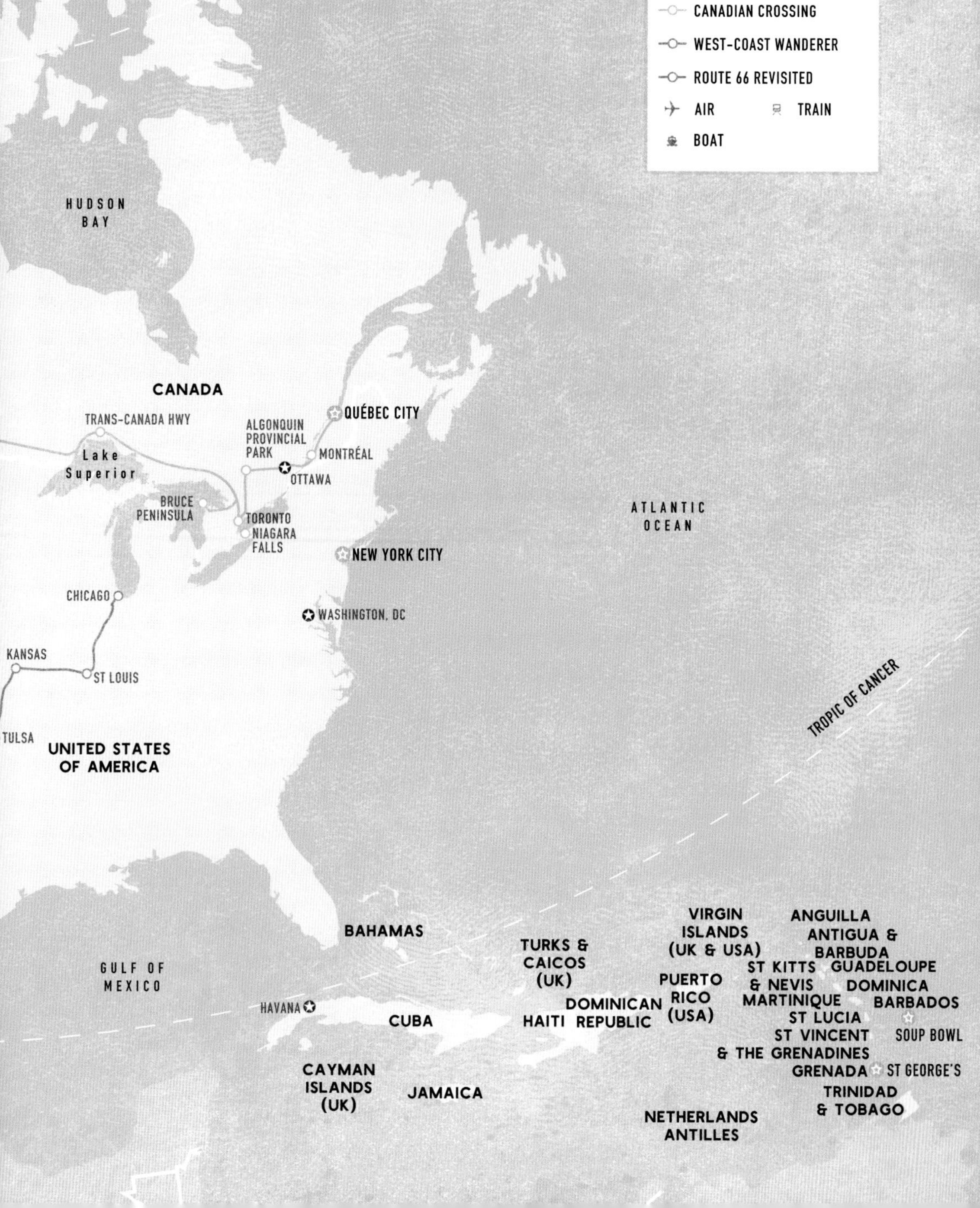

GREENLAND
(DENMARK)
HIGHLIGHT
CANADIAN CROSSING
WEST-COAST WANDERER
ROUTE 66 REVISITED
AIR
TRAIN
BOAT
HUDSON
BAY
CANADA
TRANS-CANADA HWY
Lake
Superior
ALGONQUIN
PROVINCIAL
PARK
QUÉBEC CITY
MONTRÉAL
OTTAWA
BRUCE
PENINSULA
TORONTO
NIAGARA
FALLS
NEW YORK CITY
ATLANTIC
OCEAN
CHICAGO
WASHINGTON, DC
KANSAS
ST LOUIS
TULSA
UNITED STATES
OF AMERICA
TROPIC OF CANCER
GULF OF
MEXICO
BAHAMAS
HAVANA
CUBA
CAYMAN
ISLANDS
(UK)
JAMAICA
TURKS &
CAICOS
(UK)
HAITI
DOMINICAN
REPUBLIC
VIRGIN
ISLANDS
(UK & USA)
PUERTO
RICO
(USA)
ANGUILLA
ANTIGUA &
BARBUDA
ST KITTS
& NEVIS
GUADELOUPE
DOMINICA
MARTINIQUE
BARBADOS
ST LUCIA
SOUP BOWL
ST VINCENT
& THE GRENADINES
GRENADA
ST GEORGE'S
TRINIDAD
& TOBAGO
NETHERLANDS
ANTILLES

Second Line street parades are a Sunday tradition in New Orleans

Reaching velocity on the slopes of Whistler, British Columbia, Canada

There are few more famous city signifiers than the Golden Gate Bridge in San Francisco

which includes the halfway point and the sculpture junkyard of cars stuck in the ground. There's more cow-poking in **New Mexico** as the road passes **Acoma Pueblo** and **Santa Fe**, and in **Arizona** you'll find the longest uninterrupted section of the original route as well as several small towns on a serious nostalgia binge. **California** is the home stretch with the original McDonald's, and at the end of the road is Los Angeles County's **Santa Monica**, where the beach and boardwalk await.

WHAT TO DO?

HIGHLIGHTS

- Hitting the streets of **New York City** (USA) to experience its staggering number of museums, parks and ethnic neighbourhoods that are scattered over its five boroughs.
- Gazing at iconic wildlife and marvelling at geologic wonders – geysers, fluorescent hot springs, fumaroles – in the world's first national park, **Yellowstone** (USA).
- Wandering over the Golden Gate Bridge and into the diverse districts of **San Francisco** (USA), with great indie shops, fabulous restaurants and bohemian nightlife.
- Hiking, biking, rafting or mule riding in the mighty depths of the **Grand Canyon** (USA).
- Exploring **Hawai'i Volcanoes National Park** (USA), checking out the crater and forests thick with tree ferns by day, then by night witnessing the magical glow of lava pouring into the sea.
- Skiing or boarding down the saw-toothed, white-topped **Canadian Rockies** straddling the British Columbia–Alberta border.
- Revelling in the world's most beautiful urban playground, **Vancouver** (Canada) – ski, kayak, sail, hike, and travel your taste buds.
- Absorbing the atmosphere, romance, melancholy, eccentricity and intrigue of French-speaking **Québec City** (Canada), with its 350-year-old stone ramparts, glinting-spired cathedrals and jazz-soaked corner cafes.
- Watching the world go by in the harbour of **St George's** (Grenada), a buzzing little horseshoe-shaped inlet bobbing boats, busy cafes and a sprinkling of shady spots.
- Surfing the **Soup Bowl** (Barbados), an east-side break that has crashed on to the world surf scene.

GET ACTIVE

The USA, Canada and the Caribbean have world-class terrain for just about any outdoor pursuit you care to mention. No matter what makes you tick, you'll find a perfect spot to do it and plenty of gung-ho folks to do it with.

Snowsports

Snowboarding is almost as popular as skiing on northern American slopes. Canada's main slopes are in the Rockies, which straddles the border of Alberta and British Columbia border, and at Whistler (North America's largest ski resort). Ontario and Québec have some more subdued slopes. In the USA, the Rocky Mountain states (Colorado in particular) are known for the white stuff, including Aspen, Vail, Big Sky and Jackson Hole. Mammoth and Lake Tahoe in the Sierra Nevada are California's major downhill destinations. To get off the beaten track, take on Alaska's slopes around Juneau, Anchorage and Fairbanks.

Surfing & Kitesurfing

The USA has its stamp all over surfing, from the big kahunas of Hawai'i to legendary Californians such as Malibu, Rincon and Mavericks. Waves reach monstrous proportions, mostly on O'ahu's North Shore, between November and February. Beginners get the basics at gentle Waikiki and then go gawk at the world-class big-wave pros. Maui attracts top international windsurfers like moths to a flame. Canada has some chilly surfing off the east coast in Nova Scotia and out west in British Columbia off Vancouver Island at Tofino.

Except for Barbados, which is further out into the open Atlantic, the islands of the Eastern Caribbean aren't really great for surfing. Once you head north and west, however, you can find surfable swells.

Hawaii is also a great place for kitesurfing, particularly at Waipulani Beach in Maui. San Francisco also catches the sweet summer winds that make the bay a good place to try kitesurfing, while Oregon has Hood River and Texas offers South Padre Island – both good spots to be blown away. The favourable winds and good water conditions found throughout the Caribbean have boosted the popularity of windsurfing and kitesurfing in the region.

© Putt Sakdhnagool / Getty Images

Havasu Falls is one of the Grand Canyon's innumerable sights

Trekking, Hiking & Rock-Climbing

If you're looking for a purely hiking holiday with a taste of the whole region, the Pacific Crest Trail zigzags from Canada to Mexico taking in the natural wonders of California, Oregon and Washington along the way. The USA has even more long-distance trekking options, ranging from the multiday Appalachian Trail to shorter strolls around Yosemite National Park. Desert trails and canyoneering in the southwest can be a good option in winter, and the mile trek down to the Grand Canyon is a must. At the other end of the thermometer, Alaska offers epic tracks including the Resurrection Pass Trail and Chena Dome Trail west of Fairbanks. The Chilkoot Trail is another classic, which starts in Alaska and climbs into British Columbia, Canada.

Elsewhere in Canada, Ontario's Killarney Provincial Park has a long-distance trail around the tops of its rounded mountains. Other vertically oriented regions include Gaspésie Park and Mont Tremblant Park (Québec), Gros Morne National Park in Newfoundland and Cape Breton Highlands National Park in Nova Scotia. More hard-core trekking can be had in Pukaskwa National Park and on the Trans Canada Trail (can you spare a few years?), which at almost 24,000km is the world's longest recreational trail. There are incredible day-hike options throughout the country, many within striking distance of major cities such as Vancouver.

The Caribbean is not renowned for trekking, but Cuba has some good options such as the three-day trek over the Sierra Maestra via the 2000m-high Pico Turquino.

Rock-climbing and mountaineering are popular in California's Yosemite National Park (El Capitan and Half Dome are legendary big-wall climbs), the Sierra Nevada and the Rockies. Canadian climbing meccas include Collingwood, Sault Ste Marie and Thunder Bay in Ontario, Banff and Jasper in Alberta, and Squamish in British Colombia. In Alaska, Denali (6096m), the highest peak in North America, is the site of organised expeditions in late spring and early summer.

Diving

Keeping a US toe in the Pacific Islands, Hawaii has awesome diving, with caves, canyons, lava tubes, vertical walls, WWII shipwrecks and the sunken volcanic crater of Molokini all awaiting you. There's casual snorkelling in Hanauma Bay Nature Preserve. Elsewhere in the USA, the Great Lakes, the Florida Keys (where you can dive with sharks) and southern California all feature top-notch underwater action.

The Caribbean is a diver's dream. The wide variety of dive sites are easily accessible with excellent local dive operators, and many resorts cater just to divers. Incredible sites include: Little Cayman's Bloody Bay Wall (Cayman Islands), Saba Marine Park (Saba), Bonaire National Marine Park (Bonaire), Statia Marine Park (Sint Eustatius) and the reefs and wrecks galore in Grenada.

Cycling & Mountain Biking

Mountain biking is huge in the USA, from the forest trails of the Pacific Northwest to the desert around Moab in Utah and the epic routes of the Rockies. Cycle-touring hotspots include the forests of New England, the Atlantic coast's offshore islands, the swamps of southern Louisiana, and California's west coast and wine country. In Canada, the North Shore of Vancouver is legendary in mountain-biking circles, with the Laurentian Mountains of Québec and the Rockies of Alberta and British Columbia being other prime destinations. Cycling is the most budget-friendly way to get around on the Caribbean islands.

WILDLIFE

Whale watching is popular in New England (USA) and further north in Nova Scotia and Newfoundland (Canada). There are numerous places to see whales in the Caribbean and along the Californian coast. Orcas (aka killer whales) are often spotted spyhopping off Vancouver Island, Haida Gwaii and all the way up the west coast into Alaska. Beautiful beluga whales can be seen in Hudson's Bay (Canada). Manatees can be seen in Florida, which is also a good place to dive with sharks.

Bears rule the roost in northern Canada (beware the hefty polar bears in Churchill, Manitoba). Wolves, mountain lions and grizzly bears flourish in famous North American national parks such as Glacier and Yellowstone, which harbours the greatest unfenced concentration of charismatic (and photogenic) megafauna in the lower 48 states.

FESTIVALS

- **Festival San Sebastián** (Puerto Rico) This famous street party, Fiestas de la Calle San Sebastián, draws big crowds to Old San Juan for a week in mid-January.
- **Sundance Film Festival** (USA; www.sundance.org) The legendary festival brings Hollywood stars, indie directors and avid film-goers to Park City, UT, for a 10-day indie extravaganza in late January.
- **Québec City Winter Carnival** (Canada; carnaval.qc.ca/en) Features ice sculptures, music and dogsled racing. Held in February.

• **Trinidad Carnival** (Trinidad) A year in the making, this is the biggest party in the Caribbean. Steel-pan bands, blasting *soca* and calypso music, and outrageous costumes. Late February or early March.
• **Mardis Gras** (USA; www.mardigras neworleans.com) Held in late February or early March, the finale of Carnival on Fat Tuesday in New Orleans' is legendary.
• **South by Southwest** (USA; www.sxsw.com) Each March, Austin, TX, hosts one of the biggest music festivals in North America, one that carries influence worldwide. It's also a major film festival and interactive fest – a platform for ground-breaking ideas.
• **Stratford Theater Festival** (Canada; www.stratfordfestival.ca) Four theatres stage contemporary drama, music, operas and, of course, works by Shakespeare between the months of April and November.

With a twist and a dash, a mixologist goes to work in a Brooklyn bar

• **Chicago Blues Festival** (USA; www. chicagobluesfestival.us) It's the globe's biggest free blues fest – it kicks off in June with three days of the music that made Chicago famous.
• **Montréal Jazz Festival** (Canada; www. montrealjazzfest.com) Two million music lovers descend on the city late June, when the heart of downtown explodes with jazz and blues for 11 straight days (many concerts are free).
• **Summer Solstice** (USA) Almost continuous daylight, with midnight baseball, axe-tossing and tree-climbing competitions held in June across Alaska.
• **Reggae Sumfest** (Jamaica; www. reggaesumfest.com) The biggest of all reggae and dancehall festivals, held in late July in Montego Bay Jamaica. .
• **Festival Acadien** (Canada; https:// festivalacadien.ca) Acadians tune their fiddles and unleash their Franco-Canadian spirit for two weeks in early August. Held in Caraquet, New Brunswick.
• **Burning Man** (USA; www.burningman.com) Thousands of revellers, artists and free spirits descend on Nevada's Black Rock Desert in late August for a week to create a metropolis of art installations, theme camps and environmental curiosities.
• **Dark Sky Festival** (Canada; https:// jasperdarksky.travel) In late October, this festival in Jasper fills two weeks with events celebrating space. Hear talks by astronauts, see the aurora borealis reflected in a glacial lake and gaze through a telescope into the great beyond.

NIGHTLIFE

There are endless possibilities and places to enjoy the nights in the USA, Canada and the Caribbean. Here are a few top locations:
• **Austin** (USA) Home to more than 200 live

music venues, Austin proudly wears the music crown. And there are bejillions of bars in Austin. The legendary 6th St bar scene has spilled onto nearby thoroughfares, especially Red River St.

• **Barbados** Barbados loves to *lime* (party). The main nightlife on the island is concentrated around St Lawrence Gap, but there are also good venues in Holetown.

• **Boston** (USA) Irish pubs, a dynamic craft-beer movement and a red-hot cocktail scene. Boston's nightlife is also richer thanks to the huge population of students who keep it real.

• **Chicago** (USA) Chicagoans love to hang out in drinking establishments. Blame it on the long winter, when folks need to huddle together somewhere warm. Blame it on summer, when sunny days make beer gardens and sidewalk patios so splendid.

• **Halifax** (Canada) Halifax rivals St John's, NL, for the most drinking holes per capita. The biggest concentration of attractive bars is on Argyle St, where temporary street-side patios expand the sidewalk each summer.

• **Kingston** (Jamaica) Kingston is the best town in Jamaica for bar-hopping and clubbing, and you'll never want for after-hours action.

• **Las Vegas** (USA) The Strip is ground zero for some of the country's hottest clubs and most happening bars, but Downtown's Fremont East Entertainment District is the go-to place for Vegas' coolest non-mainstream haunts.

• **Los Angeles** (USA) From post-industrial coffee roasters and breweries to mid-century lounges, classic Hollywood martini bars and cocktail-pouring bowling alleys, LA serves its drinks with a generous splash of wow.

• **Miami** (USA) Miami has an intense variety of bars to pick from that range from grotty dives to beautiful – but still laid-back – lounges and nightclubs. The live music scene is fantastic.

• **Montréal** (Canada) Maybe it's the European influence: this is a town where it's perfectly acceptable, even expected, to begin cocktail hour after work and continue well into the night. A great Jazz music scene to boot.

• **New Orleans** (USA) New Orleans doesn't rest for much. But the city isn't just an alcoholic lush. A typical night out features just as much food and live music as booze.

• **New York City** (USA) Everything from terminally hip cocktail lounges and historic dive bars to specialty tap rooms and Third Wave coffee shops. Then there's the legendary club scene, spanning from celebrity staples to gritty, indie hangouts. Head downtown or to Brooklyn for the parts of the city that, as they say, truly never sleep.

• **Portland** (USA) After dinner, Wharf St transforms into one long bar. Other places are along Fore St, between Union and Exchange Sts, and the northern end of Middle St. If you want something more low-key, try the West End or Munjoy Hill.

• **San Francisco** (USA) SF bars and clubs are there to oblige. But why stick to your usual, when there are California wines, Bay spirits and microbrews to try? DJs set the tone at clubs in SF, where the right groove gets everyone on the dancefloor – blending LGBT and straight in a giddy motion blur.

• **St John's** (Canada) George St is the city's famous party lane. Water and Duckworth Sts also have plenty of places to drink, but the scene is slightly more sedate. Don't forget to try the local Screech rum.

• **Toronto** (Canada) The Toronto pub and bar scene embraces everything from sticky-carpet beer holes, cookie-cutter franchised 'British' pubs and Yankee-style sports bars to slick martini bars, rooftop patios, sky-high wine rooms and an effervescent smattering of LGBT hangouts.

• **Vancouver** (Canada) The regional craft-beer scene keeps many quaffers merry. For a night out with locally made libations as your side dish, join savvy drinkers supping in the bars of Gastown, on Main St and around Commercial Drive.

ROADS LESS TRAVELLED

Alaska, and Canada's three territories – Yukon, Northwest Territories and Nunavut – are truly wild. Explore, hike, canoe and learn about Inuit traditions. Northern British Columbia also has some undiscovered provincial parks: Moose and mountain-goat mecca Stone Mountain, Muncho Lake with a dazzling blueness, and Liard River Hot Springs with soul-warming hot tubs to soak away the road. Canada's far eastern province of Newfoundland and Labrador is another entertaining option. The island of Newfoundland is perhaps the friendliest place on the continent, and across the Strait of Belle Isle is Labrador, an undulating, rocky, puddled expanses of 293,000 sq km that sprawls toward the Arctic Circle. If you ever wanted to imagine the world before humans, Labrador is the place.

If you're looking for warmer options, the Caribbean has a few escape hatches from the tourist traps: the 'emerald isle' of Montserrat, a perfect haunt for nature lovers; Saba, a divers' paradise; Sint Eustatius (Statia), a haven for endangered species and aquatic life; and St-Barthélemy (St Barts), home to the historical Port of Gustavia and exquisite beaches.

WORKING

Getting a job in the States can be difficult. If you're from the United Kingdom, your best bet is to secure a J1 visa through sponsorship by an exchange group such as Bunac (British Universities North America Club; www.bunac.org), which organises a variety of work and camp jobs. For Australians and New Zealanders, there is a Student Work and Travel Pilot Program visa valid for a year (more info at http://travel.state.gov).

Canada, as part of the Commonwealth, offers a working holiday visa, the International **Experience Canada** (www.international.gc.ca), for 18- to 35-year-olds.

The Caribbean isn't a particularly great place to look for work, due to its high unemployment rate and low pay. Crewing on a boat is one of the few opportunities in the area. You can start with Florida-based **Crewfinders** (www.crewfinders.com).

Working in North America without a visa isn't advisable, and border-security staff have been known to refuse entry to jobseekers if they find evidence that they'll be working in the country.

See the Jobs section (p115) for more information.

WHEN TO GO?

Most of the USA and southern parts of Canada are visitable year-round. Warm temperatures and generally sunny skies are the norm between June and September, though things can get very hot and humid at times, especially in the far south. During this period Alaska and Canada's far north have a brief thaw and plenty of rain, with 24-hour daylight in early summer. The northwest coast can also be sopping wet, though much of the precipitation falls during winter (great for the ski resorts, where it falls as snow between December and March). The great North American prairies – lying in the Midwest between the Rocky Mountains and eastern seaboard – are fairly dry year-round and stay well below freezing point in winter. Florida enjoys a tropical climate and California's southern coast is comfortable year-round. Hawaii's balmy weather is near perfect, with northeasterly breezes – the rainiest period is between December and March.

The Caribbean delivers warm weather, except during hurricane season from August to September. From mid-December to mid-April, the Caribbean is at its busiest, though see Road Less Travelled (opposite) for some quiet options. May, June and November are better times to visit the traditionally busy islands.

WHAT TO EXPECT?

LOCALS & OTHER TRAVELLERS

It's just as common to see Canadians and Americans travelling around their own countries as it is to see international visitors. Most international visitors head for the big cities – New York, San Francisco and Vancouver are high on many must-visit lists, though national parks are becoming more popular. If you're backpacking you'll meet more travellers in Cuba, Jamaica and the Dominican Republic than in the eastern islands, which are less budget friendly.

You'll find that Americans are friendly (expect people to chat to you at bus stops and bars), polite (they seriously say 'sir' and 'ma'am') and very helpful people (handy when you're presented with 50 choices of bread in a café). The rich history of immigration (forced or voluntary) gives America a unique sum-of-its-parts identity. Afro-American culture is strong, with Mexican and Latin American culture becoming increasingly influential. Don't underestimate the power of US patriotism with flags waved at every baseball or football game and many students swearing a pledge of allegiance to the US before starting lessons.

Most Canucks (Canadians) live in the far south of the country where the climate is less harsh, and where the land is traditionally more arable. This means that 90% of the population is within 160km of the US border. That said, culturally, the general population is closer to the former colonial powers the United Kingdom and France (Québec is the centre of French loyalists) than to their southern neighbours. Compared with the US citizens, Canadians are often considered a little more reserved, more laid-back and more outward looking (they are far from boring). More than 20% of the country's population is foreign-born, with British Columbia having long welcomed Japanese, Chinese and South Asian immigrants – more than a third of Vancouver's population is now of Chinese heritage.

Toronto is incredibly diverse too, with visible minorities making up more than half of the city's population. Canada's aboriginal community is a proud one and it's playing a larger role in tourism as its people push to retain or regain their traditional cultural roots. This group, consisting of First Nations (those of North American Indian descent), Métis (those with 'mixed blood' ancestry) and Inuit (those in the Arctic), makes up 4.3% of the population.

The Caribbean is a region of staggering cultural diversity. In many ways it's where the modern world was first born, where the peoples of the Americas, Europe and Africa first met – a product of globalisation before the term was even invented.

FOOD

In a country of such size and regional variation, you could spend a lifetime eating your way across America and barely scratch the surface. Owing to such scope, dining American-style could mean many things: from munching on pulled-pork sandwiches at an old roadhouse to feasting on sustainably sourced seafood in a waterfront dining room.

Mexican food in California is generally just as good as you'll get south of the border. The cuisine of the Deep South, Louisiana in particular, fuses its immigrant flavours (which include French, Sicilian and Native American Choctaw) with the bounty of the New World to produce dishes such as shrimp rémoulade, *beignets* (deep-fried doughnut) and *pain perdu* (sweet French toast).

Canadian cuisine is nothing if not eclectic, a casserole of food cultures blended together from centuries of immigration. *Poutine* (French fries covered in gravy and cheese curds), Montréal-style bagels, salmon jerky and *pierogi* (dumplings) jostle for comfort-food attention. For something more refined, Montréal, Toronto and Vancouver have well-seasoned fine-dining scenes, while regions across the country have rediscovered the unique ingredients grown, foraged and produced on their doorsteps – bringing distinctive seafood, artisan cheeses and lip-smacking produce to menus.

Caribbean fare includes loads of seafood, but you'll also get a chance to build up a list of exotic fruits, such as *soursop* (a prickly-skinned fruit with tingly ice-cream flavoured flesh), guava and naseberry (usually used in ice creams and jams).

LANGUAGE

English is the lingua franca across North America, but it can be difficult to understand the Creole patois in the Caribbean. French and English are both official languages in Canada, but only in Québec will you need your French phrasebook. Spanish is spoken in Cuba, the Dominican Republic and Puerto Rico. Thanks to immigration from Latin America, 'Spanglish' is increasingly spoken in El Norte (aka the USA) and Spanish is the USA's second most widely spoken language.

COMMUNICATION

Travellers will have few problems staying connected in tech-savvy USA or Canada. Most hotels, guesthouses, hostels and motels have Wi-Fi (usually free, though luxury hotels are more likely to charge for access), and countless cafes offer free Wi-Fi. Some cities have Wi-Fi-connected parks and plazas. Internet cafes are limited to main tourist areas.

Internet access and Wi-Fi is generally easily found throughout most of the Caribbean.

The North American mobile-phone (or 'cell') system uses GSM 1900 or CDMA 800. The geek-free translation is that unless you have a tri-band model phone, you're better off renting or buying a pay-as-you-go option for the length of your stay.

HEALTH

North America is a pretty healthy place, which is just as well since being ill costs a fortune. You may have to get special insurance to cover you in the USA, so double-check that your coverage includes the States.

Outdoors, there's a small risk of tick-borne diseases (such as Rocky Mountain fever and Lyme disease), giardiasis (known locally as 'beaver fever'), caught by drinking contaminated water, and the odd case of rabies in the northern wilderness. Sharks are a rare health risk to surfers in Florida and northern California.

In the Caribbean a few more travel precautions are required. Some fresh water is contaminated with schistosomiasis (bilharzia) or leptospirosis, and mosquitoes in some areas carry dengue fever.

Consult the Health & Safety section and seek professional medical advice for more travel-health information.

SAMPLE COSTS

	USA (US dollar, US$)	Canada (Canadian dollar, C$)	Jamaica (Jamaican dollar, J$)	Dominican Republic (Dominican peso, RD$)
Hostel: dorm bed	US$20-40	C$25-40 (US$19-30)	J$2700-3385 (US$20-25)	RD$600-1000 (US$12-20)
Midrange hotel: double room	US$100-250	C$80-250 (US$61-191)	J$12,000-27,000 (US$90-200)	RD$25,000-50,000 (US$50–100)
Street snack	Hot dog US$2.50	*Poutine* C$6-9 (US4.50-6.90)	Jerk pork J$300-500 (US$2.20-3.70)	*Pastelitos* RD$50 (US$1)
Budget meal	US$10-25	C$13-20 (US$9.95-15.30)	J$500-650 (US$3.70-4.80)	RD$250-500 (US$5-10)
Midrange restaurant: main	US$15-25	C$15-25 (US$11.50-19)	J$1900-3200 (US$14-23.50)	RD$250-750 (US$5-15)
Cappuccino	US$3.50-5	C$3-5 (US$2.30-3.82)	J$350-500 (US$2.60-3.79	RD$50-100 (US$1-2)
1.5L bottle of water	US$1.50-3	C$1.50-3 (US$1.15-2.30)	J$150-250 (US$1.10-1.90)	RD$20-100 (US$0.40-2)
1L Petrol (gas)	US$0.78	C$1.25 (US$0.96)	J$144 (US$1.06)	RD$60 (US$1.20)

ISSUES

Despite its seemingly apocalyptic list of dangers – violent crime, riots, guns, earthquakes, tornadoes – the USA is actually a pretty safe country to visit. The greatest danger for travellers is posed by car accidents (buckle up – it's the law). For the traveller it's not violent crime but petty theft that is the biggest concern. When possible, withdraw money from ATMs during the day, or in well-lit, busy areas at night. When driving, don't pick up hitchhikers, and lock valuables in the trunk of your car before arriving at your destination.

Canada is one of the safest countries in the world. Pickpocketing and muggings are rare, especially if you take precautions.

In terms of individual safety and crime, the situation is quite varied in the Caribbean. Exercise extra caution in urban areas such as Pointe-à-Pitre (Guadeloupe), Fort-de-France (Martinique), some areas of Kingston (Jamaica), Port-au-Prince (Haiti) and downtown Port of Spain (Trinidad). You should check the latest on the safety in these regions by using government warning sites. August to September is hurricane season in the Caribbean (and southern USA), with many places closing in August.

Borders are pretty easy-going throughout the region, though the US Department of Homeland Security can occasionally shake down the odd traveller. If anything is out of order or if they suspect you of intending to work illegally, they'll send you straight home. Beefed-up domestic security means that there are strict limits on what you can carry on domestic flights; check the **Transport Administration Authority** (www.tsa.gov) for details.

GETTING THERE

AIR

Chicago, Dallas, Los Angeles, New York, Miami, San Francisco and Washington, DC are the USA's major international hubs, but flights into other US cities won't cost much more. Toronto, Montréal and Vancouver are the major Canadian air hubs. If you're coming from Australasia or Southeast Asia, it may be cheaper to hop on a flight to Hawaii and get a domestic flight within the US.

Most capital cities in the Caribbean serve as transport hubs, though access varies. Many North American airlines fly direct to the more popular islands. UK airlines serve former British colonies like Barbados and Antigua; French airlines serve the French-speaking islands; and Dutch carriers fly to Aruba, Bonaire, Curaçao and Sint Maarten. There are no direct flights from Australia, New Zealand or Asia.

Transatlantic alliances and code-share agreements mean that reaching many major Caribbean and far-flung North American destinations, such as Hawaii and Alaska, often requires at least one change of planes (in order to get the cheapest deal). Ask about the possibility of free stopovers on these routes.

Major local airlines include:

- **Air Canada** (www.aircanada.com)
- **Alaska Airlines** (www.alaskaair.com)
- **American Airlines** (www.aa.com)
- **Delta Airlines** (www.delta.com)
- **United Airlines** (www.united.com)

These budget carriers might be an option:

- **Air Transat** (www.airtransat.com)
- **Allegiant Air** (www.allegiantair.com)
- **Frontier Airlines** (www.flyfrontier.com)
- **JetBlue Airways** (www.jetblue.com)
- **Liat** (http://book.liat.com)
- **Southwest** (www.southwest.com)
- **Spirit Airlines** (www.spirit.com)
- **Sun Country Airlines** (www.suncountry.com)
- **WestJet** (www.westjet.com)

SEA

You can also travel to and from this region on a freighter, though it will be much slower and less cushy than a cruise ship. Nevertheless, freighters aren't spartan (some advertise cruise-ship-level amenities), and they are much cheaper (sometimes by half). Trips range from a week to two months; stops at interim ports are usually quick. For more information, try **Cruise and Freighter Travel Association** (www.travltips.com) and **Maris Freighter Cruises** (www.freightercruises.com). Another option is to score passage across the Atlantic or Pacific on a yacht while working as crew.

SPECIALIST OPERATORS

- **Backroads** (www.backroads.com) Designs a range of active, multisport and outdoor-oriented trips for all abilities and budgets.
- **Go Native America** (www.gonativeamerica.

com) A US-based organisation that offers tours into Native America.

- **Green Tortoise** (www.greentortoise.com) Try their hostel-hopper that goes between San Francisco, Los Angeles and Las Vegas, with trips further afield to Alaska, Baja Peninsula and Mexico.
- **Road Scholar** (www.roadscholar.org) This non-profit organisation offers study tours in nearly all provinces and many states for active people over 50, including train trips, cruises, and bus and walking tours.
- **Salty Bear Adventure Tours** (www.saltybear.ca) Backpacker-oriented van tours through the Canadian Maritimes with jump-on/jump-off flexibility.
- **TrekAmerica** (www.trekamerica.co.uk) Trips taking in a combination of big cities in the US and Canada, national parks, out-of-the-way towns and remote beaches.

BEYOND THE USA, CANADA & THE CARIBBEAN

The most obvious route out of the region is overland south into Mexico and Central America. There are no longer scheduled ferries between Netherlands Antilles or Trinidad and Tobago with Venezuela, though it may well be possible to find passage to each if you're prepared to wait around at nearby ports. It's also possible to catch a boat from Jamaica and other Caribbean islands to Central America (normally Belize, Honduras or Panama).

FURTHER INFORMATION

WEBSITES

- **Caribbean Journal** (www.caribjournal.com) Regional news and travel features.
- **Destination Canada** (en.destinationcanada.com) Official tourism site.

CENTRAL PARK STROLL IN THE SNOW

I was a naïve first-time traveller in New York City. It was the mid-90s, and despite the 1987 film *Wall Street* painting the city as a playground for capitalism's winners, New York was still very much a mecca for aspiring actors, writers and musicians living in studio apartments and freezing warehouse conversions. It was a little bit gritty, everyone talked loudly and the subway didn't feel very safe to this 21-year-old kid from Melbourne (blame the 1990 thriller *Jacob's Ladder*).

Before I left Australia my parents' friends and my friends' parents all told me the same thing: 'Whatever you do, don't walk through Central Park at night.' But one night I found myself on wrong side of the park, and being young, stupid and rather reckless, I decided to cut through anyway. When I got to the middle I stopped for a moment to look around me. I did a slow 360-degree turn and took it all in: the park was completely white with fresh snow, the only other tracks were a squirrel's dancing around a tree, and the apartment windows above were lit up like fairy lights. And then, in the stillness, the snow started to silently fall from the sky and wet my cheeks.

It was a moment of pure beauty and elation. I was in New York. It was magical. And the world seemed full of possibility.

The Take Away

Sometimes it pays to ignore the wisdom of your elders. Flouting such advice resulted in this magical moment and, as luck has probably been on my side most of my life, it has since led to others. And lastly, beauty can be found wherever you look for it.

Tasmin Waby – taken from Lonely Planet's *The Best Moment of Your Life*

- **Eater** (www.eater.com) Foodie insight into two-dozen American cities.
- **National Park Hotel Guide** (www.nationalparkhotelguide.com) A guide to hotels throughout the wilderness of the USA and Canada.
- **National Park Service** (NPS; www.nps.gov) Gateway to America's greatest natural treasures, its national parks.
- **Parks Canada** (www.pc.gc.ca) Lowdown on national parks.
- **Punch** (www.punchdrink.com) Quirky guides and helpful insights on how to drink well in America's cities.
- **Road Trip USA** (www.roadtripusa.com) Great guide to the USA's best off-the-beaten-blacktop road trips.
- **Travel.org** (www.travel.org/na.html) Huge North American travel directory.

BOOKS

- **Blue Highways** A classic of American travel writing by William Least Heat-Moon.
- **Bury My Heart at Wounded Knee** The book that brought Native American experience to the mainstream. By Dee Brown.
- **Claire of the Sea Light** Edwidge Danticat interweaves fables of Haitian family life.
- **Dear Life** A collection of short stories by the Canadian 2013 Nobel Prize laureate Alice Munro.
- **Dread: The Rastafarians of Jamaica** Beyond the ganja (marijuana), this is a deep examination of Jamaica's cultural cornerstone by Joseph Owens.
- **On the Road** Jack Kerouac's brilliant blueprint for American road trips with the odd drug-fuelled detour.
- **The Illegal** Lawrence Hill writes about a marathoner in a fictional land running from the law; takes on race and immigration.
- **The Lost Continent** American travel writer Bill Bryson turns his pen on his own country with some chuckle-worthy observations.
- **The Underground Railroad** Colson Whitehead's Pulitzer Prize–winning novel chronicling a young slave's bid for freedom.

FILMS

- **Traffic** (2000) The US war on drugs from both sides of the Mexican border.
- **Les Invasions Barbares** (The Barbarian Invasions; 2003) An intellectual Québec film (in French) following a son's efforts to make his father's last days perfect.
- **Hollywood North** (2003) A mockumentary about the Canadian film industry.
- **Into the Wild** (2007) After university a top student gives away his life savings and hitches to Alaska to see the country.
- **Twelve Years a Slave** (2013) This violent and moving historical drama takes a new look at the United States' history of slavery.
- **Boyhood** (2014) Richard Linklater's coming-of-age tale, shot over the course of 12 years.
- **Room** (2015) Canadian-Irish film about a mother and son who are finally released after years of captivity.
- **Sleeping Giant** (2015) Teenagers surviving summer in an isolated Ontario cottage community.
- **The Revenant** (2015) A semi-biographical film that captures some of America's wilderness.

Opposite: seen here in the Dominican Republic, surfers are synonymous with the Americas' shores

SUPER

MEXICO, CENTRAL & SOUTH AMERICA

Latin America is an epic destination that lures first-time travellers with its extraordinary terrain and captivating history. The region stretches from the arid northern border of Mexico to the glacial southerly tip of Patagonia in South America. But in-between these distant frontiers lie idyllic beaches, lush jungles, pristine lakes, pulsating cities and towering mountains.

The heady mix doesn't stop there – add the voices of the ancient Aztec, Mayan and Incan civilisations, and you have yourself a potent cocktail of potential travel experiences. Mexico's magnificent Aztec heritage is a huge draw, while Guatemala, Belize and Honduras form the heartlands of the complex and learned culture of the Maya. Further south in Peru, trekkers can uncover the breathtaking beauty of Machu Picchu at the heart of the former Inca Empire.

Ecotourism is still rightly huge, which is why Costa Rica continues to grab headlines for all the right reasons. Indeed, vast swathes of the country are either private reserves or national parks, and the government has progressive environmental policies. But there are other countries that also boast spectacular landscapes and an array of amazing creatures – as well as fewer tourists. The Honduran Bay Islands, Belize and Guatemala's Lago de Atitlán are prized for their diving and snorkelling, while the wild Andes mountain range (and all the activities that come with it) stretches from Colombia to the tip of Patagonia like a continental backbone. And of course, the lungs of the New World are the lush and fertile Amazon jungle that carpets so much of the interior.

People lose their hearts to Latin American cities too. Buenos Aires' wide, grand boulevards, and the sensual melancholy melody of its tango, have cast a spell on many a visitor, while the *joie de vivre* and sights of Rio de Janeiro and Brazil's legendary Carnaval are known the world over.

Whether you find yourself taking a siesta in a hammock on the Mexican Riviera, or trekking along the ancient Inca Trail, you could easily amble around the region for months and never tire of it.

ITINERARIES

A trip from Mexico to Argentina is entirely within the realm of possibility and remains one of the planet's great overland adventures. However, it takes time, energy and a whole lot of patience to travel the vast expanse of two continents. For those with less time, however, you can still cover a lot of ground in a few months, especially if you focus your energy on a particular area or two. Although it's hard to generalise a region as varied as Latin America, it helps to break things down: think Mexico, Central America, the Andes and Amazonia.

CANYONS, BEACHES & YUCATÁN

Mexico is as varied as its world-famous cuisine, which means that you can kick off your travels in a few tourist hotspots. If you're coming down from the States, **Tijuana** is the country's notorious gateway. But Mexico is much more than cheap tequila and donkey shows, which you'll quickly learn once you start surfing the wilderness beaches of **Baja California**.

If you cross the border at Texas, consider riding the legendary **Copper Canyon Railway** (Ferrocarril Chihuahua Pacífico), which cuts through canyons and winds around dizzyingly high cliffs on its way from **Chihuahua** to the Pacific. Once you have arrived on the coast, **Mazatlán**, **Puerto Vallarta** and **Acapulco** are traditional destinations for sun-worshippers and siesta-seekers.

If you want to combine some quality beach time with visits to spectacular ruins, the **Yucatán Peninsula** is just the place. A few nights in **Cozumel** and **Cancún** could be followed by a healthy dose of visits to pre-Columbian sites, including the stunning cliff-top ruins at **Tulum**, and the famous Mayan sites of **Uxmal** and **Chichén Itzá**.

Continuing on the same theme, don't miss the Indiana Jones–esque lost jungle city of **Palenque**, before kicking it colonial style in either **Oaxaca** or **San Cristóbal de las Casas**.

CENTRAL TEMPLES & SEA DIVES

After scaling temples in Guatemala's **Tikal**, the crown jewel of the old Mayan cities, celebrate in the beautiful volcano-ringed colonial city of **Antigua**. This is a great place to spend a few weeks studying Spanish in an affordable language school if you so choose, but be sure to press on to the **Copán** ruins within **Honduras**.

A jaunt out to the **Bay Islands** for a spot of diving or snorkelling is an understandably popular diversion. In neighbouring **Belize**, the **Blue Hole** is also an unforgettable site for diving. In this narrow waist of the Americas, it's not difficult to make rapid headway down through **El Salvador** and **Nicaragua**. Surfers rave about the empty beaches of **La Libertad**, while history buffs are happy to brave the potholed roads of **Nicaragua** for a chance to see the colonial city of **Granada**.

For many, the trail stops at the eco-haven of **Costa Rica**, where you can explore the rainforests of **Monteverde**, laze on the beaches of **Montezuma**, or visit the hot springs of the volcano at **Arenal**. But those who continue south to **Panama** are richly rewarded. From the chic clubs of **Panama City** to the Caribbean climes of **Bocas del Toro**, this country remains bewilderingly underexplored.

Some intrepid explorers decide to skirt round the dangerous no-man's-land of Darién Gap by freighter or yacht, but it's far safer to get a flight if you're continuing on down to South America.

ANDEAN HIGHS

Many travellers, lured by the **Galápagos** Islands, pick up the travellers trail in **Ecuador**. Ecuador's capital, **Quito**, is a stunning city more than worthy of its World Heritage status. There is also a memorable **Devil's Nose** (El Nariz del Diablo) train journey leading from **Riobamba** to **Durán** on the coast, which is worth working into your jaunt around Ecuador – it's often referred to as South America in miniature.

Heading south to **Peru**, almost all travellers will pass through **Lima** (once a fallen colonial city, now a rejuvenated capital with thriving cultural and culinary life) on their way to the **Inca Trail**. Alternatively, the Southern Railway to **Cuzco** provides a wonderful rickety ride close to **Machu Picchu** itself.

TROPIC OF CANCER
MEXICO
GULF OF MEXICO
ZÓCALO
MEXICO CITY
SEE ENLARGEMENT
BELIZE
BELIZEAN CAYES
TIKAL
HONDURAS
GUATEMALA
TEGUCIGALPA
EL SALVADOR
NICARAGUA
MANAGUA
SAN JOSÉ
COSTA RICA
PARQUE NACIONAL CORCOVADO
SEE ENLARGEMENT
PACIFIC OCEAN
EQUATOR
GALÁPAGOS ISLANDS

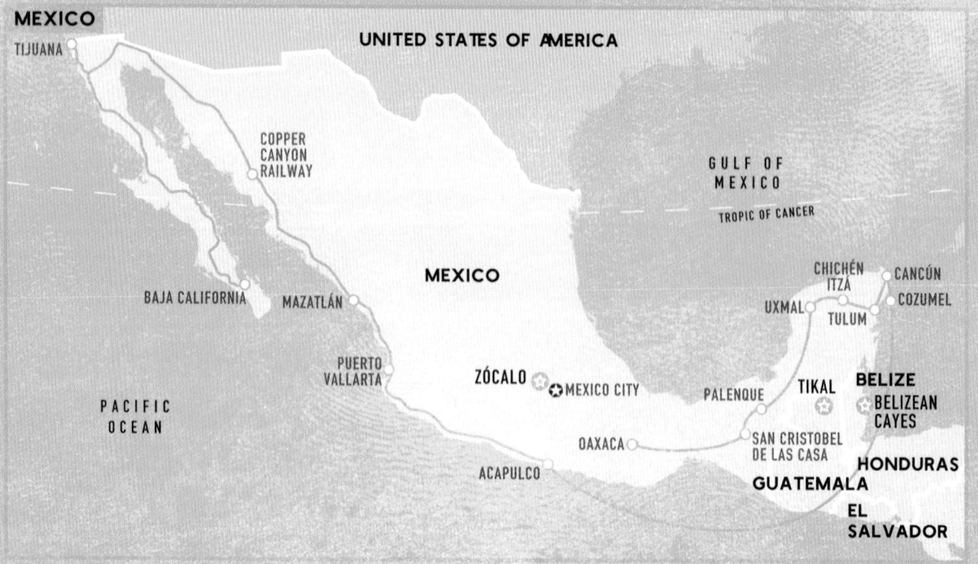

MEXICO, CENTRAL AMERICA & SOUTH AMERICA

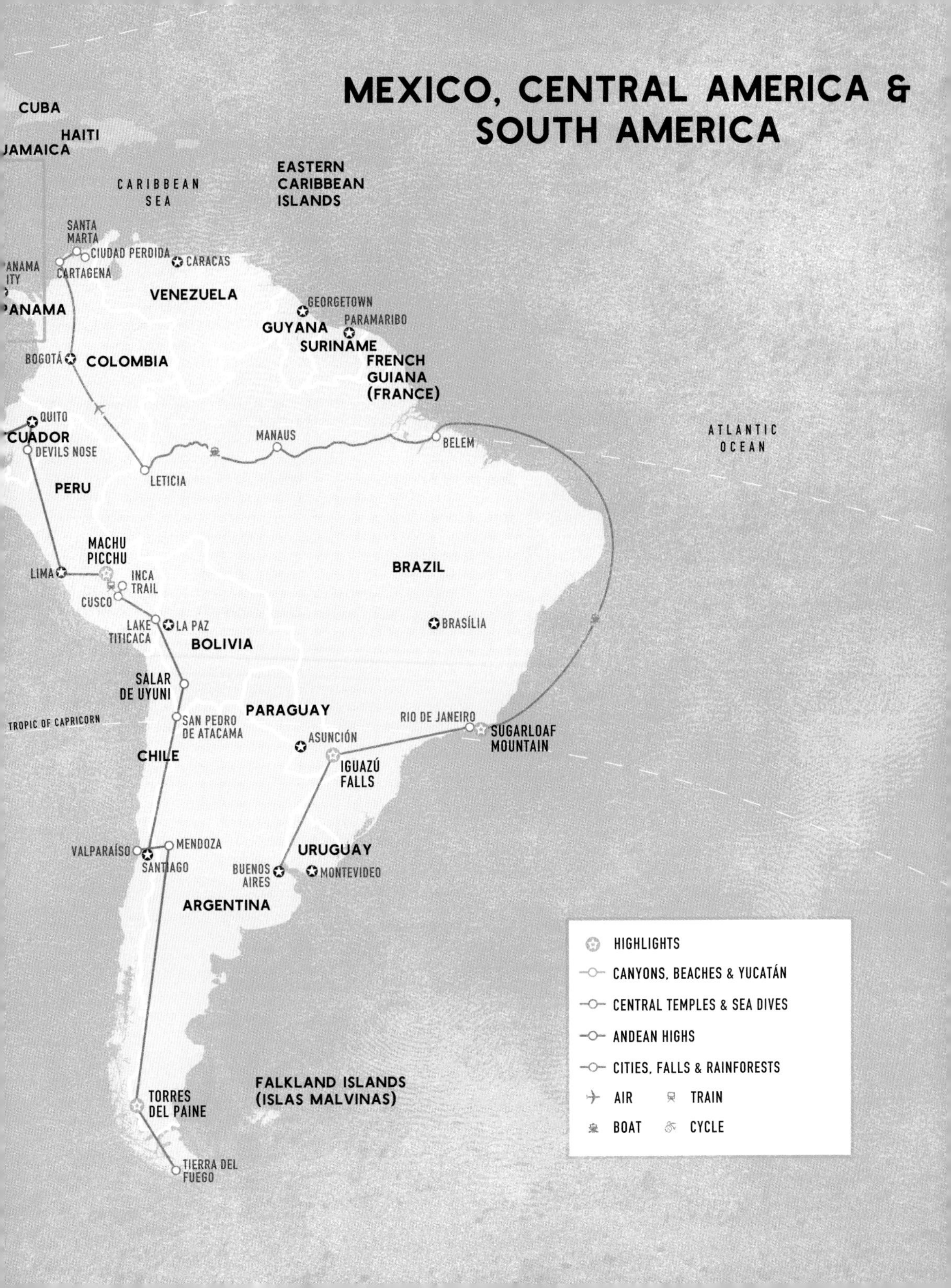

CUBA
HAITI
JAMAICA
CARIBBEAN SEA
EASTERN CARIBBEAN ISLANDS
SANTA MARTA
CIUDAD PERDIDA
CARTAGENA
PANAMA CITY
PANAMA
CARACAS
VENEZUELA
GEORGETOWN
PARAMARIBO
GUYANA
SURINAME
FRENCH GUIANA (FRANCE)
BOGOTÁ
COLOMBIA
QUITO
ECUADOR
DEVILS NOSE
MANAUS
BELEM
LETICIA
ATLANTIC OCEAN
PERU
MACHU PICCHU
LIMA
INCA TRAIL
CUSCO
BRAZIL
LAKE TITICACA
LA PAZ
BOLIVIA
BRASÍLIA
SALAR DE UYUNI
TROPIC OF CAPRICORN
SAN PEDRO DE ATACAMA
PARAGUAY
RIO DE JANEIRO
SUGARLOAF MOUNTAIN
ASUNCIÓN
CHILE
IGUAZÚ FALLS
VALPARAÍSO
SANTIAGO
MENDOZA
URUGUAY
BUENOS AIRES
MONTEVIDEO
ARGENTINA
FALKLAND ISLANDS (ISLAS MALVINAS)
TORRES DEL PAINE
TIERRA DEL FUEGO

HIGHLIGHTS
CANYONS, BEACHES & YUCATÁN
CENTRAL TEMPLES & SEA DIVES
ANDEAN HIGHS
CITIES, FALLS & RAINFORESTS
AIR
TRAIN
BOAT
CYCLE

Restoring El Palacio in Palenque, Mexico's ancient Mayan city

Costa Rica's rich variety of wildlife includes colourful hummingbirds

The mountainous terrain of Parque Nacional Torres del Paine in Chile

From there, the laid-back, altitudinous climes of **Lake Titicaca** draw in a lot of travellers, as do the breathtaking **Bolivian Salar de Uyuni** salt plains and Chile's laid-back oasis of **San Pedro de Atacama**.

Most travellers to Chile arrive in **Santiago** at some point, either by bus or by plane. After savouring a sophisticated glass of Chilean red or white, it's a short hop to the port city of **Valparaíso**, a syncopated, dilapidated, colourful and poetic place – it truly is a wonderful mess. Next, pivot for the exhilarating trans-Andean bus ride over to the colonial Argentinian city of **Mendoza**. Finish by venturing to the very tip of the continent to see the majestic **Torres del Paine** and/or the stark **Tierra del Fuego**.

CITIES, FALLS & RAINFORESTS

Start off in **Buenos Aires**, the cosmopolitan capital of Argentina. Here you can eat steak, sip wine, savour ice cream, dance the tango, explore its famed nightlife and take in its grand French- and Italian-style palaces. Next, move north to a different type of giant, the thundering **Iguazú Falls** on the edge of Amazonia. From here it's back to metropolis madness in **Rio de Janeiro**, with its golden beaches and lush mountains, samba-fuelled nightlife and spectacular football matches – welcome to the *Cidade Maravilhosa*.

Enjoy hopping along the coast northwards to **Belém**, from where you'll start your journey into the **Amazon**. The rainforest is almost like a continent unto itself, with a whole network of mini-routes within its borders. However, one of the best ways to tackle this huge landscape is by taking an unforgettable river trip from Belém to Brazil's jungle city of **Manaus** and beyond to **Leticia** in Colombia. Move north to **Bogotá** for some spellbinding street art and incredible museums before flying to **Cartagena**. Rejuvenated and alive with colour and flair, this is the most important colonial city on Colombia's Caribbean.

Finish at the coast's second city, the sultry seaside port of **Santa Marta**, South America's oldest European-founded town. It has a charming, if somewhat gritty, historical centre that has plenty of great bars and restaurants. If you have the time and legs for it, make the multi-day trek to **Ciudad Perdida** in the **Sierra Nevada de Santa Marta**.

SENSE OF PERSPECTIVE

Strange as it sounds, nothing is more liberating – exhilarating even – than to experience a true sense of insignificance. When the world is writ large, it provides context for the petty worries of life back home. In Chilean Patagonia, you're there on nature's terms, just a dot on the landscape.

Adrian Phillips

WHAT TO DO?

HIGHLIGHTS

• Heading deep into the jungles to discover the lost city of **Tikal** (Guatemala), one of the great wonders of the Mayan world.

• Getting your dive on in the **Belizean Cayes** (Belize), the site of the world's second largest barrier reef.

• Coming face to face with rare wildlife in **Parque Nacional Corcovado** (Costa Rica), a biodiversity hotspot.

• Snapping pics of Sugarloaf Mountain in **Rio de Janeiro** (Brazil), the quintessential sight of this spectacularly located city.

- Following Darwin's storied tracks through the world's wildest wildlife in the far-flung **Galápagos Islands** (Ecuador).
- Exploring the end of the world at **Torres del Paine** (Chile), home to turquoise lakes, granite pillars and pristine glaciers.
- Entering a seemingly alien landscape when you drive on the world's largest salt flats at **Salar de Uyuni** (Bolivia).
- Trekking along the Inca Trail to **Machu Picchu** (Peru), one of the wonders of the ancient world.
- Standing in awe at **Iguazú Falls** (Argentina, Paraguay, Brazil) – it's loud, angry, unstoppable and impossibly gorgeous.
- Viewing Mexico in a single frame at the **Zócalo** (Mexico), which blends colonial architecture with Aztec ruins.

GET ACTIVE

Latin America has its fair share of hammock-strung beaches, which is good news – you'll want a siesta after getting your adrenaline fix.

Caving (spelunking)

Central America has a labyrinth of caves, many of which were used as ceremonial sites by the Maya. Lanquín is the best known in Guatemala, and has a spectacular exodus of bats at dusk, but there are more at B'omb'il Pek, Candelaria and Rey Marcos. Mexico's Cuetzalan cave system is renowned amongst cavers, as is Sótano de las Golondrinas, which is reputedly the world's second-deepest cave entrance. In South America, northeast of Brazil, close to 200 deep underground caves are known to exist in the Terra Ronca region, one of the largest networks in Latin America – many caves are still unexplored. The area around Bonito is also a rich playground for cavers.

Cycling & Mountain Biking

With an increasingly large network of paved secondary roads and heightened awareness of cyclists, Costa Rica has emerged as Central America's most comfortable cycle-touring destinations. In the rest of the region and Mexico, poor road surfaces, careless motorists and other road hazards are deterrents.

Cycling South America is a challenging yet highly rewarding alternative to public transport. While better roads in Argentina and Chile make the Cono Sur (Southern Cone; a collective term for Argentina, Chile, Uruguay and parts of Brazil and Paraguay) countries especially attractive, the entire continent is manageable by bike, or – more precisely – by mountain bike. An increasingly popular biking option is to cycle the spectacular forests and lakes of southern Chile and Argentina.

Diving & Snorkelling

Belize has the planet's second-largest barrier reef, some crystal-clear waters and breathtaking dive sites. Cozumel in Mexico is also known as a great destination for lovers of underwater life. If you're on a tight budget, you could head to the Honduran Bay Islands, particularly Utila, which offers cheap PADI courses. But don't ignore the Pacific coast – there is still some memorable diving here, including off Panama's Coiba Island. Down in South America, the best diving is off the Galápagos Islands. Only experienced divers take the plunge here, but they get a privileged glimpse into a world of sea lions, hammerhead sharks and eagle rays.

Snowsports

Some world-class slopes are located in Chile and Argentina. The most renowned resort is Chile's Portillo, just over an hour and a half away by car or bus from Santiago. Termas de Chillán, just east of Chillán, is a more laid-back spot with several beginners' slopes, while Parque Nacional Villarrica, near the resort town of Pucón, has the added thrill of skiing on a smoking volcano. On Volcán Lonquimay, Corralco has great novice and expert terrain, as well as excellent backcountry access. Volcanoes Osorno and Antillanca, east of Osorno, have open terrain with incredible views and a family atmosphere.

In Argentina, there are three main snow-sport areas: Mendoza, the Lake District and Ushuaia. Mendoza is near Argentina's premier resort, Las Leñas, which has the best snow and longest runs; the resort Los Penitentes is also nearby. The Lake District is home to several low-key resorts, including Cerro Catedral, near Bariloche, and Cerro Chapelco, near San Martín de los Andes.

Surfing

The Pacific Ocean off Central America has some great surfing. Costa Rica draws its fair share of jet-setting surfers, especially since you can choose from two oceans. The Pacific has more consistent waves, but the swells on the Caribbean coast can be more impressive during the right season. El Salvador is often overlooked, but its beaches have some great breaks – mainly in the La Libertad region. The powerful Mexican Pipeline break at Puerto Escondido in Baja California is also a big draw for wave fans. In South America, try the Chilean town of Pichilemu for more low-key (and colder) surf, while Brazil's coastline is almost one uninterrupted line of surfing nirvana.

Trekking & Mountaineering

Pick any spot in Central America, and chances are there will be a volcano looming nearby. One of the most accessible is Volcán Pacaya near Antigua, Guatemala. A stream of tourists treks to the summit for a noxious waft of sulphur and the chance to stride on the volcanic ash.

If the Andes look awesome from below, they are even more breathtaking once you are in amongst them. Among the cognoscenti, the peaks in Peru are thought to provide the best climbing opportunities. The Cordillera Huayhuash is one for hard-core climbers, while the Cordillera Blanca includes some of the more popular peaks around the town of Cuzco.

In the north of Chile, San Pedro de Atacama is a popular launching point for treks. Further down, many *andinistas* (as opposed to alpinists) get tempted by the mountains that encircle Santiago. Los Leones is a good one for the enthusiastic but inexperienced climber. On the other hand, Argentina's Mt Aconcagua (6962m) is the highest summit in the western hemisphere, and should only be undertaken by the very experienced – it can take weeks simply to acclimatise to the thin air.

Whitewater Rafting

When it comes to water sports, Costa Rica, once again, got there first in Central America. The Reventazón and Pacuare rivers in Costa Rica are in a stunning virgin-forest setting. However, other countries are now getting in on the whitewater action. Both Honduras and Guatemala have some decent rafting opportunities with varying levels of difficulty. In Mexico, visit the state of Veracruz for some hair-raising rafting.

Chile arguably has the best (and most challenging) rapids in South America, with exhilarating runs for both rafters and kayakers on the Maipó, Trancura and Futaleufú rivers. Just across the Andes in Argentina, Mendoza offers plenty of scope to satisfy white-water thrill-seekers. There's also rafting just outside of Cuzco in Peru, and Ecuador's many rivers bubble with possibilities.

WILDLIFE

Latin America hogs more than its fair share of all creatures great and small. In Central America, you can banter with spider monkeys in Nicaragua, recoil from tarantulas in El Salvador, and view a kaleidoscopic range of birds, from macaws to the elusive quetzal, in Guatemala. Costa Rica, with its rainforest-canopy walkways, is the most developed nation for wildlife-spotters, but the ecosystem is equally broad in most of its neighbours. For instance, Panama has around 940 different types of birds to spot.

In South America you are even more spoilt for choice. The Amazon has an estimated 15,000 animal species, with around 1800 species of butterfly alone! Less feted, but with far more visible wildlife, the Pantanal wetlands in the west of Brazil teem with pumas, anacondas, giant river otters and a myriad of other exotic creatures. The same accessibility is also available in the Esteros del Iberá marshlands in Corrientes (Argentina), while the Península de Valdés in the same country is a great place to watch whales.

Then, of course, there are the legendary Galápagos Islands, where a couple of the hardiest giant tortoises may even have been around to welcome Darwin ashore back in the old days.

Sundowners by the sea wall in Cartagena, Colombia

FESTIVALS

From sacred indigenous ceremonies in Peru to Carnaval in Rio, Latin Americans are never ones to shirk an opportunity for a full-blooded celebration. Try to fit as many of the following into your trip as possible:

- **New Year's Eve** (Chile) Not, strictly speaking, a festival, but the spectacular fireworks extravaganza and New Year's celebration at Valparaíso is one of the finest of its kind anywhere.
- **Fiesta de la Virgen de Candelaria** (Bolivia & Peru) Celebrated across the highlands on February 2nd, it features music, drinking, eating, dancing, processions and fireworks. Copacabana (Bolivia) and Puno (Peru) are best.
- **Carnaval** (Brazil) The February carnivals in Rio, Olinda, Recife and Salvador are some of the most spectacular festivals on earth. Parades, dancing, music and song combine for the most hedonistic of celebrations.
- **Semana Santa** (Guatemala) The Easter celebrations in the delightful colonial town of Antigua include colourful parades, elaborate ceremonies and beautiful yet fragile decorations.

• **Inti Raymi** (Peru) The 'sun festival' of Cuzco (24 June) culminates with a re-enactment of the Inca winter-solstice observance at Sacsayhuamán.
• **Guelaguetza** (Mexico) Oaxaca is thronged for this fantastically colorful feast of regional dance on the first two Mondays after July 16, with plenty of other celebratory events accompanying it.
• **Tango BA Festival y Mundial** (Argentina; www.tangobuenosaires.gob.ar) World-class tango dancers perform throughout Buenos Aires during this two-week festival.
• **Bolas de Fuego** (El Salvador) Local scallywags paint their faces like devils and throw fireballs at each other – just a bit of (potentially harmful) fun. Held on August 31 in Nejapa.
• **Festival of Yamor** (Ecuador) Otavalo's biggest shindig in early September has fireworks, parades and an all-round party atmosphere. The Reina de la Fiesta procession is a highlight.
• **Día de Los Muertos** (Day of the Dead; Mexico) Mexicans welcome the souls of their dead back to earth across the country (Pátzcuaro is especially colourful) on 2 November.
• **Día de Nuestra Señora de Guadalupe** (Mexico) The day (12 December) of Mexico's patron saint, Guadalupe. Festivities culminate with a huge procession and party at the Basílica de Guadalupe in Mexico City.

NIGHTLIFE

The variety of nightlife across this broad region is a compelling reason to lose some sleep. Here are some places to start trying.
• **Antigua** (Guatemala) The bar scene jumps, especially on Friday and Saturday evenings when the hordes roll in from Guatemala City for some Antigua-style revelry.
• **Bogotá** (Colombia) Bohemian barrios west of Av Caracas, such as Parkway in La Soledad, have become stomping grounds for craft brewing and other hipster-associated trendiness in the last few years.
• **Buenos Aires** (Argentina) The nightlife is legendary. In some neighborhoods, finding a good sports bar, classy cocktail lounge, atmospheric old cafe or upscale wine bar is as easy as walking down the street. BA boasts spectacular nightclubs showcasing top DJs.
• **Cartagena** (Colombia) There's a long-standing bar scene centred on the Plaza de los Coches in El Centro for salsa and vallenato, while most of the hotter and hipper action can be found in thumping Getsemaní these days.
• **Guadalajara** (Mexico) The Chapultepec area is always hopping, with both local *antros* (literally 'dens,' but meaning dives) and international-style bars and clubs.
• **Jericoacoara** (Brazil) Everything starts at the cocktail *barracas* (carts) on the beach at the foot of Rua Principal. From early evening, *caipirinhas* and *caipifrutas* are mixed up with exotic fruits.
• **Mancora** (Peru) The party starts along Piura, then moves to the dancehall bars along the beach. Loki has a DJ party on Friday and Saturday nights.
• **Medellín** (Colombia) Parque Lleras in El Poblado has a dense tangle of upscale restaurants, bars and clubs. For a more bohemian experience, check the options around Parque del Periodista.
• **Mexico City** (Mexico) Nightlife is sophisticated in the capital and includes everything from swanky cocktail bars to exclusive *mezcalerías* (bars specialising in mezcal).
• **Montañita** (Ecuador) Street-cart sellers dole out tropical cocktails, beers and shakes until late most nights. Lost Beach Club throws big dance parties, with DJs from Ecuador and abroad.
• **Rio de Janeiro** (Brazil) Any night of the week

you'll find plenty of ways to experience Rio's electrifying nightlife: open-air bars by the lake; festive outdoor drinking spots on the colonial streets of Centro; beachfront kiosks; stylish lounges and nightclubs; and warm and welcoming *botecos* (small open-air bars) that are scattered all across the city.

- **São Paulo** (Brazil) The Vila Madalena area is a solid option for all, while Itaim Bibi is the drinking ground for the wealthy. Baixo Augusta is the edgiest nightlife district, where LGBT+ mingle with artsy hipsters. Artists, journalists and bohemians have claimed the Pinheiros area.
- **Tamarindo** (Costa Rica) The main drag has the festive feel of spring break, with well-oiled patrons spilling out onto the beach, drinks in hand. Almost every hour is happy hour, all around you.

ROADS LESS TRAVELLED

There are many times there are more options of things to do off the well-travelled path than on it, and new opportunities are cropping up year after year. Crater Azul in Guatemala has recently opened for visitation – this crystal-clear spring-fed tributary allows for stunning underwater photography and swimming. It's a 90-minute boat ride from Sayaxché past a mix of farms, fields, and forests.

Trekking to the 'Lost City' (Ciudad Perdida) in the Sierra Nevada de Santa Marta of Colombia is a fantastic option to the Inca Trail. If you are still set on Machu Picchu, try trekking the Salkantay Route instead. Even some of the major festivities have excellent alternatives. While carnival in Rio is epic indeed, experiencing it in smaller Brazilian centres such as Olinda, Recife and Salvador is also incredible, as it is in Mexico's Mérida, Campeche and Isla Cozumel.

VOLUNTEERING

Latin America is awash with volunteer positions, with something to suit almost everyone. You could work on social and environment programmes in Costa Rica, fundraise for development organisations in Brazil, teach kids in Guatemala (clear criminal background check needed), conserve sea turtles in Costa Rica, support women's groups in Chile – the range of options are simply huge.

Before arriving, many first-timers prefer to sort out their volunteer work through an organisation in their home country, which is good for peace of mind. These groups usually arrange projects before you arrive, and provide backup and support in case things go wrong. However, don't rule out the possibility of finding volunteer work once you are in the region. It often works out to be cheaper in the long run, and you can get a feel for a project before you agree to join in. For more on how to organise a volunteering trip, get a copy of *Volunteer: A Traveller's Guide to Making a Difference Around the World*.

WORKING

Speaking English as a first language is no longer the guaranteed ticket to employment it once was. Many language schools no longer take on teachers without a degree or a TEFL qualification, and they should also require a clear criminal background check if you're working with children.

Possibilities also exist for crewing on foreign yachts that stop along the Pacific, especially on the Guatemalan, Costa Rican, Venezuelan, Ecuadorian and Peruvian coasts. Deck hands are occasionally taken on by yachts at either end of the Panama Canal. In popular tourist areas, jobs for tour leaders, trekking guides, hostel managers, bar hands or shop workers do crop up – but wages are typically minimal. More options are covered in the Jobs section (see p115).

WHEN TO GO?

The busiest time for tourism tends to be from December to March, when many North Americans seek shelter from cold, northerly climes. July and August are also popular. In such a vast region with great geographical extremes, there is, unsurprisingly, a huge variety in climate. And the best time to go will depend largely on what you plan to do. There are no seasonal patterns that apply everywhere in Latin America, so be careful to check the weather cycles for each of your destinations when you are planning your trip.

WHAT TO EXPECT?

LOCALS & OTHER TRAVELLERS

Travelling around Mexico quickly reveals that Mexicans are a vastly diverse bunch, from the industrial workers of Monterrey to the rich sophisticates and bohemian counterculture of Mexico City, and indigenous villagers eking out subsistence in the southern mountains. But certain common threads run through almost everyone here – among them a deep vein of spirituality, the importance of family, and a simultaneous pride and frustration about Mexico itself.

Central and South America is an even more diverse patchwork, with a mix of European-, Amerindian- and African-descended groups – most of which have intermixed with each other. A large proportion of the regions' population are in fact *mestizo* (Spanish-Amerindian mix) or Caucasian (European). Most of the remaining population is made up of dozens of distinct indigenous groups, from the once-mighty Maya to the barely-surviving Maleku. A small but

LEARNING TO LOVE SOLITUDE

'You emerge from this marvellous novel as if from a dream, the mind on fire...' the back cover review by *New York Times* journalist John Leonard could not have been more apt.

I was sitting outside a café in Mendoza, Argentina, sipping an early-evening glass of deep, rich, fruity Malbec. Sycamore leaves flitted across a wide pavement still warm from the gentle late summer sun. A plate of empanadas sat on the table, each a little warm, flaky pastry parcel of beef, chicken or cheese. And next to them lay a yellowed, second-hand copy of *One Hundred Years of Solitude* by Gabriel García Márquez.

I'd bought it from a bookseller under Waterloo Bridge years before, but had never even opened the cover. But now I had time: ill health and bereavement had forced an abrupt, six-month sabbatical from work. Yet through a fog of grief and despair I'd found the courage to book a ticket around the world, beginning in Argentina but with little idea of where to go or what to do.

For no other reason than Malbec being my favourite wine, I grabbed an overnight bus to Mendoza when I landed in Buenos Aires. As I lay in my seat watching a spectacular electrical storm light up the 2am sky over the Pampas, tears rolled down my tired cheeks. In London I'd been too scared to do anything alone – did I now have the courage to travel solo for six months?

Then, suddenly, unexpectedly, on that warm pavement, I was alone and at peace.

Looking back conjures a feeling of utter contentment. I felt awake, alive and empowered for the first time in years – it gave me the courage to go forward.

Abigail Butcher

significant percentage descends from African slaves and immigrant workers.

In Mexico and Central America there is a large North American travelling contingent, while in South America you'll find slightly more Europeans. Plenty of Aussies and Kiwis travel in Latin America, and there is a growing number of Korean and Japanese visitors.

FOOD

Throughout most of Latin America, food tends to centre on the hearty and healthy staple combination of rice and beans. But fresh fruit (especially in the tropics) is never far from the menu, nor is fresh seafood along the coasts. That said, there are a few noteworthy culinary hotspots. In the north, Mexico has richly varied regional cuisines, and the Caribbean side of Central America, where cooks tends to work with more spice and coconut milk, is worth a feast or two. Lima (Peru), the gastronomic capital of South America, is where you will find some of the continent's most sublime culinary creations: from *cevicherías* (ceviche counters) and corner *anticucho* (beef-heart skewer) stands to outstanding molecular cuisine. You'll also find some of the world's most sumptuous steaks in the Argentinian pampas.

LANGUAGE

Spanish is the official language in every Latin American country with the exception of Brazil (Portuguese), Belize (English), Suriname (Dutch), French Guiana (French) and Guyana (English). Speaking English in Latin America is on the rise and is often spoken in big cities and tourist areas, but learning the rudiments of the Spanish and/or Portuguese is strongly advised. There are also hundreds of indigenous languages still being used in Latin America, although the number of speakers are dwindling.

COMMUNICATION

Wi-Fi access is widely available, with many hotels, hostels, cafes and guesthouses offering free service. As it's easy and cheap to purchase a local SIM card with mobile data for your smartphone or device, internet cafes aren't as prevalent as they once were.

HEALTH

If you're going to a tropical region of Latin America, the list of recommended vaccinations can seem intimidating. Don't let this faze you – the most serious condition you're likely to encounter is a bad case of the runs. Malaria, however, is a risk, especially in lowland tropical areas, while yellow fever is endemic in Panama and most of the top half of South America. If you are going on a jungle trip, do take proper precautions.

Climbers should be wary of altitude sickness, which can be fatal. If you start feeling its effects, go down the mountain immediately. In the desert, the tropics or on a mountain, the sun can be dangerous – make sure your skin is properly protected.

ISSUES

While Latin America is no longer the hotbed of civil unrest it once was, some countries still have shaky political situations. Venezuela's fortunes since the death of former President Hugo Chávez in 2013 have been decidedly poor, and the country, once a beacon for left-wing causes around the world, is now in a state of near economic collapse. Endemic corruption, poor governance, the world's highest inflation rate (82,766% at last count) and spiralling crime levels have led most governments to warn their citizens against visiting. Similar warnings are in place for Nicaragua, which has been in a state of violent political unrest since April 2018.

SAMPLE COSTS

	Mexico (Mexican peso, M$)	Costa Rica (Colón, ₡)	Guatemala (Quetzal, Q)	Brazil (Brazilian real, R$)
Hostel: dorm bed	M$200 (US$10.50)	₡4550-8525 (US$8-15)	Q90-110 (US$12-15)	R$50-80 (US$13-20)
Midrange hotel: double room	M$630–1500 (US$33-80)	₡28,400–56,800 (US$50-100)	Q350-600 (US$47-80)	R$175-350 (US$45-90)
Street snack	*Tacos de carne asada* M$12-20 (US$0.63-1.05)	*Patí* ₡600-1000 (US$1.05-1.76)	*Dobladas* Q5-10 (US$0.67-1.34)	*Aacarajé* R$8-13 (US$2.04-3.31)
Budget meal	M$70-130 (US$3.70-6.90)	₡1700-4000 (US$3-7)	Q30-50 (US$4-6.68)	R$15-30 (US$3.83-7.66)
Midrange restaurant: main	M$100-200 (US$5.25-10.50)	₡5700-8500 (US$10-15)	Q50-100 (US$6.68-13.36)	R$30-75 (US$7.66-19.14)
Cappuccino	M$30-50 (US$1.59-2.65)	₡700-2200 (US$1.25-3.85)	Q15-25 (US$2-3.36)	R$4-8 (US$1.02-2.04)
1.5L Bottle of water	M$10-19 (US$0.53-1)	₡750-1500 (US$1.32-2.64)	Q3.50-10 (US$0.46-1.34)	R$1.75-5 (US$0.46-1.28)
1L Petrol (gas)	M$18.64 (US$0.99)	₡625 (US$1.10)	Q6.41 (US$0.86)	R$4.77 (US$1.22)

On brighter fronts, the recent progress in Colombia has been extraordinary. The FARC's (Revolutionary Armed Forces of Colombia) surrender and conversion to democracy looks to have put the country on a path to long-term peace. While it's undeniable that there are still tensions in discrete areas (for which there are still travel advisories), Colombia today is racing ahead to become one of the hottest, most exciting destinations on the continent, and tourism is playing an increasingly large role in that. Colombian confidence hasn't been so high in living memory, and most visitors will find this infectious.

While the vast majority of Ecuador and Peru are considered to be safe for travellers, there are warnings against visiting the areas in the immediate vicinity of their respective borders with each other and also their borders with Colombia.

Elsewhere, Mexico's drug war is undeniably horrific and frightening, but the violence that has been building over the past three decades is almost exclusively an internal matter between the drug gangs; tourists have rarely been victims. That said, petty and violent crime is an issue in Mexican and other Latin American cities, which includes some tourist areas. Be vigilant, don't keep any more money than is necessary with you, and stick to tried and trusted routes.

GETTING THERE

You'll most likely need to fly into the region, though it is of course possible to fly to the USA, and then overland into Latin America.

AIR

Latin America is extremely well connected via a number of international travel centres. Working from roughly north to south, you can choose to start your travels in Mexico City, San José (Costa Rica), Panama City, Bogotá (Colombia), Quito (Ecuador), Lima (Peru), Rio de Janeiro (Brazil), Santiago (Chile) or Buenos Aires (Argentina), as well as several other lesser-known hubs.

Besides the many international airlines based around the globe that fly into the region, here are the major local airlines:

- **Aerolíneas Argentinas** (www.aerolineas.com.ar)
- **Avianca** (www.avianca.com)
- **Latam Airlines** (www.latam.com)

Budget airlines operating in the region include:

- **Amaszonas** (www.amaszonas.com)
- **Azul** (www.voeazul.com.br)
- **EasyFly** (www.easyfly.com.co)
- **Gol** (www.voegol.com.br/en)
- **Peruvian** (www.peruvian.pe/pe/en)
- **Sky Airline** (www.skyairline.com)
- **Tame** (www.tame.com.ec)
- **Viva Air** (https://vivaair.com)

SEA & OVERLAND

If you're planning on travelling from Mexico to Argentina, you will most likely need to bypass the Darién Gap, which for all intents and purposes blocks the overland route between Panama and Colombia. One option for doing this is to snag a life on a sailboat from Puerto Lindo in Colón to Cartagena via the San Blas Islands (of course, you can always fly!). Otherwise, travelling by sea is not a particularly practical option.

Travelling overland through Latin America is a wonderful way of exploring the region, especially since border crossings are generally safe and secure. Some travellers even buy cars before hitting the open road, but you really need to be confident you know your stuff, both mechanically and your driving skills, to even contemplate this option.

Specialist Tour Operators

- **Adventure Life** (www.adventure-life.com) A US-based operator which organises responsible tours, including Andean trekking, Amazon exploring and multisport itineraries. It uses bilingual guides, family-run hotels and local transportation.
- **Ancon Expeditions** (www.anconexpeditions.com) Panama-based, it offers quality service and employs some of the country's best nature guides, many with decades of experience and speaking multiple languages.
- **Andean Trails** (www.andeantrails.co.uk) UK-operator who specialises in South American adventure tours, whether mountain biking, climbing, trekking and rafting.
- **Intrepid Travel** (www.intrepidtravel.com) A global small-group tour provider who uses sustainable practices.
- **Journey Latin America** (www.journeylatinamerica.co.uk) Cultural trips and

treks in the Cordilleras Blanca and Huayhuash and to Machu Picchu.

There are plenty of flights to Australia and New Zealand from Chile, Brazil and Argentina. You may get a stopover in the South Pacific, but the cheapest way to arrange this is with a round-the-world (RTW) ticket. Flights to North America (Miami is the cheapest destination) are frequent and often good value. There are also some cheap deals to Johannesburg from São Paulo and Buenos Aires – it could even be worth getting a return ticket if you fancy a quick blast in a different continent.

FURTHER INFORMATION

WEBSITES

- **Bolivian Express** (www.bolivianexpress.org) English magazine focusing on cultural coverage.
- **Brasil** (www.visitbrasil.com) Official site of Brazil's Ministry of Tourism.
- **Degusta Panama** (www.degustapanama.com) Website and app with locals' restaurant picks.
- **Essential Costa Rica** (www.visitcostarica.com) The Costa Rica Tourism Board website has planning tips and destination details.
- **Latin America Press** (www.lapress.org) News on political issues from across the region.
- **Latin American Network Information Center** (www.lanic.utexas.edu) One of the best resources for Latin America.
- **Visit México** (www.visitmexico.com) Official tourism site with plenty of helpful ideas.
- **Mexico Cooks!** (www.mexicocooks.typepad.com) Excellent blog on Mexican life.
- **Pacunam** (www.pacunam.org) Guatemalan foundation focusing on Maya archaeology, conservation and sustainable tourism.
- **Planeta** (https://planeta.com) Regional articles, events, reference material and links, with an emphasis on sustainable travel.

MY FIRST NIGHT IN THE JUNGLE

The jaguars didn't bother me much during the day. Adonis, our local guide who was leading us deep into the Guatemalan jungle, assured us they were elusive, shy creatures. The most recent time he'd seen one was more than a year ago when caught a pair in the act of jaguar love. Last week, he'd spotted some spoor, which was probably as close to the animals as we would get, he said.

But his reassurance meant little that night as I cowered in my hammock under the stars. Now my mind turned every rustle into a prowling big cat full of murderous intent (probably to get back at the rude human who had interrupted a moment of feline passion). And, if it wasn't a jaguar poised to spring, it was a poisonous fer-de-lance viper, picking which of my buttocks to sink its fangs into.

Tiredness calmed my overactive imagination and I dozed. Next day, big surprise: no death by either snakebite or jaguar mauling. We packed up our stuff and continued towards our destination, El Mirador, the site of the tallest temple in the Mayan world, and two days' trekking from the small village of Carmelita at the end of the road.

Although we may have questioned why we had left a perfectly nice Honduran beach to come here, that night no doubts remained. Just before sunset we took our places at the top of the unexcavated temple mound. A Mayan astrology priest had probably sat in the same place 2000 years before and honed his knowledge of the galaxy. Tonight, the howler monkeys screeched their farewells to the setting sun as spectacular pink shades streaked the western skyline. The sky darkened and the stars shimmered into life.

Jolyon Attwooll

• **Santiago Times** (www.santiagotimes.cl) Daily English-language update on Chilean current affairs, with a broader South American perspective too.
• **Sernatur** (www.chile.travel/en.html) The national tourism organisation of Chile.
• **The Bubble** (www.thebubble.com) Dissects current events in Argentina and Latin America, with a dose of pop and media culture.
• **Tico Times** (www.ticotimes.net) News source relied upon heavily by expats in Costa Rica.

BOOKS

• **A Mayan Life** The first published novel by a Maya author (Gaspar Pedro Gonzáles) and an excellent study of rural Guatemalan life.
• **El Narco** Ioan Grillo's exposé on Mexico's drugs war, researched in some of the most dangerous territories.
• **Empire of Blue Water** Stephen Talty's intriguing pirate history and *New York Times* bestseller.
• **Gabriela, Clove and Cinnamon** Tale set in Bahia, by Brazil's greatest writer, Jorge Amado.
• **In Patagonia** Bruce Chatwin evocatively writes of Patagonia's history and mystique.
• **One Hundred Years of Solitude** Gabriel García Márquez's masterpiece on the metaphorical history of Latin America.
• **The Old Patagonian Express** Paul Theroux tells of a train journey from Boston to Patagonia; written in a cantankerous fashion.
• **Touching the Void** Joe Simpson brilliantly captures the drama of an Andes mountaineering disaster.
• **Voyage of the Beagle** (Charles Darwin) Describes the trip that stirred the English scientist to form his theory of evolution.

FILMS

• **Amores Perros** (2000) Gritty groundbreaker that set director Alejandro González Iñárritu and actor Gael García Bernal on the path to stardom.
• **Y Tu Mamá También** (2001) Follows an uncensored coming-of-age road trip through the Mexican countryside.
• **City of God** (2002) A harrowing yet artistic portrait of life in the slums of Rio from the 1960s to the mid-1980s.
• **The Motorcycle Diaries** (2004) An epic retelling of a young Che Guevara's motorcycle trip through South America.
• **Qué tan lejos** (2006) Road movie about two young women on a journey of self-discovery in the Andean highlands.
• **Heli** (2013) Amat Escalante won Cannes' best-director garland for this tale of a young couple caught up in the drugs war.
• **Relatos salvajes** (Wild Tales; 2014) Black comedy showcasing six short, entertaining stories.
• **Ixcanul** (2015) Multi-award-winning film about a young Kaqchikel girl's coming of age in Guatemala.
• **A Fantastic Woman** (2017) Transgender identity and society.

Opposite: a bird's-eye view of Mexico's Unesco-listed San Miguel de Allende

MIDDLE EAST

The Middle East is a grand epic, a cradle of civilisations and a beautiful, complicated land that's home to some of the planet's most hospitable people.

In the Middle East, history is not something you read about in books. Here, it's a story written on the stones that litter the region, from the flagstones of old Roman roads to the delicately carved tombs and temples from Petra to Persepolis. This is where humankind first built cities and learned to write, and it was from here that Judaism, Christianity and Islam all arose. Wherever you find yourself, the past is always present because here, perhaps more than anywhere else on earth, history is the heart and soul of the land.

The Middle East's cities read like a roll-call of historical heavyweights: Jerusalem, Beirut, Istanbul, Esfahan... These ancient and now modern metropolises are places to take the pulse of a region. It is here that you find the stirring, aspirational architecture that so distinguishes the three great monotheistic faiths. And then there are cities like Dubai and Tel Aviv, whose embrace of all that is modern signals the region's arrival in the 21st century.

Beyond city limits, this is a land of rivers (the Tigris, Euphrates), even mightier deserts (the Empty Quarter and peerless Wadi Rum) and green landscapes of exceptional beauty. Exploring these wilderness areas – from snow-capped summits in Turkey, Iran and Lebanon to the kaleidoscopic waters of the Red Sea – is another key piece of the region's appeal.

Perhaps the Middle East's greatest treasure, however, is its people. Their warmth and genuine hospitality bears scant resemblance to what you may have read in the headlines. If you don't believe us, you'll be missing out on one of the most soulful travel experiences available on earth.

ITINERARIES

There are two stumbling blocks to overland travel in the Middle East: the troubled nations of Iraq and Syria. Traditionally Saudi Arabia has been a road block too, though out of choice, not conflict. However, in 2018 they started issuing tourist visas for the first time. It's still not clear how the tourism industry will develop in this very conservative country.

AMMAN TO CAIRO & BEYOND

Amman is a great starting place, an agreeably cosmopolitan city with a handful of Roman ruins offset by brilliant restaurants. **Jordan** may be small, but there's a lot to pack in, including a visit to the **Dead Sea** – it's an easy day trip from the capital. A detour to **Jerusalem** takes you to the Middle East's spiritual heart. Returning to Jordan, spend some time exploring fabulous **Petra**, arguably the Middle East's most beguiling ancient city. Futher south, Petra's rival to the title of Jordan's most spectacular site is **Wadi Rum**, a soulful red-hued desert landscape that rewards those who spend a couple of days exploring, either by camel or 4WD.

From there it's down to the **Red Sea**, where you'll find diving and snorkelling that is some of the best in the world, either at **Aqaba** or across the waters from Egypt's Sinai Peninsula at laid-back resorts such as **Dahab**. The clamour of **Cairo** and the **Pyramids of Giza** is not far away, not to mention the sophistication of **Alexandria** or the antiquities of the **Nile Valley**.

ISTANBUL TO SHIRAZ

Travelling east across Turkey from **Istanbul** is a gradual process of leaving Europe behind and entering the Middle East. Crossing Turkey's border with Iran takes you onto the old **Silk Road**. The bazaar at **Tabriz** is a roiling introduction to the country, and while **Tehran** wouldn't win any beauty contests, it resonates with the intriguing contradictions of modern Iran. Further south, the beautiful blue-tiled **Esfahan** is a living monument to the glories of ancient Persia. The mud-brick architecture of **Yazd** will draw you in, while at journey's end, **Shiraz** is studded with fine mosques. Between the two lies the astonishing ruins of **Persepolis**.

THE GULF & ARABIAN SEA

The Qatari capital **Doha** was already well on its way to becoming a Dubai-style regional hub prior to the country landing the 2022 Fifa World Cup, but since then development has truly boomed. The city makes for a dynamic gateway to the Gulf. Explore the surrounds before heading to the **United Arab Emireas** (UAE), and its two burgeoning cities **Abu Dhabi** and **Dubai**. The latter has been transformed into one of the world's most glamorous, most talked-about cities. Continue to the coast around **Khor Fakkan**, which is spectacular. Similarly grand is the nearby **Oman** exclave of **Musandam Peninsula**. By boat, road or by air, head to **Muscat**, the capital of Oman which surrounds a beautiful arc of bay and is home to a souq (market) without peer. Travel inland to **Jebel Shams**, the Grand Canyon of Arabia, visiting nearby **Bahla**, the home of potters, genii and a Unesco-listed fort that has opened to the public after years of restoration. Cross the arid plains of central Oman to **Salalah** where, if you arrive in July and August, it is so green you'll think you've been spirited off to Europe – except, that is, for the grazing camels. Finish at **Mughsail** on Oman's most spectacular bay, ending in a set of sheer cliffs that reaches towards the Yemeni border.

SKIPPING THE STAMP

As anyone who has an Israeli stamp in their passport will not be allowed to enter Iran or Lebanon (or Iraq or Syria when they're considered safe to visit), ask to have a small loose-leaf card stamped instead when coming and going from Israel. Israel tend to allow this as standard, but retains the right to stamp your passport if it sees fit. Also be aware that entry and exit stamps from Jordan and Egypt may still give the game away.

WHAT TO DO?

HIGHLIGHTS

- Feeling history resonating with profound force amid the Ottoman and Byzantine glories of the Blue Mosque, Aya Sofya and Topkapı Palace in **Istanbul** (Turkey).
- Returning to the glories of the Achaemenid Empire at the ruins of **Persepolis** (Iran).
- Following in the footsteps of pilgrims to **Jerusalem** (Israel and the Palestinian Territories).
- Hot-air ballooning over **Cappadocia** (Turkey), a fantastical lunarscape honeycombed with cave dwellings.
- Emerging, Indiana Jones–like, into glorious rose-red, rock-hewn **Petra** (Jordan), an ancient Nabataean city.
- Relishing the bars, bistros and boutiques of cosmopolitan **Tel Aviv** (Israel and the Palestinian Territories).
- Imagining yourself as Lawrence of Arabia in **Wadi Rum** (Jordan).

MIDDLE EAST
ITALY
IONIAN SEA
GREECE
AEGEAN SEA
ISTANBUL
ANKARA
TURKEY
CAPPADOCIA
SEA OF CRETE
SYRIA
CYPRUS
LEBANON
BEIRUT
MEDITERRANEAN SEA
ISRAEL & THE PALESTINIAN TERRITORIES
DAMASCUS
TEL AVIV
GULF OF SIRT
JERUSALEM
AMMAN
ALEXANDRIA
DEAD SEA
JORDAN
CAIRO
PETRA
PYRAMIDS OF GIZA
AQABA
WADI RUM
DAHAB
LIBYA
EGYPT
LUXOR
RED SEA
NILE VALLEY
CHAD
HIGHLIGHT
AMMAN TO CAIRO & BEYOND
ISTANBUL TO SHIRAZ
THE GULF & ARABIAN SEA
AIR
TRAIN
BOAT
SUDAN
ERITREA
ETHIOPI

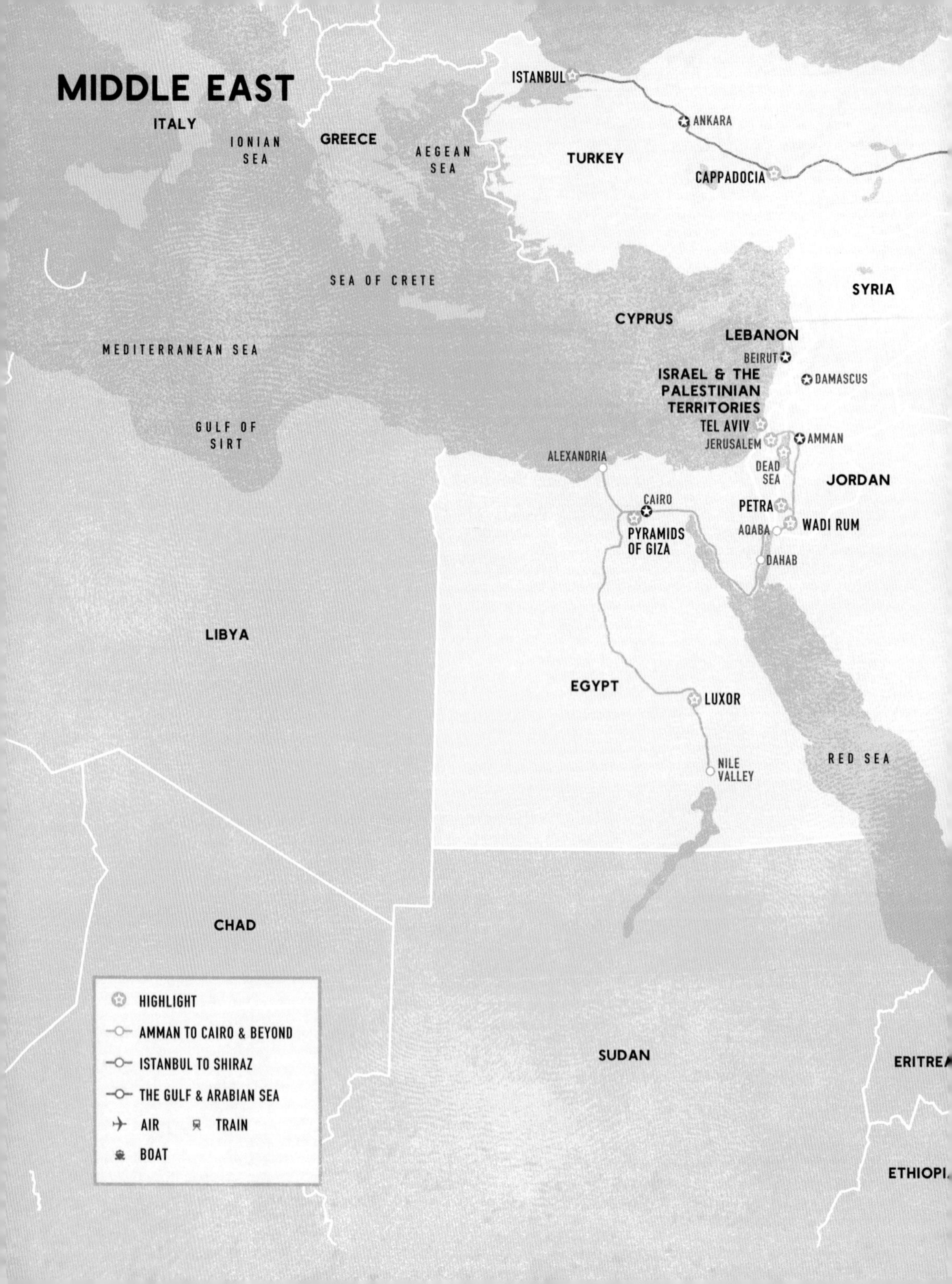

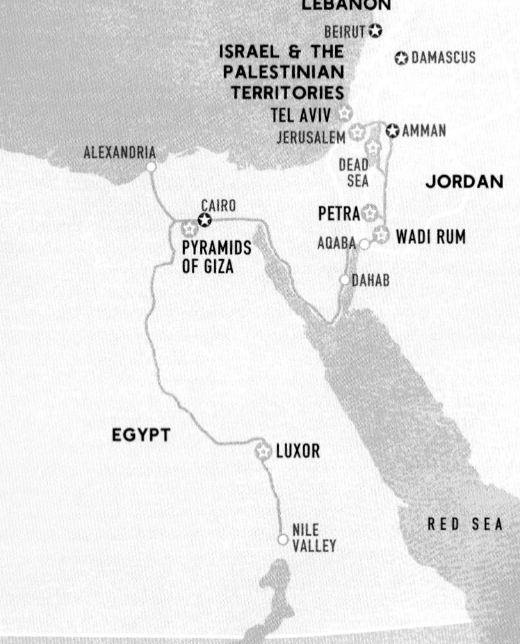

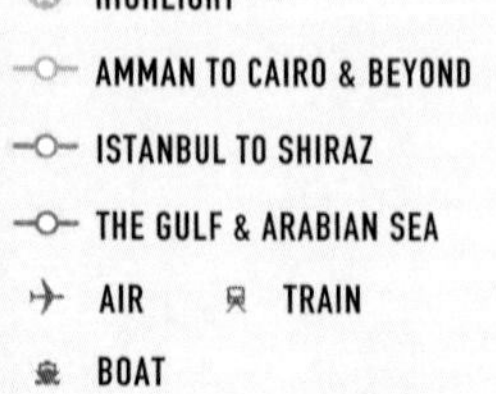

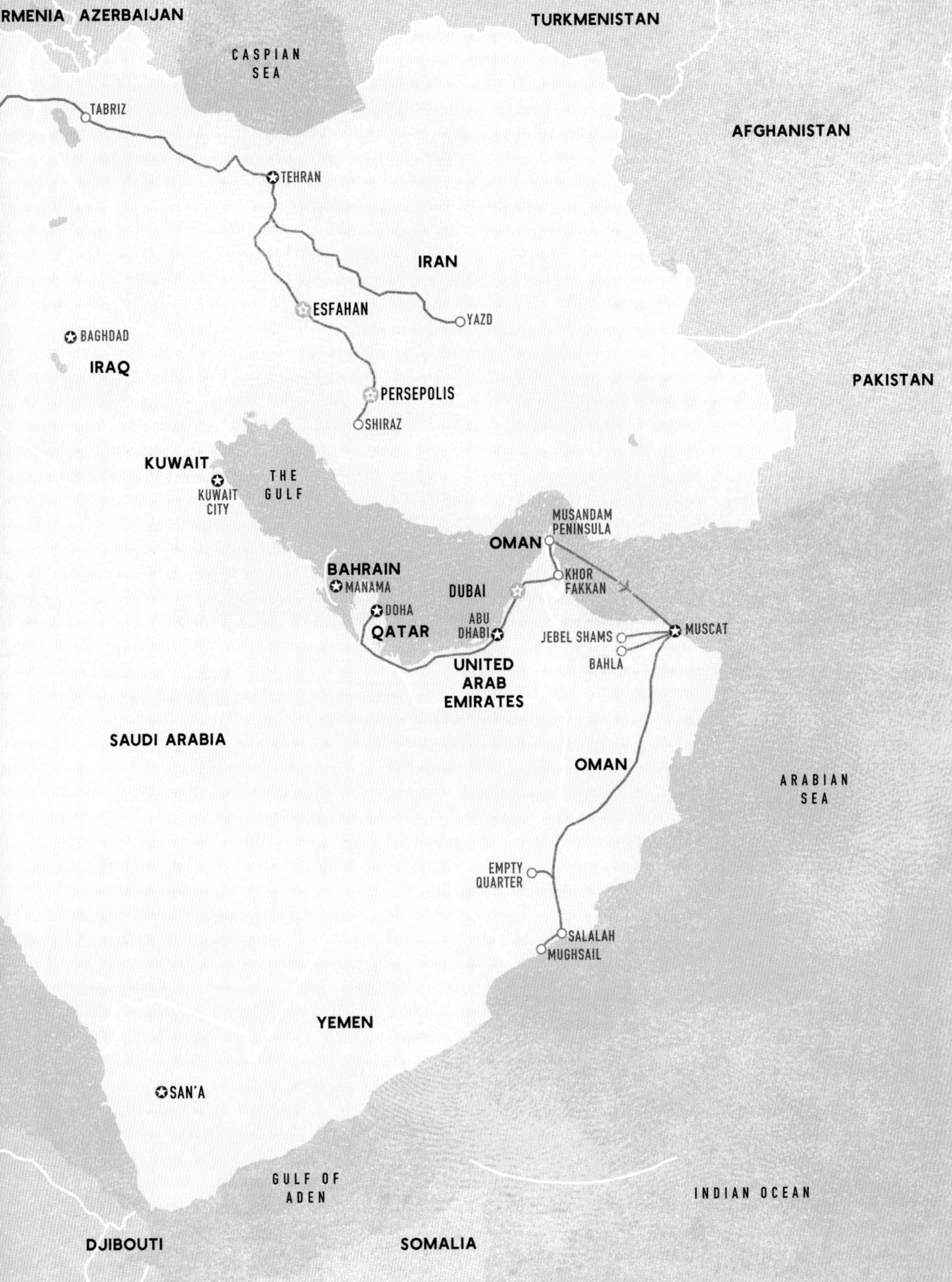

ARMENIA
AZERBAIJAN
TURKMENISTAN
CASPIAN SEA
TABRIZ
AFGHANISTAN
TEHRAN
IRAN
ESFAHAN
YAZD
BAGHDAD
IRAQ
PAKISTAN
PERSEPOLIS
SHIRAZ
KUWAIT
KUWAIT CITY
THE GULF
MUSANDAM PENINSULA
OMAN
BAHRAIN
MANAMA
DUBAI
KHOR FAKKAN
DOHA
QATAR
ABU DHABI
MUSCAT
JEBEL SHAMS
BAHLA
UNITED ARAB EMIRATES
SAUDI ARABIA
OMAN
ARABIAN SEA
EMPTY QUARTER
SALALAH
MUGHSAIL
YEMEN
SAN'A
GULF OF ADEN
INDIAN OCEAN
DJIBOUTI
SOMALIA

A colourful canopy tops a row of cafes in Beirut, Lebanon

Istanbul's New Mosque (Yeni Cami) is actually around 400 years old

A herd of camels traipse through the Wadi Rum desert in Jordan

• Seeing the future in **Dubai** (United Arab Emirates), one of the 21st century's most exciting cities.
• Wondering at the wisdom of the ancients in blue-tiled **Esfahan** (Iran).
• Floating in the **Dead Sea** (Jordan and Israel and the Palestinian Territories), one of the world's great natural experiences.
• Embracing ancient Egypt at **Luxor**, home to the greatest concentration of Egyptian monuments anywhere.

GET ACTIVE

Diving, scaling summits of rock and of sand or skiing the slopes, there's not much you can't do in the Middle East.

Camel Trekking & 4WD Safaris

The deserts of Wadi Rum (Jordan) and the Empty Quarter (Saudi Arabia, United Arab Emirates and Oman) are among the most spectacular on earth. In Jordan, UAE and Oman a camel is the perfect vehicle for desert contemplation, though make sure the animals are cared for and healthy (this tends not to be the case for camels, donkeys and horses used for visitor experiences around Petra in Jordan, and their use is not recommended). For deeper access into the wilderness, 4WD adventures are the way forward.

Cycling & Mountain Biking

Mountain biking is popular in Israel, Jordan and to some extent in Lebanon (Mt Lebanon Range). The only drawbacks? The heat can be a killer (avoid May to September) and you should be self-sufficient as spare parts are scarce.

Snowsports

Beirut is famous for the fact that there, you can swim in the Mediterranean in the morning, then ski on Mt Makmal, northeast of Beirut, in the afternoon. A no less improbable experience awaits in the Alborz Mountains north of Tehran, where there are no less than five ski resorts. And for the truly improbable, there's the black run in Dubai, which hosts the world's largest indoor ski slope.

Trekking, Mountaineering & Rock-Climbing

Jordan is a trekkers' and climbers' paradise, most notably in and around Wadi Rum, Petra and the Dana Biosphere Reserve. Makhtesh Ramon Nature Reserve and the canyons and pools of Ein Avdat in Israel's Negev Desert are great trekking areas; while the rugged mountains of Oman offer some of the best climbing and caving in the Middle East. North of Tehran it's possible to reach the summit of Mt Damavand (5671m) – the Middle East's highest peak – on a three-day trek. The surrounding Alborz Mountains also offer some marvellous trekking and mountaineering to the adventurous traveller. When not affected by travel advisories, Mt Sinai, in Egypt, attracts hikers and pilgrims for exceptional sunsets.

Water Sports

The Red Sea is world renowned for underwater splendour. Coastal towns in the Gulf of Aqaba and Sinai (security permitting) offer easy access to some of the region's best dive sites, together with a wide variety of other water sports, both above and below the waterline. Practically all of the big beach resorts in Dubai maintain state-of-the-art water-sports centres that offer both guests and non-guests a range of ways to get out on the water. The menu may include waterskiing, jet-skiing, wakeboarding, parasailing and power boating. Or, for something completely different, try pearl diving in Bahrain.

WILDLIFE

Occupying the junction of three natural zones, the Middle East was once a sanctuary for an amazing variety of mammals. But most mammals have been hunted into extinction, with only a few vestiges surviving. Listed here are a few ecotourism projects and wildlife reserves that now protect the region's most charismatic fauna:

• **Hai-Bar Yotvata Nature Reserve** (Israel and the Palestinian Territories) Observe African asses, addax, ostriches and oryx in the wild.

• **Ras Mohammed National Park** (Egypt) One of the Red Sea's few protected areas teems with marine life.

• **Shaumari Wildlife Reserve** (Jordan) Take a safari to see wild Arabian oryx in this ground-breaking reserve.

• **Mujib Biosphere Reserve** (Jordan) An enclosure for the Nubian ibex and the chance to see caracal.

• **Shouf Biosphere Reserve** (Lebanon) If you're (extremely) lucky, you might see wolves, wild cats, ibex and gazelle.

• **Sir Bani Yas Island** (UAE) Once Sheikh Zayed's private retreat, this nature reserve has 13,000 free-roaming indigenous and introduced animals.

FESTIVALS

Major festivals in the Middle East fall into two categories: religious ones that change according to the lunar calendar, and which are marked by feasting and religious observance, and cultural festivals that attract an international audience.

Religious Festivals

• **Ras as-Sana** (Islamic New Year) The start of the Muslim year is marked by family feasts and a few public festivities.

• **Eid al-Moulid** (Moulid an-Nabi) The Prophet Mohammed's birthday. Celebrated with feasts and large gatherings of extended family.

• **Ramadan** Muslims fast during daylight hours and enjoy the sharing of food after sunset.

• **Eid al-Fitr** The end of Ramadan is marked by family gatherings, feasting and the buying of new clothes.

• **Eid al-Adha** Muslims undertake *haj*, the pilgrimage to Mecca.

• **Eid al-Kebir** (Tabaski) Commemorates Abraham's willingness to sacrifice his son on God's command; rams are eaten in great quantities.

• **Nevruz / No Ruz** (Turkey and Iran) Kurds and Alevis celebrate the ancient Middle Eastern spring festival on 21 March with much jumping over bonfires, huge parties and general jollity.

• **Easter & Christmas** The region's Christians attend church services and gather for celebratory feasts and, in some countries, processions at Easter.

• **Pesah** (Passover) Honours the exodus of the Jews from Egypt and lasts for a week.

• **Purim** (Feast of Lots) Celebrates how the Jewish people living in Persia were saved from massacre.

Other festivals

• **Muscat Festival** (Oman; https://en.muscat-festival.com) A month of top-class acrobatic acts, international craft shopping and Omani heritage displays across the city for a month in January/February.

• **Cappadox Festival** (Turkey; www.cappadox.com/en) Cappadocia's three-day arts festival in May merges music, nature walks, art exhibitions, yoga and gastronomy into an extravaganza of Turkish contemporary culture.

• **Midburn** (Israel and the Palestinian Territories; www.midburn.org/en) The region's answer to Burning Man sees thousands of people descend on the Negev in May to celebrate art, music and radical self-expression.

• **Jerash Festival** (Jordan) Taking place within Roman ruins, this much-loved festival of culture and arts brings ancient Jerash to life through plays, poetry recitals, opera and concerts. It runs over 17 days from mid-July to mid-August.

NIGHTLIFE

You wouldn't come to the Middle East for its nightlife, but the situation is more nuanced than you might think. Bars are commonplace in urban and coastal Turkey, Beirut and Christian areas of Lebanon, Amman in Jordan, and throughout Israel. In the more liberal countries on the Arabian Peninsula, such as Bahrain and some parts of the UAE, bars, cocktail bars and even pubs can be found. In others, such as Qatar and Oman, usually only certain mid- or upper-range hotels are permitted to serve alcohol. Wine is served in most licensed restaurants in Bahrain, Oman, Qatar and the UAE. Alcohol is forbidden in Iran, Saudi Arabia and Kuwait.

Tel Aviv is undoubtedly the home of the Middle East's most vibrant party scene, but Dubai also has some terrific nightlife. Amman also has sophisticated venues beloved by middle-class locals and travellers alike.

ROADS LESS TRAVELLED

The issues of terrorism and inter-state conflict within the Middle East over the past two decades have hampered many visitors in their quest to explore parts of the region. For instance, Syria was once considered to be one of the friendliest countries in the world to visit, but, tragically, over the past few years it has simply been a no-go zone. Unfortunately, these issues have also needlessly scared off many people from visiting places in the region that don't pose such a threat. So, with the exception of Dubai, Abu Dhabi, Doha and parts of Israel, Turkey and Jordan, this region is all on the road less travelled.

WORKING

The Middle East is the sort of place where you keep your CV stashed and just get down to the serious business of travelling. Short-term job possibilities are limited to teaching English and working in backpackers hostels (especially Israel) and in the kibbutz or moshav systems in Israel.

For archaeology buffs, joining a dig in Israel and Jordan between May and September, is a possibility but it also require months of advance planning (see Fancy a Dig, p146).

WHEN TO GO?

The best times to visit the Middle East are during the spring and autumn. Summer is just way too hot, especially in the desert regions and along the Gulf and Red Sea coasts. Winter can bring some surprisingly miserable weather to the northern Middle East.

The coasts of the Red Sea, Arabian Sea and the Gulf range from hot to extremely hot, often with 70% humidity; summer daytime temperatures can exceed 50°C/122°F. The shores of the Mediterranean enjoy a milder, more European climate. Much of Iran is above 1000m and, together with highland areas in Lebanon, northern Israel and the Hajar Mountains of Oman, these parts experience very cold winters. Southeastern Iran and southern Oman are affected by Indian monsoonal systems from March to May and July to August.

Apart from climate, you'll need to factor in Ramadan, when the region is on a go-slow.

WHAT TO EXPECT?

LOCALS & OTHER TRAVELLERS

The Middle East is dominated by two very Islamic characteristics: honouring guests with boundless hospitality and conservative codes of social behaviour.

At some point on your visit you'll be sitting in a coffeehouse or looking lost in a labyrinth of narrow lanes when someone will strike up a conversation and, within minutes, invite you home to meet their family and share a meal. Or someone will simply approach and say with unmistakable warmth, 'Welcome'. These spontaneous, disarming and utterly genuine words of welcome can occur anywhere across the region. And when they do, they can suddenly (and forever) change the way you see the Middle East.

At the same time, the social conservatism requires a careful adherence to local norms; so do as the locals do, and dress and behave more modestly than you might at home and always err on the side of caution. As with anywhere, take your cues from those around you. Blending in by wearing what locals do will not only show respect, but it may also make your path a more enjoyable one.

Historic links ensure that British travel to much of the region and French travellers are

© Fatma Barlas Özkavalcıoğlu / 500px

Hot-air balloons above Cappadocia during the annual festival in Turkey

© Mark Read / Lonely Planet

A worshipper at rest inside Istanbul's Rushtem Pasha mosque

more common in Lebanon. American travellers are drawn to Israel. Europeans, Aussies and Kiwis also frequent the region but, as a general rule, the Middle East attracts far fewer travellers than Europe or Asia.

In some areas, such as the Arabian Peninsula, most foreigners are those who have a job in the region. That said, destinations where travellers congregate in larger numbers include Wadi Musa (around Petra in Jordan), Jerusalem and Cairo.

URBAN MYTHS – DANGERZONE?

Outbreaks of violence and acts of terrorism against Western targets in the Middle East are rare, although you should always check out the latest security warnings. OK, so you probably shouldn't be planning a trip to Iraq or Gaza any time soon, and rambling around the Israel–Lebanon border is not a smart move. Turkey's extreme southeast, close to the Iraq border, should also be avoided, and check the security advice before heading to Yemen. But the region's problems are invariably localised, leaving most places safe to visit. Isolated acts of terrorism aside, personal safety is rarely an issue. You're far less likely to be mugged on the streets of Tehran or Cairo than in London.

FOOD

The Middle East is a feast for the senses and your taste buds are in for a treat. Mezze is the Middle East's answer to Spanish tapas and Italian antipasto and is almost infinite in its variety from Lebanon to Egypt. Dips (such as hummus and baba ghanoosh) are staples, as are *shawarmas* (kebabs/kababs), *falafel* (mashed chickpeas with spices), fresh salads, *fuul* (fava beans cooked with garlic and

AT THE WESTERN WALL

Countless hands were caressing Jerusalem's Western Wall, which blushed gold in the late afternoon sun. I watched as women pressed their tear-stained cheeks against the wall, planting kisses on its bare stone.

Standing a few feet back, I struggled to wrap my mind around its history over the past two millennia. The Western Wall supports the outer part of Temple Mount, where the Second Temple stood before its destruction in 70 CE. Built from hand-chiselled blocks as long as 14m, it's a wonder of ancient architecture. To Jewish people, this is the holiest place of prayer on earth. It's also part of the world's most contested sacred site: to Muslims, the wall adjoins the Noble Sanctuary, the holiest place in Islam after Mecca and Medina.

With a flutter of trepidation, I stepped forward and placed my palms on the sun-warmed stone. Every fissure in the wall was jammed with tightly folded pieces of paper. Some had fallen onto the ground, unfurling to reveal prayers of joy, despair and gratitude in innumerable languages. Many people believe that prayers placed in the wall's cracks are channelled directly to God. Squeezing my eyes shut, I marvelled at my tiny place within this tide of pulsating humanity. Moments passed – time is impossible to measure at the Western Wall.

Overwhelmed by the crowd, I finally stepped back from the wall. Worshippers flowed around me to fill every available space. I could hear women's murmurs of prayerful longing rising to a crescendo. My heart thudded its reply.

Anita Isalska

garnished with herbs and spices), piping hot bread and the sweetest of sweets. There are subtle culinary differences from country to country. But they all share an emphatic belief in the importance of good food.

LANGUAGE

Arabic is the official language everywhere except Iran and Israel, where Farsi (Persian) and Hebrew, respectively, are spoken. English is widely spoken in the region, and Lebanese still speak a little French.

COMMUNICATION

Wi-Fi access is increasingly the norm in many hotels. It's also getting easier to connect in upmarket cafes and restaurants. In some cities, like Tel Aviv, there aren't many places where you can't connect. There are still internet cafes in major cities and larger towns, but they're dwindling in number due to availability of Wi-Fi.

Given its reputation for political censorship, there are surprisingly few websites that are blocked by governments in the region, although Iran is a significant exception; in the latter tens of thousands of sites fall foul of the censors.

Mobile networks in Middle Eastern countries all work on the GSM system, and it's rare that your mobile brought from home won't automatically link up with a local operator. Local SIM cards are widely available.

COSTS

The region's surfeit of oil and government subsidies mean that transport costs are generally low, and the basic necessities of life remain quite reasonable. The cheapest places to travel are Egypt, Jordan and Iran, where you can travel in luxury quite cheaply. Lebanon is also relatively inexpensive, unlike Israel, the Gulf States and Oman.

HEALTH

Prevention is the key to staying healthy while travelling in the Middle East. Infectious diseases can and do occur in the region but are usually associated with poor living conditions and poverty and can be avoided with a few precautions. The most common reason for travellers needing medical help is as a result of accidents – cars are not always well maintained, seatbelts are rare and poorly lit roads are littered with potholes. Medical facilities can be excellent in large cities, but in remote areas may be more basic.See the Health & Safety chapter and seek professional medical advice.

ISSUES

For a region with a reputation for being so volatile, remarkably little changes when it comes to the bigger picture. War continues in Syria and in parts of Iraq, Israel and the Palestinians seem as far away from a peaceful resolution as ever, while Iran continues to be everyone's favourite bogeyman. Turkey has experienced more turmoil than it has become used to, but remains essentially stable, as does Jordan, while Egypt and Lebanon are at peace, if only just.

GETTING THERE

The Middle East, with Dubai and Doha leading the way, is fast becoming a transport hub for air travellers, either as entry points to the region or as stopovers en route elsewhere.

AIR

The region's major air hubs are Abu Dhabi, Bahrain, Beirut, Cairo, Doha, Dubai and Istanbul.

Major airlines based in the region include:

- **EgyptAir** (www.egyptair.com)

SAMPLE COSTS

	Israel (New Israeli shekel, NIS)	Egypt (Egyptian pound, LE)	Jordan (dinar, JD)	UAE (UAE dirham, Dhs)
Hostel: dorm bed	100NIS (US$27.50)	LE50-180 (US$2.80-10)	JD7-10 (US$10-14)	Dhs70-120 (US$19-33)
Midrange hotel: double room	250-500NIS (US$69-138)	LE540-1800 (US$30-100)	JD40-90 (US$56-127)	Dhs500-1000 (US$136-272)
Street snack	*Falafel* 7-10NIS (US$1.93-2.75)	*Kushari* LE6-10 (US$0.34-0.56)	*Shawarma* JD1 (US$1.40)	*Shawarma* Dhs7-15 (US$1.90-4.10)
Budget meal	45-75NIS (US$12.40-20.68)	LE40-100 (US$2.23-5.60)	JD4-7 (US$5.65-9.87)	Dhs20-40 (US$5.45-10.90)
Midrange restaurant: main	35-70NIS (US$9.65-19.30)	LE50–150 (US$2.80–8.40)	JD5-10 (US$7-14)	Dhs30-90 (US$8.15-24.45)
Cappuccino	7-15NIS (US$1.93-4.14)	LE17-40 (US$0.95-2.25)	JD1.25-4 (US$1.75-5.65)	Dhs13-25 (US$3.54-6.80)
1.5L bottle of water	3-10NIS (US$0.83-2.75)	LE4-6 (US$0.23-0.34)	JD0.35-0.60 (US$0.50-0.85)	Dhs2-5 (US$0.55-1.36)
1L Petrol (gas)	6.30NIS (US$1.74)	LE5.40 (US$0.30)	JD0.85 (US$1.20)	Dhs2.25 (US$0.61)

- **El Al** (www.elal.co.il)
- **Emirates** (www.emirates.com)
- **Etihad** (www.etihad.com)
- **Gulf Air** (www.gulfair.com)
- **Middle East Airlines** (www.mea.com.lb)
- **Qatar Airways** (www.qatarairways.com)
- **Royal Jordanian Airlines** (www.rj.com)
- **Turkish Airlines** (www.turkishairlines.com)

Budget airlines operating within the region:

- **Air Arabia** (www.airarabia.com)
- **flydubai** (www.flydubai.com)
- **Jazeera Airlines** (www.jazeeraairways.com)
- **Pegasus** (www.flypgs.com)
- **SunExpress** (www.sunexpress.com)

SEA & OVERLAND

Ferries shuttle reasonably regularly from Greece and Cyprus to Israel. Routes also connect Egypt with Jordan and Saudi Arabia, and Sudan with Saudi Arabia.

An Istanbul street vendor waits to greet potential customers

Overland transport between Turkey, Iran, Lebanon, Jordan, Israel, Egypt and, to a lesser extent, Sudan, is plentiful. Travelling overland is also straightforward between the UAE and Oman. However, it is simpler, quicker and cheaper to fly between the other countries of the Arabian Peninsula.

SPECIALIST TOUR OPERATORS

- **Backpacker Concierge** (www.backpackerconcierge.com) Operating in Egypt and Jordan, it offers excellent tours, with great connections to Bedouin groups.
- **Crusader Travel** (www.crusadertravel.com) Diving and adventure tours from Israel, Oman, Jordan and Turkey.
- **Exodus** (www.exodus.co.uk) Small-group tours to Egypt, Iran and Jordan.
- **Explore Worldwide** (www.exploreworldwide.com) Small-group tours to Egypt, Iran, Israel, Jordan and Oman.
- **The Imaginative Traveller** (www.imaginative-traveller.com) Iran, Israel and the Palestinian Territories, Jordan, Oman and Turkey are all covered by their tours.
- **Intrepid Travel** (www.intrepidtravel.com) Small-group tours to most of the region, including the UAE.
- **Oasis Overland** (www.oasisoverland.co.uk) Offer various Egypt and Jordan itineraries on its overland trucks.
- **Zahara Tours** (www.zaharatours.com) Specialising in small-group cultural and adventure tours in Oman.

BEYOND THE MIDDLE EAST

Standing as it does at the crossroads of three continents, the Middle East can be a launch pad for an epic overland journey. Egypt enables you to travel south into the heart of Africa and on to Cape Town. An alternative is the so-called 'hippie trail', running from Turkey to Iran, the Indian subcontinent and on to Kathmandu. If you're flying, Dubai is good for cheap deals to the Indian subcontinent and acts as a gateway to Indian Ocean destinations such as the Maldives and Seychelles, which can be hard and expensive to reach from beyond the region. A final option is to head north through southern and eastern Europe.

FURTHER INFORMATION

WEBSITES

- **Al-Bab** (www.al-bab.com) Arab-world gateway with links to news services, country profiles, travel sites and maps.
- **Al-Bawaba** (www.albawaba.com) News, entertainment and Yellow Pages directories, with online forums and kids' pages.
- **Bahrain Tourism** (www.culture.gov.bh) Official government tourism site.

- **Destination Oman** (www.destinationoman.com) Practical information.
- **Dubai Tourism** (www.visitdubai.com) Dubai's official tourism site.
- **I Love Qatar** (www.iloveqatar.net) Expat-run guide to the country with news and listings.
- **Israel Ministry of Tourism** (www.goisrael.com) Background, events and a virtual tour.
- **Tehran Times** (www.tehrantimes.com) Iran's English-language news site and newspaper.
- **See You In Iran** (www.facebook.com/SeeYouinIran/) Worth signing up to this FB group posting all kinds of useful stuff for Iran travellers.

BOOKS

- **A History of the Arab Peoples** Albert Hourani's highly readable sweep through centuries of Arab history.
- **A Strangeness in My Mind** Orhan Pamuk writes of 20th-century Istanbul through the eyes of an Anatolian street hawker.
- **Arabian Sands** Wilfred Thesiger writes of his crossing of the Empty Quarter – it's an all-time travel classic.
- **City of Lies** Ramita Navai writes of contemporary Iran along Tehran's longest street, Valiasr.
- **From the Holy Mountain** William Dalrymple writes of an engaging trip through Turkey, Syria, Israel and the Palestinian Territories.
- **Jerusalem: One City, Three Faiths** Karen Armstrong provides a balanced study of the city claimed by Jews, Muslims and Christians.
- **Mezzoterra** Ahdaf Soueif's searing critique of Western stereotypes and the gritty realities of the Arab-Israeli conflict.
- **Nine Parts of Desire** Geraldine Brooks takes an outsider-insider look at the role of women in the region.
- **No Knives in the Kitchens of This City** Aleppo at war provides a backdrop to Khaled Khalifa's story about a family facing its own disintegration.
- **Seven Pillars of Wisdom** A great read by TE Lawrence, one of the Middle East's most legendary figures.
- **The Innocents Abroad** Mark Twain's 1869 effort is still many people's favourite travel book about the region.
- **The Last Palestinian: The Rise and Reign of Mahmoud Abbas** Grant Rumley and Amir Tibon's well-paced unauthorised biography of the Palestinian leader.

FILMS

- **Lawrence of Arabia** (1962) David Lean's masterpiece captures all the hopes and subsequent frustrations in the aftermath of WWI.
- **Once Upon a Time in Anatolia** (2011) Acclaimed evocation of the Turkish soul and steppe.
- **A Separation** (2011) Oscar-winning film that portrays the angst of modern Iran.
- **Omar** (2014) Oscar-nominated film about the fatal entwining of Palestinians and Israelis.
- **Rosewater** (2014) Jon Stewart's acclaimed dramatisation of Iran's Green Movement.
- **Taxi** (2015) Jafar Panahi's brilliant 'docu-fiction' gives a voice to ordinary Iranians in a Tehran taxi.
- **Going To Heaven** (Saeed Salmeen Al Murry; 2015) Sweet drama following 11 year old Sultan and Saud as they set out from Abu Dhabi to Dhubai on a mission to find Sultan's grandmother.
- **The Salesman** (2016) Asghar Farhadi's Oscar-nominated study of modern Iran through a troubled relationship.
- **Eshtebak** (Clash, 2016) Captures the essence of the Arab Spring in Cairo.

AFRICA

Africa. There's nowhere like it on the planet for stunning wildlife, majestic landscapes, ancient history and rich traditions that endure. Prepare to fall in love.

This frequently misunderstood continent is home to 54 countries, each unique, each with an array of different life-changing experiences. In that sense it's impossible to talk of Africa as a single entity. How could it not be so with more than one billion Africans and well over 2000 different languages?

To grasp the diversity it's a place you need to explore, work at and put something into in order to get the maximum out. Not that this is an easy proposition of course, especially since the sheer scale of the continent can quickly overwhelm even seasoned travellers (the continental USA is smaller than the Sahara Desert). You have to be up for some hard journeys, and there are a few ugly and frantic cities, with plenty of poverty. But within them you'll find fascinating Africans, both rich and poor, who have embraced the future, bringing creativity and sophistication to the fore.

It will shake you to the core, and leave you reeling for more – but it's all worth it, one hundred times over. Pack your bags and check your expectations – you're in for a long and bumpy road. But, we promise that once you've visited the birthplace of humankind, you'll never look at life the same way again.

ITINERARIES

Africa is the second-largest continent on the planet. It is home to dense jungles, bone-dry deserts, sprawling savannahs, jagged mountains and seething cities. Trying to break down this hulking continent is also no small task, though it helps to think of Africa as having roughly five regions: north, south, east, west and central.

SOUTHERN SAFARI

Start in **Cape Town**, a gorgeous beach-meets-mountain city. Next taste your way through the vineyards of the **Winelands**, and whale-watch your way along the **Garden Route**. Continuing east through the **Wild Coast** to **Durban** is a remarkable experience (stop to surf the legendary breaks of **Jeffrey's Bay**). Head north for the stunning summits of the **Drakensberg** and on to the mountain kingdom of **Lesotho**, or fly to **Kruger National Park** – it's 19,485 sq km of wilderness is home to unthinkable numbers of wildlife, including the 'Big Five' (lion, leopard, elephant, rhino, buffalo).

Fly to Namibia's capital **Windhoek**, from where you can strike out westward to **Swakopmund** for a skydive over the Atlantic and the **Namib Desert**, and to visit **Sossusvlei** for a climb up some of the world's tallest (and most stunning) dunes. Or move north to **Etosha National Park**, which is another of Africa's top safari destinations.

Next is the Botswana's **Okavango Delta**, one of Africa's greatest natural wonders. Herds of elephants (tens of thousands strong) then wait at **Chobe National Park**. From here it's a short trip to the famed **Victoria Falls**, which straddles the Zimbabwe and Zambia border. Intense whitewater rafting is one of dozens of adrenaline activities at the falls – have your fill before heading north to **Lusaka**. For leopard sightings aplenty visit **South Luangwa National Park**, or instead flake on a tranquil beach at **Lake Malawi**.

CLASSIC EAST AFRICA

Another classic African gateway is **Nairobi**, the capital of Kenya. After some museums, Giraffe House and the elephant orphanage, make a beeline for **Masai Mara National Reserve**. Between July and October the great wildebeest migration is taking place, but there is wildlife year round. Next stops include **Lake Victoria** at **Kisumu** and the central African rainforest at **Kakamega** before entering Uganda.

Stop at East Africa's adrenaline-sports capital of **Jinja**, then it's a short hop to **Kampala**. Move west to track chimps in **Kibale Forest National Park** and trek in the **Rwenzori Mountains**. Head south for an unforgettable gorilla encounter in **Bwindi Impenetrable National Park** or in Rwanda's **Volcanoes National Park**. Take in Kigali before moving east into Tanzania for a safari in **Serengeti National Park** and a climb of **Kilimanjaro**. From here, it's back to **Nairobi**, though it's worth a detour south to **Zanzibar** for beach action.

Check out sacred, glacier-capped **Mt Kenya** before travelling to **Lake Nakuru** for rhinos galore. Continue up the **Rift Valley** into the bleak wilds around **Lake Turkana** before crossing into Ethiopia. After a stop in **Addis Ababa**, you'll swoon at the rock-hewn churches at **Lalibela**, the castles of **Gonder** and the ancient city of **Aksum**.

COLONIAL FOOTSTEPS

When the dust settled from the colonial scrabble for Africa in the 19th century, elements of French, Spanish and British culture embedded in the north and west of the continent. This legacy provides a fascinating counterpoint to the indigenous cultures of Islam and animism.

From **Tangier**, make your way to the charming Spanish-flavoured medina of **Chefchaouen**. The elegant medina of **Fez** and the vibrant souqs of **Marrakesh** recall a time when Morocco was the centre of the learned world. For nature-lovers, a visit to the graceful red sand dunes at **Merzouga** is a must, while windsurfers and kitesurfers should flock to the coastal town of **Essaouira**.

A long journey south through the **Western Sahara** takes you to **Nouâdhibou** in Mauritania. If the security situation permits then you can detour to see Africa's biggest monolith, **Ben Amira**, and the Saharan caravan towns, **Chinguetti** and **Ouadâne**. Head to the capital, **Nouakchott**, then across the border to charming **Saint-Louis** in Senegal.

Dakar is one of West Africa's cultural capitals, with Parisian trappings and great live music and nightlife. Africa's smallest mainland country, The Gambia, is next. It was once a sliver of the British Empire within French colonial Africa. Bounce from the capital **Banjul** to the lively **Atlantic Coast** resorts and the easy-to-reach and well-managed **Abuko Nature Reserve**.

WILD WEST

From Cameroon's capital, **Yaoundé**, head west to the chocolate-coloured beaches around **Limbe**, where the Limbe Wildlife Centre is home to rescued gorillas, chimps and drills. After exploring **Mt Cameroon** head south to the lovely white beaches of **Kribi**. Even better for wildlife enthusiasts, continue down the coast to **Ebodjé**, with its nesting turtles and impressive ecotourism project.

From **Ebolowa** venture across the Gabon border. The capital **Libreville** is organised, clean and expensive. From here you can make a train trip to see elephants and spectacular scenery at **Lopé National Park**. Another highlight are the surfing hippos and beach-

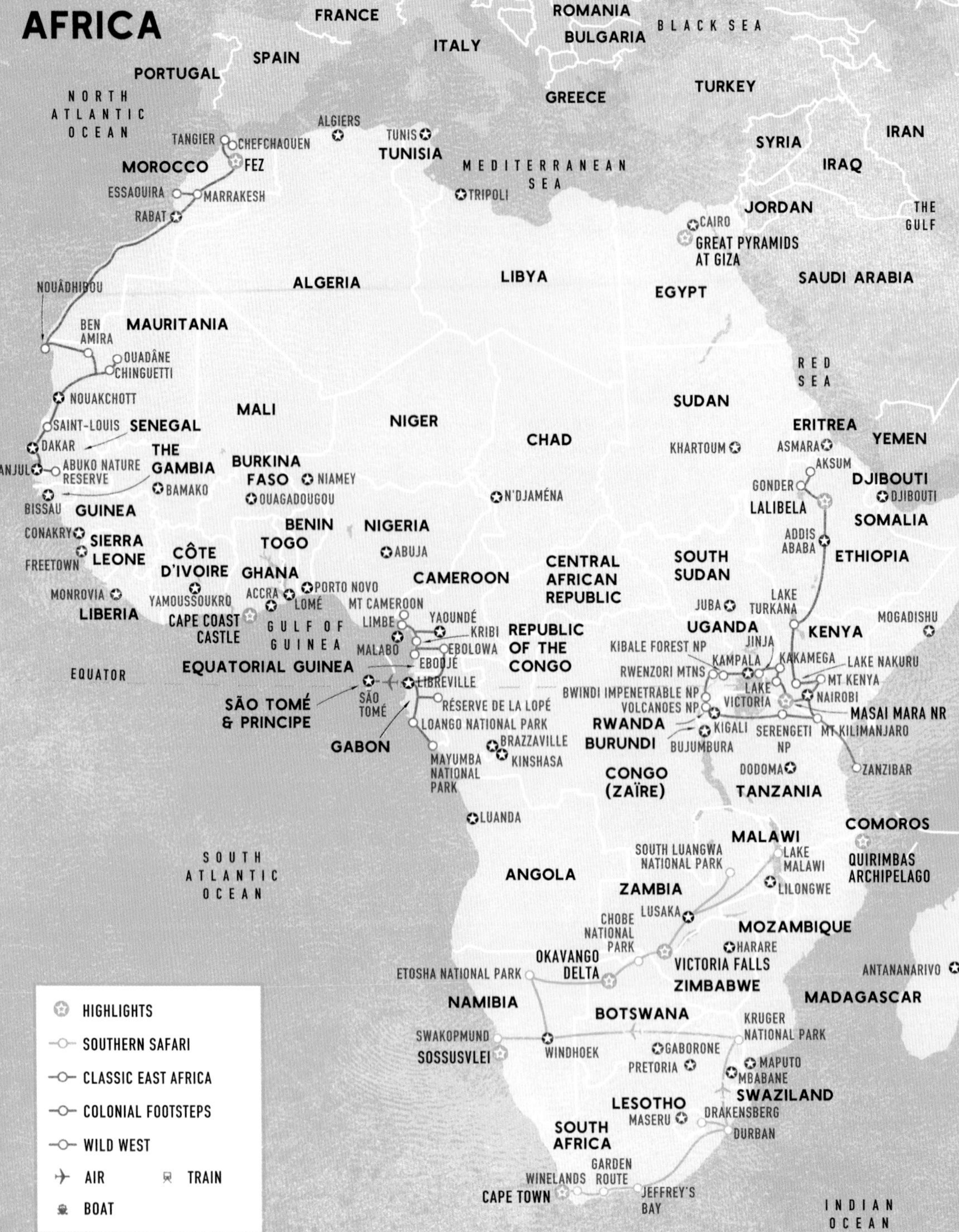
AFRICA
FRANCE
ROMANIA
BULGARIA
BLACK SEA
ITALY
SPAIN
PORTUGAL
GREECE
TURKEY
NORTH ATLANTIC OCEAN
ALGIERS
TUNIS
TANGIER
CHEFCHAOUEN
TUNISIA
SYRIA
IRAN
MOROCCO
FEZ
MEDITERRANEAN SEA
IRAQ
ESSAOUIRA
MARRAKESH
TRIPOLI
RABAT
JORDAN
THE GULF
CAIRO
GREAT PYRAMIDS AT GIZA
ALGERIA
LIBYA
EGYPT
SAUDI ARABIA
NOUÂDHIBOU
BEN AMIRA
MAURITANIA
OUADÂNE
CHINGUETTI
RED SEA
NOUAKCHOTT
MALI
SUDAN
SAINT-LOUIS
SENEGAL
NIGER
ERITREA
DAKAR
CHAD
YEMEN
THE GAMBIA
KHARTOUM
ASMARA
BANJUL
ABUKO NATURE RESERVE
BURKINA FASO
NIAMEY
AKSUM
GONDER
DJIBOUTI
BAMAKO
DJIBOUTI
BISSAU
GUINEA
OUAGADOUGOU
N'DJAMÉNA
LALIBELA
SOMALIA
BENIN
NIGERIA
CONAKRY
SIERRA LEONE
TOGO
ADDIS ABABA
ETHIOPIA
FREETOWN
CÔTE D'IVOIRE
ABUJA
CENTRAL AFRICAN REPUBLIC
SOUTH SUDAN
GHANA
CAMEROON
MONROVIA
ACCRA
PORTO NOVO
YAMOUSSOUKRO
LOMÉ
MT CAMEROON
JUBA
LAKE TURKANA
LIBERIA
CAPE COAST CASTLE
GULF OF GUINEA
LIMBE
YAOUNDÉ
REPUBLIC OF THE CONGO
UGANDA
KENYA
MOGADISHU
KRIBI
MALABO
EBOLOWA
KIBALE FOREST NP
JINJA
EQUATOR
EQUATORIAL GUINEA
EBODJÉ
KAMPALA
KAKAMEGA
LAKE NAKURU
RWENZORI MTNS
LIBREVILLE
LAKE VICTORIA
MT KENYA
SÃO TOMÉ & PRINCIPE
SÃO TOMÉ
BWINDI IMPENETRABLE NP
NAIROBI
RÉSERVE DE LA LOPÉ
VOLCANOES NP
MASAI MARA NR
LOANGO NATIONAL PARK
RWANDA
KIGALI
SERENGETI NP
MT KILIMANJARO
GABON
BRAZZAVILLE
BURUNDI
BUJUMBURA
KINSHASA
MAYUMBA NATIONAL PARK
CONGO (ZAÏRE)
DODOMA
ZANZIBAR
TANZANIA
LUANDA
COMOROS
MALAWI
SOUTH LUANGWA NATIONAL PARK
LAKE MALAWI
QUIRIMBAS ARCHIPELAGO
SOUTH ATLANTIC OCEAN
ANGOLA
ZAMBIA
LILONGWE
LUSAKA
CHOBE NATIONAL PARK
MOZAMBIQUE
HARARE
OKAVANGO DELTA
VICTORIA FALLS
ETOSHA NATIONAL PARK
ZIMBABWE
ANTANANARIVO
NAMIBIA
MADAGASCAR
BOTSWANA
KRUGER NATIONAL PARK
SWAKOPMUND
GABORONE
SOSSUSVLEI
WINDHOEK
PRETORIA
MAPUTO
MBABANE
SWAZILAND
LESOTHO
MASERU
DRAKENSBERG
SOUTH AFRICA
DURBAN
GARDEN ROUTE
WINELANDS
CAPE TOWN
JEFFREY'S BAY
INDIAN OCEAN
HIGHLIGHTS
SOUTHERN SAFARI
CLASSIC EAST AFRICA
COLONIAL FOOTSTEPS
WILD WEST
AIR
TRAIN
BOAT

© Justin Foulkes / Lonely Planet

The fort of St Sebastian on São Tomé & Principe

Fancy glamping in the southern Serengeti? One of the luxury tents at Namiri Plains Camp, Tanzania

The local residents of Sabi Sand Game Reserve, which flanks South Africa's vast Kruger National Park, include elephants and leopards

going elephants of **Loango National Park**, which also hosts lowland gorillas. From here you can continue to **Mayumba National Park** to view humpback whales and go body surfing.

Finish the trip with a jaunt to one of Africa's smallest countries, São Tomé & Príncipe – stand-up paddle board in in the spectacular **Baía das Agulhas** (Bay of Spires), watch nesting turtles at **Praia Jalé** and lounge on the deserted and generally perfect sands of **Praia Banana**.

WHAT TO DO?

HIGHLIGHTS

- Looking over the city of **Cape Town** (South Africa) from a well-earned perch atop iconic Table Mountain.
- Journeying through the surreal beauty of the reed-lined channels within the **Okavango Delta** (Botswana) by traditional *mokoro* (a dugout canoe).
- Standing in awe before magnificent **Victoria Falls** (Zambia and Zimbabwe), one of the natural wonders of the world.
- Being humbled by the wildebeest migration in **Masai Mara** (Kenya) and the **Serengeti** (Tanzania).
- Trying to comprehend the horrors of the slave trade while touring the **Cape Coast Castle** (Ghana), one of West Africa's many such forts.
- Chilling out on the mind-blowing beaches of the **Quirimbas Archipelago** (Mozambique), a place of both great beauty and history.
- Stepping into the rock-hewn underworld of **Lalibela** (Ethiopia), where the past has been frozen in stone.
- Walking among the skeletons of an ancient forest on the floor of Deadvlei, with the dunes of **Sossusvlei** (Namibia) as a backdrop.
- Putting on your very best Indiana Jones hat, and penetrating the depths of the **Pyramids of Giza** (Egypt).
- Navigating the winding, narrow alleys of the old medina in **Fez** (Morocco), one of North Africa's most enigmatic cities.

GET ACTIVE

Africa is all about getting into the wilds – but make sure you're doing so by heading out in the presence of qualified guides and/or tour operators.

Diving & Snorkelling

Arguably, Africa's best diving and snorkelling is found in the Red Sea. Egypt is the most obvious place to get your feet wet, though nearby Djibouti is one of the best places on the planet to dive with whale sharks. Of course, the whole east coast of Africa is peppered with great dive locations, especially Mozambique. Far-flung São Tomé & Príncipe is another exotic place to dive, while the shores of Lake Malawi are cheap and decidedly more humble in scale.

Whitewater Rafting & Kayaking

Whitewater rafting on the Zambezi River below Victoria Falls (Zambia/Zimbabwe) is simply incredible – it's one of the hardest commercially run set of rapids in the world. Those on the Nile in Uganda are also mad, but they've been dampened by recent dam works. You can also raft in Kenya, Namibia and Swaziland. The Okavango Delta in Botswana and the Zambezi River in Zambia are the ultimate locations for multi-day water-borne safaris, while Lake Malawi is a good place for renting canoes. Pole-propelled *pirogues* (dugout canoes) can give you a taste of local life on the West African waterways – exploring the thatched huts of Ganvié, perched on stilts above Lake Nokoué in Benin, is a classic African experience.

Surfing & Kiteboarding
Between April and July, there's world-class surfing to be had all along the coast of South Africa. The most famous break on the continent is at Jeffrey's Bay, which dishes out a fierce ride that can last several minutes. However, you'll find less crowds (and sometimes no-one at all) if you go beyond the surfer trail and explore Madagascar, Mozambique, Senegal, Liberia and Namibia.

If you prefer to surf with a kite, Mauritius, Cabo Verde, Kenya and Morocco are now emerging as internationally recognised kitesurfing destinations.

Trekking
Mt Kilimanjaro (5895m) and Mt Kenya (5199m), the continent's highest and second-highest peaks, are both tremendous challenges (the latter requiring technical climbing), as are peaks in the Rwenzoris (Uganda), Simiens (Ethiopia), Drakensberg (South Africa) and Atlas (Morocco). Namibia's Fish River Canyon is a great 86km trek, though it's open only from early May to mid-September (soaring heat makes it unsafe the rest of the year). In West Africa, Mt Cameroon is worth a climb, as are areas of the Fouta Djalon Highlands (Guinea). The continent has many curious little corners where you can pick up a guide, shoulder a pack, walk through beautiful countryside and meet local people on their own terms. Donkeys, horses or camels will extend your range, or could be your sole means of transport if you're truly out in the wilderness.

Safaris
Going on safari (Swahili for 'journey') is undoubtedly an African highlight. East and Southern Africa have the highest density of the wildlife-laden parks and reserves. The wildebeest migration (July through October) between the Serengeti and Masai Mara reserves on the Tanzanian–Kenyan border is one of the world's great wildlife spectacles. Safaris are possible year-round, but best at the end of the dry season when animals are concentrated around dwindling water sources. At the end of the rains, the grass can be just too damn high to see much. Budget camping safaris are easily arranged, but going cheap often means missing out on a top guide.

A CANOE SAFARI ON THE ZAMBEZI

Despite the natural theatrics and sense of danger, the experience was full of peace and absolute wonder. I was witnessing the world's most iconic species of wildlife living their unique lives on their terms.
I was a guest in a world that was not mine. And it's impossible to forget that.

Aurelia India Burwood

WILDLIFE

Don't focus all your attention on the safari centres of Kenya and Tanzania, or the mountain gorilla enclaves of Uganda and Rwanda – parks and reserves crawling with iconic safari species are also found in Botswana, Malawi, Mozambique, Namibia, South Africa, Swaziland, Zambia and Zimbabwe.

There are also other lesser-known highlights to enjoy: the wondrous weirdness of Madagascar's wildlife; lions in Benin; great white sharks and whales off South Africa; lowland gorillas in Gabon and the Congo; forest elephants in Ghana; chimpanzees in Guinea; and geladas, Ethiopian wolves and walia ibex in Ethiopia.

FESTIVALS

Festivals take place across the continent and almost every nation hosts a handful of religious and cultural events. Islamic festivals are widely celebrated in the north, west and coastal regions of East Africa. The end of Ramadan and Eid al-Adha are celebrated big-style in Foumban (Cameroon) – expect horse racing and all-night parties. Christian festivals are common elsewhere in Africa. Here are some of the highlights:

- **Cape Town Minstrel Carnival** (South Africa) The Mother City's most colourful street party runs for a month from 2 January. It's the Cape's equivalent of Mardi Gras.
- **Voodoo Festival** (Benin) Held on 10 January across Benin; the celebrations in the voodoo heartland around Ouidah are the largest and most exuberant.
- **Leddet & Timkat** (Ethiopia) The Ethiopian Christian Orthodox festivals are celebrated in grand style in Addis Ababa, Aksum, Gonder and Lalibela. They mark the birth and baptism of Jesus on 7 and 19 January respectively.
- **Fêtes des Masques** (Côte d'Ivoire) Held in the villages around Man each February, the region's most significant mask festival brings together a great variety of masks and dances from the area.
- **Sauti za Busara** (Tanzania; www.busaramusic.org) Swahili songs from every era fill the night, and dance troupes take over the stages of Stone Town and elsewhere on Zanzibar for four days every February.
- **Festival Pan-Africain du Cinema** (Fespaco; Burkina Faso; www.fespaco.bf/en) This festival is held over nine days in Ougadougou during late February/early March in odd-numbered years.
- **Maitisong Festival** (Botswana; www.maitisong.org) Botswana's largest performing arts festival is held annually over seven days from mid-March to early April in Gaborone. Expect outdoor performances of music, theatre, film and dance.
- **Saint-Louis Jazz Festival** (Senegal; www.saintlouisjazz.org) Hands-down the most internationally renowned festival in West Africa, attracting major jazz performers to this Unesco Heritage-designated town every May.
- **National Arts Festival** (South Africa) Feel South Africa's creative pulse at the country's premier arts festival from late June to early July in studenty Grahamstown.
- **Festival of the Dhow Countries** (Tanzania; www.ziff.or.tz) East Africa's largest cultural event showcases the literature, music, culture and art of coastal countries and is held in July. The Zanzibar International Film Festival is part of the programme.
- **Lake of Stars Music Festival** (Malawi; www.lakeofstars.org) 'Glastonbury on the beach': this brilliant three-day Malawian festival bubbles with stellar UK and African bands, and a host of celebrated global DJs.
- **Kampala City Festival** (Uganda) This fun and frenetic street festival runs through the first week of October with parades and performers celebrating Ugandan culture. Art, fashion and music appear on stages across the city.
- **Oktoberfest** (Namibia) Windhoek stages this feast of food, drink and merrymaking.

NIGHTLIFE

Across such a huge continent, it's unsurprising that the nightlife available runs the gamut from hole-in-the-wall dives and sophisticated drinking dens to operatic experiences and roving cultural street parties. Here are a few of the top sites.

- **Accra** (Ghana) As the night grows older, every bar and lounge in the city can turn into a club.

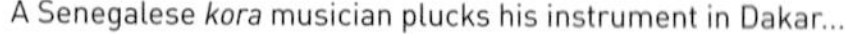

A Senegalese *kora* musician plucks his instrument in Dakar...

...while a percussive ensemble bring the house down across town

Boats arrive at the tiny, car-free Île de Gorée off the coast of Dakar, Senegal

These range from stylish skyscraper rooftops to bustling street parties.

- **Cape Town** (South Africa) There's a great drinking and club scene here, but the nightlife also embraces cabaret and comedy venues, and live music as well as hybrid events such as First Thursdays (roving art-gallery focused street party) and Tuning the Vine (roving wine party).
- **Dakar** (Senegal) There are bars to suit every taste, but the glam venues are mainly in Les Almadies. Live-music venues with dance floors are extremely popular, but nights on the dance floor don't start before 1am. And always – always – overdress.
- **Johannesburg** (South Africa) Jo'burg is an excellent place to see live music, especially across the jazz-tipped and electronic spectrum. Its bar scene is ever-revolving and you'll find everything from crusty bohemian haunts to chic cocktail lounges and conservative wine bars.
- **Lagos** (Nigeria) As they say in Lagos, what happens in Gidi stays in Gidi. In other words, Lagos' nightlife is legendary.
- **Maputo** (Mozambique) Its thriving nightlife scene includes a large and frequently changing selection of cafes, pubs, bars and clubs.
- **Nairobi** (Kenya) Escape the clutches of the ubiquitous sports bars and head to Westlands for a good time.

Outside of the large cities noted above, there are some more casual hang-outs dotted around the continent where younger travellers seem to congregate, kick back and let the good times roll. These include: Cape Maclear and Nkhata Bay (Malawi); Chefhaouen (Morocco); Kokrobite (Ghana); Swakopmund (Namibia); and Tofo (Mozambique).

ROADS LESS TRAVELLED

There aren't too many places in Africa that feel like the beaten path, which is what makes it so very special. The continent is such a mammoth place, and with the number of travellers there being a fraction seen in other areas of the world, you won't often be around fellow travellers when not in a big-name city or famous national park.

WORKING

For those without specialist skills and training, getting paid work in Africa is hard, and usually you'll need to spend a lot of time chatting up the expat community. A few travellers get lucky and land tourist-industry jobs (tour guiding, bar work etc) in East and Southern Africa's backpacker destinations, but don't expect great (if any) wages. Travellers with a degree can sometimes get teaching work, most commonly in private schools.

WHEN TO GO?

The equator cuts right through the middle of Africa and the continent enjoys an enormous variety of climates, so there's never really a bad time to visit – the weather is always perfect somewhere.

The rains in West Africa begin between March and June and finish between September and October – their exact timing is influenced by distance from the coast. Temperatures are generally higher just before the torrential downpours begin.

North Africa has seasons similar to southern Europe, but summer is terribly hot, even in the High Atlas. Winters can be cold, grey and nasty.

In East Africa the 'long rains' occur between March and May, while the 'short rains' are between October and December. June and July are the coolest months, with temperatures and rainfall varying less along the coast. Primetime for wildlife runs from July to October and late December through February.

© Daniel Di Paolo

Served with a smile, fresh fish on the African coastline

The southern African summer (which runs from November through March) is hot and wet, while winter can be surprisingly cold at night. Wildlife safaris in this region are best at the tail end of the dry season (July through October) when animals congregate around dwindling water resources. That said, Kruger National Park is still incredible to visit at any time of the year.

WHAT TO EXPECT?

LOCALS & OTHER TRAVELLERS

Africa attracts a huge cross section of nationalities, though the French are more prevalent in West Africa, where French is an official language. East and Southern Africa's huge tourist profile ensures the widest variety (and number) of nationalities, including the most English-speakers.

While most people come to Africa for the wildlife and massive landscapes, they often leave speaking about their love of its people. The warmth and generosity offered by this incredibly diverse group of humans is something no visitor forgets – it's partly why travellers rarely just visit Africa once. And while there are invariably bad eggs that do pose threats, you will often feel (particularly if travelling alone) like you have a community of people looking out for your wellbeing.

As happens in many tourist hotspots around the world (though here it is the exception rather than the rule), hospitality sometimes comes with a catch, and travellers are exploited for income rather than offered genuine friendship.

FOOD

Whether it's a group of Kenyans gathering in a *nyama choma* (barbecued meat) shop to consume hunks of grilled meat, or Ghanaians dipping balls of *fufu* (pounded yam or cassava with a doughlike consistency) into a steaming communal bowl of stew, there are two things all Africans have in common – they love to eat and it's almost always a social event. African food is generally bold and colourful, with rich, earthy textures and strong, spicy undertones.

Each region has its own key staples. In East and Southern Africa, the base for many local meals is a stiff dough made from maize flour, called – among other things – *ugali*, *sadza*, *pap* and *nshima*. In West Africa millet is also common, and served in a similar way, while staples nearer the coast are root crops such as yam or cassava (*manioc* in French).

In North Africa, bread forms a major part of the meal, while all over Africa rice is an alternative to the local specialities. In some countries, plantain (green banana) is also common, either fried or cooked solid. A sauce of meat, fish, beans or vegetables is typically added to the carb base. If you're eating local-style, you grab a portion of bread or dough or pancake (with your right hand), dip it in the communal pot of sauce and sit back, beaming contentedly, to eat it.

Across Africa many cheap restaurants serve rice and beans and other meals suitable for vegans. For vegetarians, eggs are usually easy to find – expect to eat an awful lot of egg and chips – and, for pescetarians, fish is available nearer the coast. Be aware that in many places chicken is usually not regarded as meat, while even the simplest vegetable sauce may have a bit of animal fat thrown in.

LANGUAGE

Africa is a place of, quite literally, thousands of languages, but English is widely spoken, except in West Africa where French is the most common second language. Portuguese is good for Angola, Mozambique and São Tomé & Príncipe, while Swahili is the trading language of East Africa, just like Hausa in West Africa and Arabic in North Africa. A number of pidgins and creoles (mixtures of local and European languages) are spoken on the coast of West Africa.

COMMUNICATION

Although things are improving, many connections (both Wi-Fi and and in internet cafes) can be excruciatingly slow. There are still cybercafes in most capitals and major towns, but these are disappearing as Wi-Fi becomes more widespread. Many hotels and hostels also offer internet access. Midrange and top-end hotels increasingly offer Wi-Fi; sometimes you have to pay but most often it's free.

Local SIM cards can be used in European and Australian phones.

COSTS

Compared with most of the developing world, Africa is expensive. Travellers commonly blow big chunks of their budget on 4WD hire and internal flights. However, you should try to save some cash for something worthwhile, such as going on safari or arranging an expedition.

The actual cost of living (food, transport etc) varies only a little around the continent, and our table (p321) should give you a rough idea.

HEALTH

As long as you stay up to date with your vaccinations and take some basic preventive measures, you'd have to be pretty unlucky to succumb to any serious health hazards. Africa certainly has an impressive selection of tropical diseases on offer, but you're infinitely more likely to get a bout of diarrhoea (in fact, you should bank on it), a cold or an infected mosquito bite than an exotic disease such West Nile fever or Ebola.

Precautions should start with antimalarials, as Malaria is a problem from the southern fringes of the Sahara right down to South Africa. Yellow fever is endemic across West, Central and parts of East Africa, so getting vaccinated is wise – you'll need to show a Yellow Fever Vaccination Certificate when applying for some visas.

Schistosomiasis (bilharziasis) is present in many beautiful (and inviting) lakes and waterways, including the ever popular Lake Malawi. The risk to tourists is pretty low, but if you do get wet (especially after tramping through standing water on reedy shorelines) dry off quickly and dry your clothes well.

When it comes to injuries (as opposed to illness), the most likely reason for needing medical help in Africa is as a result of road accidents – vehicles are rarely well maintained, the roads are potholed and poorly lit, and drink driving is common.

ISSUES

Crossing borders in Africa is relatively easy and usually straightforward. At remote frontiers and disputed borders, bureaucratic obstacles and demands for 'fines' can be thrown your way. Unfortunately corruption is a common occurrence in many parts of Africa. When asked for a 'fine' always politely request a receipt to document your payment before you hand over money – this tends to reduce the need for the transfer of funds.

Since the fall of Gaddafi in Libya, the Sahara has become a much more dangerous place to visit, with large parts of Chad, Mali, Niger, Algeria and Mauritania off limits to travellers. Boko Haram's rise in parts of West Africa has also curtailed travellers' security in northern parts of Nigeria and Cameroon. All of the Burundi, Central African Republic, Somalia, South Sudan and large parts of the Democratic Republic of the Congo are also off limits due to insecurity.

On the bright side, the political deadlock between Ethiopia and Eritrea seemed to miraculously turn the corner in 2018, which led to the long-awaited opening of the border between the two countries.

As is the case with destinations around the world, check your government's up-to-date travel advisories before travelling.

GETTING THERE

Africa has a number of international air hubs, which makes it pretty easy for travellers the world over to arrive there by plane. European travellers also take advantage of the numerous intercontinental ferries that ply the Mediterranean Sea.

AIR

The five most popular gateways for international arrivals into Africa are Johannesburg and Cape Town (South Africa), Cairo (Egypt), Addis Ababa (Ethiopia) and Casablanca (Morocco). In East Africa, the most popular arrival city is Nairobi – it receives more visitors than the Tanzanian airports of Dar es Salaam, Kilimanjaro and Zanzibar combined. In West Africa, Accra (Ghana) and Lagos (Nigeria) are the busy gateways, as is the new airport in Dakar (Senegal).

The major local airlines that cover inside and outside of the continent include:

- **Arik Air** (www.arikair.com)
- **EgyptAir** (www.egyptair.com)
- **Ethiopian Airlines** (www.ethiopianairlines.com)
- **Kenya Airways** (www.kenya-airways.com)
- **Royal Air Maroc** (www.royalairmaroc.com)
- **South African Airways** (www.flysaa.com)

Local and budget airlines include:

- **Air Botswana** (www.airbotswana.co.bw)
- **Air Namibia** (www.airnamibia.com)
- **Fastjet** (www.fastjet.com)
- **Fly540** (www.fly540.com)
- **Kulula.com** (www.kulula.com)
- **LAM Mozambique** (www.lam.co.mz)
- **Malawi Airlines** (www.malawian-airlines.com)
- **Mango** (www.flymango.com)

SEA & OVERLAND

Frequent ferries link Spain and France with Morocco (and the Spanish enclaves of Ceuta and Melilla), France with Algeria and Tunisia, Italy with Tunisia, and Egypt with Jordan. It's also still possible to reach Africa by cargo ship, with **Freighter Expeditions** (www.freighterexpeditions.com.au) offering routes between Europe and both West and South Africa. They also sail to South Africa via Madagascar from Singapore.

SAMPLE COSTS

	South Africa (Rand, R)	Kenya (Kenyan schilling, KSh)	Morocco (Dirham, Dh)	Senegal (West African franc, CFA)
Hostel: dorm bed	R175-300 (US$12-20)	KSh1500-2000 (US$15-20)	Dh70-200 (US$7.36-21)	CFA5000-12,000 (US$8.75-21)
Midrange hotel: double room	R700-1400 (US$48-96)	KSh5000-15,000 (US$50-150)	Dh400-800 (US$42-84)	CFA30,000-90,000 (US$52.50–157.50)
Street snack	Bunny chow R40-70 (US$2.75-4.82)	*Nyama choma* KSh200-500 (US$2-5)	*B'sara* Dh5-10 (US$0.53-1.06)	Baguette sandwich CFA2000-3000 (US$3.50-5.25)
Budget meal	R100-150 (US$6.89-10.33)	KSh200-500 (US$2-5)	Dh25-40 (US$2.63-4.20)	CFA1500-5000 (US$2.60-8.75)
Midrange restaurant: main	R75-200 (US$5-13.77)	KSh500-1000 (US$5-10)	Dh70-150 (US$7.37-15.78)	CFA3000-6000 (US$5.20-10.40)
Cappuccino	R20-30 (US$1.40-2.10)	KSh200-300 (US$2-3)	Dh12-20 (US$1.26-2.10)	CFA1000-2000 (US$1.75-3.50)
1.5L Bottle of water	R20-30 (US$1.40-2.10)	KSh60-130 (US$0.60-1.30)	Dh7-15 (US$0.74-1.58)	CFA400-500 (US$0.70-0.88)
1L Petrol (gas)	R14.70 (US$1)	KSh104 (US$1.04)	Dh10.50 (US$1.10)	CFA670 (US$1.17)

The only land access to Africa is across the Sinai from Israel to Egypt. However, you can only cross at the Taba–Eilat border post, not at Rafah in the troubled Gaza Strip.

SPECIALIST TOUR OPERATORS

There are operators who run budget-friendly, months-long overland truck trips across vast tracts of Africa. The list of safari operators in East and Southern Africa could fill this book, but here are a few select choices:

- **&Beyond** (www.andbeyond.com) Stunning lodges, incredible service and impressive conservation programs.
- **Expert Africa** (www.expertafrica.com) A reliable, experienced and knowledgeable operator with a wide selection of itineraries.
- **IntoAfrica** (www.intoafrica.co.uk) Praised for 'fair-trade' trips providing insights into African life and directly supporting local communities
- **Naturetrek** (www.naturetrek.co.uk) Extensive portfolio of wildlife-centric safaris.

• **Robin Pope Safaris** (www.robinpopesafaris.net) Excellent safaris in Malawi and Zambia.
• **Safari Drive** (www.safaridrive.com) Provide you with the 4WD, camping kit and safety equipment for your own self-drive explorations in Southern and East Africa.
• **Wilderness Safaris** (www.wilderness-safaris.com) Lodge-based tours in remote areas, it also offers fly-in safaris and activity-based trips.

BEYOND AFRICA

From South Africa, flying is your main option and there are occasionally good deals to Australia, India and South America. Or why not take the chance to visit St Helena, one of the most remote islands on the planet (and the place of Napoleon's exile and death)? It used to be accessible only by mail ship from Cape Town, but there are now flights from Johannesburg.

If you're finishing your African adventure in Egypt, it's easy to continue into the Middle East before heading east into Asia or northeast towards Russia. You could also go by rail through China or Europe. From Morocco, Europe is a short ferry trip away. Cheap flights to India can often be found in Nairobi and Dar es Salaam.

FURTHER INFORMATION

WEBSITES

• **Africa Geographic** (www.africageographic.com) Nature-focused Africa online mag with good wildlife and birdwatching info.
• **Africa Centre** (www.africacentre.org.uk) A cultural centre and education resource for all things African.
• **All Africa** (www.allafrica.com) A real gateway to Africa, this website posts around 1000 articles a day, collated from more than 125 different news organisations.
• **BBC News Africa** (www.bbc.com/news/world/africa) A comprehensive daily review of the leading African news stories.
• **Regional Tourism Organisation of Southern Africa** (www.retosa.co.za) Promotes tourism in the region.
• **Safari Bookings** (www.safaribookings.com) Fantastic resource for booking your safari, with expert and traveller reviews.
• **Sahara Overland** (www.sahara-overland.com) The best practical guide for travellers to the Sahara, with useful forums and route information.
• **Travel Africa** (https://travelafricamag.com) Features articles on every corner of the continent and a useful 'safari planner'.

BOOKS

• **A History of Africa** A comprehensive yet digestible overview of the entire continent by JD Fage.
• **Dark Star Safari** The famed travel writer Paul Theroux weaves pessimism and anger into his trans-African tale.
• **Disgrace** JM Coetzee's harrowing Booker Prize winner about post-apartheid South Africa.
• **Don't Let's Go to the Dogs Tonight – An African Childhood** Alexandra Fuller's stunning memoir of life and loss, and a family's unbreakable bond with Africa.
• **In the Footsteps of Mr Kurtz** (Michela Wrong) Tells the sorry tale of Mobutu's reign in the Democratic Republic of Congo (formerly Zaïre).
• **Lions in the Balance: Man-Eaters, Manes, and Men with Guns** Craig Packer's behind-the-scenes look into the politics of lion conservation in Tanzania.
• **Things Fall Apart** A timeless dramatisation of the collision between traditional culture and Europeans in 19th-century Nigeria, written by Chinua Achebe.

• **Travels in West Africa** Mary Kingsley's remarkable account of a woman's travels in 19th-century West Africa.
• **We Wish to Inform You That Tomorrow We Will Be Killed with Our Families** Philip Gourevitch's searing study of Rwanda's 1994 genocide.

FILMS

• **Out of Africa** (1985) Depicts a somewhat idealised image of colonial Kenya, starring Meryl Streep and Robert Redford.
• **Hotel Rwanda** (2004) The true story of one hotel manager's efforts to save thousands from the genocide.
• **Tsotsi** (2005) Academy Award–winning film about life in the black townships of Johannesburg, South Africa.
• **The Last King of Scotland** (2006) Forrest Whitaker brings the violent and bone-chilling dictatorship of Idi Amin to life.
• **Invictus** (2009) Covers the historic 1995 Rugby World Cup in South Africa.
• **Mandela: Long Walk to Freedom** (2013) Condensed but enjoyable biography, covering Madiba's journey to South Africa's presidency.
• **Half of a Yellow Sun** (2013) Stirring love story and evocation of Nigeria's Biafran civil war in the 1960s.
• **Savage Kingdom** (2016) Fantastic wildlife documentary showing the rivalry between predators in the Savuti region of Botswana.

FACE TO FACE WITH SEVEN LIONS

It was mid-afternoon and I was battling siesta-hour drowsiness under the hot equatorial sun. My feet were up on the bumper of the Land Rover, and I'd had my head down in my laptop screen for well over an hour. I knew there were hypnotic views down to the shimmering plains, but I was in Uganda's Kidepo Valley National Park as a volunteer, and I needed to get map data uploaded if I had any chance to explore the area that afternoon.

Suddenly a harsh cough broke my concentration, like claws slashing a mosquito net, and I instinctively looked up to find myself staring straight into the amber eyes of a lion. It was less than 50m away, and after a quick scan of the granite outcrops, I realised she was not alone... there were six others.

Yet given their relaxed, lazy-looking state – paws coyly crossed – I didn't make a dash for it. That would have felt rather melodramatic as they'd clearly been there a while. Instead I slowly sidled around the Land Rover to ease the door open for a bolthole. I then aimed a hissed whisper over my shoulder towards the tents where my three teammates were dozing: 'Hey guys... some visitors here you might want to meet...'

The lions remained at ease even when we started barbecuing sausages as dusk fell, though they must have been hungry as I was woken that evening by the bellowing of a panicked buffalo being taken down by this Kidepo pride.

Mark Eveleigh

RUSSIA, CENTRAL ASIA & THE CAUCASUS

Bigger than Africa and Australasia put together, this vast region could use Texas as a handkerchief. Central Asia alone (the famous 'Stans': Kazakhstan, Uzbekistan, Kyrgyzstan, Tajikistan, Turkmenistan and Afghanistan) is about the size of Europe; Russia spans half the globe. It's an area that makes many wonder how they know so little about a place so big.

Throw in Belarus, the Caucasus and Ukraine and this is an area of huge contrasts, covering everything from permanently frozen tundra to baking desert, and embracing Christianity, Islam and Buddhism. The ghosts of great empires still haunt historic centres from St Petersburg (Russia) to Samarkand (Uzbekistan), and outside the cities there are enough blanks on the maps, enough wilderness, to keep you exploring for years.

And if you like history and a diverse culture, you'll be mesmerised. Russia has European tradition plastered over with grim Soviet aesthetic, and a confusing catch-up capitalism that sees Hummers rolling over medieval streets and past onion-dome churches.

Central Asia is completely different. The Eurasian steppe quickly turns to untamed jagged mountains, expansive deserts, and lush alpine valleys dotted with the yurts of Mongolian-looking horsemen. Down in the plains and valleys lies a string of ancient Silk Road cities and Islamic architectural treasures that stretches from Tbilisi (Georgia) to China. Reality may not quite gel with romantic images of camel caravans, *caravanserais* (pit stops for trade caravans as they travelled across the Silk Road) and turbaned Silk Road merchants, but in some places you can definitely get the sense that you are travelling directly in the footsteps of Marco Polo.

ITINERARIES

Train travel is the best way to get around the region, though packing a Dostoevsky-sized novel is essential for the epic rides, and you should expect anything under second class to be cramped, uncomfortable and insecure. In Russia and the west, boat travel on canals, rivers and lakes is a great way to get about. There's also a ferry service from Baku (Azerbaijan) to Turkmenbashi (Turkmenistan). Flying saves time and takes the tedium out of Central Asia's long distances but it is arguably the least safe mode of transport in the region.

TRANS-SIBERIAN RAILWAY

The Trans-Siberian railway links Moscow to Vladivostok on the Pacific coast, clanking through eight time zones and across 9289km of mountain, steppe, forest and desert. It's possible to do it in a single run over seven days, but it's much better to take a month and break up the journey. Before crossing the Urals and leaving European Russia, spend a day or so in **Yekaterinburg**, a historic, bustling city well stocked with interesting museums and sites connected to the murder of the last tsar and his family. Siberia's capital of **Novosibirsk** offers big-city delights, including the gigantic Opera & Ballet Theatre. Flush with oil wealth, happening **Krasnoyarsk**, on the Yenisey River, affords the opportunity for scenic cruises along one of Siberia's most pleasant waterways. Check out historic **Irkutsk** before reaching the magnificent **Lake Baikal**. Allow at least three days to soak up the charms of this beautiful lake, basing yourself on beguiling **Olkhon Island**. Hop off the train at **Ulan-Ude**, where Russian, Soviet and Mongolian cultures coexist; from here you can venture into the steppes to visit Russia's principal Buddhist monastery, **Ivolginsk (Ivolga) Datsan**. Situated on a stunningly attractive natural harbour, the port of **Vladivostok** is worth a couple of days' sightseeing after disembarking from the train.

Another option is the Trans-Mongolian railway, which branches south two-thirds along the route, passing through **Mongolia** en route to **Běijīng**. If you don't plan to stop in **Ulaanbaatar** to soak up traditional (and modern) Mongolian culture, you can take the Trans-Manchurian route, which cuts through **northern China** instead of Mongolia.

GOLDEN RING

The Golden Ring (Zolotoe Koltso) allows the exploration of historic old towns (such as **Suzdal** and **Yaroslavl**), Russian Orthodox churches and magnificent monasteries northeast of **Moscow**. It's not going to take months (a week would take in the highlights), but will give you a real taste of what old Russia must have been like.

SILK ROAD

This ancient trade route links **Xī'ān** (China) to the Mediterranean via a tangle of alternate routes. Ours starts at **Ashgabat**, then heads overland to **Merv** and the **Silk Road** cities of **Bukhara**, **Samarkand** and **Tashkent**. From here dip into the fertile **Fergana Valley** before swinging north on the mountainous road to **Bishkek**. Skip the border with Kazakhstan into cosmopolitan **Almaty** and then catch the train on to **Ürümqi** in China. Alternatively, from Bishkek cross the rugged **Torugart Pass**, visiting the *jailoos* (summer pastures) around **Kochkor** and the *caravanserai* of **Tash Rabat** before crossing over to **Kashgar**.

WHAT TO DO?

HIGHLIGHTS

- Exploring the bazaars, bathhouses and medieval Ark in **Bukhara** (Uzbekistan), easily Central Asia's most interesting town.
- Trekking past turquoise lakes and meeting local Tajik shepherds in the stunning **Fan Mountains** (Tajikistan).
- Discovering treasures in the Hermitage, the top art house of **St Petersburg** (Russia).
- Rambling through **Khiva** (Uzbekistan), the last independent khanate with fortifications frozen in time amid the desert.
- Paddling for as long as you can in **Lake Baikal** (Russia), the Pearl of Siberia ringed by daunting mountains.
- Meeting **Merv** (Turkmenistan), a maze of ruins where you can reconstruct ancient empires from the leftover foundations and pottery shards.
- Marvelling at the stone minarets and ancient architecture of **Samarkand** (Uzbekistan), one of Asia's most beautiful cities.
- Falling for the cultural heart of Ukraine in the historical centre of **Lviv**.
- Hanging out in cosmopolitan **Almaty** (Kazakhstan) before you try to scale the majestic Tian Shan ranges.

RUSSIA, CENTRAL ASIA & THE CAUCASUS

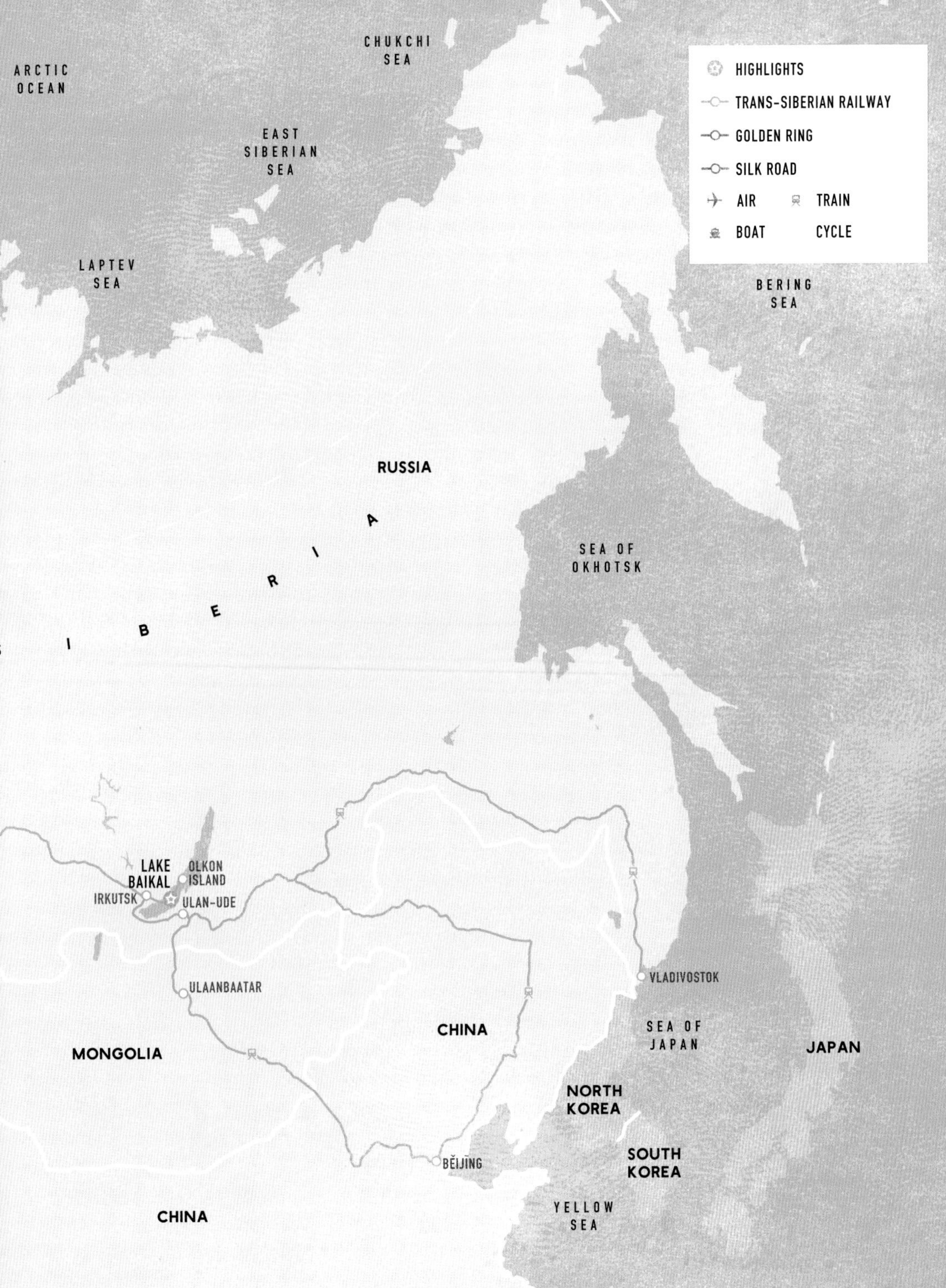
ARCTIC OCEAN
CHUKCHI SEA
EAST SIBERIAN SEA
LAPTEV SEA
BERING SEA
HIGHLIGHTS
TRANS-SIBERIAN RAILWAY
GOLDEN RING
SILK ROAD
AIR
TRAIN
BOAT
CYCLE
RUSSIA
SIBERIA
SEA OF OKHOTSK
LAKE BAIKAL
OLKON ISLAND
IRKUTSK
ULAN-UDE
ULAANBAATAR
VLADIVOSTOK
CHINA
MONGOLIA
SEA OF JAPAN
JAPAN
NORTH KOREA
SOUTH KOREA
BĚIJĪNG
YELLOW SEA
CHINA

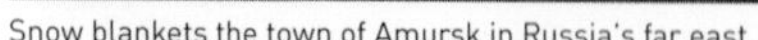

Snow blankets the town of Amursk in Russia's far east

A train departs Komsomolsk-na-Amure on the 4300km BAM railway

The Cathedral of the Holy Spirit in Minsk, the capital of Belarus

• Getting under the skin of **Minsk** (Belarus), the friendly and accessible capital that's a showcase of Stalinist architecture.

GET ACTIVE

With soaring peaks, rolling pasturelands, desert tracts and the Arctic, there is a thrilling and irresistible range of terrain to embrace the outdoors in Russia and Central Asia. New adventure-travel possibilities continue to crop up, and if you like extreme in the extremities, there are expeditions into the Arctic, Siberian wilderness and mountains of Central Asia.

Trekking, Mountaineering & Rock-Climbing

The wilder and more difficult the terrain, the more it will inevitably draw mountaineers and trekkers. And Central Asia is no exception, with fantastic walking and trekking actually kicking off right at some city limits, notably in Almaty in Kazakhstan and Bishkek and Karakol in Kyrgyzstan. Further afield, the alpine valleys of the Fan Mountains in Tajikistan and pyramid peaks of Khan Tengri and Tian Shan range in eastern Kyrgyzstan provide impressive goals for climbers, trekkers and mountaineers. Eastern Tajikistan and remoter parts of Kyrgyzstan offer more ambitious treks and never-climbed peaks for the truly intrepid.

Other good mountains with scope for adventure include:

- **Carpathian Mountains** (Ukraine)
- **Lapland Biosphere Reserve** (Russia)
- **Elbrus Area** (Russia–Georgia border)
- **Altay Mountains** (southern Russia and Western Mongolia)
- **Ural Mountains** (central Russia) – the divide between Europe and Asia
- **Sayan Mountains** (Mongolian border)
- **Kamchatka Peninsula** (Russia)

RIDING THE TRANS-SIBERIAN RAILWAY

I was nosing around a paint-peeled train station near Lake Baikal. Keeping the grease-smeared locomotive in sight – I never knew how long these pit stops would last – I watched transfixed as a gaggle of local women tried on fur coats hawked by some travelling merchants. Laughing and strutting, they had no intention of buying but they knew how to have a good time.

Rejoining my girlfriend in our drab, Formica-lined little cabin, I feverishly jotted the scene into my journal. It was the first of many long, rapidly scribbled entries.

After a bleary-eyed year teaching English, we'd dragged ourselves onto the Trans-Siberian in Běijīng. We wanted to recuperate and decide what to do next with our lives. On this six-night Moscow-bound trundle, rocking to sleep under gold-streaked sunsets, thinking was a perpetual pastime.

Autumnal larch trees and painted wooden houses flashed past, as we talked of the future; avoided the angry-looking *provodnitsa* attendants; and gorged on baked fish or buttered potatoes from station vendors.

I also filled my dog-eared journal with microscopic handwriting, fearful of exhausting the pages. Eventually, as smoky factories and grubby row houses slid into view, we crawled into cold, mist-fingered Moscow.

By then, my detangled brain had made a life-changing decision, consigning my teaching career to the buffers. Weeks later, I felt a jolt of excitement when my Trans-Siberian travel story appeared in a London newspaper. A new track had opened ahead of me – and I've been writing ever since.

John Lee

Father and child cross the plains near their village in rural Kyrgyzstan

Cycling & Mountain Biking

Kyrgyzstan is the biggest hub of cycling in the region, with several tour companies offering supported biking trips over the Torugart Pass, although diehard do-it-yourselfers will find Irkeshtam Pass logistically easier. The Kegeti Canyon and pass in northern Kyrgyzstan is another biking location favoured by adventure-travel companies. The Karkara Valley offers quiet country back roads. From here you can cycle around the southern shore of Issyk-Köl and then up into central Kyrgyzstan. Mountain bikes can be rented in Karakol and Arslanbob for local rides, though most travellers on multiday trips bring their own bikes.

A growing number of diehards organise their own long-distance mountain-bike trips across Central Asia. The most popular route is probably the Pamir Hwy in Tajikistan, which is a spectacular but hard trip.

If downhill mountain biking is your thing, the ski resort of Chimbulak near Almaty in Kazakhstan turns into a mountain-biking playground in summer.

Horse & Camel Trips

Ride the ranges like a traditional Kyrgyz cowboy with Central Asia's rich culture of nomadic horsemanship. Trips will vary from a couple of days to three-week-long expeditions, but Kyrgyzstan and Kazakhstan are good places to start. You can saddle up with these operators:

- **Asia Adventures** (www.centralasia-adventures.com) Operating horseback trips in Kyrgyzstan, Turkmenistan and Uzbekistan.
- **Pegasus Horse Trekking** Organise horseback tours to the Ornok Valley in Kyrgyzstan.
- **Shepherd's Way** (www.kyrgyztrek.com) An eco-tourism pioneer operating out of Barskoön, Kyrgyzstan.
- **Wild Frontiers** (www.wildfrontiers.co.uk) UK-based, but run horseback trips in Kyrgyzstan and Georgia.

Snowsports

Ski facilities are found outside Almaty in Kazakhstan and in the central Caucasus region around Elbrus (5642m). Russia has several solid downhill ski resorts including Abzakovo, Asha, Baikalsk, Kirovsk, Dombay and Krasnaya Polyana (site of the alpine events at the 2014 Winter Olympics). Skiing is growing quickly in Kyrgyzstan, with several small ski bases in the valleys south of Bishkek (particularly local favourites Chunkurchak and Zil). And the relatively modern Karakol Ski Resort has three new chairlifts and equipment rental. Where Kyrgyzstan really shines, though, is in freeride potential. For epic adventures, try heli-skiing in the Caucasus and Kamchatka.

The Kola Peninsula north of Moscow, the Altay Mountains on the Kazakhstan–Russia border and the Carpathians in Ukraine provide cross-country skiing par excellence, and locally made gear of reasonable quality is readily available here.

Other Activities

You can explore Siberia by ferry on the Irtysh, Yenisey and Ob rivers, or float down the Volga from Nizhny Novgord to Volgograd (former Stalingrad). Boating around the Black Sea coast is popular between May and mid-October. The remote Altay area of Russia has some of the region's most intense whitewater rafting. If you fancy a dogsled trek in the wilds, check out **Baikal Dog Sledding Centre** (http://baikalsled.blogspot.com) around Listvyanka in winter. You can go caving in Kyrgyzstan and Kazakhstan, where local speleological societies lead guided hiking, caving and mountain expeditions. In Siberia, a Russian sauna (complete with the optional back-beating with birch twigs and a naked roll in the snow) is an experience you won't forget in a rush. You can dive in the icy Siberian Lake Baikal (Russia) or within the Arctic Circle with diving operators such as **RuDive Group** (www.dive.ru).

WHEN TO GO?

Generally, the region has an extreme continental European climate. Summers are very warm, but Russia's long, dark, very cold winters are truly extreme – much of the country is well below freezing point for over four months of the year (November to March). In February and March the sun shines, there's a lack of humidity and it doesn't feel so cold. The coast bordering the Sea of Japan experiences a northern monsoonal climate, which means there's a 30% to 40% chance of rain each day between May and September.

WHAT TO EXPECT?

LOCALS & OTHER TRAVELLERS

Tourist hang-outs are tough to find, though you'll discover plenty of travellers in Russia's Golden Ring, on the Trans-Siberian railway and, to a lesser extent, around Lake Baikal and the Black Sea coast, and in the Central Asian towns of Bukhara, Samarkand and Bishkek.

From gold-toothed Turkmen in shaggy, dreadlocked hats to Kyrgyz herders whose eyes still hint at their nomadic past, Central Asia presents a fascinating collection of portraits and peoples. The most noticeable divide is between the traditionally sedentary peoples, the Uzbeks and Tajiks, and their formerly nomadic neighbours, the Kazakhs, Kyrgyz and Turkmen.

For the people of ex-Soviet Central Asia it's been more than a turbulent quarter-century since independence in 1991. Each of the republics have grappled with economic collapse, population shifts and resurgent Islam. All are reinventing their past, rehabilitating historical heroes and reinforcing their national languages in an attempt to redefine and shore up what it means to be Central Asian. Despite years of political repression and faltering economies, life is improving slowly, if unevenly, across the region.

In Russia itself, the diverse people you might encounter include a Nenets reindeer herder in Siberia, a marketing executive in Moscow, an imam in Kazan or a Buddhist Buryat taxi driver in Ulan-Ude. Generally speaking, Belarusians are quiet, polite and reserved people. Because they tend to be shy, they seem less approachable than Russians and Ukrainians, but they are just as friendly and generous (often more so) once introductions are made.

Generally, attitudes are conservative, particularly in Central Asia, which is staunchly Muslim. The Orthodox Church is enjoying a revival in Russia, Georgia and Armenia.

FOOD

Russia's glorious culinary heritage is enriched by influences from the Baltic to the Far East. The country's rich black soil provides an abundance of grains and vegetables used in a wonderful range of breads, salads, appetisers and soups that are the highlight of any Russian meal. Its waterways yield a unique range of fish and, as with any cold-climate country, there's a great love of fat-loaded dishes.

The same can be said for Central Asia, with common lard-heavy menu choices of *shorpa* (mutton fat in a bowl), *shashlik* (mutton fat) kebabs and *plov/pilau* (mutton fat in rice). Vegetarians really suffer here, and it's not a place many visit for the food. That said, the situation in Central Asia has improved in

SAMPLE COSTS

	Russia (Russian rouble, R)	Belarus (Belarus rouble, BR)	Kazakhstan (Tenge, T)	Kyrgyzstan (Kyrgyzstani, som)
Hostel: dorm bed	R700-800 US$10.40-11.87	BR5-12 (US$2.43-5.84)	2800-3500T (US$7.76-9.70)	400–700som (US$5.83-10.20)
Midrange hotel: double room	R1500-4000 (US$22-59)	BR50-100 (US$24.30-48.60)	8200-22,800T (US$22.75-63.25)	2060-3450som (US$30-50)
Street snack	*Blini* R100-200 (US$1.50-3)	*Draniki* BR7-10 (US3.40-4.87)	*Baursaki* 50-75T (US$0.14-0.21)	*Manty* 40-60som (US$0.58-0.87)
Budget meal	R500-1000 (US$7.42-14.84)	BR10-20 (US$4.87-9.74)	1500-2500T (US$4.16-6.93)	200-450som (US$2.91-6.56)
Midrange restaurant: main	R300-1000 (US$4.45-14.84)	BR10-20 (US$4.87-9.74)	1500-3000T (US$4.16-8.32)	250-700som (US$3.64-10.20)
Cappuccino	R125-250 (US$1.85-3.70)	BR2.05-4.10 (US$1-2)	600-800 (US$1.66-2.22)	80-140som (US$1.17-2.04)
1.5L Bottle of water	R35-70 (US$0.52-1.04)	BR0.94-1.55 (US$0.45-0.75)	100-200 (US$0.28-0.56)	25-35som (US$0.36-0.51)
1L Petrol (gas)	R42.50 (US$0.63)	BR1.33 (US$0.65)	162.50T (US$0.45)	41som (US$0.60)

recent years, particularly in the cities, where you can find a rush of pleasant open-air cafes, and openings of Turkish, Korean, Chinese and Western restaurants. And come summer across the city landscapes markets groan with fruit – the region's melons, grapes and nuts are world class. But probably the best way to appreciate regional cuisines, and the region's extraordinary hospitality, is still a meal in a private home.

LANGUAGE

Russian is the second language of the majority of the population in Central Asia, where numerous Turkic ethnic languages (and occasionally Persian) are also used locally. Learning the Cyrillic alphabet is a must, as even a few characters will help you decipher the Russian, Central Asian, Ukrainian and Belarusian languages. English, however, is not widely spoken, so you'll need to learn some language before you go. Lonely Planet's Russian and Central Asia phrasebooks will get a battering if you're travelling through the area.

COMMUNICATION

Wi-Fi is available in almost all hotels and many restaurants and cafes, especially in Russia, Kazakhstan, Kyrgyzstan and Uzbekistan (but much less so in Turkmenistan). You may find it easier to bring a smartphone and get a SIM card with a data package.

If you have an 'unlocked' GSM-900 phone, buy a local SIM card and top that up at booths in every village.

COSTS

Russia, Central Asia and the Caucasus are all fairly budget-friendly destinations, though you can easily break the bank if you so choose, particularly in big cities such as Moscow or St Petersburg.

HEALTH

Stomach and digestive problems are by far the most common health problems faced by visitors to the region. A diet of mutton, bread and *plov* seems to induce diarrhoea and constipation in equal measure. Exposure to malaria, rabies and encephalitis is rare and depends largely upon the location and/or months of travel, but check with your travel clinic regarding vaccinations well in advance of your trip. More common during the searing summer months is heat exhaustion, so make sure you keep cool and hydrated in the 35°C heat. Most short-term travels to the main tourist areas remain problem-free.

ISSUES

With President Putin following a more aggressive international political agenda, including his country's implied involvement in the election of Donald Trump in 2016 and the poisoning of former spy Sergei Skripal and his daughter Yulia in the UK, tensions surrounding the possibility of a new Cold War are clearly brewing. And there's also Russia's military backing for separatists in eastern Ukraine to throw into the mix, where, several years on from the annexation of Crimea, heavy fighting continues.

The Central Asian republics (particularly Uzbekistan) point southwards to turbulent Afghanistan and the threat of Islamic insurgency to justify their increasingly repressive government policies. Isolated bombings in Uzbekistan, Turkmenistan and Tajikistan have underscored the threat but it's hard to say whether armed attacks are the cause for all the repression, or rather a consequence of it.

Despite claims of Central Asian fraternity, tensions persist among the 'Stans'. Disputes over water, electricity and gas supplies are increasingly rising to the surface. Uzbekistan, Kazakhstan and Turkmenistan are rich in energy reserves but are chronically lacking in water, while mountainous Kyrgyzstan and Tajikistan control the upstream taps but regularly run out of electricity. The chronic lack of trust means that regional issues such as the Aral Sea, the drug trade from neighbouring Afghanistan and economic cooperation rarely get the international attention they so desperately require.

At the time of writing there were several no-go zones for travellers, such as Afghanistan, so make sure to check the government advisories prior to travel. Remember that the size of this region is immense, so you'll find that it will always be easy enough to plot a wide path and still avoid trouble.

STILL ALIVE

You can't say Ukrainians look at the positive side of things. Rather than the chest-beating and drum-thumping of most national anthems, Ukraine's national tune is rather downbeat and is titled *Ukraine Has Not Yet Died*.

GETTING THERE

Vexing visa arrangements and border boredom are bound to start your journey to the region. You can come by land from Iran, China and Europe, though flying into the region's hubs – Kiev, Moscow, Almaty and Baku – is a more common way in.

AIR

Many flights into the region won't appear on your standard RTW ticket. Moscow is serviced by dozens of airlines, and destinations in Central Asia are becoming more accessible. Majar local airlines servicing the region include the following:

- **Aeroflot** (www.aeroflot.com)
- **Air Astana** (http://airastana.com)
- **Belavia** (https://en.belavia.by)
- **Rossiya Airlines** (www.rossiya-airlines.com)
- **S7 Airlines** (www.s7.ru)
- **Ural Airlines** (www.uralairlines.com)
- **Uzbekistan Airways** (www.uzairways.com)

SEA & OVERLAND

By land there are hundreds of routes into the region from all directions. Trains are the easiest option. Before you make any plans, carefully check out the border crossings you want to use.

Despite an incredible network of ship canals and sea ports, there are only a handful of

REMOTE MOUNTAIN RESCUE IN KYRGYZSTAN

From our vantage on the valley's slopes, we could see points of light approaching around the mountain's curve until a face finally emerged from the darkness.

Much earlier, after a day and a half under stormy skies, even the steep scree slope below the pass wasn't enough to prompt a second-guessing on a third attempted ascent – it must be the right valley, and dark clouds were moving in fast.

We had been tempted by the unexplored pass, and after reaching the crest, a harrowing descent of snow, rocks and a butt-first slide led to a distinct thought: 'I'm glad we don't have to do that again.'

Several hours downhill, atop the sheer face of a waterfall, a nagging suspicion became a growing realisation. This was not the path. Not the way. How do we get out, get home? There was frustration, self-recrimination, but also a quietly gnawing fear of a steep, unsafe, unroped ascent on a pass that we never should have come down.

Miracle mobile phone reception allowed a measured message home that belied our growing concern:

'We won't be home tonight. What's Kyrgyzstan's emergency number?'

A few static-crackled phone calls later, we sat, waited, and hoped help was coming... But darkness fell, and with it our spirits.

That is until that face eventually materialised. After a long drag on his cigarette, a hand was extended along with two simple words: 'I rescuer.'

We clipped into harnesses. The feeling, the moment, the relief; all sublime.

Stephen Lioy

scheduled services into Russia (from Japan) and only a minimal amount of traffic that crosses the Black and Caspian Seas.

SPECIALIST TOUR OPERATORS

These local and international operators can get you out and about in the region:

- **Ayan Travel** (www.ayan-travel.com) Turkmenistan and Uzbekistan tour specialists.
- **Eastern Europe/Russian Travel Centre** (www.eetbtravel.com) This organisation has offices in Sydney, Australia and Christchurch, New Zealand.
- **Go To Russia Travel** (www.gotorussia.com) Offers tours and a full range of travel services; has offices in Atlanta, San Francisco and Moscow.
- **Kalpak Travel** (www.kalpak-travel.com) Specialises in tours to Central Asia, with several Turkmenistan itineraries.
- **Outfitter KZ** (www.outfitter.kz) Excellent Kazakhstan tours. It's happy to work with individual travellers.
- **Passport Travel** (www.travelcentre.com.au) Australia-based, this agency has plenty of experience organising trips to Russia including trans-Siberian itineraries.
- **Real Russia** (http://realrussia.co.uk) London-based firm specialising in Russian visas and travel.
- **Russian Gateway Tours** (www.russian-gateway.com.au) Offers tours across Russia, including Crimea.
- **Salom Travel** (www.salomtravel.com) Has good tours of the 'Stans.
- **SilkOffRoad** (www.silkoffroad.kz) These motorcycling pioneers organise superb biking tours of Kazakhstan and Central Asia.
- **Young Pioneers** (www.youngpioneertours.com) Lower-cost guided tours of Turkmenistan and all the surrounding 'Stans'.

Mongolian shepherds perfect their skills at a tender age

BEYOND RUSSIA, CENTRAL ASIA & THE CAUCASUS

From Russia and Central Asia you can branch out almost anywhere. Once you've travelled overland to Europe, you can roll on into the Middle East or Eastern Europe. Head for western China to follow the Karakoram Hwy (one of the world's most breathtaking overland trips) down into the Indian subcontinent, or take the Tran-Manchurian railway all the way to Běijīng.

FURTHER INFORMATION

WEBSITES

• **Advantour** (www.advantour.com) Useful tips and detailed info on attractions by Uzbekistan-based agency.
• **Belarus Tourism** (www.belarus.by/en): Country facts and travel guide.
• **Caravanistan** (www.caravanistan.com) Peerless online travel guide to Central Asia.
• **EurasiaNet** (www.eurasianet.org) Good news source and portal for Central Asia.
• **GoKG** (http://gokg.asia) News and info from around Kyrgystan, and up-to-date info on events of interest to visitors.
• **Pamirs** (www.pamirs.org) Excellent travel info for exploring the Pamirs in Tajikistan.
• **Tajikstan Official Tourism Portal** (http://tdc.tj) Electronic e-visas are available from here.
• **Visit Azerbaijan** (http://azerbaijan.travel) Arts, history, travel and gastronomy of Azerbaijan.
• **Visit Kazakhstan** (www.visitkazakhan.kz) Official tourism website.
• **WayToRussia.Net** (www.waytorussia.net) Good travel-agency guide.

BOOKS

• **A Short Walk in the Hindu Kush** Eric Newby's funny take on the region is no lazy stroll.
• **Journey to Khiva** Following the footsteps of Britain's 19th-century spies, Philip Glazebrook digs deep in Central Asia and the Caucasus.
• **Nothing Is True and Everything Is Possible: Adventures in Modern Russia** Darkly entertaining tales of contemporary Russian life by TV producer Peter Pomerantsev.
• **The Railway** (Hamid Ismailov) A satirical novel about the end-of-the-line town of Gilas in Soviet Uzbekistan; so good they banned it in Uzbekistan.
• **The Last Man in Russia** (Oliver Bullough; 2013) A spot-on portrait of modern Russia, told through the tumultuous and tragic life of an Orthodox priest.

FILMS

• **Luna Papa** (1999) A Central Asian coming-of-age tale that shows off the region's markets and people.
• **Russian Ark** (2002) If you can't get to St Petersburg's Hermitage, this film will walk you through it with insights into Russia's history.
• **Tulpan** (2008) Kazakh drama about life on the steppe, as the main character tries to woo his prospective wife Tulpan.
• **My Perestroika** (2010) Robin Hessman's film focuses on five Russians and the effect of the past 20 turbulent years on their lives.
• **The Desert of Forbidden Art** (2010) Excellent documentary about Igor Savitsky and the 40,000 items of Soviet art he secretly collected in Karakalpakstan.
• **Bolshoi Babylon** (2015) Behind-the-scenes documentary exposing the violent rivalries in Russia's most famous ballet troupe.
• **Loveless** (2017) The winner of the Jury Prize at Cannes in 2017, Andrei Zvyagintsev's Oscar-nominated follow-up to *Leviathan* is another critique of contemporary Russian society.

DIRECTORY
PART FOUR

BRITISH & IRISH TRAVELLERS

PAPERWORK

GETTING A PASSPORT

- **Citizens Information** (http://www.citizensinformation.ie/en/travel_and_recreation/passports)
- **UK Passport Service** (www.gov.uk/browse/abroad/passports)

VISAS FOR TRAVEL

- **CIBT Visas** (http://cibtvisas.co.uk) Comprehensive visa agency.

INSURANCE

- **Blue Bear Travel Insurance** (www.bluebeartravelinsurance.co.uk)
- **Columbus Travel Insurance** (www.columbusdirect.com)
- **Insure and Go** (www.insureandgo.com)
- **STA Travel** (www.statravel.com)
- **Staysure** (www.staysure.co.uk) Good platform for pre-existing medical condition cover
- **World Nomads** (www.worldnomads.com)

MONEY & COSTS

DISCOUNT CARDS

For information on the International Student Identity Card (ISIC) and International Youth Travel Card (IYTC), see p38. The local affiliates of Hostelling International (HI) can supply you with a card for use in any country:

- **Irish Youth Hostel Association** (https://anoige.ie)
- **UK Youth Hostels Association** (www.yha.org.uk).

HEALTH & SAFETY

The British Foreign & Commonwealth Office (FCO; www.gov.uk/foreign-travel-advice) provides safety advice by country. Ireland's **Department of Foreign Affairs and Trade** (www.dfa.ie/travel/travel-advice) provides similar advice to its citizens.

VACCINATIONS

- **Fit For Travel** (www.fitfortravel.nhs.uk) Details where to get immunised and offers other pre-travel tips.
- **NHS** (https://www.nhs.uk/conditions/travel-vaccinations) Web pages with information on immunisation and its benefits.
- **Travel Doctor** (www.traveldoctor.co.uk/vaccines.htm) Lists immunisation recommendations and requirements; also has good clinic list.
- **World Health Organization** (www.who.int/ith/en) WHO's last word on health everywhere around the globe.

FIRST-AID & OTHER TRAVEL-SAFETY COURSES

- **Adventure Lifesigns** (www.adventurelifesigns.co.uk)
- **British Red Cross** (www.redcross.org.uk)
- **Irish Red Cross** (www.redcross.ie)
- **Objective** (www.objectivegapyear.com)
- **St John Ambulance** (www.sja.org.uk)
- **Wilderness Expertise** (www.wilderness-expertise.co.uk)
- **Wilderness Medical Training** (www.wildernessmedicaltraining.co.uk)

TRAVEL CLINICS

- **Globetrotters** Health Clinics (www.globetrotterstravelclinics.com) Clinics in

Hounslow and Southall.

- **MASTA** (www.masta-travel-health.com) Travel clinics all over Britain.
- **Nomad Travel Clinics** (www.nomadtravel.co.uk) Clinics in London, Bristol, Birmingham, Manchester, Cardiff, Bath and Bishop's Stortford.
- **Tropical Medical Bureau** (TMB; www.tmb.ie) Plenty of clinics across Ireland.

GET PACKING

Good outfitters (most with online stores) include:

- **AlpineTrek** (www.alpinetrek.co.uk) Online store with great deals on equipment.
- **Arc'teryx** (https://arcteryx.com) Top-end outdoor equipment. Canadian brand with store in Picadilly.
- **Blacks** (www.blacks.co.uk) Affordable gear.
- **Cotswold** (www.cotswoldoutdoor.com) Outdoor stockist.
- **Nomad Travel & Outdoor** (www.nomadtravel.co.uk) Some shops include travel clinics so you can get immunisations while browsing backpacks.
- **Pyramid** (www.pyramidtravelshop.co.uk) Good for health supplies.

TAKEOFF

- **HM Revenue & Customs** (www.hmrc.gov.uk) Search this site for the latest information on customs regulations on bringing duty-free and more back with you to the UK.
- **Office of the Revenue Commission** (www.revenue.ie) Customs information for Irish travellers.

STAYING IN TOUCH

PHONE

With Wi-Fi widely available, there are plenty of internet VOIP calls and messaging apps available. The following UK-based app may also come in handy:

- **Tesco International Calling** (http://tescointernationalcalling.com) This app allows free texts and cheap international calls or free app-to-app calls, whether or not you are a Tesco Mobile customer.

TRANSPORT OPTIONS

AIR

Online Bookers

For online booking portals, see p30.

SPECIALIST TRAVEL AGENTS

- **Austravel** (www.austravel.com)
- **Flight Centre** (www.flightcentre.co.uk)
- **Trailfinders** (www.trailfinders.com)
- **TravelBag** (www.travelbag.co.uk)
- **STA Travel** (www.statravel.co.uk)
- **Hayes & Jarvis** (www.hayesandjarvis.ie)
- **USIT** (www.usit.ie)

ROUND-THE-WORLD (RTW) TICKETS

- **Great Escapade** (www.thegreatescapade.com) UK-only RTW tickets (for more information, see Round-The-World, p88).

BUDGET AIRLINES

Here are a few reliable airlines from the UK's ever-changing budget market:

- **Aer Lingus** (www.aerlingus.com)
- **BMI Regional** (www.bmiregional.com)
- **EasyJet** (www.easyjet.com)
- **FlyBe** (www.flybe.com)
- **Jet2** (www.jet2.com)
- **Norwegian Air Shuttle** (www.norwegian.com)
- **Ryanair** (www.ryanair.com)
- **Tui** (www.tui.co.uk)
- **Wow Air** (http://wowair.co.uk)

OVERLAND

• **AA Ireland** (www.theaa.ie) Apply for your international driving license here.
• **Interrail** (www.interrail.eu) Budget train tickets and passes, with discounts for those under 28 years of age.
• **RAC** (www.rac.co.uk) Issues international driving licences.

JOBS

TEACHING ENGLISH

• **Bell Language School** (www.bellenglish.com) Runs CELTA programs in the UK with affiliated language schools worldwide.
• **British Council** (www.britishcouncil.org/teach-english) Has advice about training and job searches, and a language-assistants program for those with no experience or qualifications.
• **EF English First** (www.englishfirst.com) An international school with several UK training branches offering TEFL and TESOL courses and good placements afterwards.
• **Inlingua International** (www.inlingua-cheltenham.co.uk) Offers TESOL training in Cheltenham, with the option to work at schools upon completion.
• **International House London** (www.ihlondon.co.uk) Offers good distance programs in CELTA courses with jobs in partner schools globally.
• **Saxoncourt UK** (www.saxoncourt.com) Offers CELTA training in London, with placements in private language schools in 20 countries upon completion.
• **Via Lingua** (www.vialingua.org) Offers TEFL certificate training plus job placements.

TOURISM & HOSPITALITY

Ski Jobs

• **Crystal Ski Holidays** (www.crystalski.co.uk) Operated by TUI, it has plenty of seasonal work.
• **Fish & Pips** (www.fishandpips.co.uk) Boutique chalet company with openings in Méribel (France) for resort managers, chefs, hosts, drivers and resort assistants.
• **Inghams** (www.inghams.co.uk) It recruits resort managers, resort administrators and reps, along with chalet and hotel staff.
• **LeSki** (www.leski.com) A small, niche operator that offers work in chalets in France.
• **Mark Warner** (www.markwarner.co.uk/recruitment2) Recruits UK and Irish residents for chalet and ski-host work at European resorts as well as summer jobs at Mediterranean resorts.
• **Natives** (http://jobs.natives.co.uk) A great site for ski season work, complete with a helpful forum to get advice.
• **Neilson** (www.neilson.co.uk) Openings range from children's club staff and qualified nannies to hospitality staff, kitchen workers, management and ski reps.
• **Work a Season** (www.workaseason.com) Has winter jobs as instructors, reps and chalet and catering staff, mostly in Europe, with some in Canada.
• **VIP Ski** (www.vip-chalets.com) Operates luxury chalets across the Alps.

INTERNSHIPS & WORK PLACEMENTS

• **ABN AMRO** (www.abnamro.com) International bank accepting graduates for internships at its European offices.
• **BUNAC** (www.bunac.org/uk) Offers several overseas programs (including cultural exchange).
• **Changing Worlds** (www.changingworlds.co.uk) Provides work placements in Australia and New Zealand.
• **English-Speaking Union** (www.esu.org) For UK undergrads only, this program has limited internships in the US and French parliaments.

- **FreshMinds** (www.freshminds.co.uk) Recruits high-performing graduates for corporate research projects.
- **InterExchange** (www.interexchange.org) Does work-exchange programs to the US for under-28-year-olds.
- **IST Plus** (www.istplus.com) An organisation offering internships in the US, Canada, Australia and New Zealand. Teaching placements in China and Thailand.
- **USIT** (www.usit.ie) Ireland's top student travel company organises work-abroad programs.
- **Visitoz** (www.visitoz.org) Offers work placements on Australian farms.
- **Work & Travel Company** (www.worktravelcompany.com) Does a variety of work programs in Australia, New Zealand and the UK that can be good for continuing university students.

AU PAIRS & NANNIES

See Finding Au Pair or Nanny Work on p136.

CAMP COUNSELLORS

See Finding Camp Counsellor Work on p139.

VOLUNTEERING

Organised Programmes

See Finding Organised Volunteer Programmes on p143.

Structured & Self-Funding Volunteer Programmes

See Finding Structured & Self-Funding Volunteer Programmes on p144.

Do-It-Yourself Volunteer Placements

See Finding a Do-It-Yourself Volunteer Placements on p146.

Useful websites

- **British Overseas NGOs for Development** (BOND; www.bond.org.uk) Forums and information about the UK's contribution to international development.
- **Comhlámh** (www.comhlamh.org) Irish site that has lots of information about international volunteering.
- **Scotland's International Development Alliance** (www.intdevalliance.scot) A network of numerous Scottish-based volunteer organisations.

COURSES

For a rundown of global opportunities, see Courses on p148.

EXCHANGE PROGRAMMES

- **En Famille Overseas** (www.enfamilleoverseas.co.uk) Family-stay exchanges in France, Germany, Italy, Spain and around the UK.
- **English-Speaking Union** (www.esu.org) Offers scholarships and other opportunities in the USA and Canada.

See Further Education (p152) for further options.

NORTH AMERICAN TRAVELLERS

PAPERWORK

GETTING A PASSPORT

- **US State Department** (http://travel.state.gov)
- **Immigration, Refugees and Citizenship Canada** (www.canada.ca)

VISAS

Here are a few services that will apply for visas on your behalf (most will also help you out with passports):

- **Travel Document Systems** (www.traveldocs.com)
- **Travel Visa Pro** (www.travelvisapro.com)
- **Travisa** (www.travisa.com)

- **US Visa Connection** (www.usvisaconnection.com)
- **Visa Central** (http://visacentral.com)
- **Visa HQ** (www.visahq.com)

INSURANCE

- **AIG Travel Guard** (www.travelguard.com)
- **Generali Travel Assistance** (www.generalitravelinsurance.com)
- **HTH Travel Insurance** (www.hthtravelinsurance.com)
- **IMG** (International Medical Group; www.imglobal.com)
- **Travelex** (www.travelexinsurance.com)
- **Wallach & Company** (www.wallach.com)

MONEY & COSTS

DISCOUNT CARDS

For information on the International Student Identity Card (ISIC) and International Youth Travel Card (IYTC), see p38.

These local affiliates of Hostelling International (HI) can supply you with a card that you can use in any country.

- **Hostelling International USA** (www.hiusa.org)
- **Hostelling International Canada** (www.hihostels.ca)

HEALTH & SAFETY

The US Department of State – Bureau of Consular Affairs (www.travel.state.gov) provides individual country advice and the Worldwide Caution Alert. Register with the **Smart Traveler Enrollment Program** (https://step.state.gov) to be sent regular updates. The **Government of Canada** (https://travel.gc.ca/) also provides advisories by country, along with other useful travel information.

VACCINATIONS

- **CDC Vaccination** (www.cdc.gov/vaccines) Information on US vaccination programs.
- **World Health Organization** (www.who.int/ith/en) WHO's last word on health everywhere around the globe.

FIRST-AID COURSES

- **American Safety & Health Institute** (www.hsi.com/medicfirstaid) A portal to centres across the US that offer accredited courses.
- **American Heart Association** (www.heart.org) Has CPR courses.
- **American Red Cross** (www.redcross.org)
- **Canadian Red Cross** (www.redcross.ca)
- **Healthy World** (www.healthy.net) Features a series of online treatments for the basics.
- **Wilderness Medical Associates** (www.wildmed.com) Specialising in first-aid and survival skills for the great outdoors.

OTHER TRAVEL-SAFETY COURSES

- **School for Field Studies** (www.fieldstudies.org) Offers a variety of international health and safety courses.

TRAVEL CLINICS

- **American Society of Tropical Medicine and Hygiene** (www.astmh.org) Has a directory of travel clinics (under 'Clinical Consultants Directory').
- **Public Health Agency of Canada** (www.phac-aspc.gc.ca) Navigate to Travel Health and find their list of travel clinics.
- **Traveler's Medical Service** (www.travelersmedical.com) Clinics in Washington and New York.

GET PACKING

Here are a few equipment suppliers:

- **Magellans** (www.magellans.com) Online

travel supplies store.

- **REI Co-op** (www.rei.com) Equipment for travel, and whatever that throws at you, be it climbing, cycling, snowsports or yoga.
- **US Outdoor Store** (www.usoutdoor.com) Good backpacks and specialised outdoor sports gear.

TAKEOFF

- **US Customs and Border Protection** (www.cbp.gov) Details what you can take and bring back, including duty-free limits.
- **Canadian Border Services Agency** (www.cbsa-asfc.gc.ca) Duty-free and customs limits for Canadians.

STAYING IN TOUCH

PHONE

With Wi-Fi widely available, there are plenty of internet VOIP calls and messaging apps available. The following options may also come in handy:

- **AT&T** (www.att.com/esupport/traveler.jsp) Has useful information and several options for calling cards and web-based calling.
- **Telestial** (www.telestial.com) Specialises in inter-national cell phones including prepaid SIM cards and handset rental.
- **United World Telecom** (www.uwtcallback.com) Services include calling cards, callback, VOIP and global SIMs and phones, and you can keep your own phone number.

TRANSPORT OPTIONS

AIR

Online Bookers

For international online booking portals, see p30. Some US-focused sites include:

SPECIALIST TRAVEL AGENCIES

- **Liberty Travel** (www.libertytravel.com)
- **Travelcuts** (www.travelcuts.com)
- **Travelosophy** (www.itravelosophy.com)

ROUND-THE-WORLD (RTW) TICKETS

- **Airtreks** (www.airtreks.com)

BUDGET AIRLINES

As well as major airlines, North America and the Caribbean have the following cheap ways to around:

- **Air Transat** (www.airtransat.com)
- **Allegiant Air** (www.allegiantair.com)
- **Frontier Airlines** (www.flyfrontier.com)
- **JetBlue Airways** (www.jetblue.com)
- **Liat** (http://book.liat.com)
- **Southwest** (www.southwest.com)
- **Spirit Airlines** (www.spirit.com)
- **Sun Country Airlines** (www.suncountry.com)
- **WestJet** (www.westjet.com)

OVERLAND

Car & Motorbike

Apply for an international driving licence from these organisations:

- **AAA** (www.aaa.com) Add your zip code and you'll get your nearest regional office in the USA.
- **CAA** (www.caa.ca) For Canadians.

JOBS

TEACHING ENGLISH

- **Dave's ESL Cafe** (http://eslcafe.com) Loads of jobs, especially in Northeast Asia, but also in Southeast Asia.
- **Language Magazine** (http://languagemagazine.com) US language-teaching magazine with Job Shop for US opportunities.
- **TESL Canada** (www.tesl.ca) Official TESL site with links for schools and teachers throughout Canada.

TOURISM & HOSPITALITY

See Your First Resort on p124.

INTERNSHIPS & WORK PLACEMENTS

- **Abroad China** (http://abroadchina.net) Offers internships in China.
- **Alfa Bank Fellowship** (https://alfafellowship.org) Placements in Moscow for US citizens.
- **Alliance Abroad** (www.allianceabroad.com) Organises internships both in the US and internationally.
- **BUNAC** (www.bunac.org/uk) Offers several overseas programs (including cultural exchange).
- **Connect 123** (www.connect-123.com) Offers internships in Argentina, Australia, China, Ireland and Spain.
- **Cross Cultural Solutions** (www.crossculturalsolutions.org) Offers programs throughout South America.
- **Cultural Vistas** (www.culturalvistas.org) Portal for placements in the US and international businesses.
- **European Internships** (www.europeaninternships.com) Portal to a variety of opportunities across Europe.
- **Institute for Central American Development Studies** (www.icads.org) Has social-justice positions in Central and South America.
- **Intern Jobs** (www.internjobs.com) Portal for internships worldwide.

AU PAIRS & NANNIES

See Finding Au Pair or Nanny Work on p134.

CAMP COUNSELLORS

See Finding Camp Counsellor Work on p139.

GENERAL JOB SITES

- **Escape Artist** (www.escapeartist.com) Has three different e-zines aimed at North Americans moving overseas; one has good coverage of jobs.
- **Overseas Jobs** (www.overseasjobs.com) Search portal for North Americans looking for overseas work.
- **Monster** (www.monster.com) One of the largest employment sites in the world.

VOLUNTEERING

Organised Programmes

See Finding Organised Volunteer Programmes on p143.

Structured & Self-Funding Volunteer Programmes

See Finding Structured & Self-Funding Volunteer Programmes on p144.

Do-It-Yourself Volunteer Placements

See Finding a Do-It-Yourself Volunteer Placements on p146.

COURSES

- **Amerispan** (www.amerispan.com) Offers study options in several different languages.
- **Center for Study Abroad** (www.centerforstudyabroad.com) A Seattle-based outfit offering study programs that can get credit in your school.
- **Centers for Interamerican Studies** (http://cedei.org) Offers exchanges and courses in South America, including the popular 'Semester in the Andes'.
- **School for Field Studies** (www.fieldstudies.org) Does courses in conservation that can be credited to some college courses.
- **University of Minnesota Learning Abroad Center** (www.umabroad.umn.edu) A self-service centre for studying abroad that's not just for U of M students.

EXCHANGE PROGRAMMES

- **American Institute for Foreign Study** (AIFS;

www.aifs.com) College study exchanges with five different countries.

• **Council on International Educational Exchange** (www.ciee.org) The first port of call for North Americans studying overseas – with courses on languages, culture, business and more.

• **Swap Canada** (www.swap.ca) Solid site for Canadians who want to go on exchanges overseas.

AUSTRALASIAN TRAVELLERS

PAPERWORK

GETTING A PASSPORT

• **Australian Passport Information Service** (www.passports.gov.au)

• **New Zealand Department of Internal Affairs** (www.passports.govt.nz)

VISAS

• **VisaHQ** (www.visahq.com.au)

• **Visa Link** (https://visalink.com.au)

INSURANCE

• **Cover-More** (www.covermore.com.au)

• **iTrek** (www.itrektravelinsurance.com.au) Policies for up to 18-months.

• **Worldcare** (www.worldcare.com.au) Offer coverage of many pre-existing medical conditions.

• **World Nomads** (www.worldnomads.com)

MONEY & COSTS

DISCOUNT CARDS

For information on the International Student Identity Card (ISIC) and International Youth Travel Card (IYTC), see p38.

These local affiliates of Hostelling International (HI) can supply you with a card that you can use in recognised HI hostels in any country in the world.

• **YHA Australia** (www.yha.com.au)

• **YHA New Zealand** (www.yha.co.nz)

HEALTH & SAFETY

The Australian government issues travel warnings on the website of the **Department of Foreign Affairs and Trade** (www.smartraveller.gov.au). The **New Zealand Foreign Affairs and Trade** (www.safetravel.govt.nz) is also good for safety advice on the Pacific islands.

VACCINATIONS

• **Immunisation Advisory Centre** (www.immune.org.nz) General information on Kiwi immunisation policy.

• **Immunise Australia Program** (www.immunise.health.gov.au) General information on Australian immunisation policy.

FIRST-AID COURSES

• **First Aid International** (http://cpr.com.au) Offers courses and kits.

• **Emergency First Aid** (www.emergency.com.au) Kits and courses in Melbourne only.

• **Red Cross New Zealand** (www.redcross.org.nz)

• **St John Ambulance Australia** (www.stjohn.org.au)

OTHER TRAVEL-SAFETY COURSES

• **RedR Australia** (www.redr.org.au) Offers training in humanitarian-relief fields.

TRAVEL CLINICS

• **Travel Clinic** (http://travelclinic.com.au)

• **Travel Doctor** (www.traveldoctor.co.nz) Several branches throughout New Zealand.

• **Traveller Medical & Vaccination Clinic** (www.traveldoctor.com.au)

GET PACKING

- **Go Go Gear** (www.gogogear.com.au) Online travel goods store.
- **Kathmandu** (www.kathmandu.com.au)
- **Paddy Pallin** (www.paddypallin.com.au) Outdoor specialist with good tents.

TAKEOFF

- **Australian Customs Service** (www.customs.gov.au) Look for the 'Know before you go' PDF for details on what you can take out and bring back.
- **New Zealand Customs Service** (www.customs.govt.nz) Information on what you can take when departing and returning to New Zealand.

STAYING IN TOUCH

PHONE

With Wi-Fi widely available, there are plenty of internet VOIP calls and messaging apps available.

TRANSPORT OPTIONS

AIR

Online Bookers

For online booking portals, see p30.

SPECIALIST TRAVEL AGENCIES

- Flight Centre Australia (www.flightcentre.com.au)
- **Flight Centre New Zealand** (www.flightcentre.co.nz)
- **Student Flights** (www.studentflights.com.au)
- **STA Australia** (www.statravel.com.au)
- **STA New Zealand** (www.statravel.co.nz)

BUDGET AIRLINES

- **Jetstar** (www.jetstar.com.au)
- **Tiger Air** (www.tigerair.com)

OVERLAND

Car & Motorcycle

- **Australian Automobile Association** (www.aaa.asn.au) Find your state's association on this umbrella website.
- **New Zealand Automobile Association** (www.aa.co.nz)

JOBS

TEACHING ENGLISH

- **Australasian Training Academy** (www.ataonline.edu.au) TESOL certification.
- **Dave's ESL Cafe** (http://eslcafe.com) Loads of jobs especially in Northeast Asia, but also in Southeast Asia.
- **Languages International** (www.languages.ac.nz) Teacher training in Auckland and Christchurch.

TOURISM & HOSPITALITY

See Your First Resort on p124.

INTERNSHIPS & WORK PLACEMENTS

- **Professional Pathways Australia** (http://professionalyeareducation.com.au/ppa.html) Monash University's link to international and local internships.
- **Student Exchange Australia New Zealand** (http://workandtravelusa.com.au) Has internships and summer work in the US.

AU PAIRS & NANNIES

- **Au Pair in America** (www.aupairamerica.com.au) Great for US jobs.
- **Australian Nanny and Au Pair Connection** (www.australiannannies.info) Places internationally.
- **Charlton Brown** (https://nannies.charltonbrown.com.au/our-services) Provides childcare training for professional nannies.
- **JCR** (www.jcraupairs.com.au) Strong

international links make this a good option for overseas placements.

- **Smartaupairs** (www.smartaupairs.com.au) International placements.
- **Nannies Abroad** (www.nanniesabroad.co.nz) Recruits Kiwis for nanny jobs internationally.

Additional options are found on p134.

GENERAL JOB SITES

Like recruitment companies, the following site can help you with your job quest:

- **International Working Holidays** (www.iwh.co.nz) Work options for Kiwis, from nannying and camps to hospitality and ski-resort jobs.

VOLUNTEERING

Organised Programmes

See Finding Organised Volunteer Programmes on p143.

Structured & Self-Funding Volunteer Programmes

See Finding Structured & Self-Funding Volunteer Programmes on p144.

Do-It-Yourself Volunteer Placements

See Finding a Do-It-Yourself Volunteer Placements on p146.

COURSES

EXCHANGE PROGRAMMES

- **AFS Australia** (www.afs.org.au) Offers high-school and university exchanges.
- **Society for Australian-German Student Exchange** (www.sagse.org.au) Scholarships to visit Germany for short-term study.
- **Student Exchange Australia New Zealand** (http://studentexchange.org.au) Offers semester-, summer- and year-long programs.
- **Youth For Understanding** (YFU; www.yfu.com.au/exchange) Runs several programs for under-25-year-olds.

INDEX

ACKNOWLEDGEMENTS

Matt Phillips
Author
Raised in Vancouver and now at home on the banks of the Thames in Hammersmith, London, Matt is no stranger to big trips. He has made plenty of them: the first inspiring his love of life and his second thrusting him out of a career working as a geologist in underground gold mines and into a life of travel writing. He has happily never looked back. When he's not managing Lonely Planet's sub-Saharan Africa content as a Destination Editor in London, he's travelling to write about everything from epic adventures to responsible travel in Africa, Asia, Europe, Australia and the Americas.

Thanks from Matt
A huge thanks to all the Lonely Planet writers who have walked the streets, hiked the trails and gathered all the valuable information that I had at my disposal for this important title. A big thanks to Tasmin Waby for her ever-present ear and valuable advice. A shout out to Imogen Hall for helping with contacts in relation to family travel, and for the following families who helped out: Caz and Craig Makepeace; Stuart, Sue and Annabel Norman; and Fleur Bainger & Co. And last but not least to Amanda Pirie for adding a smiling face to my late nights in the office.

Martin Heng
Contributing author
Martin Heng is Lonely Planet's Accessible Travel Manager. He has published a number of accessible travel titles, including a guide to Rio de Janeiro that was supplied to all athletes participating in the 2016 Paralympics. He also maintain the world's largest collection of Accessible Travel Online Resources, which was featured in the UNWTO's Good Practices in the Accessible Tourism Supply Chain. His most recent publication is an Accessible Travel Phrasebook, featuring disability-specific words and phrases in 35 languages. In 2014, he was a keynote speaker at the UNWTO-sponsored global accessible travel summit.

4th Edition

April 2019

Published by
Lonely Planet Global Limited
CRN 5543153
www.lonelyplanet.com
ISBN 978 1 78868 129 2
Printed in Singapore
10 9 8 7 6 5 4 3 2 1

Stay in touch lonelyplanet.com/contact

Lonely Planet Offices
Australia
The Malt Store, Level 3,
551 Swanston St,
Carlton, Victoria 3053
T: 03 8379 8000
Ireland
Digital Depot, Roe Lane (off Thomas St), Digital Hub, Dublin 8, D08 TCV4
USA
124 Linden St, Oakland, CA 94607
T: 510 250 6400
UK
240 Blackfriars Rd,
London SE1 8NW
T: 020 3771 5100

Managing Director, Publishing
Piers Pickard
Associate Publisher
Robin Barton
Commissioning Editor & Editor
Matt Phillips
Proofing & Captions
Nick Mee, Christina Webb
Art Direction and Design
Daniel di Paolo
Cover Design
Tina García
Mapping
Wayne Murphy
Print Production
Nigel Longuet

Paper in this book is certified against the Forest Stewardship Council™ standards. FSC™ promotes environmentally responsible, socially beneficial and economically viable management of the world's forests.